THE CULTURE AND S

Also by E. John B. Allen—

From Skisport to Skiing:

One Hundred Years of an American Sport,

1840–1940

THE CULTURE AND SPORT OF

Skiing

FIS-WETTKÄMPFE
1933 INNSBRUCK
6. BIS 13. FEBRUAR

FROM ANTIQUITY TO WORLD WAR II

E. JOHN B. ALLEN

UNIVERSITY OF MASSACHUSETTS PRESS AMHERST

LC 2007004223

ISBN 978-1-55849-601-9 (paper); 600-2 (library cloth)

Designed by Richard Hendel
Set in Scala and Scala Sans by dix! Digital Prepress, Inc.
Printed and bound by Thomson-Shore, Inc.

Library of Congress Cataloging-in-Publication Data
Allen, E. John B., 1933–
The culture and sport of skiing : from antiquity to World
War II / E. John B. Allen.
    p.   cm.
Includes bibliographical references and index.
1. Skis and skiing—History.   2. Skis and skiing—
Social aspects.   I. Title.
ISBN 978-1-55849-600-2 (cloth : alk. paper)—
ISBN 978-1-55849-601-9 (pbk. : alk. paper)
 GV854.1.A45 2007
796.93—DC22   2007004223

British Library Cataloguing in Publication data are available.

Frontispiece (p. viii): After his Greenland crossing on skis
and his return from the attempt on the North Pole, for
Norwegians Fridtjof Nansen became the reincarnate Viking,
embodying the secular religion of nationalism.

CONTENTS

Dr. Fridtjof Nansen.

die „FRAM"

Nansen
Polarreise
1893-96

No. 746

Nansen auf
Schneeschuhen
Grönland
durchquerend.

ILLUSTRATIONS

This book had its origins many years ago. On sabbatical leave from an American university in 1976, I left an Innsbruck exhibition of old skiing prints fascinated and determined to acquire some. Here was *my* sport depicted in a sixteenth-century Olaus Magnus woodcut with a man and a woman striding off to church, a couple of children on their backs and, in a quite extraordinary seventeenth-century print taken from Johannes Schefferus's *Lapponia*, a man on two skis of unequal length. There was a wealth of late nineteenth-century illustrations, mostly from German magazines and periodicals. I was struck! Antiquarian sellers of Innsbruck and Salzburg laughed at me; it would be near impossible to find such material, and even if I did, I would never be able to afford such treasures. Very soon afterward, I was in Munich. During a massive rainstorm, as I ran from one shop awning to another, I slipped into a vast indoor flea market. Facing me just inside the entrance were two 1930s paintings, originals for ski clothing advertisements. Was I receiving some sign? With some misgivings—I had just bought a car and was planning a family trip through Europe—I bought one of the paintings. It was unsigned but I was told that it was by Thea von Wurmburgh (I have never been able to find out anything about her). I walked around the flea market, bought three old postcards of skiers, Fritz Heinrich's *Ski-Spiele,* and at the exit came upon a dealer selling military magazines. He asked me if I was a collector. I hesitated, having the second of those quasi–life decision vignettes of myself, then said *jawohl!* So I returned to Innsbruck with my secondhand Opel, the painting, three postcards, the little ski games book, and two *Kriegsausgaben,* and Heide only blinked.

Back in the United States, I hunted around in secondhand bookshops, bought a few mostly "how to ski" books from the 1930s, started to read them and to look for literature of a more academic nature on the history of skiing. There was hardly anything. After many years of investigating, giving talks and papers, writing a few articles, my book *From Skisport to Skiing: One Hundred Years of an American Sport, 1840–1940* was published in 1993.

Much of early American skiing was immigrant driven—Norwegians in the Midwest, and in the 1930s, especially in the northeastern United States, the influence of Austrians was overwhelming. In order to understand this background, I took research trips to Scandinavia and to central Europe. It soon came to me that I was, perhaps, writing first what should have been the second book. The more I gathered about European ski history, the more I realized that up until the Second World War, American skiing was dependent upon its European origins and upon the immigrants themselves. The history of European skiing began to intrigue me more and more.

The problems with writing European ski history are quite different and more complex than those met with in analyzing American skiing. First, there is the enormous time span, some six thousand years. On a practical level, languages present difficulties. The two major ski languages of Europe, German and French, I can manage. I can muddle along in Spanish and less so in Italian. Course work in Norwegian I supplemented with intermittent translation, but I fail completely in the Eastern European languages. Luckily, during the Cold War, a number of *Hausarbeiten* (seminar papers) and theses were written at the Sporthochschule für Körperkultur in Leipzig by Eastern European students who used their own language sources and yet wrote their theses in German. Once the obligatory Marxist arguments are out of the way, there is much of interest for anyone searching for East German, Rumanian, Bulgarian, and Russian skiing.

There are other cultural conundrums: In Norway, people changed their surnames when they moved to a different farm, and place-names changed as well: Norway's capital Christiania changed to Kristiania in 1897 and to Oslo in 1925. I have used Christiania for the period before 1925.[1]

In the course of our European *Wanderschaft*, I have found that each nation has seen its ski history through its own eyes: the Norwegians are proud of their land being the cradle of skiing; the British know that they are responsible for downhill and slalom; the Austrians are sure that their method of instruction was best—in fact, they are sure that they are the Number One skiing nation, something that is disputed, of course, by the Germans, the French, and the Italians. Finns claim cross-country as their high ground. There are other nationalistic causes. For Austrians, up to the Second World War, ski history also revolves around two particular instructors (*pace* Bilgeri), Mathias Zdarsky and Hannes Schneider. For Germany it is the racers, especially the dominant female of the 1930s, Christel Cranz. And as to the British, their man is Arnold Lunn. Jakob Vaage, Norway's long time Holmenkollen museum curator now passed on, once wrote a book to dispute Lunn's claim that the British were really responsible for the advent of modern skiing. He titled it *Norwegian Skis Conquer the World (Norske Ski erobrer Verden)*. There is nothing reticent about these nationalists.

Hans Heidinger, who took over the Mürzzuschlag Wintersportmuseum in Austria from its founder Theodor Hüttenegger in 1982, once said to me, "Perhaps only an American could write an objective history of Europe's skiing," someone who was not socially, politically, and economically bound up with a nation's skiing. I have to confess that I was born in Britain, but I have spent my historical-academic life in the United States. To this day there are very few ski histories by academics. There are many journalistic accounts, though, some of them extremely good, and a mass of club reports usually produced for an anniversary or promotion of one sort or another. Recently, particularly from Scandinavia and Germany, have come some academic investigations; but on the whole, the output is small. I have researched in fifteen countries and corresponded with historians in four more to write this history. Much of the research has been in primary documents, and for secondary materials, I have visited libraries with major and minor holdings, some museums, and occasional private collections besides making use of that most wonderful of institutions, interlibrary loan. I should like to express my gratitude to Joyce Bruce of Plymouth State University for the heavy-duty work and to the regretfully unknown inter-librarians at the other end of my requests. The students at the Help Desk of the Information Technology Service at Plymouth State University have always been most courteous with their technological assistance.

I have many people to whom I owe thanks for friendship, hospitality, translation, understanding, and wonderful late night conversation. Parts of this book have been read by some of those listed below; others have photocopied material for me or replied to questions. I know how long it can take to answer what seems like a simple request. I am extremely grateful for all the help I have been given, in Austria: Marliese Buchta, Dietmar Scholl, the late Franz Klaus, Hans and Helga Heidinger, Rudi Müllner, Hannes Nothnagl, Herbert Schneider, Hannes and Irene Strohmeyer, Christof Thoeny; in Canada: Bob Barney; in the Czech Republic: Karel Danek; in Finland: Merja Heiskanen, Pekka and Teija Honkanen; in France: Jean-Jacques Bompard, Pierre Chauvet, Gilbert and Francine Merlin, Roger Tangueley, Thierry Terret; in Germany: Gerd Falkner, family Gelbert, Arnd Krüger, Manfred Lämmer, Joachim Rühl, the late Erich Sanktjohanser, Martin and Ute Schwer, the late Ekkehart Ulmrich; in Great Britain: Elisabeth Hussey; in Italy: Gigliola Gori, Angela Teja; in Japan: Hiroshi Arai; in Latvia: Juris Baldunčiks; in Norway: Karin Berg, Arnold Dalen, Rune Flaten, Matti Goksøyr, Leif Torgersen, the late Jakob Vaage; in Poland: Iwona Grys, Janusz Ślusarczyk, Wojciech Szatkowski; in Slovenia: Borut Batagelj, Aleš and Vlasta Guček; in South Africa: Floris van der Merwe; in Sweden: Kenneth and Margareth Åstrom, Jan Lindroth, Bengt Soderberg, Leif

Yttergren; in Switzerland: Max Triet; in the United States: Anbarth Andersen, Anne Anninger, Elizabeth Aprea, Martha (Ki) Clough, Jacqueline Downing, Kirby Gilbert, the late Helen Harris, Phil Haskell, Nils Larsen, Liz Lambregtse, Harold Leich, Jeff Leich, Xiaoxiong Li, Morten Lund, Emiko Ohnuki-Tierney, Einar Sunde, Hans Susskind, and Henry Yaple. As I write such a list, my wife and I think back on wonderful times; ski history has made us friends all over the world. I owe thanks for sabbatical leaves from Plymouth State University and for a travel grant from the Deutsche Akademische Austausch-Dienst.

I have presented parts of this book at conferences of the International Society for Sport and Physical Education (ISHPES), at sessions of the Committee for European Sport History (CESH), the British Society for Sport History (BSSH), and at the North American Society for Sports History (NASSH). I thank all who offered critiques. For seeing the manuscript to press, I should like to thank Carol Betsch and Clark Dougan, and for his copyediting, Michael Shally-Jensen. Special thanks to Richard Chisholm, Annie Coleman, John Fry, and Allen Guttmann, who gave the entire manuscript a critical reading. For errors that remain, I am responsible.

One special word: My native-speaker, German wife, Heide, also has enjoyed pilgrimaging to ski history places, visiting the archives, libraries, and museums. I am fortunate to have such a helpmate. Besides sorting out the more involved of German paragraphs, she has given this manuscript the first of its editorial overhauls. The book is better for the trimming. It is to Heide that *The Culture and Sport of Skiing* is dedicated.

THE CULTURE AND SPORT OF Skiing

Introduction

Let your skis be the great adventure
Taking you on the brisk morning wind
To feel the slope and smell the pine . . .
Everything else is mere literature.
—*Easter at Val d'Isère 1937*

Que tes skis soient la bonne aventure
Eparse au vent crispé du matin
Qui va sentant la pente et le pin . . .
Et tout le reste est littérature.[1]

 The present historical survey covers the period from antiquity
to 1940. The ending date, at the beginning of the Second
World War, is of importance for two reasons. One: the Russo-
Finnish war was a winter war where simple, utilitarian skis,
familiar to hunters a thousand years before, proved more
successful than the technologically advanced Soviet tanks and
artillery weapons. This mix of ancient and modern in military competition brings my history to a fitting end. Second:
although the worldwide diffusion of skiing was starting here and there in the
late nineteenth century, it remained largely a preoccupation of individuals and
groups, and skiing did not become globalized until after 1945. Today, around
the world, between twenty and twenty-five million people ski. This study is an
analysis of how skiing became a modern sport.

The modernization thesis is an extremely complex phenomenon that has
been much criticized in the last twenty years. Postmodernists consider the
twentieth century so replete with horrors that any progress stemming from
the eighteenth-century Enlightenment appears spurious. Knowledge, truth,
and sundry other certainties that appeared in western historiography of
the nineteenth century are considered dubious. Postmodernists have taken
Friedrich Nietzsche's dictum at face value: humans do not discover truth but
invent it.

This history of skiing is not invented, but I do take into account many of the
postmodernists' concerns, particularly those bearing the label "culture." Why
did skiing have such powerful yet different meanings for societies like Norway
and France? Eric Hobsbawm's "invented tradition," in which social cohesion,
legitimacy of authority, and the inculcation of a set of beliefs converge, helps
to explain the Norwegian case. The establishment of ruling institutions with
authority—a hegemony of elites and their ideas and actions—affects Norway's

ski history in a totally different way than does, say, the British presence in Switzerland.

Why people skied and the meaning they attributed to this activity is one of the central concerns of this book. One of the joys of delving into this sport's history (really, most sport history) is that it lies at the intersection of cultural history, anthropology, sociological discussion, linguistics, and the "special histories," as Roberta Park called them, of literature, gender, and ethnicity.[2] Sometimes, however, a single factor such as Fridtjof Nansen's crossing of Greenland in 1888 produces totally unexpected results and makes nonsense of the postmodernists' dismissal of the role of the individual.

Nansen became an instant icon, with very little argument about his persona. He embodied Norwegian nationalistic hopes. In the historical context, the psychological importance of his skiing and its impact on Norway's politics is the "thick" part of Clifford Geertz's anthropological "description."

To sum up my perspective: I have rejected the postmodernists' siren call to be inventive, imaginative, and creative. "Where once we were exhorted to be accurate and factual," wrote Gertrude Himmelfarb in the *Times Literary Supplement,* "we are now urged to be imaginative and inventive. Instead of 'recreating' the past, we are told to 'create' it; instead of 'reconstructing' history, to construct or 'deconstruct' it."[3] I have not invented this history; it is based on the factual record. This history is not one that I have imagined, although I have used my imagination in writing it. And the creative part is in the ordering and organization of the cross-disciplinary use of wide-ranging source materials, to the end that the reader has my interpretation of how and why skiing became a modern sport.

What emerges from this chronological narrative is that the history of skiing had a long period where utilitarian activity was its major focus—from c. 4000 BC to 1890. Skis were homemade, most of them rough transportation for hunting, gathering, getting in the wood supply—instruments for winter survival. Then came the ever-widening spread of skiing as sport, mostly by aristocrats and wealthier middle classes from c. 1890 to 1940. This period was one in which the sport of skiing took on its modern forms, not merely because it became part of the industrial world's leisure commodity, but also because the domination of one style, Nordic, for which skis were manufactured for touring, cross-country trips and races, was replaced by another, Alpine. The manufactured ski made especially for the Alpine type of skiing, associated with "downhill" and "slalom," required the boot to be held tightly to the ski; and in order to turn fast, steel edges were fixed at the sides of the bottom of the ski: an instrument made specifically for a sporting purpose.

Riding on these skis were skiers: anyone who used skis in any way. In the prehistoric period to 1890, this meant a hunter, people headed to church, mail carriers, a skier on skis for any useful purpose. There was no special word for a skier who ran in a cross-country race or for one who jumped, because for centuries the ideal skier was one who could do everything on skis. Specialization was dismissed as unworthy. Only when the Alpine disciplines became prominent in the 1930s, and especially among those who raced, would a skier perhaps become a "downmountain specialist," a "*Slalommeister*," or one of the well known "*Kanonen*"—the big guns. "Ski jumper" also became a designation for someone who specialized in that form of skiing. In the Norwegian Holmenkollen competition, all who competed had to ski cross-country and jump. Only in 1933 was a man allowed to enter one or the other of the twin events.

All these changes take place over a period of decades. In the 1936 Olympic Games, for example, there was only one gold medal awarded to the winner of the combined downhill and slalom events, because the traditional emphasis on the all-around skier was still strong enough to preclude one gold medal for the winner of downhill and another, separate gold medal for the winner of the slalom. Norwegian Laila Schou Nilsen was the surprise winner of the women's downhill, but she received comparatively little recognition because she placed only fifth in the slalom, even though the two combined showings were enough to earn her a bronze medal.

I do not mean to be gratuitous by saying that skiing was managed, accomplished, and performed on snow. Snow is a remarkably different substance at different times of the day. It can become a sheet of ice and it can fall as three feet of fluffy powder and everything in between. When it is cold, it does not necessarily stick to the bottom of skis; in the spring sun, it can ball up mercilessly and make skiing impossible. In the early centuries, skiers hunted when conditions were right. Those conditions could easily change since expeditions could last for days, weeks, months, even more than a year. From very early on, skiers understood the use of animal skins fixed to the undersides of their skis, the hair slanting backward to enable them to glide forward but not slip back. Attaching "skins," as they are still called today, was one of the earliest technical innovations when the snow demanded it.

Only when people started skiing over and over again in the same place, did they come to manage the snow. Or, rather, they began to employ someone to rake the snow smooth and fill in the *Sitzmarks*. As the wealthy sported on skis, hotel management made their winter holidaying as easy as possible. To make a sport easy was a goal very different from the idea that a sport should make you healthy, or that skiing might provide a way out of a political problem—in this case Norway's freedom from Sweden.

When racing across country, skiers followed the same track, and there were rules about when the person in front of you should move aside to let you overtake. Essentially, however, the natural snow provided the trail. Only when alpine downhill and particularly slalom competitions took place did the snow become tracked like a toboggan run. What to do, since one of the conditions of modern sport is to have equality of competition? The first runner would have a very different descent than the thirtieth. Arnold Lunn, who invented modern slalom, experimented with two sorts of runs, one on tracked snow, which he came to think of as Cresta skiing (after the famous Cresta toboggan run) and later as Marxist skiing (everyone skiing in exactly the same way in the same place), and the other on new snow. But, of course, that did not work as the new-snow track soon became like the first one. This being only one example of the experimental nature of the sport in the interwar years, it nevertheless shows how the winter culture of skiing was becoming a modern sport. As with any sport undergoing change over the years, skiing retained much of its pre-modern elements at the same time that it modernized.

One other natural factor played an important role: mountains. Cross-country skiers did not think in terms of mountains but rather of trails that might go up and down, sometimes quite steeply; but cross-country was exactly that—one skied over the landscape. In Alpine skiing (the adjective is derived from the Alps of Europe), mountains are the prime ingredient. When Norwegians first arrived on skis in the Alps, they told their European friends that this was not the place to ski. Zermatt, so well known for its Matterhorn, was long considered not a ski venue; it was just too steep. When an American rope-tow tinkerer in the mid-1930s was asked to put a tow up to the top of a mountain, he had to readjust his whole outlook. To climb up mountains had been the goal and joy of mountaineers, and some had even attempted peaks in winter. But skiers used mountains as play spaces, something antithetical to the serious business of climbing. As skiing's sporting and social attractions grew, mountaineers found themselves being run off what they considered their property.

Mountaineers billeted themselves in mountain huts; skiers came up from the Palace Hotels. The natural, physical world of the mountaineer was invaded by social sportsmen and sportswomen, both out to enjoy the pristine world of the high mountain winter landscape. But then came the return trip: for the mountaineer, the long slog across the snowfield; for the skier, the exhilarating *schuss* that came as a reward for the exhausting climb. As the technical capabilities of conquering mountains by railways and lifts increased, the mountaineer disdained such mechanical aids, whereas the skier took to them with such a relish that lines formed at "rush hour" and the huge *téléférique* cabins were jammed full. The problems of urban living were brought to the mountains.

This was urban living for the well-to-do. But in the 1930s, the beginnings of skiing-for-all, the Dopolavoro, Hitler Youth, and Sport for All were started in Italy, Germany, and France. In a way, this was not new. The European military establishments had long shown an interest in finding young men who could already ski to join the ski troops when the tocsin for war sounded. This was how it was in Norway, and what Norwegians did, said, and wrote about skiing was considered holy writ for the first fifty years as skiing became a sport.

In *The Culture and Sport of Skiing,* the first four chapters cover the history from the bog ski artifacts to the end of the nineteenth century. This is the utilitarian period of ski use. Fridtjof Nansen's crossing of Greenland in 1888 and his attempt to reach the North Pole on skis in 1894, paradoxically highlighted two opposing factors. The expeditions enshrined the utilitarian use of skis that became at the same time so enthralling to the aristocracy and bourgeois that they took to skiing as a sport.

The ski sport is then analyzed in terms of nationals, British, French, and German: how the British trespassed upon Switzerland in their own class-rooted, hegemonic way; how the shrill enjoyment of gallic skiing was somewhat in response to a fear that the Prussians might invade again, causing army officers and bourgeois elites to take control of French skiing; how the Germans and Austrians, already showing a desire for unity, organized their sport. The heart of each chapter's analysis is a modernization thesis directly related to the major country involved in the years before 1914. From time to time, where relevant, I have tied in similar or different goings-on elsewhere. Women's skiing in this masculine sport receives its own treatment for the time period and owes particular insights to theories of gender. Since much of French, German, Austrian and Italian skiing was related to military defense, it is fitting that the Great War brings Part II to a close.

The French found "winning the peace" in the postwar period extremely difficult. Despite the publicity and kudos for hosting the first Winter Olympic Games and for prodigious lift construction and resort building, there grew in France a feeling that they were not, indeed, winning the peace. To some extent it is remarkable that the Olympic Winter Games—Nordic events held only at Chamonix, St. Moritz, and Lake Placid, new icons of what winter industrialization could produce—ever took place.

The fact that the 1932 Olympics was awarded to the United States indicated that skiing was becoming a worldwide sport. Two waves of immigrants shaped how America skied. The Norwegians brought their form of skiing with them from the mid-nineteenth century on, and in the snow belt of North America, skiing became embedded as part of winter culture, even as ethnic tensions surfaced. Austrian skiers came in the 1930s, along with a few Germans and Swiss. Their style and philosophy of skiing was very different, "Alpine" rather than "Nordic," and essentially social in nature. I deal with the spread of these alpine skiers in the Americas and in the East, in Asia, Australia, and New Zealand: the beginnings of the globalization of the modern sport.

A number of these immigrant skiers were fleeing from fascism. Utilizing Antonio Gramsci's hegemonic theory, I show how Mussolini and Hitler co-opted the sport of skiing under the Nazi and Fascist movements. Anti-Semitic policies were carried through in the clubs of Germany and Austria, and caused a major rethinking about whether sport was free from politics as the 1936 Winter Olympics were held in southern Germany. Not only was this a Nazi Olympics, but it was also the first Games where competitions were open to women skiers, and where Alpine events of downhill and slalom were on the program. However, it is the politics of these Olympics to which most of the analysis is devoted. Hannes Schneider's case illuminates the politicization of the sport of skiing. In the 1930s, with the dominance of his teaching method, the success of his films, his personal visits as far afield as the United States and Japan, he had become *Skimeister* to the world. With the *Anschluss* in March 1938, his imprisonment and subsequent release to the United States bring a special focus on politics, money, and the sport.

When politics and diplomacy fail, war usually follows. This was the case with the Soviet expansion into Finland. The Russo-Finnish war, on the periphery of World War II yet central to ski history, brings this history to a close. The Finns, using simple ski equipment, brought the technologically superior Russians to a halt in the snows of 1939–40. Western observers marveled at the Finns, reveled in their skiing exploits, found a satisfaction that their sport was achieving such magnificent results, not caring to realize that the Finnish defense owed nothing to the sport of skiing as they thought of it.

CHAPTER 1 Archaeology and Myth

The find was made in the Autumn of 1924 by Forest Inspector
August Högdahl, in a sedge marsh 2 km. east of the most south-
east farm in Kalvtråsk village at a depth of 1.5 meters. One ski
disintegrated in transport.—Gösta Berg, on the finding of an old ski,
now dated to 3200 BC

God of skiers Ullr "is such a skier that no one can race for a wager
with him."—Snorri Sturluson, the younger Edda, 1223

Skiing as we know it today has utilitarian origins dating back
six thousand years, which gives it one of the longest histories
of any sport. Prehistoric rock carvings in northern Norway
and Russia depict skis as necessary for survival in lands that
were covered for much of the year in snow. Our knowledge is
further enhanced by fragments of skis and a few poles found
in the bogs of Scandinavia and Russia. Documents in the form
of reports, sagas, and illustrations add to the limited material.
These sources provide a scant record for the beginnings of what became a
worldwide sport. But they have been made to provide the most compelling
authority for the promotion of a national identity for Norway. The study of
skiing's archeology and mythology not only entails the chasing of the historical record, but is relevant for the period that culminated in Norway's political
freedom from Sweden in 1905, and is also pursued right up to today.

Facts and the interpretation of the 1994 Lillehammer Olympic torch journey bring some of this interplay into focus. The sacred flame (sacred only
since 1936 when the Nazis invented this tradition) was lit using stone flints
in the hearth of ski pioneer Sondre Norheim's home in Morgedal. (In a children's brochure, Norheim is called "the God of Skiing," and as you come into
Morgedal today, a tourist sign welcomes you to the "Cradle of Skiing"). When
this same torch passed through the Sami village of Mortensnes, locals staged
a play showing quite clearly that the ski was a Sami invention that had been
stolen by Norwegians. Ethnic frustrations of the Sami community are quite
evident, and in the lighting ceremony, the tradition of Norway, and particularly
of Morgedal as the cradle of skiing, is being upheld.[1]

The climatic conditions in these snowbound lands made hunting in winter a difficult requirement for the survival of its inhabitants. It was time-consuming enough in summer, but unless means were found to travel on top of the snow—and to enable high speed in the process—hunting was nearly impossible in winter. Some 250 artifacts provide evidence that a variety of skis were used to glide on snow. A typical ski was a board some 160 centimeters long, 10 to 15 centimeters wide, with the front end curved up and a foothold in the middle. This form of skis did not change much over the first five thousand years. A heavy staff, which doubled as a weapon, completed the equipment. Snowshoes were in use as well, but they did not prove as effective in deep snow.

Today, in the museums of Norway, Sweden, Finland, and Russia, these bog finds provide a major source for understanding the cultural importance of skiing in the period from c. 4000 BC to c. 1000 AD. Whole typologies of skis have been constructed based on minute numbers of finds. Most of the 250 skis were discovered when the shovel of a farmer, ditch digger, road mender, or fence maker turned up bits of wood remarkable enough to spur the digger to tell local authorities of the find. The earliest remains were dug up in 1897, the latest in 2003.[2] It is unlikely that many more will be found; peat is no longer a source of heat, and ditch digging and dredging are done by machines that do not recognize so fragile an archeological treasure. Though the small numbers of artifacts in existence are scant evidence indeed upon which to base a history, the development of Carbon-14 dating techniques since 1926, pollen analysis and dendrochronological comparisons, increasing geologic knowledge and better understanding of botanical science, provide growing certainty about them. The actual dating, of course, is of the wood, most commonly pine; but early skiers used whatever wood was available.

Finnish and Swedish scholars were at the forefront of early ski research. Under the guidance of Karl Wiklund, Professor of Ugric-Finnish languages and ethnologist at Uppsala University, the remains of the skis from the bogs were studied and categorized in the 1920s and 1930s. The making of the ski, the foot placement, and the attachment were analyzed. The origin and influence of one type of ski on another created the hottest debate. Finnish professor Toivo Itkonen critiqued Wiklund and put forward his own claims, as did the Norwegian Nils Lid. There were others too. Each produced a typological schema of skis, and each was criticized in turn.[3] Our understanding of the prehistoric culture represented by these skis relies on these scholars' studies, and no one looking into the history of early skis can neglect their work.

Wiklund proposed Eastern, Western, and Southern varieties of skis. The Eastern ski, often called Arctic, had hide covering its underside as its most prominent feature. Such skis were used in Siberia until very recent times. The Southern ski—short and broad with front tip rounded and curved upwards—had a concave foot placing and holes in the raised side of the ski through which straps were threaded to provide for keeping the foot in place. This ski was widely distributed in Sweden, Finland, eastern Norway, the Baltic States, and Russia. But it is clear that there were many other ways of classifying the bog skis. One Finnish scholar tried a method based on decoration, others on the number of holes for the foot placement, others on whether the back end was cut straight off or rounded, and so on.

The bog skis, dated from 4700 BC to 1000 AD, came from a period when a tribesman knew only which type of ski was best for hunting, and which for going into the forest to cut wood. It is modern anthropologists and sociologists and the like who have classified these artifacts. Although the bulk of Gösta Berg's *Finds of Swedish Skis in Bogs* was researched and written before the Second World War, it appeared in English only in 1950. Berg's classification of four ski types as Arctic, Bothnic, Scandic, and Southern immediately became the most important analysis, and his book remains to this day the most well known on the subject.[4]

The analysis and classification of ski types in different nations, of their early diffusion across snow countries of Europe and Asia, and particularly of the influence of one sort of ski upon another, not only gave rise to hot debates among the ethnological scientists of the late nineteenth and early twentieth centuries but had political, psychological, social, and economic ramifications. The origin of a ski, how it was used, its place in the winter culture, could single out a particular nation, or even a region of a nation, as providing the basis for nationalism. It could prove that the world owed a certain deference to that country or region.

Indeed, when the serious study of skiing began, it was rooted in a nationalistic ethos that played out in different ways in different nations. At that time, all over the Western world, and to a lesser degree in Africa and Asia under imperial tutelage, new foundations were being discovered and invented to give authenticity to the concept of nationalism: folk stories, language, race, religion, myth, and legend were studied in turn. For countries like Norway and Hungary, which were not independent states in the late nineteenth century, these foundations were of political importance—in Norway's case, to free itself from Sweden. Some countries sought in skiing an antidote to the poor health of the nation, others stressed skiing as a winter necessity for military preparedness. Thus, the study of these artifacts, thousands of years old, took on more than antiquarian interest and scientific knowledge. This national guardianship continues to this day, especially in Norway and its Telemark region.

Scandinavian researchers have classified only Scandinavian skis. Skis discovered in other parts of the world defy the neatness of their systems. The Caribou Eskimos, in northern Canada, for example, used a narrow snowshoe-like board. Drawings of Siberian Samoyed and Ostyak from the seventeenth to the nineteenth centuries show semi-snowshoe, semi-ski footgear.[5] If we look at the center of the ski on which the foot rests, we recognize similarities in geographically separate parts of the world. Not a few skis have two small pieces of wood attached on either side to help hold the foot in place. Their widespread distribution is as impressive as the longevity of their use. Such skis have been found north of Bergen, Norway, as they have been in Latvia (at Vecpicbalga) as well as in Bloke, Slovenia (seventeenth-century type) and in California (nineteenth century). The Norwegian Furnes ski (c. 2200 years BP) is quite different, having a gouged out area in which the boot is placed, leaving the sides high. The same type of ski has been found as far away as Korea, where it may have been used in the marshes. Only one find has retained its binding, the Mänttä ski from Finland, dated to c. 500 AD. Part of a heel strap was still attached that had been made from badger skin. The pelt of the animal had also supplied an underlining to the ski. A similar binding was still in use in the 1890s in Norway.[6] Cultural traditions are hard to break if they work well.

Russian finds have until recently remained behind closed museum doors. In 1936, Soviet academics showed an initial interest in ski history, but political upheavals and war ended that effort. In the 1960s, a symbolized skiing figure was found on a fragment of a Don Abashevo pot, and in a burial ground near Omsk, a dagger with a tiny figure of a skier on the hilt was unearthed. At Vis I and II in the Lake Sindor region, thirty-nine pieces of wood with tracings on them were dated to 6300 BC–5000 BC. The excavations at Vis I have produced hunting artifacts, tools, fishing gear, sledge runners, and skis. The most remarkable feature is a moose head carved on the front underside of what was obviously part of a ski. Here was an early form of brake, or a device to stop the ski sliding backward. Gregoriy Burov believes that the moose's head was also a symbol for speed.[7]

Grooves on the underside of skis—to make the skis run true—are another distinguishing feature appearing first in early Sami skis. Many of the grooves are wide and shallow, while others are quite narrow. Some run the length of the ski and others are quite short. Grooved skis appear to have been fairly common in much of Scandinavia and in Finland,[8] yet ungrooved skis were also made right into the twentieth century. American miners in gold rush California thought that one of them had invented the grooving of skis along with a specialized tool to do the work.[9]

There has been much discussion about the origin of the ski pole. It is so obvious to us that two poles are more efficient than one that we find it curious that until recently, only one was used. The few pieces that have been saved from the bogs indicate that they were part of a stout staff, about six feet long. On one end, the hunter might fit a leather-covered knife. Another was fashioned into an elongated sort of spoon, probably for scooping up water, finding moss under the snow for domestic reindeer to eat, or disemboweling an animal killed on a hunting expedition.[10]

The use of the staff as a hunter's weapon explains why only one was carried; both hands would be needed to deal with an animal. But for skiing along and going uphill, two poles would have made the day easier. And there was a tenth-century precedent from east of the Urals where ice skaters pushed themselves along with two poles.[11] Also in 1748, Wilhelm Cederhielm published a map of Lapland with a picture of skiers equipped with two poles. It is from this illustration that some assume the impetus for the use of two poles came from Finland, Finns and Lapps often being equated as experts in the art of skiing. But one pole was common the world over into the early twentieth century.

Exciting visual evidence comes from rock art. The most well known is the "Rødøy hunter," a rabbit-like man, on skis. This mythical hunter or hunter in disguise was uncovered from its Nordland moss-covered rock in 1929. It traveled the world as a postage stamp in 1966 and was used twenty-eight years later as one symbol at the Lillehammer Olympic Winter Games. Norwegians take seriously their efforts to keep alive the invented tradition of being the first people on skis. Another Norwegian rock carving at Alta, some 200 kilometers by road south of the North Cape, is similar in style to the skiers depicted on some Sami drums. The most impressive set of petroglyphs are to be found north of Lake Ladoga at Bessov Noss and at Zalavrouga in Russia, where they have been known since 1850. In 1936 they received wide recognition through the work of W. J. Raudonikas.[12] The Russian "wolf" with moon and arrows (perhaps) and the Rødøy "rabbit," with hatchet in hand, conjure up a life of magic and hunting, but definitive statements of meaning remain elusive.

The Russian pictograph called Sunduk IV depicts two armed skiers with bows. Whether it is Scythian or Hunnic (third century BC to fourth century AD) is under debate.[13] What is intriguing is that the site, 1,300 miles east of the Urals, is only 400 miles from the Altai mountains: one more bit of evidence that early skiing was part of the winter culture in the Altai region, the

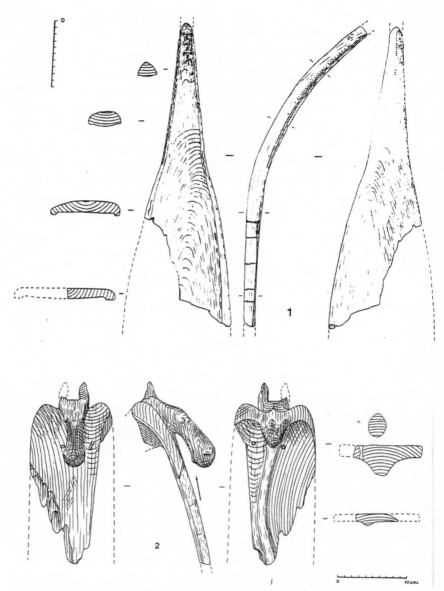

Gregoriy Burov's drawing of a moose head protruding from the underside of the tip of a ski is the most interesting of the finds unearthed in the early 1960s at the VIS I site. (Courtesy Gregoriy Burov)

borderlands of Mongolia, northwest China, and southern Russia, where skiing appears to have had its beginnings.

Another stone carving at Böksta, Uppland, Sweden, has been dated to 1050 AD, about the same time as the swan tips appear on skis. The style of the ski on the stone gives a rough idea of the date of the carving. This is also the time that ethnographers under Swedish influence mark a switch from *Förhistoricke tid* to *Fornskidor*, from prehistoric to premodern skis.[14]

Just as the small numbers of bog skis are the only primary artifacts for study, the numbers of pictographic skiers constitute a small percentage of all the rock art. It is significant that the hunter (or warrior) motif runs through all of them. Quite obviously, hunting on skis was a vital part of winter life from the Norwegian coast to the Bering Sea.

In January 2006, the Chinese *People's Daily* printed an account of rock drawings recently found near Altai (equidistant from Mongolia and Kazakhstan) that by their reckoning are 10,000 years old, but there has been no scientific corroboration yet.[15]

TALES FROM THE SAGAS

The earliest written reports of the Dinglings (hunters said to range from the Altai region to Lake Baikal in Siberia) emerged in China and date from about 200 BC. These are supplemented by an occasional remark found in Roman writings and, later, in the Scandinavian sagas and Eddas. Written accounts are few, and all are sparse in their descriptions of skiing; yet they add to the limited knowledge gained from other sources.

In the Middle Ages there is a little more to discover, mostly from the *King's Mirror*, or *Kongespeilet*. The first major source is the sixteenth-century Bishop Olaus Magnus's first-hand reports accompanied by fanciful illustrations of Scandinavian marvels. One of those marvels is skiing. In the following two centuries, western Europeans occasionally journeyed to the northlands and wrote about things unknown at home. They provided more realistic descriptions, but often skiing was still perceived as yet another one of the wild, wintry miracula of the northern lands. For most of skiing's six-thousand-year history, the source material is minimal and the descriptions are somewhat imaginative.

The Rødøy petroglyph and the Russian carvings hint at magic. Further evidence of extraordinary powers and deeds comes to us in the form of the Old Norse and Icelandic sagas and Eddas. Besides the aristocratic one-upmanship between kings Eystein and Sigurd—"I can handle skis better than you"[16]—there is much on Ullr and Skade.

Ullr (Ull) was the god of skiers providing aid and protection. He was also

Primitive rock carvings on the bank of the river Vyg near the White Sea in northwest Russia, estimated to be four or five thousand years old, first came to western attention in the work of W. J. Raudonikas in the mid-1930s. The three here belong to a group of seven on a hunting foray and show the important part skis played as a means of winter survival. (Obholzer, 5000 Jahre Ski, 1975).

the god of archers and of men in single combat and was always portrayed with a bow. His home was in Ydalir, a yew grove.[17] The best bows were made of yew. Linguistic connections such as this frequently provide solid information from the preliterate era. In southern Scandinavia, Jan de Vries found eighty place-names related to Ullr; fifty are in Norway and thirty in Sweden. The names are associated with nature, as in Ullsjö (Ullr's lake), and with culture, as in Ullin-sin (Ullr's pasture). These place-names have been dated to between 400 and 600 AD in Norway, and between 600 and 800 AD in Sweden.[18] This relationship of nature and god became increasingly important as Norwegians looked for origins while inventing their ski tradition in the nineteenth century.

Some of our knowledge of Ullr comes from the Eddas, where Ullr and Skade may be found as *Ondur-áss* (Ski God) and *Ondur-dis* (Ski Goddess), sometimes as *Ondur-goð*.[19] When these tales were written down in the thirteenth century, Ullr had virtually disappeared from the pantheon of gods, and he might have vanished into the snows forever. But skiing and its ancient associations were again brought out during the nineteenth century to provide a foundation for the new Norwegian nationalism, which would culminate in the political separation from Sweden in 1905.

Skade (Skadi) the ski goddess was quite a woman in her own right. She was the daughter of Tjasse (Storm). She exacted payment for the death of her father and was commanded to marry a god in order to become a goddess. The gods trooped by her in a manner that allowed her to see only their legs and feet . . . and she chose Njord. Njord, it turned out, was partial to the sea coast while Skade was a mountain woman. After what I suppose can be called a divorce, Skade returned to the mountains and became the ski goddess. Never physically associated with Ullr,[20] she lived a separate existence. It is from Skade that the word Scandinavia is derived.[21]

If place-names give authority to Norway's role, and if the god Njord (who gave his name to Norway) adds to that authority, it is disconcerting to some that the oldest artifacts have not been found in Norway, nor even in Sweden, but in Russia. Also, Ullr himself, always associated with Scandinavia, is identical to the Anglo-Saxon sky god, Wuldor, and was supposed to have had a German summer home on the top of an alp, where he is known as Holle.[22] But it is Frau Holle, shaking the clouds like pillows to make snow, who is better known:

Hei! hei! hei! So eine Schneeballschlacht!
Ja, das ist was für die Grossen und die Kleinen.
Wenn Frau Holle ihre Betten macht,
Ja, da braucht die liebe Sonne nicht zu scheinen.

Yea! Let's have a good old snowball fight.
It's so much fun for big and small.
When Frau Holle fluffs her bed up light
We don't need the sun's rays at all.

Skade has become Frau Holle as Ullr's name has metamorphosed into Holle. But I am getting ahead of myself, for that is a song known to German children in the twentieth century.

Ullr and Skade make impressive art deco covers for the Swedish ski annual På Skidor in 1928 and 1929. The god and goddess of skiing give historical authority to this most important of the Swedish ski journals, which began publication in 1893. (Author's collection)

Ullr, Skade, Njord, Wodin, Thor: the panoply of gods tended to disappear in the medieval world, thanks in part to Olav Tryggvason, Norway's first christianizing king (of whom we shall hear more), and later to the bishops from Rome and pastors from Wittenberg. The pagan gods were revived in the latter half of the nineteenth century and became one foundation of a romanticized national culture. Nowhere was this more important than in Norway, where for almost a hundred years after the Napoleonic wars the people were trying to free themselves from Swedish control. The interest in folk tales and songs, studies of language, the formation of the Venstre party with its political platform of nationalism—all are indications of a renewed vitality in the national culture. Skiing was put into this heady mix as a most important part of *Idræt* ("sport"), so that Fridtjof Nansen would write, "skiing is of greater national importance than is generally supposed."[23] Ullr was resurrected to provide an ancient foundation for the emerging modern state—and for the sport of skiing.

The modern term "ski" is becoming ubiquitous in all languages. You may read about 滑雪 in China, but on the slopes they put on their "skhi." Although the Finns have a Hiihtomuseo, when in conversation they use the word *suski*, or even *ski*. Through the cedars of Lebanon, locals "ski," even though the stamps depicting skiing on one's postcard to home are inscribed in Arabic. In Argentina and Austria the word is *ski*. But it was not always that way.

Because a pair of skis was often of unequal length, there were two words in Norse that meant "ski." *Andor* (variously spelled) came to mean the shorter of the two, often skin-covered for a good kick (as we would now say), and most clearly illustrated in Schefferus's *Lapponia* of 1673. The longer of the two skis, the gliding ski, is derived from Old Norse *skið*, originally meaning "a piece of cleft wood," that is, a simple board to cross the snow on.[24] Its name became attached to types of skis used on different terrain, in different conditions of snow, and in different geographical areas. Local varieties had local names. Karin Berg, in her recent *Ski i Norge* (The Ski in Norway) delineates different types of skis according to their use and geographical place. The name of the famous Telemark ski obviously derives from geographic reference. The Norwegians slid along on the *vedski* (everyday ski), the *løpski* (trail ski), the *rennski* (running ski), the *fjellski* (mountain skis), the *skogski* (skis for going in the woods), the *skareski* (for use on crusty snow), and so on.[25] This specialization was not confined to Norway. A number of Siberian tribes, the Nivkhi for example, had one sort of skin-covered skis for hunting and another form for wood cutting. The most ubiquitous was the *langski* (long ski), which has now turned worldwide into simply the *ski*. But this sort of analysis belongs to skis in the eighteenth, nineteenth, and early twentieth centuries. In earlier historical and prehistorical periods, skis were not so sophisticated.

With Norwegian immigrants of the nineteenth century spreading the knowledge of skiing worldwide, it is not surprising that the Norwegian word *ski* eventually became universal. For some decades, however, particularly in German-speaking countries and in the American West, skis were referred to as *Schneeschuhe* and (its English equivalent) "snowshoes." In early writings from Germany and California, only the context makes it clear that skis were being used rather than the Native Americans' webbed snowshoes. This is why the name of Norway's most famous skiing immigrant in the United States is Snowshoe Thompson, the Sierra Nevada mail carrier. Into the 1920s, there was discussion over the pronunciation, "whua-schu" or "ski," with obvious puns about the manly sport of "sheeing." It was not until 1984 that the

Bundesministerium for Education and Culture in Vienna decreed that "ski" was to be used, not "schi."

About poles there has been little discussion. First, there was only one, homemade of local wood. Countries that linguistically claimed a Germanic stem used a *Stock*, a *Stav*. Translated into the Romance languages, skiers used a *baton* or *batón*. Americans rejected the British "stick," used to this day, and the word "pole" became the norm after 1900. In countries where imperial skiers laid their tracks, they left their *baton* in Algeria and stick in Kashmir.

The word for "binding"—for attaching the foot to the ski—is so similar in the Germanic languages that there was no mistaking its meaning: *binding* in Norwegian, *Bindung* in German. If I dwell on Norwegian and German terms it is because those languages were the early languages of skiing. French and Italian skiers had little influence, and their words—*fixation* and *attacco*—never laid claim to universality. Since some of the makeshift iron and leather contraptions were fitted on to the skis by blacksmith and farrier, various local names such as "riggings" in the United States derived from farming.

The most difficult word, though it expresses the essence of Norwegian skiing, is *Ski-Idræt* (*Ski-Idrott* in Swedish).[26] The word *Idræt* is generally translated as *"sport,"* but it really means a great deal more. *Idræt* in its nineteenth-century meaning, when it became attached to skiing, was inspired by the nurture–nature philosophies of Jean Jacques Rousseau, romantic writers and poets, and people promoting physical exercise. This "nature" philosophy was European-wide, but in Scandinavia it took on the weighty baggage of the Old Norse sagas and Icelandic Eddas. The grisly horrors of German Hansel and Gretel stories pale in comparison with the tale of the god Loki being wrapped in his son's intestines, or our "shimmering bride" Skade suspending a snake over Loki so the venom would drip into him.[27] The sagas are full of action; gods rushed on the wind, roared across mountain ranges, descended into the deeps. Theirs was an enormously physical life. When added to the romanticized Viking image—plunderers and heroes who were almost myths themselves—*Idræt* encompassed the qualities of action, health, and strength though not the marauding. Skiing entailed, then, an attachment to old folk tradition, to active life in the outdoors, to wholesome all-around qualities blending body and soul of the individual into a good citizen; and by extension the whole community, even the nation would benefit. Skiing suited *Idræt* ideals perfectly, for was not Ullr the powerful god on skis? Had not Skade gone hunting on skis? Was not one of the attributes of a noble Viking to be the best on skis? Was it not healthful to battle the elements in the cold of winter? While skiing, was one not really living, as a man ought to live? We shall return to this

In the battle for women's suffrage in 1912, Lloyd George, Lord Haldane, and Sir Edward Grey, three of Prime Minister Asquith's cabinet, have trouble controlling their "Shees—who won't be obeyed." Asquith is munching 'anti' sandwiches. No surprise; suffragettes had thrown stones at No.10 Downing Street. (Punch, January 3, 1912. Author's collection).

Idræt concept at various points, as it is an important foundation for much of modern skiing.

The first to study the roots and changes of skiing terms, and to use that study to argue through linguistics where skiing began and how its diffusion had taken place, was Andreas Hansen, geologist, self-taught linguist, believer in the then-current scientific fad that skull measurement could predict character traits and, at the time, librarian-friend of Fridtjof Nansen.[28] Nansen, in his seminal *Paa Ski over Grønland,* published in 1890, incorporated Hansen's theory of skiing's origin and its diffusion.[29] From philological deduction he designated the Altai region the cradle of skiing. This was not an assertion to be taken lightly by Norwegian nationalists. Up to that point, everyone had assumed that skiing's birth had taken place in Norway. Nansen mapped out the way that knowledge of the ski passed from the Altai mountains, how it traveled north and east to the Bering Straits via the Tungus, Jakuts, Jukagirs, and Tsilksjers. Skis also passed north and west from the Altai, coming to the Ugrian Finns and then to the Sami lands. Nansen found a different origin for the arrival of skis in Norway and Sweden: Aryan groups brought them from the northern Caucasus through eastern Europe. Much of his theory is questionable. The Finns probably reached the present area of Finland early in the Christian era where they mingled with Scandinavian types who had fished, hunted, and skied since Neolithic times; the Riihimäki ski is about 3,500 years old.[30] As for the Sami, Nansen believed they were a direct stem coming from the Altai. Modern research has shown that the Sami have more in common with the Votyaks and Samoyeds from Russia than with any other group.[31] Professor Wiklund characterized Hansen's work as "dilettante," and others pointed out linguistic errors.[32]

This is not to say that the linguistic connections are not useful as historical facts, but to determine that the diffusion of such an important cultural artifact as the ski, a life-saving means of survival in the days before any other sort of winter transportation, depends only on linguistic ties is stretching the evidence. The idea of making skis and experimenting with them was more likely a local response to a need in many unrelated regions, not the importation of an invention from the Altai region along the lines on Nansen's map and what diffusion-oriented philologists and ethnographers claim to be the case. If the knowledge of skiing was, indeed, passed on from tribe to tribe, why did it never travel across the Bering Straits? Except for some Russian traders who tramped around on skis in the 1790s and early 1800s in what is now Alaska,[33] until Norwegians settled in the Americas in the mid-1800s, skis were unknown in North and South America.

There are premodern and modern examples of local inventiveness to draw upon. In the mid-seventeenth century, the Jesuit priest Diego de Rosales commented upon the use of reeds that the Peguenches of the southern ranges of the Cordillera near Tierra del Fuego, bound on their feet in winter. These were not skis to glide over the snow but devices employed in a walking fashion similar to snowshoes. The Austrian anthropologist Martin Gusinde later described these *xo she ke xam*i as a small bundle of reeds tied together so people could go over the deep snow.[34] Similarly inventive, Samuel Hnateck, a skilled carpenter, made primitive skis in Sils-Maria, Switzerland. He showed them off in an 1860 photograph, broad, comparatively short (170 cm.), thick planks with a simple toe strap. In the great blizzard of 1888 when the snow shut down America's eastern seaboard, an enterprising African American attached boards of a foot and a half long and a half foot wide to his boots to make his way through

Newark, New Jersey, exciting considerable merriment.[35] Necessity creates ingenuity here, just as it did for thousands of years among the various tribes of the northern latitudes.

Procopius, and I suspect the recorder of the Dinglings, can only have known of skis and their use from hearsay. We are also on the unsure winds of myth when hearing of the deeds of Ullr and Skade. The exaggerations of Kings Eystein and Sigurd contain the variations of hundreds of oral tales before being written down sometime between c. 800 and 1000 AD. The hunting motifs of some rock carvings are clear, but what to make of a rabbit on skis, or the strange figure seen on the rocks near Lake Onega? The early history of skiing is far more reliable from the artifacts extracted from the bogs, yet those few dilapidated pieces have little of the heroic about them but their age. But age is important; besides sleds, skis are the oldest transportation known to humankind, and skiing has a widespread history . . . from the Altai to Zakopane, from the Arctic to Kilimanjaro.

CHAPTER 2 Skis for a Purpose

*But it would seem a greater marvel to hear about men who are able
to tame trees and boards, so that by fastening boards seven or eight
ells long under his feet, a man is made able to pass the bird on the
wing, or the fleetest greyhound that runs in the race, or the reindeer
which leaps twice as fast as the hart. For there is a large number of
men who run so well on skis that they can strike down nine reindeer
with a spear, or even more, in a single run. Now such things must
seem incredible, unlikely, and marvelous in all those lands where men
do not know with what skill and cleverness it is possible to train the
board to such great fleetness.*—The King's Mirror, c. 1250 AD

Webbed snowshoes, ski-like sliding snowshoes, and skis
were invented for the purpose of winter survival. In the pre-
industrial world, virtually no farming or field labor could be
carried on in the depths of a snowy winter. To survive, people
ate what they had in store. They also hunted game, but their
difficulties increased in winter; birds and most animals had
the advantage of flight and speed over the human hunter. To
this day, in Canada, which is snowbound in winter, the snowshoe remains the symbol of winter.

Anthropologists have analyzed the varieties of snowshoes in the Arctic, in
parts of the Americas, in Europe, Japan, and Korea. Some were small, round
platters; others were frame-and-web contraptions of many shapes.[1] As long as
the snow was not too deep and powdery, snowshoes were excellent for check-
ing traps and hunting with bow and, later, gun, but they were too slow when
it came to a chase. Far more effective was the ski—a smooth piece of wood
fashioned to let the hunter glissade over the snow rather than sink into it. The
longer and broader the ski, the better it would carry the weight of a man on top
of the snow. In Californian gold mining days, men specifically chose skis over
snowshoes simply because snowshoes proved useless in the deep powder of
the Sierra Nevada. "We started with the Canadian snowshoes," reported one
mining engineer, "but soon abandoned them for the Norwegian skis."[2]

The world over, skis were made from local wood. Soft pine and fir, hard
birch, ash and oak were common until hickory was recognized as superior

both for flexibility and durability and became available from the southern United States starting about 1900. The early skis unearthed from the peat bogs were roughly fashioned and served as plain utilitarian instruments without any regular pattern. These unsophisticated, hand-hewn boards continued to be made long after ski factories began producing sporting skis for a mass market. In the United States, the homemade board was used in backcountry Idaho in the late 1930s. During the Second World War, Italian troops destroyed most of the old Bloke skis, primitive boards then still used by Slovenian peasants as means of transport, in order to prevent their use by partisans.[3]

THE WOODEN-BOARD PEOPLE OF ASIA

Nowhere are we more unsure of the early history of skiing than in Asia[4]— here considered to be east of the Urals, south to the Himalayan chain, and east to China and Japan. From China, a document of the West Han period (206 BC–225 AD) that has recently emerged, reports that "people of the Dingling nationality living in the Altai mountains of northwest China sped like goats in the valleys and on the flatlands wearing the 'horns of goats'—a kind of knee high fur boot under which is bound a wooden board with a hoof-shaped front tip."[5] The remark is cited again 750 years later, and over the next millennium there are only five other accounts that mention skiing. The Shiwei of northern China, "afraid of falling into pits, sped by riding on wooden boards."[6] The use of poles—"they were supported by curved sticks"—made another tribe, the "Wooden Board Tujue," able to reach "nearly one hundred meters quickly in one step." There are further references during the Sung to Yuan dynasties (960–1368). Of particular interest is the explanation of how the Baximis used horsehair under the ski "which touch the snow with its growing direction towards the back for fast skiing. . . . People run faster than a deer when going downhill, use poles when on flatland, and carry the boards in their hands when going uphill." The horse pelt was used to counter sticking snow, not—as elsewhere in the world—to aid in going up the hill. Oak skis from the Han people, undercoated with boar skin, hang in the Sapporo Ski Museum in Japan.

The first reference to skijoring, where a skier is pulled by an animal, comes from China. During the Yuan and Ming dynasties (1271–1644) "tens of dogs pull a person on a pair of wooden boards . . . galloping on the snow and ice faster than a horse." I have taken most of this material from *A History of Chinese Skiing* (in Chinese) published in 1993.[7] The one account from the Tang dynasty, written by the Persian historian, Raschid ed-Din, has been known since 1878 and published numerous times in Western languages. For years, the only thing that Westerners knew of skiing from Turkestan to Mongolia was that experienced skiers could "run circles round the inexperienced ones, especially on steep slopes."[8] With the publication of the Chinese history, and the work in English in the collected papers of the International Society for the History of Physical Education and Sports conference at Lillehammer just before the Olympic Games in 1994, the standing of the Altai region as the place where skiers first put on boards seems, in spite of so few accounts, secure until other evidence is found.

THE OUTLANDISH NORTH, C. 500–1650

The story of skiing in Medieval and Renaissance Europe (c. 500–1650) is almost without exception told as part of tales in the literature of hunting and warfare, the two finding in the god Ullr a common protector. Procopius' (c. 550) Scrithiphini hunted on skis, as did their women. Paul the Deacon's (790) men on skis "hauled in the wild animals," and Adam of Bremen's (1070) Scridfinnae "overtake the wild beasts in the snow,"[9] the onomatopeic *Scrithi* or *Scrid* meaning "swishing along."

The Old Norse sagas and the Eddas, however, form the foundation of most of what we know about medieval skiing. Through all the boastings and exaggerations, the storytelling effects and oral pictures, the poetic contrivances, literary conceits, myths and time warps, it is still possible to draw knowledge of northern Europe's ski hunters and warriors from these epics. Most of them were written for and about the ruling elite. Prowess of god and king and company was staple fare. Ullr was such a skillful skier that "no one would race for a wager with him,"[10] and Olav Tryggvason—whom we shall meet in nineteenth-century guise later—was a king better on skis than most.[11] Physical prowess was demanded of a leader, and skiing was considered one of nine requirements. Men with skiing ability were sought by kings. In the ninth century, Finn the Little, known for his excellence in skiing and archery, served King Rörik, and Atti the Fool's hunting success on skis was legendary, too.[12] Arnljot's tall tale of carrying two people behind him on his skis and "striding off as quickly with them both as if he was alone and without any weight," certainly must have challenged the imagination of the audience. Its fascination endured the centuries, giving a thousand-year authority to the Norwegian Ski Association (*Norges Skiforbund*) founded in 1908, which pictured the threesome in their publications.

Kings themselves delighted in skiing. Einar Thambarskelfir was "skilled at snowshoeing [skiing] better than any other man, and was a man of the greatest prowess and valour."[13] Sons of the King of Finland, Vighard, Starkad and

The medieval story of Arnljot Gelline carrying two people behind him on his skis was exaggerated by the Norwegian nationalistic poet (and winner of the Nobel Prize in Literature in 1903) Bjørnstjerne Bjørnson (1832–1910). Arnljot also became a three-act opera and was picked up at the end of the nineteenth century as a symbol of Norwegian skiing for the Ski Association. (Norske Skiløpere: Namdal, Nord Norge, 1960)

others are picked out for their hunting ability, particularly their twisting and turning on "wood-shod feet."[14]

Finns portrayed by Saxo Grammaticus about 1200, "are wont to glide on slippery timbers, scud along at whatever pace they will. . . . As soon as they have damaged the enemy, they fly away as speedily as they approach, nor is the retreat they make quicker than their charge."[15] (It brings to mind the Finns' patriotic war against the Soviet Union over seven hundred years later.) The records before the sixteenth century, and a few afterward, did not distinguish Finns from Lapps. Olaus Magnus, publishing in the mid-sixteenth century, complained that the older writers often used the word *Finns* to cover all the folk in the north, and modern research has confirmed this practice.[16] Lapps were considered the best skiers. An Icelandic law of 1250 condemned criminals to be chased to far-off regions where "even on skis, the Lapps cannot go."[17] Those who wrote the accounts reported what they had heard; no one before Olaus Magnus had actually seen skiing in practice. There was a tendency to lump Lapps and Finns together as barbarians living on the fringes of the world, in the land of Thule. From the comforts of Rome and Paris, it hardly mattered.

When we know so little about skiing in the Middle Ages, and so little about it in the lands to the East, mainly Russia, it is remarkable that what we do know often comes from military sources. This, in itself, would be merely of interest, but it is truly remarkable that as skiing became a national sport about 1900, in many countries of Europe military officers played leading roles in encouraging and organizing skiing. They had five hundred years of history behind them.

Two military exploits in Scandinavia are commemorated annually with thousands of participants in the Norwegian Birkebeiner race and the Swedish Vasalopp. The Birkebeiner keeps alive the memory of the 1206 rescue of the two year old heir to the throne of Norway, Haakon Haakonsen, by retracing the route from Rena to Lillehammer. The Vasa, as it is now known in the English world, commemorates the 1523 return from Sälen to Mora of Gustavus Vasa, the Swedish king, to save his country from Denmark.

The Birkebeiner has spawned an offspring in Telemark, Wisconsin, USA, one of twelve marathons on the world circuit, which the Vasalopp has recently joined. On its fiftieth anniversary, in 1972, nearly eight thousand contestants skied the c. 85-kilometer course. In 2004, thirty-four countries were represented: it has become a world sporting happening giving a social meaning to all but very few of the 43,498 participants.

Scraps of information from a wide variety of sources over a few hundred years show how widespread skiing had become for practical, day-to-day winter living and for military activity. From Norway in the fifteenth and early sixteenth centuries, reports of the military on skis include Karl Knutsen, at the head of his ski troops, who invaded Skåne in 1452 in the war against Sweden.[18] Thirty years later, troops and prisoners were dispatched on skis from Moscow, over the Urals east to Irtisch and the Ob. In Russia, some four thousand of the Service Nobility were said to have used skis to deploy from the Urals to "Lapina" at end of the fifteenth century.[19]

"In the winter they travel here [the Perm region, about 250–300 miles east of Moscow] as in most parts of Russia," reported von Herberstein in the mid-sixteenth century, "almost entirely in *artach* which are a sort of oblong wooden shoes, nearly six palms in length, which they fasten on the foot and perform their journeys with great speed." The Letts, the Poles, and the Finns of the Volga also knew skiing.[20] Few of the Russian finds from the eighth to the sixteenth centuries have been studied. Present classification remains untrustworthy until more skis become available for analysis.[21]

The *Kalevala*, the Finnish epic poem, is equally interesting as a nationalistic document as it is as a folktale of the hunter Leminkainen. Probably first printed in the sixteenth century, it is part of every Finn's heritage today. The following nineteenth-century translations show with what care skis were made for our hero. Here Lylikki, ski maker, master artist and craftsman

Whittled in the fall his snowshoes,
Smoothed them in the winter evenings,
One day working on the runners,

All the next day making stick rings,
Till at last the shoes were finished.
Then he fastened well the shoe-straps,
Smooth as adder's skin the woodwork,
Soft as fox fur were the stick rings.
Oiled he well his wondrous snow-shoes,
With the tallow of the reindeer.[22]

Elias Lönnrot, the Finnish scholar who put the *Kalevala* together from
numerous tales in 1835, discovered that the hero was not a Finn at all but actually Wilhelm Lüdecke, a German agent from the Hansa port of Visby on the
island of Gotland. In Lönnrot's second edition, he substituted Leminkainen
for Lüdecke, made him the ski-running, elk-hunting hero, and turned him
into a thoroughly Finnish character, retelling the tale from a version that had
originally come from the northeastern part of Finland.[23] Besides giving Finland a national poem, the manipulation of turning Lüdecke into a skiing hero
is indicative of the power of providing perceived local, heroic qualities of folkish nationalism in the nineteenth century. Finns had a homegrown hero while
suffering Russian overlordship.

As background for Olaus Magnus's history, the most important source
for understanding the place of skiing in Renaissance Scandinavia, we should
understand that Scandinavia, "the North"—no one was sure how far the land
actually stretched—was part of the outlandish world where demons and
anthropophagi dwelled with monster fishes, and where the eternal cold lay
frozen. So when, in the eleventh century, Adam of Bremen's Skridfinnae are
said to fly faster than the beasts, it appears as another extraordinary facet of
this unknown and fearful land of miracles. Saxo continued this mythic tale-
telling, not without adding a hint of admiration for the natural wonders of the
land. It was this pagan ambience that interested the Church, which learned
about rich mineral deposits along with serpents, pygmies, and Lapps in the
fifteenth century. Some more down to earth knowledge came from an Italian
sea captain, Pietro Quirini, ship-wrecked off the Lofoten Islands in 1432. He
spent the winter in Røst but never mentioned skis.[24] These tales were grist for
the Swedish bishop.

Olaus Magnus published the *Carta Marina* in 1539 and the *Historia de gentibus septentrionalibus* in 1555. Both deserve analysis. Although the *Historia* is
always attributed to Olaus Magnus, his elder brother, Johannes, was for much
of his life Olaus's chancellor and co-traveler. Johannes wrote his own opus,
Historia de omnibus Gothorum Sveonumque regibus. One cannot help but believe

that there was cooperation between the two. In a booklet about the *Carta,* Olaus announces both his own *Historia* as well as his brother's *Gothorum Historia.*[25] The *Carta* may have been the result of a trading investigation to Holland on which Olaus Magnus had been sent by Gustavus Vasa in 1527.[26] The *Carta* is intentionally drawn out of scale. It is a document designed, as Kurt Johannesson suggests, to give courage to the Norwegians in their fight with the Danes. The map focuses almost entirely on the peninsula of Scandinavia and more particularly on Norway and on its people. The king is urging—per the Book of Revelation—that Norwegians should stand up for themselves, and the obvious warrior types on skis all seem to be attacking, if not the Danes, then other barbarians to the east.[27]

The Church wished to gather in these lands for the Roman see, and Olaus Magnus became the spokesman for the fabled northland and its folk. His *Historia* juxtaposed fear and admiration in terms of exaggerations: fishes are monstrous, in that country snow is deepest, beasts are the wildest. Men lived in these parts but were able to do so only because they had learned from nature. Men and women skied on the hunt and for sport. "Two sorts of men are found in these places that run Races for Wagers most swiftly," as the English translation of 1658 has it. "The first is the *Wild* or *Laplander* because upon crooked Stilts or long Stakes fastened to the soles of his feet, he transports himself upon the snow in Dales and Mountains, in a dangerous way, by a winding and arbitrary motion, and he doth it with a most perfect Art, whether he be to encounter with adverse accidents, or he doth it for sport in Hunting . . . or whether he undertakes this for a prize or a glory."[28]

Olaus had witnessed skiing and detailed that one ski was longer than the other, that both front tips were pointed up and with the undersides covered with reindeer skin. His book was both an immediate and long-term success on publication in 1555; within one hundred years it went through twenty editions and was translated into French, Italian, German, and English.[29] The woodcuts make popular illustrations today because they are so quaint. It is as if men and women are shod with wooden clogs with long and pointed tips. It has been suggested that Olaus did the drawings himself,[30] but that seems far-fetched because the skis pictured in the book bear little resemblance to Olaus Magnus's description. In the third Italian edition, published in 1664, it was announced that the woodcuts were by "the great Titian and his brother Cesare Veccello."[31] Johann Schefferus, a professor at Uppsala University, and an eye-witness to much of what he wrote in *Lapponia* published in 1673 (in English the following year, and in German in 1675), dismissed the images as the "fancy and figment of an Italian painter," who had obviously not understood Lapp skiers.[32] If that is the case, it is curious that Olaus allowed such obvious falsifications.

Olaus's *Carta* and his *Historia* were published in Venice and Rome so far from the land of Thule. But knowledge of "the North" was growing in the rest of Europe. In his *Jerusalem Delivered,* the much-read Torquato Tasso (1544–95), relying on hearsay, described German "peasant girls, in groups, on thin long skis running on the Rhine and in great safety glide."[33] Giovanni Guagnini (1538–1614) of Verona had soldiered in Poland for many a year and was probably the first Italian to have actually witnessed skiing. In *Sarmatiae Europeae Descriptio,* he writes of the *narta,* short skis used by the Perms, Volga Finns as well as in the region near Moscow. The drawing that accompanies his work is more realistic than those found in Olaus Magnus, although it shows only a very small part of the ski behind the foot.[34] Whereas Olaus Magnus's skis are fantastic, one might be able to ski on Guagnini's. Only a few other reports and observations filtered south from Scandinavia when, for example, Gustavus Adolphus sent reindeer along with their Lapp herders to some German princes.[35]

There is a lack of source material from Scandinavia. Skis are first mentioned in an account of a battle in 1200 near the present capital, Oslo.[36] The Birkebeiner rescue of 1206 has become part of Norwegian national identity, known far more from the romantic-nationalistic painting of Knud Bergslien in 1869 than from any written history, and kept alive in the reenactment of the Birkebeiner marathon since 1932. After the *King's Mirror* of 1250, a Norse book of manners, there is a remarkable lack of any mention of skiing for some three hundred years. One hears of elk protection from hunters on skis in 1274, and the story-filled *Flatøybok* of 1390 retells an earlier tale from the eleventh century. That is about all that is mentioned about skiing until the postal decrees of the 1520s and 1530s.[37] After Olaus Magnus's *Historia,* there was one brief mention of skiing in a Latin poem, and in the mid-seventeenth century a tale appeared about a Lapp skier who duped some Russians.[38] Historians have been at a loss to explain the lack of descriptions of skiing. The period from 1200 to 1650 was one of Norway's troubled times when feudal overlords and folkish kings subdued areas and then were taken over themselves. The on-again, off-again skirmishing against Swede and Dane, often over the question of succession, caused continuing disruption. Only one king, Haakon IV (1223–62), was of such stature to be invited to crusade with Louis IX; he had trade and marriage connections to Castile, to England, and to the Holy Roman Emperor.[39] It was during his reign that the *King's Mirror* was written, but that is the lone literary source. It is also true that there are no *belles lettres* in the

R. Jensen copied the 1873 painting of the Birkebeiner by Knud Bergslien. In what has become skiing's most well-known picture, he depicted the saving of Norway's heir to the throne by Torstein Skeivla and Skervald Skrukka of the Birkebeiner (Birchleg) party, who carried the prince to safety from Lillehammer to Østerdalen in 1206. The original painting symbolized the growing nationalism of Norway that was evidently strong enough a decade later for Jensen to copy it exactly. When the marathon race, the Birkebeinerrennet, was founded in 1932, the course followed the supposed escape route, as it still does every year. (Courtesy Mammoth Ski Museum, Beekley collection)

fourteenth and fifteenth centuries. In the private letters that have been analyzed, the use of skis was not mentioned. Skiing was simply a way to get about for country folk in the winter, something that did not warrant commentary. And who would tell tales of skiing when the Black Death was the scourge of the land?

DEFENSE AND COMPETITION, 1650–1826

Much of the interest in skiing for the next 150 years centered on military readiness in winter. Armies began to owe allegiance to a king rather than to a local lord. Centralizing military control was a common development in early modern Europe, and one upon which the Swedish Gustavus Adolphus was able to capitalize successfully. The trend toward royal command often paralleled the notion that armies were also fighting for the cause of the state. In the period prior to the French Revolution, a military force became an arm of the increasing central control imposed by monarch and government. Where regions such as Norway wished to escape domination from what they considered foreign overlordship, incipient nationalism became an ingredient in morale building cohesion. Since Norway might require protection in winter, the use of skis was discussed.

Warfare required armies to live off the land. That being impossible in winter, they had to carry much of what they needed. Numbers of men were small, and sometimes only those on skis could maneuver at all. During the period of the great northern upheaval, there are many reports of local efforts to raise ski formations before and after Sweden's Charles XII's (1697–1718) attempt to put himself on the northern and eastern European stage.[40] We know very little about the success or failure of these troops. What has come down is the odd heroic tale such as the Lapp who led Russians on skis over a precipice. After it first appeared in 1650, "The Fatherlandish Sacrifice of a Lapp" took on a life of its own. Two hundred years later, Wergeland set the same story in Norway. A German then wrote a poem, making the hero a Norwegian and the Swedes the enemy, which Carl Luther, the influential editor of the most widely read German ski periodical, *Der Winter,* published twice during and soon after the First World War. Nansen also told the tale and Erwin Mehl reprinted it in his 1964 book.[41] The tale has been put to varied uses: to bolster incipient nationalism, folk-heroics, heritage, and modern war-spirited defense.

When Norway raised ski troops at the beginning of the eighteenth century, major changes in the way of thinking about skiing were occurring, and they point toward the modern conception of skiing as a sport. Some of the detachments were under the command of Lieutenant Jens Henrik Emahusen who later wrote out in German, the military language of the day, the well-known ski troop regulations of 1735.[42] Oberstløytnant C. Hals produced a pamphlet on waxing in 1761.[43] This was just four years before the publication of what is known as Grüner's book, with its colorful drawings of soldiers at ski drill. Reports of ski competitions followed, with detailed regulations and budgeted prize money: cross-country running, downhill races, *slalåm,* jumping, and firing at a target while going downhill. Prizes were awarded according to the military value of the event; *slalåm* and jumping rank in the middle at 10 *Riksdaler.* Cross-country, obviously the easiest, received 2–4 Rdr. Shooting on the run was rated the most difficult at 20 Rdr. At a time when a horse was worth about 10 Rdr. and a milking cow about 5 Rdr., these were no mean prizes.[44] These races were organized and timed, with rules and regulations. In short, the Norwegian army started to ski for sport in a modern fashion. And these

Six paintings of ski troops' exercises in 1765 illustrated Grüner's booklet of regulations. One wonders about the accuracy of the shot taken while skiing. In reality, soldiers skied into position and then fired standing, kneeling, or lying down. (Courtesy Norwegian Armed Forces Museum)

competitions were nothing new; they had been conducted for some years, but no exact date is known. For a long time, the birth of modern skiing in the 1860s has been associated with the Christiania bourgeois' excitement over the speed and jumping style of Sondre Norheim and his Telemark companions when they came to town. But recent work by Olav Christensen and others has emphasized that the roots of modern skiing lie at least one hundred years further back than Norheim's almost mythical leap to fame.[45]

Norwegian troops on skis proved themselves in the war of 1808 against Sweden, particularly Prince Karl August's 2,200 men.[46] But in 1826 they were disbanded. Historians can only speculate on the reasons, for no documents have turned up. When Sweden swapped the overlordship of Finland for Norway in the 1814 political rearrangements, the border no longer required watching, and troops kept over winter were expensive. Norwegian nationalists were not strong enough to demand total political freedom. That would have to wait until the latter part of the century.

ENLIGHTENED EUROPE MARVELS AT SKIING

While news of Norwegian army units on skis occasionally filtered into the Western European press, accounts from travelers also became increasingly available. At the behest of a monarch, in the interests of scientific inquiry and economic gain, Westerners probed the land of mountains and waters on the fringe of civilization in nature's everlasting snows. Dutch Captain Cornelius De Jong, who wrote about the skiing soldiers after a visit to the Trondheim area in 1797, was not by any means the first Westerner to visit the northlands of Scandinavia and Russia. In the 1650s, over one hundred years earlier, a ski had been on exhibit in Leyden, Holland,[47] although little was known about it. Regnard and de la Martinière from France, Negri from Italy, Brand from England, and the German Gleditsch, all ventured into the uncharted cold of the north in the seventeenth century. They returned with strikingly similar tales to tell. Martinière remarked on a Laplander "skating on the snow as fast as we rode in our sledges . . . on skates which were made of the bark of a tree, . . . seven feet and a half long, four fingers broad and flat at the bottom." Regnard marveled at Lapps who could outspeed the animals, that "it was impossible to conceive how they are able to hold upon the most precipitous descents and how they are able to go up the most jagged mountain," sometimes with a pole in each hand. Their women were "not less adroit than the men." The Jerawena, reported Brand, went off hunting for three or four months at a time. They skied "with such speed and easiness as a bird," and they were able to climb mountains "continually in circles" and came down at "incredible speed."[48] Here was a fact of northern life worth noting.

These Western European observers were marveling at matters unimaginable in their own lands. Although they continued to explain these wonders in the manner of the traditional miracles of the northern world begun by the medieval word spinners and continued by the sixteenth century mapmakers and writers, theirs was personal, first-hand experience. But why is there so very little information produced in Norway itself?[49] Once Norway had become part of the Danish kingdom in the fourteenth century, there were no official Norwegian reports, indeed, no Norwegian literature. The first book in Norwegian, published in Norway (there had been others published in Denmark) was printed in 1643.[50] Norwegian folktales and ballads passed down orally over the generations came to general notice only in the first half of the nineteenth century when they were collected and published.

Yet, as in so many other parts of Europe, a growing sense of some incipient national feeling was directed against the new overlordship of the Swedes. The geography of Norway, however, militated against either a cultural or a political unity. The once well-known *Norðvegr,* the North Way, was in reality the coastline from Vestfold to Hålogoland. This strip gained its cohesiveness from the sea, not from the land. To move from north to south meant the use of boats—as it does today—and anyone trying to go from east to west in winter had to have skis. Little wonder there was no "imagined community," to use Benedict Anderson's useful concept, to which Norwegians might belong. Some strong personality was needed to overcome all obstacles, to "awaken Norway from her sleep one day."[51] But no one gave a thought to the prospect of his arriving on skis.

SKIING IN ISOLATION: BLOKE

With one exception, none of the travelers to Scandinavia and the vast northern expanses of Russia had been to Carinthia, that tucked-away hilly area of the Habsburg Empire (at present, stretching across the Austrian and Slovenian border), with Bloke on an 800-meter plateau. Skiing there came to modern Western attention only in 1893; and twenty years later, Bloke skis were on display in an international hunting exhibition in Vienna. Yet a special local skiing technique had been practiced as a means of transportation by the country population of Bloke for over two hundred years, as we know from the local lord, Freiherr von Valvasor.[52]

Whether skis and skiing came to Bloke from abroad or whether they were an indigenous invention has been debated mostly in Slovenian, German, and Swedish publications. The claim of indigenous skiing in 1888 on the Trnovska plateau is hard to believe, but there is no doubt that locals in that area were on skis in the early 1890s.[53] The forester E. Heinrich Schollmeyer claimed in 1893 that skis developed there with no outside influence. Research in the 1950s came down heavily on the side of local invention, and recent work confirms this view.[54] Before paternity for Bloke skiing is established, some scholars call for further research in archeological finds, records of church and war ministries and chronicles, local ones as well as those in Swedish, Danish, Norwegian, Austrian, German, and Turkish archives.[55] Valvasor's original 1659 description of ski length and width and the manner of using the equipment has been confirmed as similar to the skis and skiing of Bloke in the nineteenth and twentieth centuries, right up to the Second World War; and it is interesting to see, now, how the old Bloke skiing is employed as the foundation for modern Slovenian skiing—another of those Hobsbawmian invented traditions.[56]

The war almost brought Bloke skiing to an end. After occupation in December 1941, the Italians defined thirty-one areas where locals could ski, but that winter in February they restricted both individual and group skiing, threatening confiscation of equipment and payment of a fine if the law was disobeyed. In 1942, they demanded that all skis be turned in to the military authorities. Failure to comply meant three months in prison and a 5,000 lira fine. This put a stop to any guerrilla winter war by the partisans. The locals, however, burned most of the skis. In 1954 of the original seven hundred, only ten pairs could be rounded up. Fortunately, a few of the older ones had already found their way to various museums, and it is upon those that modern research has relied.[57]

Valvasor's book was known to the German encyclopedist Gerhard Vieth in 1794, and a visiting bishop's report of 1820 tells of Bloke parishioners on "curious, long, narrow thin boards."[58] In today's terms, Bloke skis were neither long nor narrow: about 150 centimeters long and 12 centimeters wide. Twenty-five years later, "skiers go everywhere and even the women go to church on Sundays [on skis]."[59] Even as the beginning of the sport of skiing slowly made its presence felt in Europe in the latter part of the nineteenth century, skis continued to be used by farmers, by churchgoers—one woman kept a special pair of *Totenski des Hauses,* or funeral-going skis, on hand—by woodsmen, teachers and others for purely utilitarian purposes. As sport skiing developed in the twentieth century, the notion of usefulness continued to play an important role.

CHAPTER 3

The Norwegian Thrust

*A time will come without doubt, when the peoples of Europe will
make good use of this instrument [ski], so useful and so cheap.*
—De Latocnaye, Promenade d'un Français en Suède
et en Norvège, *1801*

*Skiing had become a truly popular sport in which a major portion
of the city's youth and a large part of its older population have
participated in their search for health and a brisk physical exercise.*
—Tromsø Tidende, *April 1843*

*A new era opened for a sport, superb at the same time captivating,
and one looks in vain for something similar the world over.*
—Fritz Huitfeldt, *February 1871*

The Industrial Revolution changed the landscape, population,
politics, and mores of Europe in the nineteenth century. From
the Urals to Uruguay, from Kosciusko to Kobe, industrialization molded much of the world into its modern mode of work
and play. It had a profound impact on skiing as well. The
change in skiing was no sudden break, and it did not happen,
as industrialization did not happen, at the same pace or time
all over the world. What had been part of a folk winter culture
became recreational enjoyment for urban civilization, although the utilitarian
use of skis continued well into the 1930s. The relationship of health to skiing
took on an increasingly prominent role as sport became an interest of nationalistic concern. Creating Norwegian nationalism was a major undertaking of
intellectuals, who incorporated skiing into song, ballad, poem, play, and story.
They literally inculcated a series of beliefs in the way folk with their regional
traditions of dialect, clothes, and type of skis embraced national identities. This
changing intellectual heritage provided the backdrop for the mass outpouring
of enthusiasm on the return of Fridtjof Nansen from Greenland and, later,
from his attempt on the North Pole.

OLD SKIS IN A MODERNIZING WORLD

Hunting on skis continued well into the twentieth century. Cultural anthropologists have recognized that traditional means continue long into a period of

change. Modernizing societies are those whose traditional forms do not simply disappear. On the hunt, for example, besides the usual elk and deer, bear and wolves were often the prey. "You kill a wolf like this," recounted Johan Turi about a hunt in mid-nineteenth-century Norway:[1]

> The active and clever Lapp will ski after it when the snow is deep. . . . And when you have caught him up, you hit him with the ski staff on the head, or on the neck under the ear, or just on the black of the nose tip which is very tender; in other places he won't feel anything however hard you hit. But the man must be quick . . . [for] a wolf is very quick at snapping at the staff with his mouth, and he snaps at the skis too, and shakes them till the man falls off them . . . then the wolf leaps upon him and bites him.
>
> To chase a wolf on skis is the very worst thing there is for ruining folks' health. Then you must ski till the blood comes into your mouth, and you get so hot you must uncover the whole of your chest. . . . You sweat so that your clothes nearest the skin are wet, and you are so tired you can hardly manage to get back.

This is from one who knows. Turi had given up reindeer herding for wolf hunting; the challenge was what counted. In the forest, in deep snow, not too hard and not too soft, as long as "you are not bitten you will catch him." Drawings from the turn of the century give the eye a view of what it must have been like.[2] The earliest extant Canadian-made skis, from 1867, were used in wolf hunting in the Northwest Territories by an immigrant Sami who was reported to have killed over half a dozen while on skis.[3]

Hunting on skis among the tribes of nineteenth-century Siberia is documented too. The accounts vary only in the description of the skis. Most comment on the distances achieved in a day. The Yupitatze, a people who lived near the Amur, for example, were able to cover about 60 miles on the shortest winter day, while Samoyeds boasted of 35 miles a day without fatigue.[4]

In Kamchatka, skis were "an appendage of the highest importance," reported Langsdorff, used for breaking trail however deep the snow for the dogs and sleds in the pursuit of sable.[5] Western missionaries on the Sakhalin Islands described the Ainu sitting astride their dogsleds with skis on their feet acting as outriggers. Sometimes they harnessed themselves to reindeer and were pulled along—another form of skijoring—but they did not mention their use for any other purposes.[6]

Numerous other tribes throughout Siberia—Ostyak and Tungus are most commented upon—made use of skis for provisioning during the winter. The

Wolves were the bane of the Sami reindeer herders, decimating their stock unless hunted down. The herder skied swiftly alongside and then hit the wolf's snout as hard as he could or used a short spear. Shown here to an English readership, the image was presented in terms they would well understand, "Sport in Lapland: A Wolf-hunt on Ski." (The Graphic, *December 22, 1900. Author's collection*)

equipment varied slightly: all skis had some form of skin, horse, deer, elk, or seal, according to availability, on the underside to prevent sliding backwards. The tales of these peoples' ability to travel over many days, their dexterity and style in hilly terrain, all attest to a continued use well into the twentieth century in those far-off stretches of the wilderness that industrialization reached late. We are not talking of large numbers of people, either; the Yakuts, around the year 1900, numbered about 200,000, the Tungus 70,000, the Ostyaks 30,000, and the Samoyeds perhaps 12,000.[7] A decade or so ago the snowmobile put a stop to the last major utilitarian use of skis in the world, namely, reindeer herding in the Sami lands.

With Russian expansion into Siberia and eventually to the Pacific, savants became interested in the tribes encountered along the way: Tungus, Yakuts, Yukagirs—in all, over 30 indigenous groups. This picture of an Ostyak in 1827 is clear on the skis but how his feet actually stayed in the contraptions is difficult to say. Although there are many extant skis from nineteenth-century Siberia, most are primitive boards rather than these somewhat akin to a kayak. (Author's collection)

THE NORWEGIAN CASE

Norway presents a different picture; it was here that skis first became a sporting instrument. Yet in the nineteenth century, Norway was hardly an industrializing nation, let alone a political state. Neighboring Sweden was more industrialized, yet Sweden tended to follow what Norwegians did where skiing was concerned. Recently Sverker Sölin has suggested that skiing was the distinguishing mark of the Sami. Only when Swedes gradually developed the Sami's "feeling for nature" did they take to skis, finding it virtuous, manly, heroic, even peaceful yet also, necessary, something standing at or near the creation of their country by Gustavus Vasa—hence the Vasalopp. The Swedish Tourist Association (*Svenska Turistforeningen*) was founded in 1885 and the Swedish Ski Association (*Svenska Skiforeningen*) ten years later. As in other countries, the promotion of skiing was deemed necessary for national defense.[8] The British ambassador Cecil Spring-Rice arrived in Stockholm at the beginning of the 1908–9 winter. "All the sports are mixed up with fighting business," he wrote to an acquaintance, "one of their great events is military dispatch carrying on skis from some remote point to another."[9] The question is not only why did the changes in skiing take place in Norway first, but also why did Norway take the lead?

When the Norwegian ski troops were disbanded in 1826, interest in skiing diminished rapidly. "The number of competent skiers declines yearly," sighed *Skilling-Magasin* in 1841.[10] If active youth and their fathers gave up skiing, literary intellectuals did not. Skiing, they argued, was peculiar to Norway, and they vowed to reactivate the past in which Ullr and the Vikings had played such vigorous roles. At the time of the disbanding of the ski troops, Norway entered a stage in intellectual and political development in which—it sounds so extraordinary—skiing played a major role. How did skiing augment intellectual philosophies and the creation of a political state to propel historic events?

In service of these broad goals, writers and editors resurrected the Norse sagas, a blend of myth and history. The role of skiing in the transformation of Norway can be understood only against a complex background of cultural and political events. As a Norwegian literary historian has commented, Snorri Sturluson's *Heimskringla* "more than any other single work . . . prepared Norway for the resumption of national existence" after 1814.[11] The raw adventure, the battle with the elements, the physical prowess of protagonists and, probably most important of all, the natural landscape and seascape where the tales of derring-do played out, were more than the local tale of this or that hero, in this or that valley, but something for the whole of Norway. At the same time, the beguiling world of the Romantics found its way from France through Germany to Norwegian academics, first in Copenhagen and then in 1811 at the University of Christiania. They created saga plays and wrote Norway's first national anthem, "For Norway's Land of Heroes" (*For norge, kjaempers Føde-land*). Actually, it was not so much a national anthem as a call to wake up and do something. In the early nineteenth century it was sufficiently rousing for Henrik Wergeland to dub it the "Norwegian Marseillaise," and for the Danes to ban it.[12] There were concerted efforts in archeology, history, folklore, and dialect study to provide a national foundation for a would-be country.

One leading problem was language. The Constitution of 1814, giving Norway a new government under Swedish control, stipulated that the laws of the land be promulgated in Norwegian. However, the Church had its own solemn language, *Kirkmål* (or more exactly *Høitidssproget*), with a base in Danish, while *Landsmål*, the formal literary expression, became popular among the intellectuals. This form was modernized about 1890 and renamed *Riksmål*. At the same time, all vied with and used local dialects. There was no one ubiquitous Norwegian language. This in itself worried the intellectuals who were much impressed with Gottfried Herder's notion that language is the soul of a people speaking. No one language, ergo no one people.[13]

But there was the memory of skiing, perhaps best exemplified in Bernt Lund's poem about the Østerdal soldier-skier, Knud from Trysil. "Trysil Knud" became enshrouded in myth and found his way into folk memory, clubs, children's books, and later into films. It inspired Andreas Aabel in 1863 to write a poem, "East of the Border" (*Der øst ved grensefjeldets side*):

Vel an! I starte, gjeve trysler!
Lad stevne nu i bygden staa
Og øv med flid de vante sysler,
La ski og kuler flittig gaa!
—forat om gang til alvors stevne
vort gamle Norge rober ud
I mote maa med mod og evne
Og staa stødt som Trysil Knud

Hurrah for skiing! Trysil folk,
Train; be ready to rid the yoke.
With gun and bullet be ye free
When Norway calls to fight on ski.
Brave band of brothers firm and good
Take courage from your Trysil Knud.

Although Knud came from Østerdal, the call was for Norway's freedom, and it was to be gained through skiing and war. Andreas Aabel's poem contained many, one might almost say most, of those nineteenth century ingredients so dear to patriotic Norwegians. It is not history, of course, but such rhymes, ballads, and songs convey what was important to the people. That same year Oscar Wergeland published a little book on skiing for clubs and schools that two years later, in 1865, he enlarged to *Skiing, Its History and Use in War* (*Skiløbningen, dens historie og kriegsanvendelse*), the first book to discuss the history of skiing.[14]

Wergeland's book was based on the premise that a state could not be built by feeble folk. Part of the ancient Viking appeal was their vigorous, action-laden lives. Vigorous action required fitness, and *Idræt* provided a concept that covered all the needs. Only recently have Norwegian scholars shown an interest in the origin of *Ski- Idræt*.[15] It makes its appearance almost as a matter of course, as a birthright of all Norwegians. Every country has these sort of self-delusions. Given the indulgence in tobacco and aquavit in those days, an *Idrætsmann* could be hard to find. One of *Idræt's* goals was the health of the individual. Trusting that goal was reached, the health of the whole nation would be bettered. Health was to be attained by taking up the outdoor activities of the ancestors. There is nothing constructed or contrived here. The purity of the old fitness-keeping regimes would ensure the purity of the natural man. This notion was then latched on to the old classical dictum of the healthy mind in a healthy body that the Romantics and later the Victorian English turned into muscular Christianity. There was no overt Christian message in *Idræt;* after all, it was partially based on Ullr and the likes of the marauding Eric Bloodaxe, but the building of a strong body to be part of the strong body politic in nature's grandeur that was Norway, had a religious—not Christian[16]—cast to it. *Idræt* would also make one into a moral, or at least more moral, being. Whether women were included was not entirely clear. Although the sagas provided evidence of strong, fit, and active women—Skade certainly knew her own mind and minded her own skis—and although Norwegian women, as others in Europe, had worked in the fields alongside their men for centuries, the *Idræt* connection was a nineteenth-century concoction of intellectuals who imbibed much from Western European ideals. These ideals placed women increasingly in the home and in a corset. Henrik Ibsen's stand for women is known far and wide; he has been translated into sixty-five languages. Less well known for her stand is Fridtjof Nansen's wife, Eva, who spoke out publicly for women's skiing in a letter to the Christiania paper, *Verdens Gang*.[17]

NORWEGIAN SKIING SPREADS SOUTH

When a few adventurous souls in the heartland of Europe started to experiment with skis, they obtained their information and, indeed, the skis themselves from Norway. Naturally, what was passed down from the north to the Alps was the general use of skis for hunting, farm work, mail delivery, and visiting when the snow precluded journeys on foot. However, there was one major new development in Continental skiing: it was discovered by the wealthy as a pastime.

People in central Europe became aware of Scandinavian skiing through personal contact or through reading about it. The personal contacts were few and only among the "better sort"—men who had traveled to Norway or had Norwegian acquaintances. Skiing articles in magazines and newspapers lay on drawing room tables rather than kitchen tables. The well-to-do and often landed group sponsored the use of skis for their workers. Right from its start in Europe skiing took on something of a class aspect, although the people who actually did the skiing were often the forester, postman, farm hand, and delivery boy,

In the 1770s, the author of *Mineralogische Geschichte des sächsischen Erzgebirges* (History of the Minerals of the Saxon Erzgebirge Mountains) had written of men using "the flat board of the Laplanders with which they can go swiftly over deep snow." But skis first came to wide notice through Gerhard Anton Ulrich Vieth's *Enzyklopädie der Leibesübungen* (Encyclopedia of Physical Exercise) published in 1794. Vieth paraphrased some of Olaus Magnus's *Historia* and asked why there was no skiing in Germany. He contemplated importing Lapp and Ostyak to show how the skis should be managed. In the same region, in about the same era, Karl August Engel in his *Erdbeschreibung von Sachsen* (Geography of Saxony) wrote of a skier as able as "the native Lapp in the use of foot boards and gliding with them as gracefully and fast over the deep snow." Some type of ski was also reported in the Riesengebirge.[18] These occasional references indicate that skis began to be recognized as practical for winter work. That their origin was cited as Lapp should not necessarily be taken as fact. As shown with Olaus Magnus, there was little distinction between the various peoples who lived in the lands to the far north. "Lapp" was almost a generic term, synonymous with anyone on skis.

Although he had included some ski instruction in the second, 1804 edition of *Gymnastik für Jugend* (Gymnastics for Youth), the influence of the renowned Johann Christoph Friedrich GutsMuths's gymnastic pedagogy did not translate into the spread of skiing. He had learned about skis from a Norwegian two years after the first edition of his book had been published in 1793. He made himself a pair of skis and, according to the yearbook of the school where he taught, experimented with them quite successfully in Thuringia.[19] The details of construction and the method of use came from practical experience, not as Vieth had done, from paraphrasing others. In spite of the failure of skiing to take hold in his area, he was an important link between utilitarian skiing and what would become the "skisport." GutsMuths's *Gymnastik* was intended for pupils in school, a very different class of people from the Norwegian peasants he had been told about. Skiing would, indeed, decades later enter the realm of life training, and after that, it was to become a sport. But for now, skiing activity in the Germanies remained minimal, carried on by a few souls here and there. Most locals in the hills and mountain valleys had never had skis, never would. Who would want to spend winter out-of-doors? Why had you spent the autumn piling up the logs for a good fire? In a later edition of *Gymnastik für*

Jugend (1847), there was no mention of skiing, not because the Stuttgart editor was out of tune with ski activity, but because there was none.

How to explain, then, the arrival of skiing in Germany some twenty years later? Again, we must return to Norway. With the decline of ski troops after the Napoleonic wars, in 1812 the Association for Norwegian Well-Being (*Selskab for Norges Vel*) took it upon itself to promote skiing. The association was obviously interested in health, but it was also worried about national defense, and particularly so on the eastern border with Sweden where skis had almost disappeared from use. The association was a civilian organization, staffed by educated professionals. As the role of skiing in the army diminished, this and other civilian associations often combined with rifle clubs and promoted skiing. Army officers frequently played central roles and later, toward the end of the nineteenth century, virtually ran the major ski organizations. Skiing, once the general mode of winter communication among farms and villages—which it would remain for years in areas untouched by road plough or rail—became a bourgeois sport. It was to these new urban clubs that individuals from the rest of Europe traveled or wrote, and it was from these clubs that individual Norwegians came to astonish the novice skiers in Germany, Austria, Switzerland and, later, in France.

Not a few Norwegian students studied mining engineering in places like the Erzgebirge, Riesengebirge, and the Harz. This educated and comparatively wealthy group brought with them the ideal of skiing as a bourgeois sport rather than skiing as a country mode of transport, even though they may have carried *Ski-Idræt* in mind. The exploit of the Norwegian mining student Herman Smith Johansen's (later to be renowned as Canada's Jack Rabbit) trip up the Brocken (Harz) in 1889 appeared as nothing but a pure Norwegian ski adventure rather than anything concocted by the bourgeois.[20] But in this era of *citius, altius, fortius* (faster, higher, stronger), it was the sporting ideal that thrived and was immediately present in early ski racing. As early as 1892 the first four places went to Norwegians in a 10-kilometer race in the Riesengebirge, as did the first four places in the jumping competition.[21] When accounts of skiing appeared in the German sporting press (these German ski meets were duly reported in Norway too), the reports were always of competitions. The Holmenkollen event—Norway's ski equivalent of the Derby, as the English papers termed it, searching for a meaningful synonym—had actually started on Huseby Hill, but its low elevation and lack of snow over the years had forced the organizers either to cancel the meet or transport snow to the jump. Up to 1881, the competition tested climbing up, coming down, jumping, and going along on the flat. In 1883, the jump became separate from the cross-country but all competitors took part in both events. Only in 1933 was it possible to enter for the jump or for the cross-country run; the all-around ideal had given way to specialization.

In 1890 the competition was moved to Ullbakken near Frogneseter, and two years later it found its home at Holmenkollen, with the jump being the centerpiece of the festivities. Thus, when students from Norway came to central Europe, the jump had already been singled out and the old ideal of taking jumps in a cross-country descent had given way to the exhibiting of skill on a prepared structure that enabled exact measurement of performance.

"Exhibiting" skill on a "prepared structure" enabling "exact measurement" all smacked of athletic specialization being acclaimed by crowds of spectators. Norwegians for whom jumping had originally been one part of the cultural *Ski-Idræt*, now found that their jumping success turned them into civilized stars of the skisport: the modernization of ski jumping turned into grand theater, and the Holmenkollen became sacred soil that was annually renewed.

Entrepreneurs—clubs, village fathers, municipal governments—built jumps in order to attract spectators, and no ski center worth its name would be without a jump or two. For the person who skied, he could take the time to become a jumper as well or else let others provide the entertainment. Part of the business of attracting a crowd in Europe and America was the advertising of this or that Norwegian who would exhibit his jumping skills. For the uninitiated, the jump was the great spectacle of the meet. In the early days of Viennese skiing, when Samson gave the first demonstrations, it was the leap of 10 meters that was remembered and retold with superlative enthusiasm in 1896.

But the majority of skiers were not going to jump. Josef Wallner, the Semmering postman who won many a race, put it correctly; the jump "did not really belong to skiing, it was an art form only for the hotel guests of the winter sports centers and the cinemas." People in Austria, before 1910, were talking of jumping for "world records" and the jump as an "attraction for the public." "Gott Ull, hide your head!" exclaimed one of the pioneers.[22] But that did not stop ski centers from building jumps, advertising jumping meets, holding competitions, and attracting Scandinavian experts. All this would last up until the Second World War. In the 1920s and 1930s, the Holmenkollen became even more important as national symbol as Alpine skiing first challenged Nordic cross-country, then almost removed it from central Europe, America, and the East.

In 1896 the Holmenkollen event was described with superlative enthusiasm. Ten years later, when an Austrian, Dr. Gustav Mikusch, journeyed to

"What daring, what skill, what wondrous pluck such a jump required, under any circumstance," the English middle and upper classes were told in 1894. "But how much more so with two wooden planks about eight feet long securely tied to the feet!" Already, the Holmenkollen meet was described as an exhibition of "Norway's national sport." (The Illustrated London News, March 10, 1894. Author's collection)

Christiania, he traveled not merely as an enthusiastic skier but as a pilgrim to the homeland of the skisport. Wilhelm Paulcke, a leading ski figure in the Black Forest (Schwarzwald) area, actually traveled to Norway as the Todtnau Ski Club's representative.[23] The town of Annenberg's skiing founders were proud to name their club Norweger in 1896. Behind all the sporting, there lay the unsubstantiated idea that all Norwegians could ski.

South of the German border, the Austro-Hungarian empire, a vast stretch of land encompassing the highest alpine redoubts and the broad *pusta* of Hungary stretching to the Tatra and the Carpathian ranges, a land of many peoples and languages, increasingly felt the pressures of industrialization while saddled with an aging Habsburg tradition matched by a Habsburg ruler who had come to the throne in 1848. The countryside was dotted with hunting estates, lodges, princely country houses, and shooting tracts. But in the latter part of the nineteenth century there were a number of small towns growing larger, it seemed, by the year. If Vienna had once been the only city, it now found itself rivaled by Prague and Budapest. If all roads led to Vienna, the new railroad joined the countries as never before, just as in Austria it joined the merchant towns of Graz and Mürzzuschlag, along with the older cities of Innsbruck and Salzburg. A new and increasingly large bourgeois class was developing among the landed elite. The new transportation systems of tram and rail made it easy for city folk to travel to the hills.

In 1880 Max Kleinoscheg, a Graz bicycling champion, started correspondence with a Trondheim cyclist, wondering if Norwegian skis would be usable in the Austrian Alps.[24] In the 1890s, the odd Norwegian provided the impetus for skiing in Austria in the same way as in Germany.[25] W. B. Samson and Baron Wedel Jarlsberg, from whom we will hear again, both resided in Vienna, the one as a baker's apprentice, the other as a Swedish diplomat, although he was Norwegian. Samson astonished the Viennese with his jumping, and Wedel Jarlsberg, Fridtjof Nansen's uncle and an unexceptional ski runner, became mentor to the city's enthusiasts.[26] By 1896 both the Austrian *Allgemeine Sport-Zeitung* and the *Norsk Idrætsblad* reported that "the heroes of the international ski competition in Vienna were five Norwegians." Skiing seemed to a visiting Norwegian "a rich man's passion."[27] This was not entirely so. As late as 1913, in Neumarkt, Styria (Steiermark), two Austrians gave a Norwegian ski course for forestry personnel and students at half price.[28] Once competitions started, once the ski organizations began to manage the races, recording results, establishing records, and building jumps—that is, once skiing turned into a modern sport—hunting on skis was reduced to remote valleys into which the new bourgeois ski men (and very few women) rarely found their way. Until competitive skiing was fully organized, it was better to heed the warning the *Österreichische Touristen-Zeitung* sent out in 1911, that all tourists and skiers should keep on good terms with hunters.[29]

The utilitarian use of skis continued on into the sporting era. Among forestry personnel skis were common. In 1891 the *Allgemeine Sport-Zeitung* described Norwegian skis for hunting, an Austrian forestry paper did the same the following year, and in the ensuing years articles extolling skis for hunting appeared in *Waidmanns Heil,* published in the market town of Klagenfurt. The effect was immediate; both Freiherr von Fürstenburg and Ferdinand Reichsritter von Poschinger immediately equipped their foresters with skis in the Böhmerwald of Bavaria. Catalogs appealed to the "hunter, and anyone working on the land or in the woods, post, forester, churchman, teacher, doctor, farmer." Occasionally one of the manufacturing catalogs, like Robert Anheger from Heidelberg, also called attention to skiing for sport.[30] Max Schneider, the editor of *Der Tourist* in Berlin, reprinted some articles. "All in all," summed up one forester in 1894, skis were not only good for forestry work, "but will become in time indispensable."[31] That same year, postmen in Styria were on skis. In St. Andreasberg in the Harz, besides forestry workers and mail carriers, local police were on skis. Later, police were given instruction in how to ski in Birkenstein. Many of the German, Austrian, and Swiss sales catalogs that started to appear in the 1890s claimed that skis were indispensable for hunting, forestry work, transport, and sport. A number of them added to the list: post and telegraph workers, messengers, officials, priests, teachers, country doctors, farmers. Some had appealing illustrations of the happy hunter and the arrival of the mail. However much the catalogs paid court to the utilitarian aspects of skiing, the greater appeal was to the economic class which had the leisure time to ski for sport, the influential *Jagdherren,* owners of hunting lodges and the estates that surrounded them, the very people who employed forester and hunter.

With the rising press of business, the efficiency of mail delivery first by courier and horse, then by railroad, caused postmasters to puzzle over more regular deliveries to snowbound communities. Norwegian postal decrees go back to the early part of the sixteenth century. Once skis became known in the rest of Europe, there were local attempts in the Harz at carrying the mails on skis. The first regular run in the Black Forest (Schwarzwald) over 7 kilometers between Menzenschwand and the Feldberg in the winter of 1891 and 1892 was deemed a success. After a winter's experimentation, the Prussian postal service in Königsberg put its postmen on skis following some instruction. How successful that was, we do not know, but there are enough remarks from Braemar in Scotland to Grindelwald in Switzerland about posts on skis in the years prior to the First World War to indicate that before reliable motor transport and snow clearing machinery, the postman on skis was a welcome sight in snowbound villages. The Swiss had such success with mountain mail carriers that in 1908, the post office paid two-thirds the cost of all equipment for their mailmen. A Semmering mailman put on a fine performance in the ski competitions held at Plötzleinsdorf, Vienna in 1894, and Josef Wallner was so good that other competitors boycotted races he entered.[32]

When Norwegians arrived in Switzerland—Conrad Wild in 1868 in Mitlödi, Glarus for one—they used skis just as they had at home. The St. Bernard hospice monks received a Norwegian pair in 1883 but did not take to them for some fun and games until 1889, and tourists in Arosa and Davos had bought some Norwegian skis too.[33] Naturally some locals had taken to skis, but the utilitarian aspect of skiing had little impact in Switzerland. The country was already accustomed to hosting a wealthy summer clientele, and it was comparatively easy to extend the hotel season for winter sport and recreation. Skiing in Switzerland was quickly understood in economic terms. In 1903 the Guide Association sent two men to Norway to learn how to ski.[34] The summer guide was on his way to becoming the winter ski teacher.

Elsewhere in Europe, too, skis made their social debut in the 1890s, after the first enthusiastic wave for the peasant, utilitarian use passed. Already there were clubs forming in towns, even in such unlikely a place as Copenhagen in 1886. The Yukki Ski Club of St. Petersburg was made up of expatriate English merchants who had lively social occasions in the Toksovo wooded hills, 20 kilometers from the city.[35] Harbinger of things to come.

SPORT FOR HEALTH

L'Illustration's full-page black-and-white photograph of three children, almost nude, one on skis, was captioned: "Miracles of the air, the snow and the sun. How in the mountain fastness one can give health to children brought up in cotton." The date was 1912.[36]

The connection between health and skiing had a history going back, like so many other facets of modernization, to the Enlightenment of the eighteenth century. If a child were immersed in nature's surroundings, the equation went, then body, mind, and soul would automatically prosper. These Rousseauian notions were picked up by others in Europe during the French Revolutionary and Napoleonic wars. In those years, army officials came to believe that to defend the new ideal of the fatherland and its physical borders a recruit had to be intellectually and physically fit. In the teachings of "Turnvater Jahn"

(Friedrich Ludwig Jahn, the "father of gymnastics"), for example, there is a mix of proscriptions for a strong mind, in this case cued to nationalistic fervor, in a strong body.

When peasants, Norwegian or any others, put on their skis, they did not think in terms of that old classical saw, *mens sana in corpore sano* ("sound mind in a healthy body"). But their bookish leaders did. One of the most important threads running through the Idræt ideal was health. Proof of good health was measured at the end of a cross-country race. In Norway in 1843, for example, a finishing racer was described as "red faced as a lobster just out of the pot." More scientifically, in the 1880s 61 percent of competitors in one race were found to be in the best condition, 22 percent in next-to-best. They had been measured "in so far as these things can be determined without giving offense," for "heavy sweating, a red face, glistening, heavy eyes, incoherent answers to questions, and heavy breathing." Another means to measure a fit Idrætsmann was blacking strips of paper with the smoke from a lamp, putting them on the pulse and measuring the rate. Should there be a tie, the fellow with the lower pulse rate would be declared the winner. This health testing lasted into the 1930s. The visiting French military team in 1930 had been particularly acclaimed because of their remarkable fresh state at the finish of the patrol race. They had, in fact, come in seventh, yet the commentary was upon the state of their perceived fitness.[37] How could the body of a Norwegian be strong when Eilert Sundt's researches into peasant family life showed a staggering 50-percent illegitimacy rate, associated in those days with immorality and poor health? Worse still was one of Wergeland's reports covering eleven parishes in 1833, where out of 1,928 children, 1,749 were illegitimate. When Bjørnstjerne Bjørnson was going to write about the peasants, he was asked if there was anything but alcoholism and illegitimacy to talk about.[38]

In the true spirit of Idræt, Johan Fischerström, follower of Rousseau, called for activities "the old Scandinavians prided themselves in" to produce "strength, manliness and toughness," and followed it up by suggesting playgrounds and physical training of the young. By 1834, with the founding of the "Olympic Club," every man's duty was not only to perfect the soul "but also to develop the body" in order to "further develop the physical and moral strength of the people." Realizing that half of the people were female, the Swedish newspaper *Dagens Nyheter* in 1867 called for young women "to profit more from the strengthening influence of the healthy *Idrott.*" The whole nation would benefit. All that was needed, the *Neu Helsingborg Post* maintained, was to awaken that spirit that "in olden times has always developed the physical and moral strength of nations."[39]

"Nations" did not exist in Scandinavia the way the *Neu Helsingborg Post* referred to them in 1836. There was schizophrenia in intellectual circles: whether a person born in Norway should hold an emotional attachment to Norwegian nationalism, or a Swede to Swedish nationalism, or a Dane to Danish nationalism, or whether this person was part of a greater bloc and should hold a belief in Scandinavianism. The people of the north were not alone in their quandary. Throughout the nineteenth century, those promoting the pan-movements, particularly in Russia and Germany, were formulating ideas in which a potent brew of nationalism, racism, and social Darwinism played sometimes conflicting, sometimes converging, always emotional roles as the cultural nations contemplated political independence. War added a powerful argument, for it proved to be the successful maker of nation-states: Italy in 1860, the new United States in 1865, and Germany in 1871. Besides, something similar to the conditions in Scandinavia could be concluded from the Austro-Hungarian *Ausgleich* of 1867, whereby the Austrian Empire became the Dual Monarchies of Austria and Hungary. British Prime Minister William Gladstone's Home Rule for Ireland, too, was of particular interest to Norwegians determined on independence from Sweden.[40]

Nationalism (one scholar has the count up to 230 different definitions[41]) in Norway's case was bedeviled by the country's ties to Denmark, its connection to Sweden, and its many dialects and languages. From 1380 until 1814, Norway had been part of a Danish empire. Then, in the aftermath of Napoleon's wars, Norway was bartered for Finland and became a province of Sweden, as Finns came under the jurisdiction of the Tsars of Russia. During the past two hundred years of Danish rule, two classes had clearly emerged in Norway: the *Konditionerte,* which can be labeled bourgeois, essentially Danish and European oriented, and the *bønder* comprising the rest, peasant farmers, often poor, sometimes quite rich in land and animals. The intellectuals who called for a "Fatherland" tended either to imagine the new state to continue the cultural impetus from Denmark or they set about finding the fire of national purity in the *bønder* soul. The *bønder* suddenly found themselves with a major role to play in the new state. These political aspirations were buttressed by an extraordinary outpouring of interest in societies to preserve Norway's history and antiquities. The formation of literary societies, the publishing of nationalistic poems, of journals with names like *Saga,* the use of domestic-made goods, and the discovery of folk costumes attested to a frantic search for a national base. The creation of Norway's national day, May 17, first celebrated in 1824, and the founding of Norway's first university, were more visual attempts to manufacture national Norway. Much investment and energy went into the propagation of linguistic nationalism with its base in the revival of Old Norse, along with the immense collecting of folktales, fairy tales, ballads, and folk songs. The Norwegian soul, it was discovered, was formed "from the quiet charm of birchwood and mountain valley, from the deep stillness of the primeval forest," as well as from "the sunbeams dancing among the trees." [42] Nature symbolism of the nineteenth century was easily transposed to the days of Viking and myth, where geography and climate made both men and gods the stuff of giants. Political theorists have noted that it is at distinct breaks in political life when national identity is being forged that heritage becomes of overriding importance. [43] The question for Norwegians was how they were different from Danes and Swedes.

The answer lay in the country's purity as a separate, pure nation-state. History provided "the holy ancestral heritage" for the educated. For the *bønder,* folk tales were the equivalent. The paintings of Adolph Tidemand and Johan Christian Dahl depicting the virile peasant about his work and festivities "revealed Norway to the Norwegians." When Ole Bull was asked who taught him to play the violin, he replied, "the Mountains of Norway." [44]

The vast range of Henrik Wergeland's (1808–48) great poetry had one underlying theme: democratic culture. Wergeland envisioned Norway's future in an educated *bønder.* The Viking gave way to Askeladen (the young Cinder Lad), a male Cinderella who bested the world by his good wit and decency. Wergeland's antagonist was Johan S. C. Welhaven (1807–73) who excoriated Wergeland's "foggy mob" and pitted his own Scandinavianism and cultural core of bourgeois mores against Wergeland's "wild and thoughtless host" he wrote about in "Norway's Dawning" (*Norges Daemring*). [45] Here was the battle for Norway's future.

Arguments about indigenous nationalism ranged over many topics, but two were particularly partisan. When Sophus Bugge described the Eddas as being informed from many lands, even the Orient, [46] it seemed as if he had undermined the very foundation of Norwegian heritage, since intellectuals believed that they could feel the pulse beat of northern antiquity in the Eddas. They found that the diction of the peasant had its roots in the diction of the sagas, "a masculine mouth," as Asbjørnsen and Moe wrote in their work on Norwegian folktales (*Norske Folke-eventyr*). [47] Others found their roots in ballads. As it strove to untangle its economic and political ties with Sweden, the Norwegian government was so determined to follow a national path that it approved Jørgen Moe as Norway's first university research fellow in folklore. [48]

How did skiing interact with these political and social changes? At the start of this nationalistic movement, not very much. In spite of the efforts of Jakob Vaage, for many years curator of the Norwegian Ski Museum, to uncover every syllable about skiing, in spite of all the books about skiing that pay court to the snippets of lore extracted from the Eddas, Sagas, poems and plays, in comparison to the total output of topics in verse and song, skiing played a minor role until other factors far removed geographically from the country of Norway came into play. It was very convenient for those who believed—and believe—that skiing played a major part in Norway's break from Sweden, that the place chosen, thanks to the expertise of the local lads, was Telemark.[49] That district, like Delcarlia in Sweden and the Lake District in England, symbolized the best of the peasantry upon which so much of national creation came to rest.

Henrik Wergeland analyzed the 1814 Eidsvoll constitutional discussions in which the difficulty of overseeing administrational matters in winter emerged. "It must become an incumbent duty for the ecclesiastical, civilian and military authorities in the whole country to encourage the young to the ideal winter practice of skiing. To go to church, to the court, to military meetings, and for private occasions, skis should be used."[50] Wergeland was no mere theorist. While working on "Creation: Man and Messiah" (*Skabelsen, Menesket og Messias*) in 1829, he made a habit of going out on skis every day.[51] From the vast collections of folk tales there are a few references to skiing in Peder Christian Asbjørnsen. The same may be said of Jørgen Moe. Berte Tuppenhaug goes fox hunting on skis in Ullensaker (Ullr's field) and Moe's *Bjørnskytten* has a word or two on hunting on skis as well. Later Knud courts his Birgit on skis, which received far wider recognition twenty years later when the *Illustrerte Tidende* portrayed the occasion. Given the vast output of the folktale collectors, there is not much to prove that skiing was part of the folk tradition. But the decline of skiing cannot be dismissed simply on the basis of a lack of accounts. There are occasional references that show skiing to have been so commonplace that one can conclude that it simply went unnoted. Asbjørnsen wrote in his *Billedmagazin for Børn* in 1839, "Now the roads were not passable, both men and women skied to Gjaestebud, wives with their little babies on their backs."[52] One of the woodcuts in Olaus Magnus's *Historia* of three hundred years before shows just this picture, and it is easy to assume that in the everyday world, skis were the means for getting about on snowy days, just as Aasmund Vinje wrote about the Telemark folk in 1853.[53]

And then there is Bjørnstjerne Bjørnson. He reinvented traditional sagas to make them even more drama filled. Bjørnson turned Arnljot Gelline from the Heimskringla's "evil doer and way-besetter" able to take two people behind him on his skis into a famed Viking warrior.[54] Bjørnson wrote, "Norway, Norway, the skiing hills' shimmering land" (*Norge, Norge, Skibakkeløbets skinnende Land*), although he himself was not an enthusiastic skier. Just to mention Bjørnson, though, was "to unfold the flag of Norway."[55] "The Song of the Fatherland" (*Faedrelandssang*) began:

Det ligger et land mot den evige sne
I revnerne kun er der vårliv å se.

There lies the land of eternal snow
As the ice cracks could spring we see.

In a recent book, Tor Bomann-Larsen has used Bjørnson's opening *Evige sne* as a symbol to show how Norwegian national culture, as the country was becoming a nation-state, was one in which snow, and thereby skiing, became the invigorating factor that gave Norway her purity, her uniqueness, and her right to be independent. It also gave her the myth to which she still clings. It was clear that Fridtjof Nansen was aware of all this when he wrote that skiing was perhaps more important for nationalism than anybody had supposed.[56]

There was, however, another line to be followed in Norway's national search, one that is best exemplified by Henrik Wergeland's great rival, Johan Welhaven, and others of a more urban and urbane turn of mind. Still wishing to preserve cultural ties with Denmark, especially where language was concerned, and seeing in the change to Swedish overlordship no great threat to Norwegian identity (in fact almost enjoying the Swedish connection during the Crimean War in which Russia posed a threat), Welhaven and his friends enjoyed conservative support. A number of the leading intellectuals were European-trained and were slightly ashamed of the dialects of the valleys, uncomfortable in a brotherhood of peasants, uneasy with the water-sprites and trolls of folk art. They concerned themselves with skiing in a minor way; Jonas Lie, writing of the officialdom in the 1880s in "Family from Gilje" (*Familien på Gilje*) has his middle class on skis on occasions. In Ibsen's well-known play, Solveig visits Peer Gynt on skis. Although the landscape and nature often formed the background to many of these works, these Europeanized writers were concerned more with psychological insights and women's rights than with finding out where the fire of nationalism had its hearth and from what source it generated its heat. Europeans know Ibsen, and know not Bjørnson; older Norwegians love Bjørnson, and are only proud of Ibsen.

These "Scandinavians," as opposed to the "patriots," had a history of lumping "the north" together; after all, "Sweden" hardly existed before 1000 AD and her literary output was confined to runes. In the medieval period, the literary production was limited to religious works along with the thirteenth-century law codes of Västergötland, Gotland, and Uppland. In the most famous of Sweden's epics, *Frithof's Saga*, published in 1820–22, Esias Tegner has made Frithof the son of a Norwegian mother. The hero, wrote one French critic in muddled thinking, "is a national type . . . a great Scandinavian."[57] Where language and literary activity was of such importance, and with a hundred years and more after-sight, it is easy to see that once a strong leader appeared on the scene, the "Scandinavians" would lose to the "patriots." The last thing they expected was that this leader would come out of the ice of Greenland, and on skis.

CHAPTER 4

Fridtjof Nansen

Though we were late in learning to ski, there is some comfort in knowing that we have learned well and, even better, that we have been able to develop it to a higher level than probably any other place.—Fridtjof Nansen, Paa Ski over Grønland, 1890

What life and vigor are displayed in that snow and winter and Norwegian youth! And what a boon it has been for the nation! But if only there were less talk of sport and records imported from outside like the foreign words themselves. It shuts out the sunshine.
—Fridtjof Nansen, Diary, February 1900

Nansen Sugar, Nansen North Pole Beer, Nansen Bread, The Champagne of Dr. Nansen, and a Nansen Ballet.
—The use of fame after Nansen's return

 Fridtjof Nansen's great feat of crossing the southern third of Greenland on skis in 1888 was hardly utilitarian in the accepted sense of the word. Prior to his escapade, the usefulness of trudging through all that ice and snow was ridiculed in the press, as well as by that enigmatic genius, Knut Hamsun. Nansen was not from the *bønder,* but from well-connected Christiania circles, although the smart set never embraced him fully. Always "something of a soloist," as a friend put it, Nansen wore his explorer's outfit and wide-brimmed hat around town.

Yet Nansen embodied a stark form of *Idræt.* He was vigorous, and healthy, and appeared to be democratic, too. One could hardly find more of a social mix than among the Greenland expedition members. Nansen's crossing of Greenland symbolized the national importance of skis, the healthy challenges of nature that would move Norwegian nationalism, the Norwegian nation and, after his polar trip, the Norwegian state to the fore and make it a political reality in 1905.[1] These were immense undertakings achieved on skis, and he came home honored and bemedaled from Denmark, Sweden, Britain, France, Germany, Russia, and Austria-Hungary. He had become a Norwegian icon, about whom there could be only one reading: nationalistic.

Nansen was happiest meeting challenges presented by a hostile ice cap, less so in personal relationships. It took him nine months of daily arctic adventuring and nightly sharing a sleeping bag with Hjalmar Johansen before he suggested they used the familiar *du* to each other, and his record with both his wives and other women was unenviable.[2] Yet, after the two great ski expeditions, he was the man chosen to deal with huge problems requiring personal attention. He won renown as Norway's first ambassador to the Court of St. James. When he took up his position as ambassador to England in 1906, the *Bystander,* a society magazine, caricatured him on skis and headlined his arrival as "The Minister from the North Pole."[3] His job in London was to insure Norway's survival as a state, and once that had become clear, he cast about for a role on a larger scale.

During the 1914–18 conflict, Nansen wrote that neutrals would be needed to "maintain the continuity of world morality," and he led the Norwegian delegation to the League of Nations. He became exactly the right man to head food relief to Russia since recognition of the Bolshevik government was quite impossible by the West. He was also given charge of the repatriation of prisoners, almost half of which were Russian, and then to deal with the famine. His Russian orientation was not by chance. He had skied across Greenland's icy wastes, and over the ice cap that was the North Pole. These outlandish places were, in some ways, similar to Mongolia where he had proposed a trip in 1917, and to much of Siberia, where he also journeyed. He drew on the expert knowledge and linguistic abilities of Vidkun Quisling. Both men were moving politically to the left, one Soviet administrator telling him he was "a Bolshevik without knowing it."[4] For someone who had much experience in the political maneuvering between Norway and Sweden twenty years before, he was curiously inept in the world of right and left ideologues. Western governments, which dominated the League of Nations and appreciated his star quality as the world's premier civil servant, could not understand how he could be taken in by the Communist crew running the Soviet Union. He was even elected— without his knowledge—an Honorary Member of the Moscow Soviet.[5]

His organizing of food relief for the new Soviet Union placed him in political and diplomatic jeopardy but he was successful. As High Commissioner for the repatriation of prisoners after the First World War, and with the creation of the Nansen passports for refugees, he is remembered worldwide. The politically charged exchange of Greek and Turkish populations on either side of the Aegean Sea required immense personal intervention. The world recognized his efforts in awarding him the Nobel Peace Prize in 1922. He promptly spent the money establishing two model farms in Russia—which soon failed. Because he had skied onto the world stage, it appears to have been assumed that anything else he undertook would have equally fortuitous results.

As Lenin's experiment failed, as the terrors of Stalin's rule became increasingly evident, as the fear of Communism grew in the countries of Europe, Nansen moved to the right, and lent his name to the *Faedrelandslaget,* which openly campaigned for a nationalist government, and his name was put forward for president.

Perhaps it was all the international politics swirling about him that made him turn once more to the Arctic, such a barren expanse of purity untramped by man. In speeches across America in 1929, he tried to raise money for an airship expedition. Audiences turned a deaf ear to his financial pitch and listened only to tales of arctic skiing derring-do. After returning to Norway, he weakened after a bout with influenza caught on a skiing break on the Oslo-Bergen *fjelle* near Geilo, and a heart attack finally killed him on May 13, 1930. On this his last ski trip, perhaps he was remembering the days of training over the same country for his Greenland crossing over forty years before.

ACROSS GREENLAND IN 1888

Why Greenland? The exploits of Eirik the Red and those who followed him in the 900s made a convincing case that Greenland was not only discovered by Norwegians, but also colonized by them right into the Middle Ages. In 1261, there was an agreement by the settlers to recognize the Norwegian king in return for trade guarantees. Archeologists have unearthed the foundations of sixteen churches and 280 homesteads, and it is well known that trade ships left Norway up to 1410.[6] Through a combination of missionary activity and Bergen fur and whaling hopes, pastor Hans Egede ran a mission-trade outpost in Godthaab (Good Hope) in 1721. Conversion of the natives proved as difficult as trade. The first was converted after eight years, and the fur trade never materialized. Egede's son remained on after his father's fifteen-year stint.[7] It seemed, therefore, that Greenland had belonged to Norway for a second time. To an ardent Norwegian, it appeared that the Danes then stole Greenland (along with the Faroes and Iceland) in 1814. And yet in 1864, a folk school was opened under Norwegian instruction.[8] By this time, others were showing an interest. Swedish Baron Nils Nordenskiold, in his successful quest for the Northeast Passage, had ventured into the interior some seventy miles, and two of his Lapps had gone twice that distance on skis.[9] The American Robert Peary had also made a reconnaissance trip in preparation for a crossing. It was time for Nansen to move.

There was another attraction to Greenland. As the world became smaller, as more and more outlandish places were discovered, competed for, and opened up by Europeans, there were fewer regions left for quest. Greenland was not

Folk skiing was common in Greenland before Nansen's crossing on skis in 1888. Locals were enjoying Shrovetide competitions in 1883. The suspended barrel took many knocks from the males of the colony before it broke. Spectators and skiers alike then scrambled for figs, raisins, and other delicacies. (Skilling Magazin, 1883. Author's collection)

just the great outdoors, the antithesis of indoors, it was about as far as anyone could travel from an increasingly industrialized, civilized, modern world. Nansen played upon two concerns of late nineteenth-century Norway: to get back at the Danes, and to perform heroic *Idræt* far from civilization's view and cheer. What he obtained was something rather different.

At the outset, Norwegians did not support the idea of the crossing. Many believed it was a crazy project.[10] The Storting (Norwegian parliament) refused Nansen's request for funds and, irony of all ironies, he obtained 5,000 *kroner* from Augustin Gamel, a Danish coffee merchant. Gamel had interested himself in Arctic research since 1883. Although the expedition was promoted as a scientific venture, Nansen did not think of it in that way. He told those who wanted to underscore its scientific value that it was simply a ski trip.[11]

Some trip. On Nansen's return he became, in his uncle's words, "this proud Viking,"[12] and other Europeans almost claimed him as part of their heritage. Nansen was a skillful naturalist, the London *Times* allowed, but, obviously more important, he was "a first class sportsman, as skater and snow-shoe runner, and a crack shot"—in short, the epitome of an English gentleman. The *Times* went on to extol his past sports performances. "Before sixteen he had taken all the medals and premiums obtainable for so young a man, and at a concours in Christiania he became champion ski runner."[13] All of this was not quite true, but the details need not concern us. Obviously Nansen was part of organized sport, and however much he might inveigh against sport, he had engaged in it, and when he was much younger, even a little unfairly.[14] He had practiced for the crossing of Greenland by skiing a couple of times from Bergen to Christiania.[15] This sort of training was different, though, from those who trained for the Huseby run (as pre-Holmenkollen competitions were called), something he found uncongenial to the *Idræt* ideal. Nansen advertised for skiers to join him on the Greenland expedition. From the forty replies (some from France, England, and Holland), he chose Otto Sverdrup, at home on the sea and in the forest, with an adventurous background. Lieutenant Dietrichson, a longtime ski tourer, became the meteorologist. Kristian Trana, a forestry worker, was the handyman. Nansen also took two unlikely Sami, Ravna and Balto, because for a time he planned to use reindeer. Besides, the "sense of locality given to such children of nature" recommended them. They came for the money.[16]

After difficulties in getting onto the landmass of Greenland itself, the crossing was very successful. From the 15th of August to the 28th of September of 1888, they slogged across the inland ice, and this was duly reported in the 6,600 copies of Nansen's book *Paa Ski over Grønland*. However, it was not merely an account of the "Norwegian Greenland Expedition," as it was subtitled. The long chapter 3, "Skiing: Its History and Development" (*Skiløbningen, dens historie og udvikling*), described and analyzed the use of skis on which the expedition's success was predicated. Other explorers had taken skis but had not used them as the main means for crossing the snow. Nansen, therefore, gave to the skis a special place in his book. And they were indeed special: two pairs made of oak and seven of birch. The birch ones had thin steel sheaths on the bottom as well as small holes for attaching skins. While the use of skins was widespread, the steel bottom was an innovation intended for use on coarse, wet snow. The expedition did not encounter such snow, nor, as it turned out, were the skins much needed.[17] But the success of the expedition seemed to prove the utility of these Norwegian skis, and the vital fact was that Norwegians had shown the world what skiers could accomplish. Even in Norway, there were few who had realized what an impact it was to have. All of a sudden, after the trip, the anti-Danish sentiment was replaced by the growing antagonism toward Sweden. The long simmering frustrations over consular representation flared up. Once the new Viking returned, it became immediately clear to the more intellectually minded that Nansen "gave life to all our national ideals" for he was "the embodiment of our pride."[18] In spite of increasing calls for political statehood, the matter of going to war with Sweden over consular representation was not an appealing prospect. How then to bring about the break from Sweden? If Nansen's expedition had made Norway realize its own worth, what else was needed to achieve independence?

FARTHEST NORTH

Exploration was in vogue among late nineteenth-century Europeans. Partially inspired by the heady mix of imperial competition (to find the source of the Nile), missionary zeal (Livingstone), national pride (Scott), Europeans had left little of the world untrodden by foot—or ski. Greenland having been crossed on skis, there was really only one (or at most two) superlative goal: the North Pole. When Nansen proposed the *Fram* (his specially constructed boat, *Forward*) expedition to the Storting, it quickly granted 200,000 kroner, about half the cost.[19]

Nansen lectured to the Christiania Geographical Society on his proposed North Pole endeavor. Although he doubted there was continuous land to ski upon, he proposed a trip "in one summer by Norwegian snow-shoe runners." Even so, once on the trip, Nansen insisted that the entire crew be proficient on skis in case the *Fram* had to be abandoned.[20]

With the *Fram* embedded in ice, Nansen, and the carefully selected Hjalmar Johansen, left the ship on March 14, 1895, taking the stronger and well-prepared skis with them.[21] The record of the struggle over difficult ice, in deep and loose snow, sometimes sticking mercilessly to the base of the skis, the abandoning of extra gear, the use of skis underneath the sleeping bags to keep clear of pools of water, all made for gripping reading. "We have not slept much of late, as we have been broken on the wheel, so to speak. . . ."[22] They turned away from the Pole at 86° 14—the farthest north reached by any man. This was the stuff of Viking deeds mitigated by the marvelous chance meeting on June 17, 1896 with Frederick Jackson, the English gentleman adventurer accoutered in a checked suit. "I raised my hat," wrote Nansen. "How do you do?" Once Jackson realized it was Nansen, "By Jove! I am devilish glad to see you!" A snowy reenactment of Livingstone and Stanley. The front page of the *Illustrated London News* caught the attitudes precisely: "To have approached the North Pole within 226 miles is a grand feat of enterprise."[23] Nothing about

After months of harrowing skiing over the ice pack, Nansen was fortunate to come upon the English gentleman-explorer Frederick Jackson on Cape Flora, Northbrook Island (Ostrov Nortbruk), in the Franz Josef archipelago, in 1896. The relationship between the two remained strained for some years because Jackson played the role of savior, something Nansen never admitted. (The Graphic, September 12, 1896. Author's collection)

scientific value; the physical quality of the three-year adventure was what counted.

The return of Nansen was a Europeanized world event. For Norwegians, it was a national festival. Quite by chance, Nansen arrived in Norwegian waters at the same time that Otto Sverdrup brought the *Fram* home. It was, however, a welcome home for Nansen. The *Fram*, Sverdrup and the crew—even Johansen—were minor actors compared with the reincarnate Viking in his long ship. And more: just as Norway's medieval king Olav Tryggvason had brought Christianity to Norway in the *Ormen Lange*, so Nansen brought the message of nationalism in the *Fram*. He was received with religious grandeur. The vast crowd sang the old Lutheran favorite, "*Vor Gud han er saa fast en borg*" (A mighty fortress is our God), as Nansen set foot on land. "Thousands and thousands of men and women felt that the love of their fatherland had grown in their hearts during those three long years," wrote an author of one children's book on Nansen.[24] The revered poet Bjørnstjerne Bjørnson welcomed Nansen saying he had freed Norwegians in two ways, internally in a spiritual fashion, and externally from Sweden. Henrik Angell said the same thing in a different way. "Nansen got cold for Norway, not for Sweden."[25] There was yet another coincidence; the failed Swedish balloon expedition to the pole also arrived home at the same time. Nansen's triumphant return was compared to André's "balloon between [the Swede's] legs"—and considered a splendid omen.[26]

Nansen's trip from the north of Norway took three long weeks of coastal celebrations as he made his way south to the capital. It was almost as if Nansen were a crowned head of state. Indeed, in Christiania, some of the welcoming celebrations would be repeated when in 1905 Norway embraced her first king in modern times.[27] His reentry coincided with renewed debates over Norway's having her own consular representatives abroad. This time, though, Norwegians had a world figure of unparalleled stature to make their case. Even the Swede Sven Hedin's Tibet exploration paled in English eyes compared with the feat of the man who had gone "Farthest North." Norway became free thanks to Nansen's polar skiing and, one must add, because the last thing Western diplomats needed, occupied with the Russo-Japanese war as well as problems emerging over Morocco, was a further northern disruption. There was general pressure for a peaceful solution, and it is to the credit of Norwegian Prime Minister Christian Michelsen's compromise and Sweden's Oscar II's that there was no war.

Nansen's crossing of Greenland received immediate journalistic notice, of course, but the German translation of *Paa Ski over Grønland,* published in 1891 as *Auf Schneeschuhen durch Grönland,* became a major influence in the development of skiing in the rest of Europe. Men who were to become the impetus behind ski development in their own spheres attributed their excitement for skiing just to reading Nansen's book. It was not so much the actual technique of skiing or its history in the long chapter 3 as simply that such a daring endeavor on skis had been accomplished. The book held special appeal to city men, men of the professional classes and military officers. It appeared just when the bourgeoisie began to delight in outdoor sports that required a certain amount of physical effort. Croquet had given way to tennis, rambling was secondary to the sterner stuff of mountaineering, walking was replaced by more vigorous bicycling. But tennis, mountaineering, and cycling were summer sports. In winter, gymnastics had become popular, especially among Germans, but was possible only in the gym halls. Skating, already with its city clubs and rinks, was too ritualized, confined by wall boards all around. Skiing, especially on the vast ice pack of Greenland or the Pole, combined muscular endeavor with the promise of excitement and danger in nature's endless winter wonderland, Friedrich Nietzsche's *Gefahr und Spiel* (danger and play) in action. Of course, the good bourgeois of Munich or Vienna were not going to compete with Nansen, but on skis, little adventures seemed to beckon from any snowy hillock.

Nansen's feat and his book had the effect of "a liberation from the hesitating uncertainty of the first skiing pioneers," judged Anton Fendrich, one of the many who would write on skiing. Theodor Herzog's father gave him a copy of *Durch Grönland,* "but if only he had known what he'd done!" Georg Blab, who later wrote a popular ski manual, explained like "many others, so it was with me, that the impulse to practice the sport came through Dr. Fridtjof Nansen's epoch-making book." "Ski" was a new word then, judged the Düsseldorf *Festschrift,* and went on to pay court to Nansen's *Crossing of Greenland.* The Ski Club Todtnau secured the great man as an Honorary Member. Hauptmann Vorwerg, Oscar Norwerg, and, most important, the Berliner Max Schneider—whose entrepreneurial activities as writer, manufacturer of equipment, and even ski real estate developer spread wide—were all influenced by reading Nansen's account, and they, in turn, influenced many others.[28]

The reports of Nansen's skiing across Greenland had the same effect in Austria. In Kitzbühel, Franz Resch read Nansen, experimented with skis, influenced friends, climbed Kitzbühel's Horn in the winter of 1893, and organized the first race two years later. Mathias Zdarsky, earliest of the Austrian ski technicians and hardly a man to proffer gratuitous accolades to Norwegians, let alone admit to their influence, wrote in 1900 that Nansen's *Greenland* "is the beginning of a huge widening of the skisport. One can say that the general international public cannot say enough thanks to this hero for his keen matter, which puts into play a new cultural factor." Six years later he had not forgotten Nansen: "We skiers build a monument to Nansen in our hearts that will stay forever." Josef Müller, known as *Skimüller,* who wrote extensively on the skisport in Austria, recalled that the Austrian Ski Association (*Österreichische Ski-Verein,* ÖSV) was "guided by Nansen's super sketch of skiing and its joys which brought to notice this still unknown sport." [29]

One thrust of this widespread Norwegian influence developed in Vienna. The other connection was with enthusiasts in the Styrian market towns of Graz and Mürzzuschlag, southwest of the capital. Max Kleinoscheg, who had received a pair of skis from fellow cyclist, Nicolay Noodt from Trondheim in December 1890,[30] in turn impressed his friend, Toni Schruf who owned Mürzzuschlag's Hotel Post. Together they climbed the Stuhleck on skis, formed the Styrian Ski Runners Association (*Verband Steirischer Skiläufer*) in 1892, got in touch with Nansen, opened the first ski touring hut, named it the "Nansen Hut," and created the first international ski meeting in 1894 at which Norwegians were spectacularly successful.[31] Later came the Nordic Games (*Nordische Spiele*), at times called the "Nansen meet," at which winners received "Nansen medals." These games were run in the odd years so they did not conflict with the *Nordiska Spelen,* Sweden's bid to compete with Holmenkollen's annual meet. The Nordic Games also included exhibitions of ski-related equipment.[32] Dr. Blessing, the doctor on Nansen's Polar expedition, was a visitor in 1897, and Nansen himself accepted honorary membership in Kleinoscheg's and Schruf's association. They were still corresponding with Nansen in 1930, remembering the early days.[33]

In Norway, the Norwegian Ski Association became curious enough to find out what was happening to their own sport in Austria. Lieutenant Karl Roll had clear instructions: to see whether "they" ski like "us" or whether it was an "acrobatic sport." Roll's report, published in *Norsk Idrætsblad* and then reprinted in the Association's *Aarbog* paid court to Wedel Jarlsberg's influence in getting the Viennese started, in bringing over the first of many Norwegians, in this case W. Samson from the Ski Club Skuld. Roll commented on the fact that you had to travel at least an hour from Vienna to ski—he was thinking of Semmering and Mürzzuschlag—and realized that time and money were a must. He counted many of the Austrian Ski Association members among the aristocracy. He had much to say about their skis: they were mostly made of ash, turned up high and "not beautiful." Local factories produced skis as early as 1894 "after Norwegian originals," as advertised by Heinz Kurz in Langenlois, about 75 kilometers northwest of Vienna. Roll marveled at the prizes given at the "Ski-Derby": a grandfather clock and a silver service. In spite of the fact that there was no instruction, Roll was amazed at how well the Austrians performed and hoped the Association would grow and send representatives to the Holmenkollen meets in future years.[34]

Considering the influence of "Nansen fever" in the German-speaking countries, it is quite remarkable how little effect the French translation of Nansen's book (1893) had. This is all the more surprising in view of the growing popularity of the French Alps, their therapeutic as well as their physical attractions, and the appeal of Europe's highest mountain, Mont Blanc, with its fabled history of climbing attempts and celebrated first ascents.

With all the enthusiasm created by Nansen among the outdoor sports-minded, one major problem plagued early European skiers: they did not know how to ski and wanted instruction. Nansen did not tell people how to ski in his Greenland book. Not one of the imported so-called instructors from Norway was able to explain what he was doing or how. Leif Berg described his first teaching experience at Glarus. "A sweet daughter of Eve completely covered in snow asks me to help her, and tell her how not to fall. This was a difficult question, and I thought about it for some time, and in the end said the only way was to keep standing. She laughed and promised she would try." He wondered what he had let himself in for. "It is an unusual thing I am doing here, but very nice," he mused.[35] One Austrian judged, "They had no idea of analyzing these turns. They just did them somehow, they could not say how." They showed by example, and for many learners that may have been sufficient. But the more thoughtful were ready to qualify their enthusiasm toward their Norwegian visitors:[36]

> The Norwegians were not good ski teachers. Skiing to them was self-understood. . . . They never had to think about it and never explained it, taught it. I think they themselves were not clear on how it worked. . . . They skied, jumped and turned . . . with little or no thought to technique.

"We had to discover the 'how' for ourselves," wrote Otto Lutter years later. "Ski teaching knowledge is an alpine matter." That may be a little strong; there was, after all, public advertising for learning how to ski in Christiania's *Aftenbladet* as early as January 1881,[37] but little seems to have come of the proposed ski schooling, and certainly no lasting effect filtered down to the Alps. A recent analysis of early Swiss skiing shows clearly that Nansen had no influence on the development of ski technique.[38] He was no teacher of skiing. Teaching skiing as a sport was contrary to the *Idræt* philosophy he enjoined all to cultivate. He saw skiing leave the realm of traditional culture and become a civilized pursuit. "It is not my fault *Idræt* is translated as sport," he wrote a little testily to Kleinoscheg in 1904, "practise *Idræt* and detest sport and record-striving."[39] But sport and record striving was exactly what the rest of Europe was making of his Norwegian skiing.

NORWEGIANS ABROAD

Sport in the form of jumping competitions with the ever-increasing voyeuristic appeal of greater—record breaking—lengths was particularly appealing in the United States, where there were two Fridtjof Nansen ski clubs. In 1929 Nansen himself came to the logging town of Berlin, New Hampshire, in New England. The local paper mill's magazine thrilled at his visit and reported that some were apprehensive because "for a . . . quarter of a century his countrymen have been telling us of him. We feared to see him lest his actual presence should dim the luster of his fame." But they need not have worried; his iconic stature remained: "Tall, lithe and stalwart, an ideal Viking still, although the gray of nearly seventy years borders his massive forehead, he still exemplifies his motto 'Forward,' just as he did when the 'Fram' was first named." "He ennobles whatever he touches," judged the *New York Times*.[40] The legend remained intact in far-away USA.

Norwegian immigrants took the Nansen lore with them wherever they settled: in Algiers where, in 1906, along with French officers, they startled the Arabs near Bjurdjuras in the Atlas mountains. In South Africa, once skiing became popular among a small group at Fonteintjiesberg in 1929, Norwegian H. Michelsen, working for Shell Oil became the local guru.[41] There was one Norwegian, so the legend goes, among Kiandra's gold rush thousands who first skied in Australia. Borri Winther, immigrant from Kristiansand, introduced better bindings in 1901 with the result that the "fixed boot style is in vogue." He became the Australian record holder by jumping 23.5 meters.[42] One hundred members had joined the Alpine Ski Club of Australia after only three years, a good sign of local popularity down under. In neighboring New Zealand, after reading Nansen's *Crossing of Greenland*, Marmaduke Dixon and G. E. Mannering used skis in 1893. Norwegian miners in the Otago gold fields had skied some twenty or thirty years earlier, but like so many of the "firsts," they had no lasting effect. It is true, too, that Dixon's and Mannering's use of

Dr Fridtjof Nansen.

die „FRAM"

Nansens Polarreise 1893-96

No. 746

Nansen auf Schneeschuhen Grönland durchquerend.

Ч. И. Д.

Кр. Дмитрий

A most unusual postcard of Fridtjof Nansen was printed in Germany for the Russian market. A romantic Nansen guards the national symbols of flag and crown, while the instruments of his world domination, compass and skis, pictures of Greenland, and the Fram, his North Pole boat, frame the explorer. (Author's collection) skis on Mt. Cook had no immediate effect either, but within twenty years skis were touted as a tourist attraction in that area.[43] Business was drummed up to extend the burgeoning summer tourism into winter even in those far-away colonies at the end of the British Empire.

These developments of skiing were far from Nansen's ideal, but the very success of his expeditions, and of his books, helped to turn *Ski-Idræt* into ski sport. However much Nansen might have wished to play the role of adventurer extraordinaire—he turned up in his explorer's outfit even at the Archbishop of Canterbury's garden party—he found that *Idræt* was all well and good in Greenland but sport was decidedly *de rigeur* among the elite of the rest of Europe. "Some ideas," he sniffed, "are not for exportation." [44]

CHAPTER 5 **Creating the Skisport**

In all countries there are now enough people who think of winter sport as mere business.—Winter Sports Review, 1912–13

The ski-ing field is the finest sanatorium yet discovered.
—Engadine Year Book, 1913

 If *Idræt* was not for export, skiing was. However much Nansen may have inveighed against "sport," when skiing ceased being utilitarian, when its cultural uses gave way to recreational entertainment, skisport became the new winter attraction among both the townsmen of Scandinavia and the landed wealthy and urban bourgeoisie of much of the rest of Europe. They modernized skiing, providing standardization of equipment, of competition, and of pleasure. This standardization, as Allen Guttmann showed in his influential 1978 analysis, *From Ritual to Record,* is the great mark of modernization.[1]

EXHIBITIONS

Ski meets in the nineteenth century often provided the opportunity for exhibits of equipment. When each Norwegian valley took pride in its local skis, very little change in ski design had taken place. Only when the competitions on Huseby Hill and later Holmenkollen provided something of a national exposure, did people come to realize that one form of ski was, perhaps, better than another. Prizes were awarded for the best-made skis. At the manufacturing competition held in conjunction with the Huseby meet of 1879, the one in which Sondre Norheim put up such a spectacular show, six counties were represented. Most of the ash, pine, and birch skis were made in Numedal and Telemark. No first prize was awarded, but Knut Olafsen Haugen from Kviteseid in Telemark won second prize with his ash ski. Sondre Norheim's brother's ski was awarded fourth place. The next year, twenty craftsmen competed. Hellik Gulliksen Koppang, third the previous year, a man from Numedal, won first prize for his Telemark ski. Already, then, pride in each valley's ski type was beginning to give way before the effort to make the most suitable ski. Larsen's of Christiania advertised a ski of its own manufacture "following the Telemark design" in 1886. Laminated skis made their appearance in 1891. They were not an immediate success since the glue did not hold when the skis became damp. The experimental nature of the laminated ski showed that local tradition was not so important.[2] The Swedish Ski Museum in Umeå has made a major effort to document the old ways of making skis and has produced a fascinating film of the construction process. Norway's Holmenkollen went one better: they hired Thomas Aslaksby to make skis in the old style, using old tools and craft ways. His demonstrations are very popular, yet another example of how skiing's heritage in Norway takes center stage in her winter culture.

The exhibitions at the early ski meets and elsewhere continued, and Norwegians began to exhibit skis abroad. At the 1878 Paris Exposition, Henry Duhamel found a pair of skis lined up by some Canadian snowshoes. He bought both but, quite extraordinarily, a Swede (Norwegian? This was twenty-five years before Norwegian independence) in attendance could not explain how to use them. For ten years Duhamel experimented pretty unsuccessfully; "I felt like a carp wishing to be a potato." The problem lay with the binding. "Sufficient cord," he had been told, but he was not shown how it should hold the boot secure. Only when he saw a series of photographs at the 1889 exposition was the problem solved and he ordered fourteen pairs of skis from Helsingfors (as Helsinki was called in those days).[3] It just shows what a role happenstance can play, and makes nonsense of Guttmann's sociological requirement of "rationalization" as one of the seven indicators of modern sport. It also denies the post modernists' thesis of the denigration of the individual in explanations of what happened; Duhamel became the driving force behind skiing in the Grenoble area.

Norwegian skis were also exhibited at the International Hunting Exhibition in Cleve, Holland, in 1881.[4] The Dutch repeated their success with a ten-day enlarged show in Amsterdam the following February, where "Snow, Ice and Mountain Sport" vied for attention with Riding, Hunting and Shooting, Cycling, Water Sports, Athletics, Fishing and Photography.[5] The Todtnau Ski Club put on an exhibition in the Feldbergerhof in 1891 but it had little effect outside the Black Forest. The following year German-manufactured skis were on view in the sports exhibition at Scheveningen, Holland, where Max Schneider's skis received a diploma.[6] Much later, in 1910, even the British organized a showing of English-made skis.[7]

By far the most important of the exhibitions in middle Europe, though, was the one associated with the competitions held in January 1894 in Mürzzuschlag, Austria, at which Finns, Norwegians, Swedes, Germans, and Austrians exhibited. Attended by the presidents of ski clubs from Vienna, Munich, Berlin, and Kitzbühel, the hunting lodge set, army officers, and aristocracy could inspect winter sports equipment from Vienna, Graz, Krems, Bruck a.d. Mur, Mürzzuschlag, and Munich. Clothing, medals, jewelry, sculpture and wax were also on view. Five hundred sat down to dinner in the railroad restaurant and were entertained by the band of the 47th Infantry Bicyclists. The evening ended with a speech by Baron Wedel Jarlsberg, a grand and fitting beginning to what would become the *Nordische Spiele*.[8] The races, the exhibition, the hoopla of the festival—all helped to make Mürzzuschlag a leading ski venue. Toni Schruf and Max Kleinoscheg, well aware that the Vienna crowd often went Zdarsky-way to Lilienfeld, were determined to seize the opportunity to boost their own economic potential. It seemed to work: the next year the Finns donated ten pairs of long and narrow birch skis to Schruf's and Kleinoscheg's Styrian Ski Association for members to try out on their own terrain.[9] Here was a Finnish effort to lock in the growing Austrian market, one outside Zdarsky's sphere.

MANUFACTURING, IMPROVING, AND DISTRIBUTING THE EQUIPMENT
The most important ski factory in Norway, L. H. Hagen of Christiania, in the sporting goods business since 1851, was not exhibiting at Mürzzuschlag. Nearer to home, Hagen brought six models to Stockholm in 1902 to be among 37 Swedish, 6 other Norwegian, and 9 Finnish exhibitors.[10] The *Storting*, Norway's parliament, granted 5,000 kroner to support the Norwegian section in the International Exposition in Berlin in 1907.[11] At Christiania's exhibition that same year, 41 firms displayed 176 products. Sixty-two pairs of old skis including equipment from Nansen's and Amundsen's explorations were displayed in the Norwegian Historical Section.[12] Two years after separation from Sweden, Norwegians needed their history. The historical section items, especially those of Nansen, reminded the proud group of visitors of the part skiing had played in the creation of their nation. The color blue dominated the new ski outfits, and women's dresses were bordered in nationalistic colors.[13] When Norwegian valleys all had their own colors and styles of dress and head-gear,[14] the creation of national colors was to bring cohesion to the country as a whole and to distinguish it from Sweden whose own yellow and blue had been inaugurated only in 1902.[15]

If all this might seem a bit parochial, other countries interested in skiing did take note of what the Scandinavian ski firms were producing. One of the most remarkable things about the Christiania exhibition was that there were no new bindings on view: Huitfeldt and Ellefsen dominated.[16] For the unini-tiated, meaning all non-Scandinavians, how the foot was attached to the ski remained a major problem. The Germans actually patented a safety binding in 1909, but no manufacture followed. The *Club Alpin Français* (CAF) and the French military commanders had already worried about the cost of importing skis, bindings, and wax. Addressing this concern in 1908, CAF arranged a competition for bindings to be judged on "ease of manufacture," "moderate price," adjustability," and various technical points such as "simplicity, solidity, and weight." First prize was 100 francs and an order for fifty pairs. The results were not as hoped and, as CAF explained, there was no lacking in ingenuity, but most appeared too complicated and did not answer the need for a binding that would fit most skiers. CAF promised "success at the next competition." [17] The search for a good binding, suitable for the increasing number of French skiers continued on up to World War I. [18] In 1909, at CAF's *Grande Semaine d'Hiver* at Gérardmer in the Vosges, a "national meet of ski making" brought together personnel from manufacturing concerns, military workshops, schools, and nineteen family artisans. [19] Even Spain in 1912—certainly not in the forefront of skiing—exhibited mountain climbing gear, camp equipment, and skis thanks to the effort of the *Club Alpino Español*. It seemed, wrote an enthusiastic visitor, "to raise skiing to a national sport." [20] Hardly.

Norwegian skis reigned supreme, part of the Norse mystique that had carried Nansen and the country to freedom. No one except Mathias Zdarsky in Austria questioned the supremacy of Norwegian skis. Because Norwegians exhibited perfect technique on snow, their skis, perforce, must be superior. The best proof of their success was a 112 kilometer terrain test on "original Norwegian skis ordered directly from Norway"—accomplished in thirty-four hours by an army patrol from the Wiener-Neustadt garrison. [21] When middle Europeans began making skis, one major selling point was to advertise them as "made on Norwegian lines" or like "a Nansen ski." However, such a pair "after a Norwegian model" was criticized by visiting Norwegian Captain Karl Roll in 1896 as "not very wide, turned up high, and not beautiful." [22] Far away, in America's midwestern state of Wisconsin, Axel Holter, a Norwegian immigrant, started a ski factory by ordering seven pairs of Haugen skis from Christiania, copying them, and marketing them as "the celebrated Ashland ski, none better," using the name of his home town. [23] He did not have to announce the Norwegian pedigree because his clientele, the local immigrant community, recognized the type.

There was no scientific study of what made one ski run better than another in certain snow conditions, only handed-down know-how. As the first how-to book and sales catalog in the United States put it: Since snow could be "downy, fluffy, powdery, sandy, dusty, flowery, crystalline, brittle, gelatinous, salt-like, slithery and watery," it was better to have a few different types of skis, at least such was the recommendation of Theodore Johnsen, the manufacturer. He made skis "carefully worked on true lines" and "particularly designed for firm snow or crust" out of wood "hand made of selected stock," and so on.[24] Non-immigrant folks who took to skiing in the United States had to be told; they did not know what worked best in the different conditions of the day.

Since snow came in many forms, the sliding quality of the ski was always a point for discussion. Tar burned on the bottom every year provided a base upon which any number of home concoctions were tried: candle wax, bacon rind, fish oil, rubber and bees wax, even melted down gramophone records, all had their adherents. Although there was wax for sale around 1900, it was not very efficient. Only when the Østbye brothers, Peter and Sverre, patented a soft wax called *Klister,* did skiers have a reliable ride on wet snow. For an authentic view of how waxes used to be concocted, the Norsk Skieventyr (Norwegian Ski Adventure) in Morgedal exhibits the Østbye workshop.

When Osborne Reynolds, an English physicist working on lubricants, read Nansen, it sparked his interest in "the slipperiness of ice," as he titled his paper read in 1899 before the Manchester Literary and Philosophical Society.[25] However, none of his experiments, or his conclusions, had any effect on skiers or ski makers. Science did not offer the artisan craftsman any help.

Naturally, local ski makers tried to break the monopoly of Norwegian skis at the same time that they marketed the "True Finland Ski," or the "Ski after best Norwegian pattern." Since the numbers of people skiing increased relatively rapidly in the mid-1890s, manufacturers "shot up like mushrooms from the ground in order to disappear soon after," remembered Max Schneider.[26] Jacober of Glarus, a bronze medalist at the Geneva Exposition in 1896, was the first major ski-making business in Switzerland and exported skis that same year to France and to the Italian Alpini. In Bern, Karl Knecht advertised his Schweizer Ski, and also sold Lilienfeld skis from Austria. Zdarsky was the only real renegade. In 1902–3, he countered the expertise of the Norwegian skis by listing nine faults while advertising his own ski. Todtnau, in the Black Forest, became a major ski producing town. In 1895 it sent skis to a Frenchman who founded the Ski Club of Bruyères, and also to a British officer who enjoyed them while on leave in the Jura. The mayor of Les Rousses was so impressed that he insisted on the local mail carrier doing his rounds on skis . . . and so skiing began in the French part of the Jura.[27]

On the whole, The French were late to enter the field. The Manufacture d'Armes de Sainte-Etienne was the first major establishment to make skis, finding markets outside the local area to the south in the Pyrenees. Gleize of Chambéry and Revol Neveu of Grenoble both published catalogs in 1909.[28]

Jacober Brothers of Glarus, one of the best known early manufacturers of skis, had a virtual monopoly in eastern Switzerland and supplied skis to Italian and Swiss army units. Jacober's letterhead, however, emphasized the social ambience of the new sport. (Courtesy DSV-Archiv, Nachlass C. J. Luther)

Norwegian skis continued to command respect abroad.[29] But as more and more of the middling classes took to skiing in the alpine regions of Europe, local craftsmen thrived because skis and equipment from Scandinavia were expensive, taxed, and slow to arrive. Franz Baudish, a Jungbuch (Germany) carpenter, made his first skis in 1891, and by 1893 was publishing a list of wares for sale. Richard Neumayer of Munich gave four pairs of skis to the Ampezzo section of the German and Austrian Alpine Association (*Deutscher und Österreichischer Alpenverein*).[30] This was a marketing strategy, for he had realized that an increasing number of skiers were attracted to the Ampezzo region of the Dolomites, and they were coming for sport. By 1912, Peterlongo of Innsbruck sold skis between 200 and 238 centimeters long almost solely for sport.

By that time there had been calls for a shorter ski. Bilgeri's summer ski was on view at the Frankfurt exhibition in 1909.[31] Captain Nerlinger in France found skis as short as 150 centimeters weighing 2.5 kilos best for touring in the Vosges and Jura. Wood without knots was easier to obtain in that length. They handled easily on the railway, even on the Paris *métro*. Later, the French tried to capitalize on skis made from homegrown mountain ash which, they claimed, was "much more resistant than [skis] made in Norway from imported wood from America." This new material was hickory, first used for skis in Norway in 1882. By the 1920s and 1930s it became the wood of choice.[32] The production numbers were prodigious. Staub of Zurich made 2,875 pairs in 1903–4. In 1910–11, the well-known mountaineer and skier, Professor Roget, reckoned that 3,000 pairs of skis had been sold by one firm alone, and perhaps 30,000 pairs had been bought over the season.[33]

The French military made efforts to teach their men how to make skis. On demobilization, the veteran ski trooper would go home and produce skis for his villagers, especially for the young. In that way *montagnard* children would learn to ski well before they became of recruiting age. The Touring Club de France had exactly that in mind, too. In its booklet *Ski Utilitaire*, the TCF explained that in 1909 "we researched a method of family manufacture, cheap and easy to make, so without any model a villager—he and his family—can make skis at little cost." There was a hope that this might also relieve economic distress of some of the mountain population in winter.[34]

If the *montagnards* in France and the peasants in the alpine forelands of Austria, Germany, and Switzerland were encouraged to make their own skis, the middle class, *Jagdherren* ("hunt gentry"), and aristocracy obtained theirs from suppliers in the major cities like Berenc and Løbl of Vienna, Knecht in Bern. Maison Bardin of Paris established a special shop at CAF's Morez meet in 1909. France's first catalogs appeared that year.[35] This was a wealthy crowd. Early skiers who bought from Max Schneider, for example, included a Prince, an Adjutant-Major, a painter, lawyer, two doctors, and two nobles.[36] Skiing around 1900 was already becoming a bourgeois enjoyment, and the middle and upper classes began requiring their city comforts in the snowy foreland villages of the mountains. The winter station for sport was the result. If it could retain local character, so much the better. Welcoming contestants and visitors at CAF's meet at Pau in the Pyrenees was a banner in Béarnais strung across the main street: "*Plazé a nous—Dep ha Aunous*" (*Plaisir à nous de vous faire honneur;* "It is our pleasure to honor you"), and guides were in local costume. The Béarnois created for their visitors a sense that skiing, in this part of France anyway, was rooted in folk culture.[37]

WINTER STATIONS: COMFORT FIRST

Inns and hotels as destinations for warm weather holidaying had appeared with tourism in the early nineteenth century. Other establishments opened to accommodate patients suffering from nervousness, and later tuberculosis. Mountain air was the cure-all. But hoteliers never thought of attracting winter visitors. However, with the growth of the skisport, various individuals, clubs, municipalities, regional and national associations, regional and national governments began to take an interest in the promotion of skiing and skating. In France, the government and the military as well as the controlling influence wielded by the *Club Alpin Français* and the *Touring Club de France* played major roles in the development of skiing. Particularly in eastern Switzerland, in Glarus and the Engadine, local clubs and entrepreneurial hotel keepers had large influence over wide areas, Glarus because of its pioneering activity and the Engadine because it was home to St. Moritz, a health station since the mid-nineteenth century. In Germany and Austria clubs were the driving force behind the development of skiing. Mathias Zdarsky's refusal to let his international *Alpen Ski Verein* (Alpine Ski Association) meddle with the Austrian Ski Association created two power centers.

A number of Austrian regions of the Alpine chain: Vorarlberg, Tirol, St. Anton, and Kitzbühel in the west, Mürzzuschlag, Semmering, Graz, and Lilienfeld closer to Vienna, took to skiing early on. German skiers in many and varied clubs enjoyed their newfound sport in the Eifel, Pfalz, Schwarzwald, Harz, Riesengebirge, Erzgebirge, and, of course, the Alps. Cities spawned ski clubs that journeyed to their favored grounds by train.

In Great Britain, the government stayed out of the way, but the Ski Club of Great Britain and the Public Schools Alpine Sports Club not only influenced the way the British skied and enjoyed themselves but also became actively involved in arrangements with the host nation, particularly the Swiss. They badgered the Lauterbrunnen-Mürren railway authorities to run the mountain train during the winter season of 1910–11,[38] to ensure the British colony in Mürren had the full range of skiing possibilities with ease of riding up from the valley floor. They recreated their own world by reserving entire hotels for themselves during the high season in Morgins, for example, in 1912. The Swiss owners realized that by providing an England-away-from-home, they would enjoy a repeat clientele.[39]

The hotels that remained open for winter business had to install heating. When available, it was immediately advertised. In 1907, Kitzbühel's Grand Hotel and Davos Platz's Grand Hotel Belvedere took out notices in the *Year Book of the Ski Club of Great Britain*. The Hotel Post of St. Anton joined them in 1908. At Mittendorf, Austria, inns were "warm," even if no English was spoken. In 1910, the list included Norwegian hotels at Finse and Haugerstöl, which were joined the following year by the Grand Hotel at Åre, Sweden. In 1908, CAF also commented on heating before its major ski week at Chamonix. The following year CAF provided a list of those hotels with heat at Mont Revard, Aix-les-Bains, Grenoble, Briançon, Thorenc, Peira Cava, Luchon,

Davos "Winter life" was depicted in 1896, seven years before the first English ski club was founded there. Skiing took its place along with snowballing, tobogganing, and skating. Promenading was especially important for those trying the tuberculosis cure of high mountain air and sunshine. (Author's collection)

Cauterets, Gérardmer, Chamonix and Platet-sur-Argentière. In 1912, the Swiss Federal Railways put out an extensive booklet listing 406 hotels and pensions of which 197 had central heating.[40] Heating and electricity were also a concern among Italian stations.[41]

Electric lighting, too, was often included in advertisements to the British clientele. Perhaps they were right in directing the appeal of all mod cons to the British because by 1907, according to Dr. Esmont, writing in the *Gazette Médicale,* they had brought "a prosperity so prodigious" to Swiss resorts "that it could not be imagined."[42] The French Riviera felt economically threatened by the success of the Swiss winter business. Within France itself, the newer resorts of the Pyrenees appeared to take winter tourists away from the French alpine stations.[43] Chamonix seemed immune.

CHAMONIX–MONT BLANC

It was not the mountains that had first attracted men to the Chamonix valley, but its glaciers. Typical for the eighteenth-century Enlightenment, Englishmen Windham and Pocock were the first of a long line of gentleman amateur scientists to study the glacier world. Although Mont Blanc had been first climbed in 1786 in the Romantic Age, the high lakes were the attraction, and only from about the mid-nineteenth century did alpinism take hold. There was much foreign business in the valley prior to the advent of skiing. In 1860 Chamonix welcomed 9,020 visitors, in 1865 the number was up to 11,789 with the English supplying about one third of the tourists that made Chamonix a "little London of the High Alps" and the Col de Balme the "Oxford Street or Strand of the Alps."[44] In 1860 there were seven hotels, in 1865 ten, including the 300-bed Grand Hotel Impérial. An English church was built, the telegraph arrived later, the first of the mountain huts, the Cabane des Grands-Mulets was ready in 1864. Whymper climbed the first Needle in June of 1865.[45] Chamonix was, perhaps, a curious place for Henry Lunn to launch his winter club tour business in 1898. His son, Arnold, remembered the guide "who regarded his ski with obvious distaste and terror. He slid down a gradual slope leaning on his stick, and breathing heavily, while we gasped our admiration for his courage."[46] Henry Lunn took his ski business to neighboring Switzerland where hotel and village elders were more used to dealing with foreigners in winter. The rail connections from England were simpler too.

But Chamonix's much-respected Dr. Payot took to visiting his patients on skis and crossing cols with guides and a few others whom he inspired to join in. He made the Col de Balme on February 12, 1902, and followed it up by crossing the Col du Géant over to Courmeyeur in some fourteen hours two weeks later. The following season he did the traverse from Chamonix to Zermatt,[47] thus inaugurating the *Haute Route*. This was the year that Chamonix officials published their first ski poster—which sold at auction in 1999 for £12,650 (about $19,000).

Chamonix was CAF's choice for its 2nd International Week held in January 1908. Two hotels remained open for the winter in 1902, four in 1906, and the number tripled for 1908. The hoteliers had been skeptical of CAF's enthusiasm at first, but they joined in as the day grew closer.[48] They ended up "surprised by the affluence of the visitors," whose preferences were for hotels with central heating, always something of major concern for villages and towns as they started to attract winter guests.[49]

The meet was a resounding success. The reception for the alpine troops, the gentry in their sledges made a fine show, baby carriages on runners provided a charm and calm among the physical presence of all the skiers, the lugers, and bobsled teams. The sober colors of the skiers' clothes mingled with the elegant costumes of the ladies. Troops from Norway, Switzerland and, of course, France's own *Chasseurs Alpins* were the cynosure of all. The throng included amateurs from home and abroad, and guides and porters busied themselves throughout the town: all under a radiantly blue sky with the Mont Blanc chain creating a magnificent backdrop, "a picture rarely seen and suggestive to a high degree." Chamonix had become Chamonix-Mont Blanc, a "new winter station . . . equal to the big Swiss centers," enthused one commentator in the *Revue Alpine*.[50] The resort was classed as a "station climatique" until after the war when, in 1920, it became a "station de tourisme."[51]

A new winter station? Maybe. Certainly not one to equal St. Moritz and Davos in Switzerland, nor, indeed, did the winter visitor count come anywhere near the town's influx of summer clientele. In the summer of 1907, Chamonix had welcomed approximately 170,000 visitors, averaging about 2,000 per day. Only a few more than 2,000 had been in town for the entire winter week, but it was a start to Chamonix's becoming France's premier ski and winter station.[52]

Although the numbers of visitors did not increase appreciably during the winter seasons,[53] Chamonix's standing as premier in the places to ski in France was enhanced by CAF's sixth international meet in 1912. There was comment in the French papers, of course, but also in Oslo's *Aftenposten* and in the Italian paper *Lettura Sportiva*. *Excelsior*, a French paper, put it just right: "Chamonix shows, this year, as in others, that it knows how to organize sports events."[54]

Chamonix capitalized on its renown and started advertising abroad. "Sunshine is Life" read an advertisement cued to the British in 1913. Attractive fifteen-day excursion tickets from London cost £4.0.3 in 1913. The following year the town's tourism committee decided to spend some of their advertising budget in the Algerian and Tunisian newspapers.[55] Clearly, Chamonix was branching out, but then the war delayed all these plans by four years.

WOOING A CLIENTELE, 1900–1914

Chamonix always advertised its "winter sports" attractions. Winter sports up to about 1905 were sports played in winter: the snow and ice sports, field hockey, even boxing. About this time there began a separation between ice and snow sports. Ice skating (speed, figure, and hockey), along with ice yachting, was seen as something essentially different from the snow sports: bobsledding, skiing, and ski jumping. From then on—the date is not exact, of course—skiing in all its forms took on an increasingly important role in the promotion of winter sport stations. These stations, already undergoing some change from their primacy of health stations, often tried to combine the two activities: health and sport. The advertisements in the winter number of the *Illustrierte Zeitung* of December 24, 1908, give a good indication of the changing nature and relationship between health-cure offerings and sporting activities. Among many pages of advertisements for hotels are: Dr. Wigger's Kurheim in Garmisch-Partenkirchen. Triberg (in the Black Forest) advertised itself as a "Wintersportplatz und Winterkurort." Nearby Neustadt did the same. Dr. Barner's Sanatorium was "the best spot for winter sport," while Dr. Vogeler's Sanatorium advertised solely to those with medical problems. In Bad Sachsa, the Hotel Schützenhaus was for those in need of rejuvenation (*Erholungs-bedürftige*), as well as for "Friends of Winter Sport." Schierke in the Harz, showing a photograph of a remarkably flat expanse of snow captioned "*Das deutsche St. Moritz*," called itself a "winter cure and sports center."[56] These examples are typical of the mix of attempts to lure visitors to winter recreation towns in the period up to the Great War.

The mountain cure stations still retained an appeal. At the same time, the hoteliers, and the *syndicats d'initiatives*, realized that a new clientele could be attracted, one for whom winter sports was the great appeal. For a number of years—even into the 1920s—cure and winter sports hung uneasily together, yet increasingly winter sports became more important, and among winter sports skiing began to take pride of place.

Ski stations, railroads, clubs, manufacturing concerns, shops, all set about wooing the new winter clientele with posters, special stamps, advertising locally as well as in the ski and alpine journals.

It is impossible to gauge the effect of posters. It is not clear where they were on view other than in railway stations. The few older ones that survive are, on the whole, in good condition, which would indicate a lack of display. It is curious that the French, who lagged behind the other alpine countries in ski development, produced the first ski poster in 1903. The early posters are different from the others: a woman descending a slope at ease in her ridiculous town shoes, a man and woman in a synchronized jump, strung up like two puppets with arms perfectly horizontal. Patently, the artists did not know what skiing was all about, but they catch a playful mood. Skiing was the product being advertised, and other than indicating the venue in large letters, there was little attempt at differentiation of possibilities.[57] The Austrians and Swiss tended to portray lone men on skis looking seriously at far away hills and valleys. Dressed in somber colors, the skier was purposeful. Increasingly from about 1910 on, women are shown skiing in more or less good style. A Norwegian poster from 1909 shows a lady in a fine red folk dress looking a little Viking-like batting down a slope in fine form; she is out to convince the viewers that Norway's heritage is being upheld by women and that foreigners should come and enjoy Norway's winter traditions. There is little or no social aspect to these pre–World War I posters.

Shops and manufacturing concerns put out catalogs that doubled as instructional booklets. Those from the turn of the century—nearly all extant are from the German-speaking areas—have fine drawings of happy hunters, forestry workers, and postmen all going about their winter work. Sometimes whole articles were reprinted. Yet the catalogs, whether from Berenc & Löbl of Vienna or Gleize of Chambéry, were leveled at those who would buy skis for sport.

Special stamps were produced by CAF for its annual international weeks. Cigarette companies, even the English W. H. Wills, a manufacturer of cheap smokes, printed up promotional cards containing pictures of men and women on skis. Lindt, the well known Swiss chocolate firm supplied cards, as did coffee manufacturers, margarine companies, and various advertisers, mostly German and Austrian, portrayed ski equipment and clothing on stamps.

The most ubiquitous item spreading images of the skisport around the world was the postcard. All skiing countries produced a number of cards—some colored drawings, some photographs. Much emphasis was on the social side of skiing. Thus a Swedish couple slides down a slope hand in hand; a large number of Norwegians prepare for skiing as they get off the railway up at Holmenkollen. Russian school children dash madly about; Austrians, Swiss, and Germans stand about the ski house and hut, make their way up the Feldberg, admire the Swiss mountains and light a cigarette. Czechs enjoy themselves, Finns look serious, the Italian Alpini cocky, French lovers cast glances, racers take it straight, and jumpers jump in pairs. In short, skiing is shown in all its various facets. Some well known artists had their work on postcards: the Norwegians Andreas Bloch and Axel Enders, and in the Alps, the Swiss Carlo Pellegrini was the great social recorder of skiing prior to World War I. He won the artistic contest at the Stockholm Olympic Games of 1912.[58]

Newspapers, periodicals, and club journals also did their share of advertising, but they were also important for telling the new-to-skiing what to buy, where to go, and for introducing them to a sporting lexicon. Max Schneider's little periodical, *Der Tourist* ran to ten thousand or more copies annually and did much to spread the gospel of skiing to German readers.[59] The Semmering Club of the Austrian Ski Association made Viktor Silberer, the editor of the *Allgemeine Sport-Zeitung* an honorary member.[60] Winter sports bulletins for Lower Austria (*Niederösterreich*) were published in Vienna by the County Association for Tourism (*Landesverband für Fremdenverkehr*) and covered thirty-nine centers from Annaberg to Wienerbruck.[61] Burberry's, the renowned London clothier, had Professor Roget write *Hints on Alpine Sports,* which they published in 1912.[62] A hardcover 368-page 1913–14 *Wintersport-Kalender* for Saxony, Thuringia, and the Harz listed 154 places for Saxony, of which 64 mentioned skiing.[63] All attest to an increasing interest in skiing along with an effort to attract customers to buy Burberry's and go to Saxony. Skiing had reached such growth that it merited an encyclopedia entry in 1905.[64]

For the committed skiing fraternity, the Germans, Austrians, Swiss, and British produced ski journals. *Der Winter* started publishing in 1905, became the organ of the German Ski Association (DSV) and the Austrian Ski Association (ÖSV) three years later. With the indefatigable Carl Luther as editor starting in 1914, *Der Winter* became the most important ski publication in Europe. The Swiss annual, *Ski,* was informative and wide-ranging. The Austrians, already split into a Zdarsky faction with its own journal *Schi,* competed with the Middle European Ski Association's *Ski-Chronik,* which ran from 1908 to 1913. The Ski Club of Great Britain, founded in 1903, launched its first *Year Book* in 1905, and once Arnold Lunn took it over in 1920, it became "without any contradiction the most interesting publication concerning the sport of skiing," a handsome tribute from the French.[65] Since the *Club Alpin Français* was made responsible for French skiing in 1907, CAF's journal, *La Montagne,* became France's only ski journal until *Neige et Glace* appeared in 1924 and the *Revue du Ski* in 1930. The yearbooks of the United States, Australia, and New Zealand, and to some extent Canada, were designed along the line of Lunn's *Year Book,* which held pride of place in the English-speaking world, and its position in non-English-speaking countries remained high simply because of the prominent place Arnold Lunn held in the world of skiing. Indeed, these journals were far more important than the Norwegian *Aarbok* or the handsome Swedish annual *På Skidor,* mostly because so few read Scandinavian languages. These publications show the widening appeal to a wealthy public, one that began to delight in winter sporting at home or abroad when the snow fell thick enough to make skiing a sport competitive with the Mediterranean coastal resorts.

Local authorities did much in varied ways to advertise their own locales. The St. Moritz *Winterkur-Verein,* for example, gave the local ski club 500 francs to hold ski courses in 1904–5. A private committee donated 150 pairs of skis to the Folk School in Christiania in 1910. School children in Arnsberg were given skis by the Sauerland and Winterberg Ski Clubs in 1911. School authorities in the Riesengebirge, Harz, and Braunlage made skiing compulsory in winter, in some cases as substitute for gymnastics.[66] The Tourist Bureau in Winterberg had four hundred skis for hire.[67] When a station in France held a meet, great efforts were made to attract the national press. CAF, headquartered in Paris, had access to the major dailies, but perhaps more important were the weeklies, *L'Illustration* and *La Vie au Grand Air*. Both were at the Gérardmer meet in 1910, along with four others, besides five dailies and the *Agence Havas*. The regional press was well represented, headed by the well known aviatrix and skier Marie Marvingt writing for *L'Éclair de l'Est*. This was an impressive array and an indication both of CAF's influence and the local committee's efforts to spread the doctrine of skiing. Gérardmer had its reward; it reveled in the honor the *Touring Club de France* (TCF) bestowed on the town, now a "*Station d'Hiver*."[68] The TCF also gave out various grants. The Abbé Blot, the moving force behind skiing in Besse, was quite forthright in his parish magazine. "We must attract tourists, it is up to the hoteliers to get in pairs of skis." For two weeks in late January 1908, there were twenty-eight people in town and not enough skis for the women. By April, thanks to the TCF's subvention of 50 francs, thirty-three pairs of skis were available for visitors. The Abbé was all enthusiasm. By 1911 he was thrilled that some people had come for almost a week. "It is the beginning of our ski station," he proclaimed to his sometimes unresponsive parishioners.[69]

The Abbé Blot struggled to inspire skiing in his village. Gérardmer's Société des Sports d'Hiver, too, had to persuade locals "to adopt our countryside during the winter season." Old habits—"the sweet somnolence of winter repose"—were hard to break, besides the difficulty of "putting into gear the complicated mechanism of tourism." A single abbé or municipal committees, all were striving to transform winter France.

THE MECHANICS OF TOURISM

In the years before the motorcar dominated the transport systems of Europe, the most important sector of the "complicated mechanism of tourism" was the railroad, which played a major part in developing ski stations. Although they did not have to be on a railroad line—witness Adelboden, Lenzerheide, and Arosa in Switzerland—would-be ski stations could expect large numbers of people if they could come by train. It was all very well and folksy for mailman, forester, policeman, priest, customs officer, even doctor, to be on skis, but the money came with the city people. It was not what they spent on skiing itself but rather on room, board, and entertainment that boosted the mountain village economy. But they had to get there, hence the importance of the railroad.

In some areas the railroad was already in place. Norwegians had used their trains since the 1880s: round-trip Christiania–Bryn cost less than the freight for one pair of skis in 1888. After the restaurant opened at Frognerseter and the train line to Holmenkollen was completed in 1898, the area became a recreational ski-ground for the Oslo city people.[70] In France, the Compagnie du Midi had served the thermal baths of the Pyrenees, Eaux Bonnes, Cauterets, Ax-les-Thermes, Bagnère and Luchon, and at Mont Dore too. Sometimes odd tramways or little train lines were added. Font Remeu, just off the Chemin du Fer du Midi's line, built a special *petit train jaune* up to the Grand Hotel, which opened in 1913. Superbagnère ran a special forty-five-minute train ride that took skiers up to the plateau for sport and touring from December 1912 to 1966.[71] When Lioran offered skiing, the station building acted as the warming hut.[72] In other cases, major construction was involved. In Switzerland, after sixteen years abuilding, the Jungfrau railroad, ending at 11,340 feet, opened in August 1912. It made summer skiing possible and brought the Jungfrau and Mönch peaks within three hours of walking; the Eiger took about eight.[73]

The railroad companies advertised profusely by way of posters. Posters for the Paris-Lyon-Méditerranée (the famed PLM) destinations like Chamonix and other French stations hold an immense appeal, as they catch this era in artistic ways that photograph and word cannot. For the most part they are unreliable guides to technique, not that there was much in those early years before the First World War. They project an ambiance of wealth and health, a life of leisure and sport. Posters aim at channeling desires. They opened city people's eyes to the enjoyments of winter-accessible Mont Revard, Chamonix, or to whatever destination was served by the PLM railroad.

Swiss posters were far more parochial. Nearly all of them portrayed a particular place with no information on how to get there. For that you had to rely on *L'Hiver en Suisse*, put out by the Federal Railways at Bern. The 1912 edition has photos of skijoring, jumping, cross-country, and about twenty images of idyllic villages and winter terrain, all designed to attract the winter visitor, by the federal railway, to the Swiss Jura, around Lac Léman, to the Vaudois Alps, the Valais, the Bernese Oberland, Lac des Quatre Cantons, St. Gotthard, Grisons, the Engadine, where you could sleep in one of 25,286 beds. The listing of hotels and pensions indicated those with central heating. In this era prior to antibiotica, establishments were marked if they would accept tubercular patients. Many hotels and nearly all pensions refused those afflicted with TB except at a place like Leysin, which had fourteen hotels and pensions with 423 beds available plus five sanatoria for the contagious with a further 474 beds. At Davos, all but two establishments would take TB patients, and at St. Moritz every single establishment would do so. These last two resort towns accounted for a total of 5,157 beds alone.[74] These are impressive figures, and it is little wonder that the French would say they had nothing to compare with the Swiss statistics.[75] The figures show, too, just how much ground the *Kurort* had lost to the ski center by 1912.

There was even international cooperation. When the railroads were planned to connect the Rhône valley with Chamonix, "a very serious publicity effort" by both Swiss and French would ensure a "new element of prosperity for Chamonix," as the Swiss persuaded the mayor's office in 1908.[76] This was the year of CAF's international meet at Chamonix, and the PLM was "desirous of putting the new winter station at the gates of Paris," by providing excellent connections.[77]

In 1899, pressure from Austrian skiers was enough to get the Vienna city tramway authority to permit carriage of skis and equipment on their trams. By the 1904–5 season there were regular rates, and in 1909 there was a set of rules for the transporting of skis on the city's street cars: the skis had to be held by the owner, and only on the front platform on certain days, and only four people per platform, etc.[78] In 1900, Zdarsky had suggested that accompanied equipment should be carried free on the trains. His *Alpenverein* argued successfully for special trains from Vienna to Lilienfeld. On January 14, 1906, the first regular "Sportzug" left, and continued to run on Sundays and holidays throughout that winter. It left Vienna at 6:05 a.m., arrived in Lilienfeld at 8:15 a.m., and returned at 9:40 p.m. "Finally," commented Zdarsky's journal, *Der Schnee*, "skiers need not become martyrs for their sport." It certainly paid off for the railway; 5,625 tickets were sold over the first two seasons.[79] Railroad executives in Austria capitalized on this new winter sports clientele. It was not just the Viennese wealthy who obtained these concessions. In 1905, the Linz Railroad announced a small discount for skiers. In the north of the country, the *Salzburger Tagblatt* complained that in the Tirol there was a charge for the transport of ski equipment on the trains whereas in neighboring Bavaria it was free. "So people will not come to the Tirol," it concluded.[80]

The railroads were competing for skiers. In 1910 the ticket prices of winter sports trains from Vienna were discounted between November 26 and March 31, 1911. Some were good for eight days, an indication that some Viennese

YEAR	TRAINS	PASENGERS
1905–6	81	9,166
1906–7	107	11,725
1907–8	188	19,267

Catering to the Viennese wealthy and only an hour away from the capital by train, vast hotels like the Panhans of Semmering (still in existence) were comparatively easily turned from summer vacation destinations into winter quarters as Semmering promoted winter sports from the 1890s on. (Author's collection)

might decide to stay a week at a place like Lilienfeld, Mürzzuschlag, or Semmering. For a special event, such as the Nordische Spiele in Mürzzuschlag on January 4–8, 1908, a 50% price reduction was negotiated.[81] The opening of the Lower Austria-Styrian Alpine Railway (*Niederösterreichische-Steirische Alpenbahn*), with the connection Freiland–Taunitz, brought Annaberg within reach of skiers in the winter of 1908–9. The Ministry of Public Works was giving serious thought to promoting winter tourism in Austria.[82] As the railroad reached into the valleys, so the little towns and villages had the opportunity to become ski centers if their geography and entrepreneurial engagement permitted.

In Germany the railroad from Munich to Garmisch-Partenkirchen had opened in 1889. Members of the Munich Ski Association (*Schneeschuhverein München*) and later the ski clubs made the trip in two and a half hours. The first special wintersports train ran in 1904. The following statistics show the growth of wintersports devotees from the Munich area to Garmisch at a cost of 2 Reichsmark[83]:

Trains left from urban centers. The first special train from Düsseldorf in the Ruhr took its club to Winterberg in the Rothaargebirge, from Cologne to the Eifel in December 1911. The same year a "Luxury Train for Wintersports," the Engadine Express, left Berlin at 3:05 p.m. and was in Davos at 2:15 p.m. the following day; it arrived in St. Moritz a quarter of an hour later. Düsseldorf, Köln, Berlin: the bourgeois of flatland northern Germany were keen to try the new winter activity.

The international railroad system from England, via the Channel crossing Dover-Calais, to Switzerland annually brought the English on their classy alpine winter holidays. On December 18, 1911, six hundred left Charing Cross by the afternoon express; on the same date in 1912, about a thousand were on board. It was even possible to have a weekend in Switzerland.[84] So many traveled to the continent in the pre-Christmas period in 1913 that an extra train was provided from London to Dover with an extra connecting ferry to Calais.[85]

All the railroad construction in what was supposed to be nature's own preserve brought about a conservation effort that argued against the despoliation of the mountains. Climbers like Coolidge, were involved and some alpine clubs criticized the building of railways and tunnels. A League for the Conservation of Swiss Scenery was founded in 1905.[86] But these were small voices, hardly heard above the hubbub of the burgeoning tourist industry in the years before the Great War.

SKISPORT MADE EASY

Not only railroads and a few roads were being constructed, but more and more people skied where there were lifts. We usually associate uphill devices with the 1920s and 1930s, but there were lifts prior to the First World War, some even designed and working solely for skiers.

The most mind-boggling up-mountain marvel was projected as early as 1835: a railroad up Mont Blanc. But it was never realized. The funicular from Aix-les-Bains to Mont Revard was the first mountain railway in France, inaugurated in September 1892, and gave to Mont Revard its early position of prominence for skiers. The Swiss had put a rail up the Rigi twenty-two years before, but that was not for skiers.[87]

At Pillnitz, near Dresden, an enterprising innkeeper installed a horse-drawn lift on a short slope near his hostelry, but nothing further developed. Robert Winterhalter's water-powered tow for tobogganists and skiers at Schollach in the Black Forest, was an innovation that worked well enough when the water was in spate. He went on to devise a ski lift for the Winter Fair of Baden (at Triberg) in 1910, for which he received a gold medal for distinguished service from the Grand Duke. Winterhalter's tows received publicity in Germany and in England, and patents were granted in Germany, Austria-Hungary, Sweden, Switzerland, and the United States that detailed the intricate engineering involved. According to Klaus Winterhalter, his grandfather had no professional qualifications, which made his work suspect and brought a dearth of lift business.[88] A lift up the Bödele, hard by Dornbirn in Austria, ran for a year in 1907 before being relocated to Lenk.[89] This was a lift to serve a jump. The students at Dartmouth College in the States considered such a lift in 1915.[90]

Men and women visiting snow country practiced on the slopes by their hotel. The more adventurous made it to alm, even to alp. All had a social experience on the holiday train, in the hotel, at church,[91] and on the slope, now somewhat organized for their pleasure. For those who wanted to test their mettle against nature's formidable mountain ranges, the summer guide was beginning to turn himself into the winter ski mentor. A new era began in the alpine villages of Europe. The English, who had been the world's first tourists—the word was first used about 1811—now became the vanguard of a new breed, the winter sporting-holiday maker.

CHAPTER 6

The English Play

*The few visitors who bothered to ski in Chamonix were regarded as
reckless faddists.—Arnold Lunn, 1898*

*One frequently hears a man explain a bad and nervous style by
remarking that he is a winter mountaineer, and has no time for
"fancy tricks."—Arnold Lunn, 1913*

*"To ski like an Englishman" still remains a term of anything
but praise with our continental neighbours.
—Public Schools Alpine Sports Club, 1925*

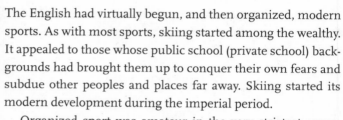

The English had virtually begun, and then organized, modern
sports. As with most sports, skiing started among the wealthy.
It appealed to those whose public school (private school) back-
grounds had brought them up to conquer their own fears and
subdue other peoples and places far away. Skiing started its
modern development during the imperial period.

Organized sport was amateur in the very strictest sense,
something one did because one loved to do it. The possibility of skiing in England and Scotland thrilled those who had not the time to
journey to the Alps. Communities in Cumberland, Yorkshire, and Durham
had been on skis since the early 1800s,[1] but thirty or forty men gliding into the
village after a working day in the mines was not something that public school
men might wish to emulate. Besides, miners scudded about on barrel staves.
Proper skiing was not going to be that sort of rudimentary fun and games. At
the time the Archbishop of Canterbury and his garden party guests were wondering how to treat Nansen wearing his explorer's outfit, England's educated
were in a peculiar frame of mind, that "tranquil consciousness of effortless
superiority,"[2] which justified their actions in spite of contrary evidence, be it
in the Boer war or the defeat of the Marylebone Cricket Club on its home pitch
by the visiting Australian cricket team. In the athletic world, a man might win
because he was faster than others, but that was not what was most important.
The upper-class Englishman was a sportsman (amateur, of course), one who
would not kowtow to people "who object to pigeon-shooting and other hunting
because they would object to every other kind of sport. Sickly humanitarian-

ism was corrupting Great Britain," as one ex-president of the Public Schools Alpine Sports Club put it in 1903 to the membership at the annual dinner.[3]

THE ELITE AND THEIR CLUBS

Skiing in Switzerland, so different from that in England, provided an outlet and outpost where the amateur superiority of the English could—yet once more—show the world the right way to conduct sport, although these skiing imperialists had little interest in inflicting their newfound winter sport on the natives.[4] In winter, among the snow-covered mountains, any thought of decadence would vanish immediately; it required character and moral commitment to get out and about in freezing weather. To some people, it may have seemed as if God had invited members of the upper class to enjoy their strenuous relaxation among His wondrous nature. Thirty percent of the male members of the Ski Club of Great Britain in 1905 were reverends.[5] It was comforting that not one of their lower-class parishioners would see them disporting on an alp; there would be no corruption of the working class.

The other mainstay of the Ski Club of Great Britain in its early days were military officers: 44 percent that same year.[6] This officer class had first conquered and was now policing the world. Since much of imperial activity was thought of in terms of sport anyway, Switzerland seemed an appropriate place to keep fit, enjoy sociable continuation of public school and officer's mess. Arnold Lunn recalled the time a Swiss hotelier admitted two Germans to his hotel. The British committee immediately met with the erring Swiss owner, and the Germans left the next day.[7] From time to time, Germans appeared to threaten British control in Switzerland, just as they challenged British naval superiority, a concern the *Times* noted in 1906 and again in 1908.[8]

The elite class of Britain was born to comfort, but this same class had the civilizing mission of taming nature and native. Outdoor sport was an antidote to a life of ease. In Switzerland they insisted on cleared pistes and favorable railway prices, and in the alpine hotels they created an England abroad. What had once been a culture of skiing, they civilized in their own image; their ski culture was bound to rub up against Norwegian *Ski-Idræt*.

Switzerland was poised, ready to receive the wealthy. It already had what we would call today a health industry. Of course, many doctors prescribed the Côte d'Azur for their nervous and exhausted patients, but in the pre–World War I days, physical exercise for many seemed a far better cure than the deckchair life on the Mediterranean coast. For the summer, hiking and mountaineering appealed. Skating, tobogganing, and, latterly, skiing were the winter attractions. As early as 1842, Dr. John Davy had drawn attention to the "robust forms commonly witnessed in the peasantry of the higher Alps." He cannot have been in the Goms valley where, even seventy-five years later, the children looked "about 70—queer little wizened trolls carrying vast buckets of manure on their backs."[9] St. Moritz, with its stunning vistas, was known for its recuperative air, and next-door Davos was publicized in the British medical journal *The Lancet* as well as in such class magazines as the *Fortnightly Review*.[10] John Addington Symonds's wife loved Switzerland "better than the South really; one feels a better human physically and morally among the snows."[11] Switzerland boasted facilities to accommodate an extended summer tourist business, with a large number of health stations that were comparatively easily converted to winter use. In 1880 the tourist bed count of Switzerland stood at 43,850. The number had doubled by 1894, and in 1912 it reached 168,625, the year that an expected 18,000 British would visit the Alps for winter sporting.[12] In the wake of the British invasion, the intimate Swiss inn gave way to luxury accommodation. As early as 1882, J. A. Symonds, the Renaissance historian, saw Davos (in 1903 to become the home of the first English Ski Club) degenerating into "an ill-drained, overcrowded, gaslighted centre of cosmopolitanism, disease and second rate gaiety."[13] The winter visitor count there stood at 13,000 by the turn of the century, almost the exact same number who visited the entire country of Norway.[14]

Symonds obviously did not like contact with the diseased. Since Switzerland's high altitude sanatoria were located where winter sporting was at its best, there was for some years an uneasy mix of the two.[15] There were so many winter enthusiasts by 1907 and probably earlier, that hotels in the Alps began advertising, like Arosa's Grand Hotel: "First Class house. No Invalids." In the Jura, "one of the healthiest places in Switzerland: No Consumptives Admitted."[16]

Starting in 1873, St. Moritz welcomed more visitors in winter than in summer. People came for their health, for skating, for bobbing, for being seen, and only marginally for skiing. The area behind one's hotel was usually sufficient for all but the true ski runner who longed, a generation later, for "the empty vast and wandering air of the heights".[17] At first only three stations in Switzerland came to be recognized centers for skiing: Grindelwald, Davos, and St. Moritz. By 1910 the list had expanded considerably, thirteen villages supplying weekly snow reports to the *Times* in 1912,[18] thanks to the influence of the two leading ski organizations of the upper class: the Ski Club of Great Britain and the Public Schools Alpine Sports Club.

The Public Schools Alpine Sports Club was not a regular club at all; it was a London-based economic venture by Henry Lunn, who reserved entire hotels for his British clientele. He gave it all the guise of an exclusive club; indeed you could join merely by being a member of Whites, Boodles, the Athaneum, or any one of the thirty-nine listed elite organizations where so much of England's affairs were decided behind the scenes. Arnold Lunn, son of the founder, initially scolded English skiers whose "minds remain for ever in England" and who were unhappy if their hotels contained foreigners.[19] But that was exactly what made his father's club so utterly successful. Through the agency of the club, Sir Martin Conway, one-time president, judged that "members formed an assemblage which seemed to produce the old kind of comradeship which formerly existed in Switzerland."[20] The old habitués had been swamped by a multitude of intruders who occupied hotels. The beauty of Lunn's club was that there were no intruders. Member Dr. Lemmon was met by a large sign "Welcome to Morgins" and enjoyed the sociable and amusing game of Coon Can with ten others. "I only know," he commented in the club's yearbook in 1914, "from the first moment I felt at home, with none of that wondering how I should like the place or the people."[21]

The wondering was never a factor; members' affiliations were listed. In 1914, of 5,432 members, of which 1,370 were women, 503 were educated at Eton (9%), 252 at Harrow (4.5%), 186 at Rugby (3.5%), 170 at Marlborough (3%), 162 at Charterhouse (3%), 117 at Winchester (2%), 102, 98, and 90 at Haileybury, Cheltenham, and Clifton (each about 2%). There were also 768 army officers, 79 naval officers, and 179 clergy. Three hundred and eleven held titles. These statistics demonstrate Henry Lunn's clientele, but among the elite were 57 members of Parliament, including a prime minister, a home secretary, a postmaster general, and a Lord Privy Seal. Imperial governors of Australia, Bombay, and Hong Kong could happily swap stories with a Field Marshal and a number of major generals. The medical officer to the Sultan of Zanzibar could compare notes with the laryngologist of H. M. Household. An international polo player, a bicycle champion, an Olympic oarsman, and a world-record-holding skater could discourse on the merits of their sports with international and county cricketers, association footballers, and rugby enthusiasts—not a few of whom were "sporting parsons," including one Rt. Rev. Bishop.[22]

This was the top drawer, and no wonder the members' families included "tutors, governesses and servants." It was, as Miss Monica Cousins explained about Campfer, close by St. Moritz, so friendly, just "one big English family."[23] The English family got into the occasional squabble over things like dancing

The pre–World War I English upper class played on the hotel slopes by day and in the evenings re-created their own country-house entertainments of amateur theatricals, fancy-dress balls, and festive nonsense as they all but took over a number of hotels in Switzerland.
(*Cleaver,* A Winter-Sport Book, *1911*)

the Chamois-shuffle or the Winkle-waddle. Happily, at Lenzerheide, exponents of the Bunny-hug consented "to modify their transports," and a rift in
the family was averted. Henry Lunn attempted to close the Mürren bars at
11 p.m., but he was not successful. Still, Mürren acquired the reputation in the
years immediately before the First World War, "as a place where grown ups
are treated like children." [24]

Mürren was where the Palace Hotel was maintained as an outpost of empire.
The British could expend their strenuous idleness on Pig Flat or Gadarene,
and in the Punch Bowl. In-group names for ski pistes were common: Mauler-
hübel (after a bottle of champagne), Martha's Meadow, and Parson's Shoulder.
Others brought immediate thoughts of home: Clapham Junction and Plum
Pudding. In 1909, the *Illustrated London News* ran a full two-page drawing of

skiers and skijoring (being pulled behind a horse on skis), entitled "When All Britain is in Switzerland."[25] It certainly might have seemed that way.

All was secure in the sports club, which spent its skiing time devising tests and competitions. According to W. R. Rickmers in 1903, the year the Ski Club of Great Britain was founded, the hotel population had "an aversion to more than gentle exertion." E. C. Richardson, writing for a Norwegian audience, put it in another way. They try it "first for the joke of the thing," and then succumb to it.[26] Norwegians would fail to comprehend how skiing might be attempted as a lark. Richardson realized, too, what Henry Lunn saw so clearly: they wanted to be with fellow countrymen in particular venues. "Any suggestion of a change is treated with undisguised hostility." The reason did not lie in the merits of the ski station, but in who was there. "It's all a question of where one's friends go," summed up another observant commentator.[27] No wonder those bent on inspiring their fellows to learn to ski properly had such a difficult time, since Mürren was the fount of right skiing. Hard to fathom, yet the Alpine disciplines of downhill and slalom emerged from this upper-class world. One man, Arnold Lunn, spent twenty years in feisty engagement before he won final acceptance in the international arena for downhill and slalom. They also emerged—another of those curious connections—from ski mountaineering.

MOUNTAINEERING AND SKI MOUNTAINEERING

Although mountaineers had chronicled their every step from 1850 on, the history of mountaineering has only recently received serious analysis. There is, however, very little discussion of winter mountaineering, and virtually no analysis of winter ascents on skis—at least in the western European languages. Since most people enjoying a skiing holiday were not about to attempt any major peak in the winter, it is an extraordinary fact that what impressed would-be skiers were the accounts of men who captured a peak or two using skis. This sort of endeavor was totally different from anything the Norwegians did. The Englishman Cecil Slingsby had hunted among the snows and glaciers of Guridalen and the pass over Riigskaret in 1880. He urged Norwegians to take up high-mountain touring on skis, but failed to find any interest among Norwegians for this sort of sport.[28]

Appreciation for the beauty of mountains was vital for mountaineering in the first place.[29] This is often attributed to Jean-Jacques Rousseau, but he "neither knew nor loved the Alps."[30] Still, his intoxicating vision of the naturally virtuous mountain folk, which he had found in Albrecht von Haller's poem *Die Alpen*, convinced the herb gardener of Chambéry to extol their virtues.

Rousseau's romantic followers searched out peasant cultures in the high mountains, believing that only such rugged and unsullied natural surroundings could produce these pure spirits.

In fact, the Swiss themselves had climbed some twenty of their own peaks before 1850: the Jungfrau, Finsteraarhorn, Wildhorn, and Piz Bernina to name four of the most recognizable. Then came the English, capturing thirty-one of thirty-nine peaks scaled between 1850 and 1865. The massive outpourings of the climbers and those whom they influenced—Whymper, Coolidge (technically American), Tyndall, Stephen, Mummery, Young, Smythe, and many others—made for the "golden age" of British mountaineering.

In winter, while the locals were floundering around in the Engadine on their homemade boards in the 1860s,[31] the tale is told (now passed into Swiss lore) that the British aristocracy made good on a bet with Johannes Badrutt, host of the Engadiner Kulm Hotel in St. Moritz. "Come back for Christmas as my guests, and if it's not as warm and sunny as I say, I will pay your expenses."[32] And so it turned out that going abroad for winter holidays joined wintering abroad for health.

Some of the upper class, imbued with Victorian muscular Christianity, came to winter in Switzerland and emulated their summer mountain escapades. They took to crossing cols, spending nights in lonely huts with their summer-guides-turned-winter-mentors, and strove for the peaks. But the vast majority of sportsmen and -women staying in the hotels were there to gaze at the mountains—just to be among them, not to struggle up them on skis, let alone fly down their slopes. As the *Times* put it in 1910, there were plenty of places right in the hotel grounds where skiing could be practiced with a minimum amount of fatigue.[33]

Among the more seriously athletic, there was a strong contingent that had little time for skis in the mountains. "I do *not* reckon 'skiing' to be any part of mountaineering," the great Coolidge dismissed Arnold Lunn at the end of a testy correspondence in 1918.[34] Coolidge was arguing from the point of view of a mountaineer, pure and simple; mountaineering required deliberateness, skiing appeared to be carefree. Lunn countered that skis were useful not merely on the snowy ascent, but were of enormous importance in saving time on the return trip. Besides, they provided a great deal of pleasure. Lunn's diaries are full of remarks such as (20 January 1904) "Down—took ten minutes in what had taken three hours up." Having dipped his skis in a handy brook, the undersides became encrusted with a thick coat of frozen snow so there would be no slippage on the way up. He reached the summit of the Elsighorn in 4 hours and 50 minutes, "50 minutes shorter than in summer time!" he gloated (9 January 1905), "way down wonderful—it is the nearest approach to flying." (11 January 1906).[35] Coolidge, that "outstanding eccentric," never gave ground, and Lunn went on his way.

In February 1904, Hugo Mylius of Frankfurt am Main climbed Mont Blanc on skis, which was widely reported in the French, Austrian, German, and Norwegian press.[36] To those who used skis to get up into the really high country, the efficiency of the skis was obvious; not only did you achieve the height more quickly, but much more impressive was the speed with which a competent ski-mountaineer descended. It was this speed that enabled men to tackle mountains that heretofore had been impossible because of the length of time taken on the return trip. The *Club Alpin Français* included a short chapter on the use of skis for mountaineering by "that fervent apostle" Dr. Payot in its 1904 publication, *Manuel d'Alpinisme*. Not that many people around Chamonix were so experienced on skis to take to the high peaks, but there was a growing interest in the region for skiing. By the beginning of the 1907–08 season there were about five hundred pairs of skis in Chamonix alone. CAF was mightily pleased with its propaganda, for it was "social and patriotic at the same time."[37]

When Norwegians first came to the Alps, almost without exception they said that the steeper regions were useless for skisport.[38] This anti-steep high mountain syndrome of the Norwegians had an effect on Europeans. When Zermatt opened for its first winter season in 1928–29, the slopes were judged "too precipitous" for skiing.[39] Yet the *Alpen-Ski*, with a trademark of the Matterhorn, was also advertised as a Norwegian ski.[40] The manufacturer of this new sort of ski for use in the Alpine lands used the advertising buzz of Norwegian models, tied them to the famed Matterhorn overlooking Zermatt, even though it was no skiing venue. High and spectacular mountains had been goals for mountaineers, now they became peaks to conquer in winter and on skis.

Much attention has been paid to Arthur Conan Doyle's crossing of the Mayenfelder Furka from Davos to Arosa in March of 1894 with the Branger brothers, a trip that they had made the year before. Conan Doyle was by no means an accomplished skier, nor for that matter were his guides.[41] But, then, no one was in those days. Still, his effort is not to be denied. However, he only received, and still receives attention because he is the author of the Sherlock Holmes mysteries. It was not so much the article in *Strand Magazine* that broadcast the possibility of skiing, but his name gave to the fledgling sport an aura of excitement. One wonders why Jerome K. Jerome, author of the utterly successful *Three Men in a Boat*, never received recognition for his skiing.[42] Besides a number of men who have been already mentioned, like Zdarsky and Bilgeri, there were others such as Christof Iselin in Glarus; Englishman E. C.

Richardson; Henry Hoek, who wrote much about *Ma bella Engadina* (hardly his; he had an Irish mother, Dutch father, and lived in Germany); the Frenchmen Henry Duhamel, Henry Cuënot, and their compatriot from the Pyrenees, Louis Falisse; Austrians Toni Schruf, Max Kleinoscheg, and Wilhelm von Arlt; and Wilhelm Paulcke from Germany. Each of them were far more important for the development of the skisport than the creator of Sherlock Holmes.

Most of those mentioned had also done what was to become ski mountaineering. A Norwegian had sent a pair of skis to the monks of the Grand St. Bernard hospice in the early 1880s, but they lay untried until 1889.[43] Olaf Kjelsberg, a Norwegian engineer in Winthertur, skied across the Pragel (1,554 m.) in 1893, which inspired the folk in Glarus to start a ski club that year. The crossing of the Pragel—not a difficult pass—was repeated with Kjelsberg by Christof Iselin, Dr. Eduard Naeff, and Alexander von Steiger.[44] In itself relatively unimportant, it proved, however, the superiority of the ski over *Schneereifen,* a type of snowshoe, for such undertakings. A very similar pattern can be observed in Styria, where the Styrian Ski Association (*Steiermark Ski Verein*) was founded by three men coming from separate sides of the *Stuhleck* to unite at the top in February 1892.[45] Wilhelm von Arlt was first up on the 3,000-meter Hohe Sonnblick in February 1894. The Grimsel, St. Gotthard, Oberalpstock, Longhin were all crossed on skis in the following two years.[46] These exploits paled in comparison with the crossing of the Berner Oberland from Haslital to Brig by Wilhelm Paulcke, Viktor de Beauclair, Drs. Ehlert and Mönnichs, and Wilhelm Lohmüller. (Ehlert and Mönnichs were later killed in an avalanche on the Sustenpass in 1898, one of the first ski deaths to be reported.)[47] This five-day tour over the Grimsel and on to the Concordia hut inspired others to take up ski mountaineering. The Todtnau archive holds a postcard telling of their triumphant Bernese Oberland success. Five years after the crossing, Paulcke himself considered this trip the proof that high-mountain touring on skis was quite feasible.[48] The *Allgemeine Sport-Zeitung,* the *Deutsche Alpenzeitung, Österreichische Alpen-Zeitung,* and *Mitteilungen des Deutschen und Österreichischen Alpenvereins* are peppered with accounts of the attempts, crossings, cols, and peaks achieved on skis in the early years of the twentieth century: the Grossvenediger (3,660 m.) in 1900, Monte Cevedale (3,774 m.) and the Sellajoch (3,304 m.) in 1901, the Fischerhorn (4,045 m.) in 1902, Mt. Blanc (4,807 m.) in 1904 (skis left at the Cabane Vallot).[49] That same year, Samuel Turner made a lone attempt on Mt. Belukha at 17,800 feet in the Altai.[50] Henry Hoek and Ernst Schottelius got to within 400 meters of the top of the Strahlhorn (4,191 m.) before they took off their skis. They reached the top on foot.

In an era when "first ascents," along with *citius-altius-fortius,* assumed a kind of physicalness to be broadcast, the old guard rejected these "artistic excursionists" on their new-fangled instruments. They were also equally unimpressed by the speed of the skiers' descents; pleasure was suspect and fun proletarian. Their dues to the Swiss Alpine Club were financing building cabins on lower slopes for skiers. It was all very irksome.[51]

Lunn kept meticulous record of his ski ascents. He was particularly keen on high traverses, one of those who had been impressed by Paulcke's crossing of the Bernese Oberland in 1897.[52] The mountaineering public, those who read the alpine journals, kept a close watch on which peaks and cols were suitable for ski excursions. Occasionally the Swiss and English daily papers took up a tale such as Lunn's traverse from Montana sur Sierre to Lenk by way of the Wildstrubel in 1908.[53] The following January, with the ambitious and boasting Professor Roget, he skied from Kandersteg to Meiringen.[54]

Mountaineers continued to question both "ski mountaineering" and "first ascents on skis" because many times the party had to divest itself of its skis some way below the summit. Lunn corresponded at length with his friend and famed mountaineer, Marcel Kurz. Towards the end of the war—Lunn looked after British, French, and Belgian internees in Switzerland from 1916 to December 1918 in his father's hotels—he came away from glorying in the achievement of the peak to enjoying the broader view from the col. "I have got beyond the stage when I wanted to make 'first winter ascents,'" he wrote to Kurz in 1917.[55] He also experimented with glacier skiing and promoted summer ski touring. "You seem to mix skiing trips on glaciers with skiing in general," Kurz replied to one of Lunn's 1917 letters; "it seems your goal has changed: you go to the high mountains now to ski exclusively," while Kurz himself never was in the high mountains "just to ski."[56] Skis remained instruments of means for Kurz, just as they had been in the earlier days for Lunn. Now Lunn was veering toward the use of skis for sport, for the thrilling enjoyment of the downhill rush that came after the col was crossed and the peak climbed. Therein lies the cause for Lunn's interest, engagement, and protracted promotion of down-mountain skiing for its own sake.

INVENTING DOWNHILL AND SLALOM

In the early days, when men talked of racing downhill, they could mean either with or without making turns. Arnold Lunn began to proselytize for downhill racing in 1913. In *Ski-ing,* published that year, he claimed that "the finest and most conclusive test of ski-ing is a downhill race without sticks" [57] (as the English called ski poles). In fact, there had been a downhill race in the German championships held at Bad Kohlgrub in 1908. This was billed as a "Great Downhill Race" (*Grosses Abfahrtsrennen*) comprising a 2-kilometer course with a 500-meter drop.[58] Racing downhill was not a thought that resided solely in the English mind nor one that was tested only by English legs—as the British accounts would have the world believe.

Lunn had little time for the old-style races across the countryside, including as much uphill work as they did downhill glide. It was not that he was against uphill expertise. But going up a hill lacked "nerve and dash," vital in the descent and proving a man's character. Since "every decent ski-runner wants to go downhill as quickly as possible," downhill races were natural and, therefore, a test of good skiing. Climbing uphill was only a test of stamina. Lunn did not have *Ski-Idræt* in mind; he thought of skiing as an adjunct to climbing, for he had been a mountaineer first, then took to skis. Once the peak had been attained, view imbibed, photograph taken, and pipe smoked, the descent should be as straight and fast as possible. Until the tree line was reached, natural obstacles such as rocks and crevasses had to be avoided, but the fastest line of descent was the straight run down, and that was the mark of a right-minded skier. In keeping with this philosophy, races were often called "straight races" up to the end of the 1920s. "Taking it straight," redolent of the foxhunt, showed spirit and dash.

If we look carefully at Lunn's ideas on downhill in the years before the First World War, much of the discussion centers on two matters. First, what actually constituted a race downhill, and second, the use of poles. Lunn's early experimental downhill competitions such as the Roberts of Kandahar, run in Montana in the Valais in 1911 and at Mürren the next year, provide clues.[59]

The ten competitors climbed up from Montana to the Wildstrubel hut in seven and half hours.[60] Lunn's account reads, "The competitors left next morning at 10 a.m." Cecil Hopkinson, leading the race at the time, met Lunn who was spectating well down the course and stopped for a chat and a drink. The course, which was not marked, comprised about 3 miles including crossing a glacier. This was followed by a short climb and then a descent of about 4,000 feet, much of it over wind-swept crust. The last 1,000 feet were a test of "tricky wood running." Cecil Hopkinson was first in 61 minutes, riding his poles on the difficult sections. This down-mountain race was as much a test of the competitors handling the changing conditions as it was of speed. Now accorded honorable status as the First Modern Downhill, the Roberts of Kandahar was very much a social affair. In the Montana hotel, a list of the odds

The illustration is as interesting for style of skiing as it is for the clothing worn for the sport in 1912. The British liked to gauge their proficiency on skis by taking tests. "Turning" was one of the great difficulties in the days when feet were not held firmly on the skis. (The Illustrated London News, January 27,1912. Author's collection)

was posted in the hall. Cecil Hopkinson did not disappoint the punters; he was the 4-to-1 favorite.

The next year's downhill was from the Wasenegg to the Brünli Bridge at Mürren. After a short climb of about 200 feet, the rest of the course was down. John Mercer's linked telemark turns aided by a free-heel binding secured a smooth and quick descent in 15 minutes.

What are we to make of these races? In the Montana race, there was only a minimal amount of organization. No starter, no official timekeeper, only a general sense of where the skiers should go. No thought was given to any possible injury and, in fact, one man cracked a collarbone near the start but finished anyhow. In both cases, the uphill sections of the courses were not specifically included as part of the test; skiers had to climb to reach the start of the path down. The racers were to get from top to bottom, as simple as that. What Lunn proposed was something new, but it was not nearly as inceptive as he believed. Norwegians had often included downhill sections in their various races, and there were even a few Norwegians, such as Sondre Norheim, who were known for their downhill skill. The downhill sections of races in Norway were merely part of the whole *Idræt;* they were not something apart, as they became in the Alps under the influence of Lunn.

Lunn believed that a "really steady stick-rider will beat all but the most brilliant stickless runners." To take a steep slope straight, the stick-rider straddled his pole. Skiing hobby-horse style was "far easier and far swifter" than descending by stickless turns and swings, but, he admonished, it was inferior skiing and aesthetics mattered. Not only is it ugly but "it does not satisfy the only true definition of style," which meant skiing in a manner that "demands the least effort and retains most control"—technique and style in 1911. Downhill racing was starting to diverge from cross-country.

If all this rings strange, we should not forget that the standard of skiing prior to 1914 and into the early 1920s was extremely low. Racing was a test of skiing skills in differing conditions of snow and slope. There was no course preparation. Competitors were "candidates" who were judged rather than racers who won and lost. Yet, the siren call of speed could be heard on alp and alm. Nor should we forget that skiing for this elite winter athletocracy was not something serious. Quite the opposite; it was a continuation of the sporting side of the upper-class house party. No one was to win with effort. Effort was damned; it indicated a show-off, and that was the last thing a gentleman—and lady—should do, hence the carelessness with which you dressed, the nonchalance with which you competed.

The leading spirit, the guiding hand, the organizational dictator behind it all was Arnold Lunn.[61] He reveled in being at the center of these matters. A born controversialist with an acute logical mind and an amusing felicity with words, he came first to the Alps as a pilgrim on some religious quest. However much Ruskin and Wordsworth may have inspired him, it was the atheist Leslie Stephen to whom he originally felt most indebted, for Lunn immersed himself in Stephen's "playground" of the Alps not only for mountaineering but also for skiing. Stephen's atheism, however, did not stand up to Lunn's search for a spiritual home, which he eventually found in Catholicism in 1933.

He never hid his spiritual-intellectual endeavors from his skiing public. He carried on very public debates with Father Ronald Knox and the philosopher Cyril Joad besides authoring numerous religious-philosophical books. Later he was a public figure in the Moral Re-armament Movement. Those who knew him only through skiing wondered at the occasional aside from St. Augustine and St. Thomas Aquinas along with the Greek and Latin quotes splashed liberally through the annuals of the Ski Club of Great Britain, which he edited for over fifty years.

His outspoken antagonism to Hitler's regime was based on Nazi persecution of human beings, and his outspoken support for Franco's fascism was his detestation of Lenin and Stalin's rabble along with his personal attachment to the Spanish royal family (who skied at Mürren). He was a "collector" of royals and not ashamed to admit it.[62] Lunn's ski world was made up of the paternalistic and social elite whose duty it was to keep the barbarian at bay, left or right, and, closer at hand on the snows of Switzerland, those whose garish costumes marked them as Cookies—package-tour Cooks travelers.

In ski matters, Lunn was the leading actor, much to his own pleasure as well as to his audience's. A well-known French journalist, Georges Blanchon, attended the Kandahar prize giving in 1937 and summed him up:

> What an exquisite man, Arnold Lunn, and what a curious personality. He is already nearly surrounded by a sort of legend. He is intimately bound up with the development of modern skiing. He is "un grand type" and one must always measure up to him. He exercises his power in such a droll way, with such good humor that only rarely does one disagree with him. . . . To end this 10th meet, everyone waited for the closing, meaning Lunn's speech. Without his speech, the Kandahar would be nothing. In the K, it is only one who presides: this is Lunn, there is only one who speaks: this is Lunn, only one who gives out the prizes: this is Lunn. He speaks of everything to everybody. It is a mix of "words" and "humor." He speaks in German, French, and English in turn—everyone laughs in unison. I laugh when everyone else does so as not to be rude.[63]

As part of his quest for the recognition of Alpine skiing, he invented the modern slalom. The word comes from the Norwegian *Slalaam*—for Lunn it was a test of skiing skills. Norwegians had a variety of *Laam*—tracks. To oversimplify (given the many dialect words) there were: *Kneikelaam* (run with bumps), *Ufselaam* (run off a cliff), *Hoplaam* (run with a jump or jumps), *Svinglaam* (run with turns), and a daredevil run mixing all the obstacles, the *Uvyrdslaam* or *Ville lamir* (wild run).[64] The *Slalaam* was a descent around natural obstacles, to prove that the all-around skier was capable of twisting and turning. This event appeared on a race program in Norway in 1879.[65] The race had not been popular, but it was reintroduced in 1906 to counter the emphasis that young skiers had begun to give to jumping. This was "a forest race, down hill all the way, the course winding among trees and rocks, and all curves being taken at top speed." In spite of the emphasis on speed, the competitors' style while negotiating the obstacles placed at difficult sections of the course was taken into account by judges.[66]

When the Norwegian skiing influence spread to Europe, races were devised specifically to include obstacles. In Germany, slalom was first introduced in the Harz in 1906. The races were often called obstacle races (*Hindernislaufen*), sometimes skill races (*Kunstlaufen*), sometimes both, indicating clearly the skill required to avoid natural or man-made obstacles. "Very interesting was the ski race, that is the slalom racing, in which leaps over a bump, swings around an obstacle and arrival in a cornered off area was demanded," is a 1913 description. In other races it was stipulated that poles were not to be used for braking.[67] Each of these various races certainly received some support, but it remained debatable which of these experiments was the true test of a good skier. The British experimented with "Bending" races where the competitors skied around the outside of twelve poles. No points were given for style. The Black Forest (Schwarzwald) races run between 1902 and 1906 provide an example of the experimental nature of early turning races. In 1902 a *Kunstlauf* was run. The next year it was called a *Kunst- oder Hindernislauf*. In 1904 there was a *Stilgemässes Laufen* (style-point race), which required a run down a steep slope with turns and swings. In 1906 for the same *Stilgemässes Laufen* specific swings were required and speed was not a consideration. Poles were not allowed.[68]

For slalom, as for downhill, Lunn's mountaineering background provided the major impulse. Once the skier had come down from the open snowfields and entered the woods, straight running became impossible. Lunn invented modern slalom to simulate tree running so the ski mountaineer could practice a safe descent to his inn on the valley floor. Little branches were actually used to define the course in the early races, then flags, and later "gates." It was only after the war that Lunn's slalom started to become popular.

There has been a long and surprisingly bitter argument over the invention of modern slalom. The supporters of the dogmatic skiing innovator, Bohemian-Austrian Mathias Zdarsky, were—and are—pitched against the followers of Lunn. Into this argument have come other factors, the most important of which were the not always friendly controversies that both Lunn and Zdarsky had with the Norwegians. Many differences, some only marginally connected with slalom, but dealing with suitability of terrain, equipment, style of skiing, rules, professionalism, and honor caused such a rumpus that challenges were thrown down in 1905 and again in 1993.[69]

Let me single out the particular arguments over slalom. The facts are these: Zdarsky mounted a *Torlauf*, an 85-gate run, on the Muckenkogel outside Lilienfeld, two hours east of Vienna by train, on March 19, 1905, with a field of twenty-four, including one woman. Styled a *Ski-Wettfahren*—a Ski Race, rather than an *Alpines Wertungsfahren*—a Judged Alpine Run, as Zdarsky had wished, the race was designed as a *Prüfungsfahren,* a Testing Run, more for technique and expertise than for speed. One of the competitors was Josef Wallner, the only competitor to use two poles, and Ellefsen bindings (rather than a pair of Zdarsky's) held him on his skis.[70] For Zdarsky, the use of one pole was religious writ and, of course, he believed there were no better bindings than his own. Wallner won by some four minutes even though he had missed a gate and had to climb back some 50 meters. A minimum amount of publicity followed this first gate-race. Although Zdarsky had written in 1900 that he believed the final test in skiing was participation in races, his skiing activities rarely included races. I have been able to find records of only two other Zdarsky slaloms, in 1906 and 1909.[71]

If Lunn had known of Zdarsky's 1905 experiment, he would have called his own creation a gate race, too.[72] Instead he used the Norwegian term *slalom,* and published debates, rules, and their changes over the years. He agitated for its inclusion into local, national, and international competitions. British clubs like the Kandahar, headquartered in Mürren, and the significantly-titled Down Hill Only—always known as the DHO—in neighboring Wengen, were founded partially to promote what was becoming known as "Alpine" rather than "Norwegian" skiing, with a commitment to downhill and slalom racing.[73] There was no instant acceptance of the new races, even by British Ski Club members and racers who held Lunn in high regard. The British championship in 1923 was actually a downhill. Held at Mürren, where one might have expected quite a field, it attracted only three competitors. But it was hardly downhill in modern terms; it included a short ascent, and one section was described as being "useful, as it rests the wearied limbs and gives an opportunity of putting into practice . . . the art of moving rapidly along the level."[74]

It is difficult to realize now, almost a hundred years later, that downhill and slalom, "turning competitions," were not popular in the mountains of Europe and certainly not in Norway. As swings had to be made in front of judges who awarded points as late as 1923, the mathematics of aesthetics caused more grumbling than raising the level of proficiency. One of the leading British organizers, pro-Norwegian stylist, E. C. Richardson, judged that "there seems to be little occasion for turning competitions of any kind" because cross-country runs and jumping provided the measure of skiing prowess.[75] "They had this weird thing," wrote visiting Norwegian Captain Kristian Krefting a few years later to *Aftenposten,* Oslo's leading newspaper, "called the Slalom Race. . . . In this they scurried round some small flags as fast as they could, turning hither and thither, breaking flags and falling down, and altogether looking quite comical."[76]

Captain Krefting may have laughed at the falling down. These were not spills. This was technique. Early skiers who could not turn well simply sat down at the flag, swished their skis round, stood up, and skied on to the next set of flags. Lunn imposed a 10-second penalty to stop this unaesthetic practice, and this remained part of the regulations for first-class ski events until 1925. Only by the mid-1920s had the standard of skiing so improved that the better skiers would lose more time in falling down than by controlling their turns through the gates.

There were other problems that Lunn tackled. Particularly difficult to control were the conditions of the course, for the first man came down in soft snow and the last on a rutted track. Since the essence of modern competition was, and is, equality of conditions, something had to be done. Hence came the idea of having two runs on two different courses, the first on stamped-out and hard snow, and the second on soft snow. For the better competitors, running positions were reversed on the second run. Such rules and regulations were available for the 1922–23 season.

Little by little, slalom spread over the Alps. Taken up by the Swiss universities, it was part of the first international universities' meet in 1925, at which a number of German students also tried the course. Lunn's innovations, technique, and ideas for course setting were translated into French and German.[77] By the second such meet, there was, according to Lunn, a general conversion "to the value of slalom as a test of technique."[78] And recognition: "Slalom" trousers made from material so rugged that, somehow, "accidents are completely suprimé," were on the market in 1932.[79] Downhill and slalom, over the years, became accepted worldwide. It would not be correct, however, to think of these Alpine disciplines as simply replacing what had gone before. Of fifty-two items in the table of contents of the 1926 Ski Club of Great Britain's *Year Book*, twenty were on ski mountaineering.[80] In a tribute at Lunn's death in 1974, Walter Amstutz, the most important of the early supporters of the Alpine disciplines, summed up Lunn's contribution: "He opened up a new epoch and it bore his personal stamp."[81] The Scandinavians, however, stood outside the general conversion and remained adamantly sure that this acrobatic tomfoolery would not sully *Ski-Idræt*.

CHAPTER 7

The French Worry

Maternity, that's the real patriotic duty of women.
—Alexandre Dumas fils, *1887*

Winter sports simply cannot stand analysis. There is much joy,
exaltation and health. It is the death of neurasthenia and all black
depressions. It is the ruin of the doctors, the end of drugs. It has power,
it widens horizons, brings happiness . . .
—Le Patriote Morézien, 1908

And how to succeed in skiing? Be French and profit from experience
elsewhere.—Commandant Hepp, 1910

 While English society was relishing the snow in "Europe's Playground," to rephrase the title of Leslie Stephen's well-known book on the Alps, the French took to skiing for rather different motives in the years running up to the First World War. Behind all the fun and games to be had on skis, uppermost in many French leaders' minds was the effort "to regenerate the race after the humiliations and anguish of 1870" as well as the creation of military ski units for the defense of the mountainous frontiers.[1] Three problems became apparent. On a national level, worry was increased by the declining fertility rates, compounding the declining population. On a local level, further concern was caused by general ill-health from disease and in-breeding among the mountain people from whom recruits for ski troops could be expected. And last, so few knew how to ski.

To improve the prospects for national defense as well as to better the physical and mental fitness of the population, the French Alpine Club (*Club Alpin Français, CAF*), a wealthy civilian organization, combined with the military to promote skiing. In France, skiing was a heady mix of serious chauvinism and social fun, of certainty of courageousness and concern about degeneracy. Fervent apostles of ski doctrine made a determined search for fit recruits. In the years before 1914, nowhere else in Europe was there such intensity in the world of skiing.

From many quarters of France there were attempts to halt the decline in population and to improve health, often thought of as two parts of one problem. In 1902, the French Assembly passed a public health law. Its execution depended on the efficiency of the Hygiene Council of each *département*. In Grenoble, for example, Isère's Council took up anti-tuberculosis measures right away.[2] Until addressed in 1908, problems with drinking water and sewage disposal continued. In the tourist regions, the government was concerned about sanitary conditions for the sake of the growing summer and winter business.[3] A law passed in 1910 gave to climatic stations the right to charge vacationers a residence tax under the condition that certain hygienic standards, which were finally guaranteed by the Academy of Physicians in 1913, were implemented. A not inconsiderable amount of money was at stake. Briançon, for example, hosted 50,000 visitors in 1909, a figure that rose to 65,000 over the following two years.[4] Around the turn of the century, a French Alpine Club's hut might have been replaced by a hotel catering to both sportsmen and ailing city people who came for the cure. "Doctors," wrote the early alpinist-skier Allotte de Fuye, "will very quickly understand . . . that influenza cases . . . should be sent fleeing from the pestilential centers to breathe the revivifying air . . . with no trace of microbes."[5] Studies showed that in a cubic decimeter of air, bacteria numbered:

55,000 in the rue de Rivoli, Paris
600 in a hotel room
25 at 560 meters altitude
0 at 2,000 to 4,000 meters altitude[6]

Addressing the sportsmen, one report detailed the relationship of red corpuscles to mountain sickness.[7] Clearly, these scientific studies gave support to the efficacy of the health-cum-sporting stations.

At the same time, wretched winter living conditions among the mountain people caused much ill health. For warmth, from December until April, peasants lived under the same roof as their animals. Captain Henri Clerc, first commander of the military ski school at Briançon (*École de Ski à Briançon*), wrote in 1905, "In certain high villages . . . one is unhappily impressed by the rickets of the race. Among 5 males one has trouble in a few cantons to find a man of 20 fit for service."[8] This degeneration of the race, he went on, was due to "the fashion of living in winter." Before 1900, washing regularly and changing clothes was rare; no nightwear was available and underclothes were scarce. The captain had recruited in these villages, had gone into "these dens [where] one cannot breathe after a few minutes." Val d'Isère was Val Misère: "Snow, always snow, then snow again and after three days no hope; the beasts are shut up for six months. For a month now the snow has kept us in our houses and all work stops. We await March and April."[9] Conditions like these could still be found in 1937.[10]

Depopulation and degeneration in the French mountains about which Captain Clerc and many others were so concerned had been public knowledge since 1895. Four percent of the population of mountainous Savoy, long known as the "fortress of goiterism," suffered from this affliction. Recruits at the Briançon garrison were taken to see the unfortunates, "emblems of beauty" as one wrote on a postcard home.[11] The decline in population was very real in some areas. Val d'Isère's birth rate declined some 22 percent over the years 1885–1914.[12] After the war, it was suggested that the low French birthrate was one of the causes of the German attack in 1914.[13] Alcoholism and tuberculosis were factors too, not only in the Alps but also in the Jura and Pyrenees.[14] As the German military threat became a reality, the urgency of combating the ill health of the mountain folk and creating a pool of youth strong enough to withstand the rigors of war both in summer and winter took on a strident tone.

In the mountain areas of France, various sporting associations were founded with the goal of improving the physique of the youth in order to have fit soldiers. The *Cercle de Gymnase de Serres* (Serres Gymmnastic Circle) was founded for "honest recreation and to encourage sentiments of virtue, fraternity and patriotism." In Gap, *Les Étoiles des Alpes* (Stars of the Alps) besides the political objective of making them feel attached to republican institutions was "to give youth a civic education as preparation for military service." Another club in 1911, was to develop the "physical and moral forces of the young, prepare in the countryside robust men and valiant soldiers and create among them friendship and solidarity."[15] The Ferry laws of 1881 made military exercises compulsory in schools, but some authorities had difficulty in finding young and vigorous instructors.[16] The Ferry laws may also have given the impetus to the burgeoning number of clubs which engaged in shooting, gymnastics, running, and swimming. Skiing thus became part of this move to combine sport, morality, health, and patriotism.

Sport, morality, health, and patriotism was exactly what the French Alpine Club expressed in its motto *Pour la Patrie par la Montagne* (For the Fatherland by way of the Mountains), which it had adopted in 1903. Once the CAF leadership had persuaded mountaineers that skiing was not just some acrobatic side show—CAF's Winter Sports Commission was created in 1906 and was

You did not need to be literate to read the message in this phallic incentive sent out in postcard form to a France desperate in its need to make up for the lack and then the loss of population before and during the war. (Courtesy Philip Ogden)

given official charge of French skiing a year later—they understood "skiing's patriotic and military reach, its moralizing force as a sport." The philosophical and practical underpinnings were based to some extent on the belief that Norwegians had taken to skiing "as part of their regeneration" during the time that they gained independence from Sweden. As part of their general preoccupation with physical education as a means to halt the degeneration of the race, the French also came to see that skiing was one means to ensure "strong men and strong soldiers."[17]

This theme of physical regeneration was not by any means merely the concern of the French Alpine Club and the military. Coddling poodles, playing with dolls, and drinking absinthe, all were given as reasons for the decline of the population. The generation of Frenchmen prior to World War I was "born tired, the product of an entire century of convulsion."[18] The census of 1881 confirmed the "increasing sterility of the French nation." Was it "*Finis Galliae?*" wondered the London *Times*.[19] Yearly births per 1,000 population between 1872 and 1880 in France were 26; in Germany 38.[20] These were disquieting statistics in this social Darwinian age. The French, wrote Max Nordau, "ascribe their own senility to the century and speak of fin-de-siècle, when they ought to say 'fin-de-race.'"[21] In 1902, one book listed 216 works on depopulation; in 1909, every one of the twenty-two works submitted for a prize contest on the causes and consequences of a low birth rate stressed France's military decline. Academic societies, politicians, and prominent writers all took up the problem in a France bombarded with books, pamphlets, posters, and postcards in which the National Alliance for the Increase of the French Population (*L'Alliance Nationale pour l'Accroissement de la Population Française*), founded in 1896, gained prominent members in Emile Zola (later to produce *Fécondité*) along with politicians of the stature of Théophile Delcassé and Raimond Poincaré. "One cannot allow the numbers of male births to fall from 500,000 in 1872 to 385,000 in 1912," declared one troubled deputy in a military service debate a year later, while at the same time the number rose "in Germany from 770,000 to 1 million." Inside or outside marriage, what France needed was "combatants and the mothers of combatants."[22]

FRENCH ALPINE CLUB IN CHARGE

The French Alpine Club was a mountaineering club. From the mid-1880s on, members practiced winter mountaineering, first without special equipment, then with snowshoes, and, before the turn of the century, with skis. Once the more conservative members were persuaded that skiing was not some madcap stunt, skis were increasingly used for mountain ascents in the Alps, pure and white in their virgin winter cover. If anything, mountaineering in winter and on skis had even more of a moral tone than climbing in summer. One finds in the reports how CAF understood skiing's "role as a moralizer," that skiing was the school of "suppleness, decision, bravery," and of "energy, sang-froid, courage, and audacity," all critical for national defense, "even the future of our race."[23] When Charles Grandmougin joined in 1884, he penned some verses whose refrain stressed the fit and willing patriotism of mountain men:

Allons plus loin encore! Luttons pour la patrie
Le corps toujours vaillant, le Coeur jamais dompté,
Et, fiers, écoutons tous notre âme qui nous crie:
Je suis la volonté.

On, on and further yet! Let's battle for France so fair.
The body always valiant, the heart never still.
Proud, we listen to our souls which cry out and dare:
I have the will![24]

In 1906, CAF was given charge of the development of skiing by the French Union of Athletic Sports Societies (*Union Française des Sociétés des Sports Athlétiques,* USDSA). It immediately sponsored a competition which it called the First International Ski Week at Mont Genèvre, near Briançon, on February 9–12, 1907. Henry Cuënot and his Winter Sports Committee obtained the cooperation of the Ministry of War which gave permission to invite the neighboring *Alpini*—Italy's Mountain Troops.[25] Some Swiss and Austrians as well as visiting Norwegian instructors competed; thus the meet was truly international. General Galliéni, the much-respected pacifier of Madagascar, and now the military governor of Lyon, supported the event and was later pictured on the front cover of *Le Monde Illustré,* one of thirteen journals and papers reporting the competitions.[26] And what days they were!

On the Briançon side of the border an Arc de Triomphe proclaimed CAF's motto: *Pour la Patrie par la Montagne,* while on the Italian side, *L'Amour de la Montagne abaisse les Frontières* (Love of the Mountains Clears Away the Frontiers) greeted their neighbors. Three thousand spectators watched the competitions for fifty-one prizes.[27] Besides various sums of money and, of course, many medals, the President of the Republic, Armand Fallières, presented a Sèvres porcelain vase which went to the winner of the amateur cross-country event, a Swiss. There was a wealth of practical prizes: skis, ice axe, aluminum lantern, alarm clock, and watches, many books, a camera, tea, tie pin, and smoking set. A number of statues were presented: a bronze "Peace and Work" for third place in the amateur cross-country run and a bronze "Eagle," appropriately awarded the winner of the jumping competition—another Swiss, followed by one of his countrymen, an Austrian, and two Italians. The civilian national champion received the military *Le Guerrier Gaulois* (The Gallic Warrior) by Frémet as well as a bronze *Coq Gaulois*—symbol of France, the Gallic cock. The journal *Armée et Marine* presented Grégoire's *Au But'* (At the Finish) to the first military team.[28] General Charbonnier accompanied General Galliéni, and three other generals were also in attendance. The Italians sent Major Ugo Porta, commander of the 3rd *Alpini,* who easily beat the French military teams. The French were "not up to the mark, all hanging on the stick," commented an Italian observer. He came to the conclusion that the French, having had Norwegian instruction for three years, "have not made much profit out of it." He compared them with the Italians, who had only three days of instruction the previous year but "who made a very good show."[29] However, all judged the meet a grand success. The band of the 159th, the famed *Quinze Neuf, Régiment de la Neige* (Regiment of the Snows), performed at the banquet. Senator Vagnat saluted the Entente Cordiale, General Galliéni congratulated all, and especially

Captain Rivas of the *École de Ski*. Major Porta raised his glass "to France and her beautiful and valiant army," and Adolpho Hess of the Turin club echoed the message on the Arc de Triomphe that the two sister nations might do away with the frontier. When the French accompanied Major Porta and his *Alpini* to the frontier, the Italian commander could only say a few words; his emotion almost got the better of him.[30]

The speeches were no mere political mouthings. The French military, which had been highly suspicious of Italian activity up to 1904, became less worried over the Italians as tension with Germany rose. In 1906, for example, France, Italy, and Great Britain signed the Tripartite Pact guaranteeing the integrity and independence of Abyssinia. The French and the British were forging their Entente. By then, the two countries were beginning to discuss military and naval commitments. Dr. Jean Charcot cooperated with Scott in 1908 and tried out his auto-sledge around the Col du Lauteret. "*L'Entente Cordiale n'est pas un vain mot*" ("Entente Cordiale is not an empty word"), commented the reporter. After Scott's death, the Alpine Garden of Lauteret was the spot selected to build the monument as "memory and admiration for the heroism of Scott and his companions." It was yet another tie in Franco-British relations. That year the French finally accepted Greenwich Mean Time as the standard. The ceremonial dinner ended with a toast proclaiming the union of the Entente Cordiale.[31] Over the years, France was cementing these relationships in the face of continuing German and Austrian threats. The CAF meets were held with the same intention; "the ski is becoming the tie between nations," enthused *La Vie au Grand Air*.[32]

The ski competitions that the French Alpine Club organized every year (in 1907 at Mont Genèvre, 1908 at Chamonix, 1909 at Morez, 1910 at Eaux Bonnes and Cauterets, 1911 at Lioran and others all over snow-covered France through to the war) were the major winter sporting events on the calendar. They were covered by large numbers of reporters from *L'Illustration, L'Auto, Armée et Marine, Le Petit Parisien, Les Alpes Pittoresques,* to name only five of twelve present in 1907. Correspondents from seventeen publications were at Gérardmer on the occasion of the awarding of the first military brevet for skiers.[33] The French Alpine Club believed, as it said in a letter soliciting prizes for the meet at Morez in the Jura, that "our contest is the most powerful means of spreading in our country, a sport which regenerated the Norwegian race."[34] This theme runs through CAF's discussions and reports. Many of these were written by Henry Cuënot, the spokesman for regeneration, and his words fell upon receptive listeners.

The annual CAF meets were heavily reliant on military support. The patronage committee for the 1910 competitions at Eaux Bonnes, for example, included the minister of war, the under-secretary to the minister of war, the military governor of Lyon, and five generals commanding the 6th, 7th, 17th, 18th, and 20th Corps.[35] At another meet, two corps alone sent 19 officers and 119 men along with a 41-instrument band.[36] At a meet in the Vosges, between two and three thousand spectators were on hand to watch eight events. The two civilian events, those for youths and women, were unimportant—the crowd had come to watch the four military races.[37] Michel Achard, in his history of skiing in the *Massif Central,* notes that there was very little interest in skiing in the region until a ski team of the 16th Regiment, stationed at St. Etienne, was formed.[38] The military continued to attract attention and made a success of the civilian meets. Of CAF's competitions at Eaux Bonnes in the Pyrenees, one observer wrote, "The most interesting to me was the military events. They gave the true, just measure of the utility of skis, the practical and national use, more than merely the sporting." [39]

This "practical and national use" of skis was precisely what was so problematic to the French military. Skis were unknown to the mountain folk from whom recruits for the ski troops might naturally be expected to come. All looked to Scandinavia as the fount of all things skiing, but there was one great difference; in Norway boys were brought up on skis so no thought had to be given to instruction. Everywhere else but Scandinavia, instruction in the basic knowledge of how to ski had to be a major part of ski troop development. By the 1890s, Russian, German, Austrian, Swiss, and Italian regiments were experimenting with ski troops. Even the English contemplated the use of skiing soldiers to guard their Himalayan frontier. In France, when the Triple Alliance of Germany, Austria, and Italy was renewed in 1887, Italian-French border relations took on a wary unease.[40] French military officers stationed in the Alpine forts naturally began to think about using skis while on patrol on the snowed-in mountain frontier. Lieutenants Monnier and Widmann, both with Scandinavian experience, and later Captain Clerc, prodded the French Ministry of War to follow their neighbors and establish ski detachments.[41] Widmann's extensive report was rejected by the military authorities, and Monnier was also told that for troops "the use of skis was too difficult. It exposed beginners to deathly falls." Besides, they were "impossible to use in hilly country." [42]

In response to the Italian *Alpini* formed in 1872, the *Chasseurs Alpins* (Mountain Troops) had been created in 1879, and with the perceived threat from Italy, the military authorities were thankful to have Lt. Monnier, a *Chasseurs* officer

French cheese makers skied their products down from the heights of the Jura to the local markets. Trust a youngster to find the fun in skiing. (Author's collection)

considered to possess "the purest spine and nerve of France."[43] Captain Clerc was another and as commander of the 7th Company of the *Quinze Neuf* was given permission to experiment with a few soldiers on skis. His second officer was Lt. Monnier. In the winter of 1901–02 the results proved sufficiently encouraging in spite of the "mediocre materiel," as Clerc wrote in his report, to suggest further experiments. Two Norwegian officers, Captain Henrik Angell and Lieutenant Finn Qual, were seconded to Briançon for the following winter. A third Norwegian officer, Lieutenant Schultz, was also on hand to help.[44] These experiments at last convinced the military governor of Lyon to sanction the *École de Ski* for the winter of 1903–04. Clerc was congratulated by his superiors and honored with the Norwegian Order of St. Olaf.[45]

In Angell's report of his time in France, "All's Well, Captain," (*Ça va bien, mon Capitaine*), he paid tribute to French élan but he was critical of poor materiel, "pitiable bindings, deplorable boots and a rucksack too big and improperly placed."[46] In these first years *"nos troupes alpines"* entered the French public consciousness as they appeared in their Basque berets (which had been worn by the mountain fusiliers of 1744), perhaps offsetting the romance of the *Alpini's* feathered hat. *La Vie au Grand Air* in 1902 described military skiing as "a new sport just come to France," and pooh-poohed the notion of the

Under the stern gaze of their Norwegian advisers, the Chasseurs Alpins file by. Before the war, Norwegian officers did not teach how to ski, but demonstrated technique, advised on equipment, and promoted their military maneuvers. (Le Petit Journal, January 19, 1908. Author's collection)

Alps being too steep to be skied. *Le Petit Journal* and *La Vie au Grand Air* both carried covers in 1901 and 1902.[47] Skiing troops were yet another proof to the public that France was ready and prepared for battle on plain or hill.

After all Clerc's good work, he requested a posting to Africa. Captain Bernard took over the command of the *École de Ski* at the time when some officials, albeit admitting that skis were useful for marching and maneuvering in the Alps, still argued that "the results were not yet in."[48] Supporting the continuation of further development, and at the same time somewhat disquieting, was the fact that the Italians had officially adopted skis for certain regiments. Captain Bernard, like Captain Clerc, was impressed by the writing and analysis of ski troops by Italian Captain Oreste Zavattari, and Lieutenant Roiti's article that had appeared in an Italian military journal was immediately translated and printed in *Le Moniteur Dauphinois* two weeks later.[49] Captain Bernard, with his officers, continued to train the mountain recruits, sometimes doing astonishing marches: 80 kilometers with 1,800 meters difference in elevation in 20 hours, from 3 a.m. to 11 p.m.[50]

As the number of recruits mounted and Bernard's work was increasingly noted outside military circles, Briançon, once known only as the high fortress town, became "the center of tourism and winter alpinism." The bourgeoisie read their glossy weeklies and were patriotically titillated when Private Marcel was killed in an avalanche. His death only seemed to increase the mystique of those who skied, for "fatigue and danger fortify youth and make it audacious." These ideals glorified such occasional tragedies for those in the *École de Ski*, "the ski school for the good of the country."[51]

Captain Rivas, Bernard's successor, wrote a *Petit Manuel* explaining how to make skis, how to wax them, and how to ski.[52] He questioned, in 1906, why there were no competitions in France when there were twelve in Switzerland alone, and six in Austria. Where were all the French skiers? The Germans could count four thousand. He set about changing French attitudes to skiing. Rivas realized that the equipment bought abroad was too expensive for the depressed mountain folks. After experimenting with and rejecting Wilhelm Paulcke's German models—Clerc had already tried out Norwegian skis, Max Schneider's from Berlin, a Russian pair and also a pair manufactured in St. Etienne in France—Rivas set up a factory that produced one hundred pairs of skis in 1906 and 237 pairs in 1907. These sold for about 15 francs, less than half the price of imported skis. Wax, a Norwegian specialty, cost between 35 and 50 centimes. Rivas could make a similar concoction for 5 centimes. Three different bindings were available.[53] The object was not just to train recruits but, more important, to have them return to their communities to spread ski lore.

"Be apostles of skiing in your villages," Rivas exhorted. "Make skis as we have taught you and you will be useful to your fellow citizens and your country. *En avant.*" The greatest necessity "for national defense [was] to get skis to the *montagnards.*" Rivas was perfectly aware that you could not create a skiing soldier in two seasons. He was proposing no less than to have mountain children grow up on skis.

Rivas began, too, to be noted in the press at home and abroad.[54] Captain Bernard continued to be active in the promotion of skiing by giving talks. Cuënot enlisted him for CAF's committee for the proposed 1907 International Ski Meet.[55] CAF's journal, *La Montagne,* ran articles on military skiing with increasing fervor. It suggested opening a second ski training center in the Pyrenees and patted itself on the back for its "patriotic work." The London *Times* remained unimpressed;[56] the enemy did not lie in that direction.

The French army skiers of the *Chasseurs Alpins,* however, continued to be hopelessly outclassed by the Norwegian military skiers. At CAF's 1908 meet at Chamonix, the Norwegians romped home in 3 hours, 28 minutes and 30 seconds. The Swiss followed 25 minutes behind, and over an hour later the French came in.[57] In 1909, the results were similar. The Norwegians won a military patrol race in 2 hours, 16 minutes. The French were third, just beaten by the Italians, yet they were still about an hour behind the Norwegians.[58] But perhaps results were not so important. What counted was the Entente between France and Italy, growing ever more cordial if we can believe the marvelous photo gracing the January 11, 1908, cover of *La Vie au Grand Air:* a *Chasseur* and an *Alpini* shaking hands across the snowy frontier,[59] just at the time when the beatification of Joan of Arc signaled that God was again with France.[60]

With the growing French-Italian friendship, some deputies in the French National Assembly thought the moment right to close down the winter posts on the frontiers in order to bring down military costs. Of course CAF objected. At Chamonix, CAF's congress proposed granting a military brevet to anyone able to pass the test, giving the successful candidate the right to choose which regiment he would join when called to the colors. CAF once more congratulated itself for making "the army stronger and consequently a France ever more powerful."[61] It was to youth, though, that the leadership looked, "impetuous and fecund youth which is little by little declining; they all come to ask of the sun, the pure air, power for the days to come or the courage to replace what the days past have extinguished."[62] There is a strain of romantic desperation as ominous war possibilities turned to probabilities. The skier-brevet was aimed at the sporting skier. Two who obtained their brevet in that first exam at Gérardmer in 1913 came from Paris and Roubaix.[63] This was

Neighbors in the Entente Cordiale for years are now official allies of one week as the Italians declared war on the Austrians in May 1915. The Alpini and Chasseur Alpin shake hands across a mountain boundary stretching from Switzerland to the Mediterranean. (The New York Times Mid-Week Pictorial, *May 27, 1915*. Author's collection)

not, then, an appeal only to the *montagnard* population from whom the bulk of recruits would come for the *Chasseurs*. CAF fully realized this and, following the proposal from "an officer who mounts guard on the sacred territory of the Vosges," launched "a patriotic appeal" for skis for mountain kids. In this way, "*L'Oeuvre de la Planche de Salut*" was born.[64] *Planche de Salut* had a double meaning that no one could miss: skis were not just "healthy boards" but were also "boards of last resort," as one might throw out to a drowning swimmer. In a few years, it was believed, the kids "will make a marvelous army of skiers perfectly trained and ready to defend the soil of the fatherland if needed."[65] Today, wrote one of the very few critics of the plan, "it is not only correct but elegant to be patriotic. The wealthy . . . add snobbism to their personal pleasure in the aid of national defense, even of the regeneration of the race." As the French-Italian relationship improved, France's border with Germany became increasingly scrutinized. Although it had been CAF's policy right from the start to spread its annual ski meets all over snow-covered France, I do not believe it was mere chance that Gérardmer, *Perle des Vosges* in happier times, was selected for the 1913 meet at which the *brevet militaire* was first awarded. The Vosges was not only considered the first line of defense but also the nearest place to Alsace and Lorraine, taken from the French by the Prussians in 1871, and the object of much of France's *revanche*[66] and *élan vitale* which, when translated into military terms, was formalized in Plan XVII. The Vosges as well as the Jura to the south took on more military importance than the Alpine redoubts.

> Soignons nos skis comme nos carabines
> Ils serviraient au moment du danger
> Si l'ennemi menaçait nos chaumines
> À la frontière, nous serions les premiers.
> Graçe à nos skis, malgré la neige
> Pour les combats, nous serions prêts
> Et la France qui nous protège
> Toujours, toujours, libre vivrait.[67]

> We look to our skis as we do to our arms;
> They will serve the moment dangers loom.
> If the enemy threatens our homes and our farms
> At the frontier there'll be no sign of doom.
> Thanks to our skis, in spite of the snows
> For the combats we're ready, and foresee
> A France which protects us 'gainst all foes
> Always, will always live free.

CAF and the military had done their propaganda work well. When war did come, the French Alpine Club's last number of *La Montagne* was proud to repeat that the club had been the first of the large associations founded after the debacle of 1870–71 for "the regeneration of French youth." The movement, at first, was simple, "then more intense, with the ultimate view in mind, the safety of the Fatherland." [68] It remained to be seen if skiing as the "school of vigor and health" [69] would suffice in the battle for the land of France and save the nation.

CHAPTER 8

The Germans and Austrians Organize

*One must wonder that it has taken so long for the ski to come
to us.—A forester, 1894*

*Enchanted by nature, in love with sport, convinced of the necessity
to establish in the Arlberg a constant meeting point for the friends
of this noble activity, the following ex-tempore members of this
excursion felt themselves moved to found the Ski Club Arlberg.
—St. Christof, January 3, 1901*

 France's children were in training to halt the German foe
again, the response to Germany's increasing militancy. The
French, and other powers, had taken note of the development
in Germany of ski troops. What they did not know was the
full extent of the German programs as troops on skis became
part of the overall military thinking among certain members
of the German military leadership. As it became increasingly
obvious that Austria-Hungary would be Germany's ally in any
forthcoming war, neighboring powers also worried about the developments
among the Emperor's ski troops. Ski troops in all countries may have provided
a panache to civilian skiing, but they made military leadership nervous about
maneuvering over snow country and in the mountainous terrain.

THE MILITARY TAKES UP SKIING

After successful experiments by Hauptmann Langenheinrich with the 82nd
Infantry stationed at Goslar, Germany, in 1891–92,[1] the War Office became
serious about outfitting ski troops. Orders for equipment went out to Max
Schneider whose publication, *Der Tourist,* the official organ of the German
Tourist Association (*Deutscher Touristen-Verein*) had lobbied for the formation
of ski troops. This civilian monthly journal propagated skiing while marketing Schneider's skis. Chief of Staff Paul von Hindenburg ordered equipment
for the Jägerbattalions from Mecklenburg, Pomerania, the Rhineland, and
Hannover who were sent to Colmar, Culm, and Schlettstadt in the 1893–94
season.[2] Von Hindenburg also obtained equipment from Todtnau in the Black
Forest.[3] A total of seven battalions with ski troops were deployed over snow-
covered Germany: Kirchberg, the Harz, Bavaria, and, most prominently, the

Freiburg area on the borders of the Black Forest where the energetic university professor Dr. Wilhelm Paulcke delighted in raising a volunteer troop. Ski troops were a novelty among the already militarized society. At home they were patronized, even lionized, especially in middle-class publications like *Das Buch für Alle* (The Book for All, sometimes translated as Literature for All). They received publicity abroad in the *Illustrated London News* and *L'Illustration*.[4] In a militant Germany, just when high society was taking to winter games with the Crown Prince in the lead,[5] here was yet another role for the most feared military of Europe. Or that is how it appeared. In fact, with the Vosges, the Alps, Carpathians, and the Eastern front to worry about, the battalions with ski troops were spread thin. There was surprisingly little knowledge until about 1910 of the fighting capabilities of men on skis. Prowess on skis was on display during military patrol races, often featured events at local meets, and long marches were reported in the newspapers. Norwegian instructors were made available. In 1913, the Swedish War Ministry presented the "Swedish Trophy," which became part of the National Championships,[6] all part of the military-social mix of the pre–World War I years.

The German War Ministry started equipping artillery regiments in 1910 and sent out an order for ten thousand pairs of skis for the 1912–13 winter. The War Ministry had taken some of Hauptmann Hermann Czant's analysis to heart.[7] Czant had been an observer to the Russo-Japanese War and his book was written as if war was about to come to Europe where "the passes of our mountains will play even a greater role"[8] and, like many, wondered what Napoleon would have been able to do if his troops had been equipped with skis. Curiously, no one seems to have recorded how the Emperor's retreating forces had been harassed by Russians on skis during the retreat in 1812.[9]

In spite of all this activity and the publicity that skiing received via the many drawings and photos appearing in the weekly journals, specialist papers, and magazines, German troops were not experienced enough to keep the Swiss in sight, so it would be "totally useless" to compete at Pontresina in 1914. They were issued with poor equipment, complained the *Münchener Zeitung*, and wore primitive clothing. No one expected they would compare with the Scandinavians, but the real problem was that neither could they get near the French or the Austrians. Or that is what they believed, and for Europe's mightiest military, it was something that should not be tested.[10]

Austrian military skiing was different from Swiss, French, German, and Italian skiing in two ways: it had a very strong social element to it, and two instructors dominated: Mathias Zdarsky and Oberleutnant Georg Bilgeri.

When Oberleutnant Viktor Sieger had the opportunity to ski in January 1893, he borrowed a pair of skis from Baron Oberländer. Two days later he joined the Austrian Ski Association (*Österreichischer Ski Verein*), whose president, a *Fürst*, bore the distinguished name of von Metternich and whose secretary was Baron Wilhelm von Wangenheim. When Sieger journeyed to Mürzzuschlag to compete in his first race twelve days later, he traveled with Baron Wedel Jarlsberg and Major Schadek and many officers of the Officers Military Gymnastics and Fencing Academy (*Militär-Turn- und Fechtlehrer-Akademie*) in Wiener-Neustadt, just returned from a 107-kilometer ski excursion.[11]

Major Oskar Schadek von Degenburg, commander of the Officer's School of Gymnastics and Fencing, had learned his skiing in Scandinavia. He wrote out by hand an *Instruction (und Belehrung) über die Verwendung der Schneeschuhe* (*Instruction [and Advice] on the Use of Skis*) ready for the 1894–95 season. A printed version was published in 1897.[12] Schadek knew Norwegian Baron Wedel Jarlsberg, and doubtless his Norwegian pedigree did not hinder the class makeup of the Austrian Ski Association, of which about 25 percent were officers and aristocracy, according to Captain Karl Roll, a Norwegian officer seconded to Wiener-Neustadt in 1896.[13] Roll had been the skiing mentor (one cannot say instructor) to the Norwegian Prince Olaf; so he, too, came with the very best social credentials. He inculcated the Norwegian method among the Viennese, unknowingly beginning the longest and often bitter feud over technique in European skiing. Other Norwegian officers followed Roll.

INSTRUCTION, CIVIL AND MILITARY

Unlike Norway, there had to be instruction. Oberleutnant Raimond Udy published the first instructional book for the military in 1894, but it does not appear to have had wide appeal.[14] Mathias Zdarsky was experimenting with his self-designed skis, one pole, and a different technique from the Norwegians. Oberleutnant Bilgeri was also experimenting with his skis, bindings, and two poles. Hermann Czant was off to observe the Russo-Japanese War and would, two years later, write his practical observations. But the various ideas, differences, and opinions were not glaringly apparent prior to the turn of the century. The military supplied an excitement to the civilian meets; society thrilled at the presence of so many officers at the Semmering competitions of 1896, and the *Allgemeine Sport-Zeitung* went out of its way to point out that the military had contributed "more than a little to the respect which the sport is enjoying."[15]

The well-to-do were the ones enjoying the sport. It was a "rich man's passion," reported visiting Norwegian, Hassa Horn in 1905, as it had been from the start.[16] Attending the 1893 Mürzzuschlag competitions were one margrave [*Markgraf*], six counts [*Gräfe*], three countesses [*Gräfinnen*], four barons, and one general. The aristocracy of Graz was there, almost the entire garrison of Wiener-Neustadt officers, and a great number of *Jagdherren*. Minister-President *Fürst* von Windischgrätz, the prince and princess of Liechtenstein, Prince Schwarzenberg und Hohenloe, and four countesses were at another meet. At Semmering in 1911, on hand were *Erzherzog* Albrecht, *Erzherzogin* Maria Alice, *Prinzessin* Croy and Zamoyska, *Graf* Paffy, *Gräfin* Dobrzenski-Kolowrat, *Gräfin* Coudenhove, *Graf* Draskovich, and *Baron* and *Baronin* Klein.[17] This aristocratic attendance remained part of the Viennese ski scene right up to the war.

It is surprising, looking back one hundred years, that there were no military competitions interspersed in these early civilian meets. The military commands were more intent on taking their soldiers off on long trips. In 1895, for example, a section of Infantry Regiment 17, stationed in Klagenfurt, was led by Oberleutnant Petternel on a four-day round tour from Klagenfurt, up the Saualpenzug (at 1,899 meters), and on to St. Martin. The third day, they skied back to Klagenfurt over flattish land in 20° weather. This trip must have greatly impressed the Swedes, for an account of it ended up in the important publication *På Skidor*.[18]

Ski troops of the Austrian Empire operated in Galicia, Hungary, in the Carpathians, and within Austria itself. In 1910, Leutnant Fritz Graf of the Innsbruck Corps was sent to study in Norway for two months. Two years later Oberleutnant Hans Osobliwy gave a four-week course to the 1st Bosnian-Herzgovinian Infranty: the Empire appeared covered.[19] These course instructors had learned their skiing in very different ways: watching Norwegians was one way. Others had come under the spell of Mathias Zdarsky, and still others were followers of Georg Bilgeri. During the war, one of the most prominent ski leaders, Josef Müller, was, at sixty-three years of age, faced with the question of which system to teach. He got around the difficulty by teaching bits of all three depending on student and terrain.[20] It seemed only to matter among the experts. How they vilified each other in the years before 1914! What was it that made the support of one technique and even philosophy of skiing so emotional? A brief background is necessary here.

For Norwegians there was nothing new about skiing, and prior to 1905 they knew there never would be. After 1905, some were not quite so set in their ideas, but the majority remained convinced that the hotel-sport coming out of central Europe was not to be confused with real skiing. The great majority, say more than 99 percent, tended to look down upon everyone else who skied. They did not have to be taught; it was a birthright and one, moreover, to which they partially owed their freedom from Sweden. With an upright stance, single pole, and *Idræt* in heart and mind, the Norwegian skier was at one with himself—and latterly herself—and nature. This philosophical baggage of *Ski-Idræt*, epitomized by Nansen, however marvelous it may have sounded to *Graf* this and *Gräfin* that, would be the last physical discomfort that the Vienna set would have embraced.

EARLIEST ALPINE SKI TECHNICIANS: ZDARSKY AND BILGERI

Mathias Zdarsky, a Bohemian Austrian who settled near Lilienfeld, a little over two hours west of Vienna by train, had an extraordinary, inquiring mind, a trained gymnast's body, a practical facility with his hands, a capacity for determined work, and a dogmatic certainty that he knew best . . . about most things, certainly about skiing—"a crazy cockerel," according to Paulcke. To the army leadership, however, he was a "private scholar in all areas of current human knowledge, [with] exemplary unselfishness, rare openness and integrity and cool and brave in danger." [21] He taught the army his Lilienfeld method from 1903 to 1911 and again during the war until he was caught in an avalanche in 1916. [22]

His *Lilienfelder Skilaufechnik* was published in 1896, the result of six years of experimentation. Richter of Hamburg was the publisher, the same who had brought out Nansen's "Greenland Crossing" in German. [23] Zdarsky was a missionary for his own ski, which he called the Alpenski, about 10 centimeters shorter than Norwegian models. He listed nine faults of Norwegian skis, although he freely acknowledged Nansen to be the founder of the modern skisport. After experimenting with two hundred bindings, he devised one with a metal spring, but, according to Arnold Lunn, it was "heavy, expensive and tended to break in cold weather." [24] Zdarsky used a single, diskless pole, and would not hear of two poles at all. This is what constituted what Zdarsky proclaimed as something new: an Alpine ski, with special bindings that owed little to the Norwegian heritage. That was one of the major contentious points. The other had to do with skiing itself. His shorter skis were easier to turn on steep slopes, and the pole was used as a brake. Zdarsky could ski on any slope, seemingly at any speed. A claim was made years later that he had achieved a speed of 108 kilometers per hour [25]—an impossibility given the equipment and the slope of the hill.

The sides were thus drawn: "Lilienfelder or Norwegian?" as a whole series of articles in the much respected ski weekly, *Der Winter*, and elsewhere debated the issue. [26] In the Black Forest, supporters of the Norwegian method blasted off against Zdarsky and his pupils from Vienna. Zdarsky was not only men-

Mathias Zdarsky leads an "Alpine" ski course on particularly flat ground around Mariazell, Austria, in 1913. All Zdarsky's courses were free, and it is believed that he must have taught about 40,000 people. His home near Lilienfeld became a pilgrimage destination for many of his followers. (Author's collection)

tor to the Vienna skiers but had his own association, called the International Alpenverein. The journal provided him with an outlet for his thoughts and arguments. He refused to join the Austrian Ski Association as well. Not a few of Zdarsky's followers were army officers, and the Lilienfeld method was endorsed as the official method for military skiing in 1907 with Zdarsky himself as the major instructor. By the first winter of the war, 1,500 men were on skis in the Carpathians, many instructed by Zdarsky.[27] He received a gold service medal from Emperor Franz Josef.[28]

Zdarsky issued a challenge to the Norwegians: to ski down three courses, each defined by flags. Zdarsky was to choose the course and to ski first. Letters flew back and forth about the worsening relationships. The Austrian Consul General in Christiania arranged for C. M. Schwerdtner to meet with Captain Roll. The stakes heightened when Rickmer Rickmers put up 10,000 marks for any Norwegian skiing with Norwegian bindings who could follow Zdarsky's tracks from the top of Mont Blanc down to Chamonix, later £150 (3,000 crowns) to be awarded to the first Scandinavian who accepted Zdarsky's conditions and defeated him.[29]

The Norwegians refused to take up the challenge but did agree to send an official observer, accomplished skier, and military officer, Lieutenant Hassa Horn. He and Zdarsky skied together for a number of days, and it became quite plain that on slopes of about 20° Zdarsky's technique was superior. Bindings appeared to play no role. The difference, then, was in the length and the form of the skis. On the final day, Zdarsky explained his teaching methods, much to Horn's approval. They are "excellent," he wrote, "Zdarsky is one of the best ski runners I have ever seen, *the* best indeed as far as turning on difficult ground is concerned." The two exchanged skis in the hope that it would "take the place of unseemly wrongles [sic] in which the real point at issue has frequently been obscured by personalities and irrelevant side issues." Faults there had been on both sides, but the time had come to move on to discussing 40-meter jumps and swinging turns in deep crusty snow on 60° slopes.[30] "It should be the duty of every Norwegian skier to drop the old ideas," Horn wrote in his report, "to contribute to furthering better understanding."[31] Brave words—but not really to be taken seriously in the club huts of Nordmarka.

Zdarsky was not new to challenges. He had issued his first in 1899, then another which he retracted in 1903, but the final one against Oberst Bilgeri—another military instructor—in 1910 was the most serious.[32]

In the mid-1890s Bilgeri was posted to Hall in Tirol, where he had found twenty pairs of skis in the barracks and was allowed to form a special ski cadre. He made a tour of the Tux and Zillertal Alps with sixteen men. He spent his spare time skiing, and as he became known he taught courses to civilians and to other military units. He added summer skiing on glaciers in 1908. Two years later he published *Der alpine Skilauf* which brought him into direct conflict with Zdarsky. He had criticized the master's grooveless skis, admitted that his own bindings were related to Zdarsky's all-metal model, and he advocated the use of two poles.[33] In explaining a Stem-Christiania turn, Bilgeri had referred to "the hind leg." Zdarsky, not one to let anything by, commented that "there would seem to be an officer in the Imperial army that has four legs." More important, "in many parts of his book ideas had been given with no attribution [to Zdarsky]."[34] Both were persuaded to back down, but bitter feelings remained and Bilgeri found himself posted to Komorn, on the Hungarian border with present-day Slovakia, about fifty miles northwest of Budapest. An inner group of officers had not appreciated his anti-Zdarsky stand. Bilgeri continued to give courses in the Tatra and Carpathian mountains. His teaching methods, especially the use of two poles, became increasingly accepted, much to the chagrin of Zdarsky. By 1912, *Der Winter* judged three quarters of the Austrian troops were followers of Bilgeri; his skiing was by "balance" whereas

Zdarsky's technique relied on "support." Zdarsky had become a prisoner of his own system. One of the most persuasive critics was an Englishman, Vivian Caulfeild.[35] But, from an Austrian *Skimeister's* point of view, who cared what an Englishman might say about his methods? What would an islander know of such things anyway? During the Great War, Zdarsky and Bilgeri (and others) continued to teach Austrian ski troops. Zdarsky was caught in an avalanche on the Marmolata on the Dolomite front from which he recovered in spite of many broken bones. Bilgeri went on to teach right up to his death (of syphilis) in 1934.[36]

CLUB SKIING

In some cases, ski sections were formed from already existing cycling, rowing, skating, and winter sports clubs. Sometimes new clubs were simply founded on their own.[37] Before the war, about 35,000–40,000 Germans were on skis, compared to about 6,000 French, 8,000 Swiss, 15,000 Austrians and perhaps 2,000 British, as a Munich paper estimated in 1912. The figures were probably about right, except for the British who numbered about 18,000.[38]

The social development of skiing was bound up with the forming of clubs. Gymnastic and rowing and bicycling organizations found a new activity in wintertime for their members to keep in trim for what they perceived as their main athletic pastime. Although the Turners could practice in a hall, winter gymnastics was never the same as being outside on the display grounds. Skating was so spatially circumscribed. Wherever snow lay in the lower hill areas, there was also a remarkable development of clubs in the period up to the Great War. Ski clubs formed in the Pfalz, Eifel, Black Forest (Schwarzwald), Harz, Riesengebirge, and Erzgebirge. An example from Thuringia is instructive, for it was not the major focus of early German skiing, nor would it ever become one; yet, belonging to the Thuringian Wintersports Association (*Thüringer Wintersport-Verband*) were sixteen groups in 1906 with 648 members. Oberhof was clearly the leader of the major clubs with 220 members, with Schmalkalden next with 108. In 1908 there were thirty clubs in the association, with 2,763 members. The smallest club in 1908 had six members (Neustadt), the largest boasted 680, of whom 435 were youngsters (Suhl).[39]

Others who first saw the pleasures of ski possibilities were middle-class townsmen, imbued with out-of-door romantic sensibilities, men like Guido Rotter who had already been involved in the Youth Hostel movement.[40] The driving influence of particular individuals often influenced early skiing in a region: in the Schwarzwald, Fritz Breuer and Wilhelm Paulcke, in the Harz Oberförster Ulrichs, retired officer O. A. Vorwerg in the Erzgebirge—although his claim is disputed—and in the alpine forelands south of Munich, August Finsterlin, although, in fact, skiing did not take off until the *Akademische Ski Club München* (Academic Ski Club of Munich) was founded in 1901.[41] These men, often with individual connections to Norway in one form or another, obtained skis, had them copied by local carpenters, smiths, and leather workers, and experimented on their own; there were no how-to books in the 1880s. They induced their friends to join them, started clubs, sang songs, enjoyed outings and promoted meets. An argument simmers whether the Todtnau or Braunlage Ski Club was the first with disputed dates of 1891 or 1892.[42] Other than local pride, it really does not make a difference; Todtnau was far more influential in giving direction to German skiing.

The social aspect of skiing was the most important. The singing of songs, often with in-group remarks, brought solidarity with good fellowship. The first one appears to come from Todtnau in 1892. One line, for example, reads *"Auf zum Feldberg! Kommt zum Mayer* [Up to the Feldberg! Come to Mayer's],*"* referring to the innkeeper. The third verse indicates what was important to these middle-class sportsmen:

> Drum ihr lieben Menschenkinder,
> Wollt ihr froh und lustig sein,
> Und gesund dazu nicht minder
> Schnallet an die Schneeschuh fein.
>
> Gather round you friendly soul,
> Happy be and glad all day.
> Good health too is the goal,
> So strap on skis and fly away.[43]

Fritz Breuer, the author of the song, also believed that he had started the skier's greeting, *"Ski Heil."*[44] This was not an unknown greeting; *Waidmanns Heil* for the foresters even found its way as the title of a woodsman's journal. *Ski Heil* remained popular until that other *Heil* of the 1930s made it suspect.

CHILDREN ON SKIS

The *Realschule* (High School) of Nordstadt zu Elberfeld (today's Wuppertal) began some sort of ski program as early as 1884; and Braunlage's gym requirements were replaced in 1896 with one day a week ski instruction, so that by 1900 "all boys and girls are on skis," reported the *Deutsche Eis-Sport* enthusiastically. Clubs, municipalities, and the government got into the business of promoting skiing for youngsters. In Oberwiesenthal, in the Erzgebirge, as early as 1903, about one hundred children were enrolled in ski courses, the school providing equipment for parents unable to afford it, as did the town of Erfurt for elementary school pupils a decade later. Guido Rotter in the Riesengebirge was instrumental in supplying city kids with skis.[45] In Altenau in the Oberharz, skiing, like gymnastics, became part of the physical education program in 1907. By 1911, students in Arnsberg were given skis by the ski clubs Sauerland and Winterberg, and the following year a course for teachers was inaugurated in Winterberg because skiing had been made obligatory in the Hochsauerland schools.[46] Teachers, men and women, from the Zellerfeld region of the Harz attended the ski teaching course organized by the Prussian Ministry of Culture in 1912. Participants came from Goslar, Halberstadt, Seesen, Hannover, and Göttingen.[47] It was the same in the Riesengebirge. The British could hardly believe that children were "compelled by law to ski!"[48] The amazement was half in admiration and half in worry; the Riesengebirge, it was pointed out, was between Prussia and Bohemia, two names that jarred the comfortable London clubman in two very different ways.

When skiing came into the public purview in the German-speaking world in the 1890s, the main thrust of those who propagated skiing was to men and women. Yet right from the start, children were not only mentioned but care was taken over their physical training. The most widely read of the early German papers that mentioned skiing, *Der Tourist,* extolled the sport as good "for men, women and children." Since this publication was often reprinted, it reached a wide readership. The above remark, for example, was published in the *Österreichische Turn-Zeitung.* Catalogs at the turn of the century advertised mostly to men and women, but there were also skis for children in different lengths.[49] There was a hope to get the children out into the countryside to better their health, but also country folk could see how they themselves might change their shut-in winter existence. This effort toward the children was made in part because the adults (who may have had a marvelous social time) often had difficulty in learning how to ski. As an old German forester put it: "It is also a '*malheur*' [commonly used French word meaning misfortune] that skiing in its final form is not so easy to learn. . . . In order to be really good, you have to start young."[50]

In Germany, health was a much-discussed topic. Max Schneider made it quite plain in his *Tourist:* "First is the healthiness of skiing for old, young, men, women in full fresh air . . . excellent for the lungs. As you do it so comes muscle building."[51] The well-known Hans Suren, widely published physical culturist and believer in nudism, came to the Winterberg Ski club's teachers course in February 1912, designed "in the interest of fostering manly youth."

An Oberhof, Thuringia, schoolmaster gathers his class for practice in 1908. In some communities skiing had replaced gymnastics in the winter curriculum, something that the military command noted as it became interested in finding recruits who could already ski for the newly established ski units. (Author's collection)

Suren spoke on the positive hygienic side of winter practice.[52] He had a receptive audience. The youth movement, the natural healing movement, nudism, naturism, and racial hygiene were all part of a "natural" culture designed to cure the ills of an industrial and over-burdened society.[53] Advocates implored adult skiers to "get the youngsters out on skis so the health of the whole fold will improve." They wrote articles such as "The importance of winter sports for the health of our people."[54] The Kaiser and his military chiefs wanted a healthy society that would breed healthy children. In 1893 the German Crown Prince along with Princes Eitel Friedrich and Adalbert of Prussia received skis for Christmas, and the six-year-old *Erbprinz* Johann Leopold von Sachsen, Coburg und Gotha was featured on skis on a postcard.[55] It was all very well for the elite to be on skis, but as the army began to take increasing interest in recruits for ski sections, the concern mounted that local boys in mountain districts should become proficient on skis. One major problem was that there were not enough lads. The German population had increased from 41 million to 56 million between 1871 and 1900, but it had only risen to 64 million by 1910.[56] In the social Darwinian climate, these were worrying statistics, not as poor as the French, but enough to make Chief of Staff Paul von Hindenburg get involved in the formation of ski detachments in 1893.[57] As war seemed a real possibility, Major Maurer, the promoter of military skiing in the Feldberg region, had children singing:

Wer will unter die Soldaten,
Der muß haben einen *Ski*

Whoever wants to become a soldier
Must have a ski [instead of *Gewehr,* a gun].[58]

However simple, the message had serious intent, made manifest in the founding of the German Ski Association (*Deutscher Skiverein*) in 1905. Written into the constitution was "the training of ski runners for the army."[59] Wilhelm Paulcke, a professor at the University of Freiburg and already an authority on all things to do with skiing and snow, proposed a Voluntary Free Corps of skiers in 1911, which gained immediate acceptance.[60]

Before the war, German military and ski association authorities worked toward the same goal: obtaining recruits who could ski their way straight into the various ski battalions. Of course, there was a difference between ski sport and ski service. Oberleutnant Czant had warned about that.[61] The efforts of schools and clubs to inculcate a love of skiing in their youngsters meant not only that those children had a good and healthy time in winter but that they were being readied for possible serious service on the snowy fronts of war.

SPREADING THE WORD

Many of the leaders of the clubs had connections to Max Schneider in Berlin. His *Tourist* was the official organ of the German Tourist Association (*Offizielles Organ des Verbandes Deutscher Touristen-Vereine*), with twenty-nine associations numbering 23,000 members in 1889.[62] If skiing arrived in Germany "out of the blue" in the 1890s, Max Schneider of Berlin was more than partly responsible. In a series of articles, often illustrated, some virtually paraphrasing Nansen, he described what skiing was, is, and should be. He explained the use of skis. That is why so many of the early printed publications included "hunting" (*Jagd*) and "mail and communication" (*Post und Verkehr*) in their titles, enough for some contemporaries to delight in skiing as a *Volkssport*. But for the most part, the utilitarian use of skis depended on the *Herren* (gentry) who read *Der Tourist,* not their woodsmen.[63] Since there was hardly anyone else writing about skiing, articles from *Der Tourist* were reprinted wholly or in part in a geographically wide range of publications, including Victor Silberer's influential

Allgemeine Sport-Zeitung and the *Deutsche Turn-Zeitung* along with a number of newspapers and manufacturers' catalogs that often doubled as instructional booklets. Connected with Norwegians, having leads all over Europe, acting as a clearinghouse and agent for all things to do with skiing, supplying skis to civilians and the military, Max Schneider alerted Germanic Europe to skiing's possibilities, promoted skiing's delights and, thereby, laid the foundation for the practice of modern skiing. He had plans to develop his own ski center: skiing terrain, jumps of different height, and a lodge were planned in Hohegeiss, the highest village in the Harz.[64] He had sold 1,350 pairs of skis by April 1893.[65] When Carl Luther competed at Holmenkollen in 1913, Norwegians talked to him as if Berlin were the center of German skiing.[66]

Areas that had always fought against the winter elements now found themselves cultivated by these new folk who arrived to ski in their undulating and hilly terrain. The personal example of Herr Strauch demonstrates how various strands come together.[67] This young man met some Norwegians while he was in Rostock. Their enthusiasm for skiing infected him. He negotiated with a herring boat captain who brought him skis from Norway. The customs agents did not quite know what to make of the twelve pairs of long boards, but Strauch got them through and tried them out in Rostock before spending Christmas in Ballenstadt am Harz. "I was a world wonder," he reported. No one had ever seen anything like it. Later that winter, he found himself featured in German cycling papers because the Rostock Cycling Club had become interested in skiing.

This tale is so typical around the turn of the century because it contains most of the ingredients of how skiing became part of winter hill life. The chance meeting with Norwegians, the enthusiasm, the individual effort and the search for skis from Norway were repeated time and again in Germany, from the Black Forest in the west to the Carpathians in the East. [68]

GROWTH OF SKIING

A beginner who was taken by the skisport would have done something like Leutnant Sieger, on skis for the first time on in January 1893. "Descended the meadow," he confided to his diary. "Watched [others] in the afternoon. Then descended three times." He sent in his membership to the Austrian Ski Association and attended meetings over the next two days. Later that same month he bought two pairs of skis at Berenc and Löbl, Vienna's best shop for such equipment in town. He tried them out the next day amid a crowd. Evidently confident enough, he registered for a race in Mürzzuschlag set for February 2. He spent the day before practicing at the Viennese suburb of Pötzleinsdorf hill—it was icy and he fell many times, hurting his chin. On race day he took the train along with aristocracy and officers from Wiener-Neustadt. In the fifth heat, he found himself in the lead. But he was a bit slow up the second hill. Once on top, he flew down the other side in a sitting position, and finished standing. "After a good fight [I] won." As winner of the heat, he took part in the final and placed fifth out of five. He continued to ski at Pötzleinsdorf on February 5, and again during the next week. This account from his diary—there are not many that have come to light—gives authenticity to the sort of skiing life that a man might pursue. The Austrian Ski Association that he had joined was a select club in that only ethnic Germans could join.[69] Racist in tone, it meant that other nationalities within the Austrian Empire, but especially the Czechs, should be kept out of the club.

The Czechs themselves had already founded a ski club in Prague in 1887 and held two contests prior to the one at Mürzzuschlag. The energetic founder, Rössler-Orovsky, inspired skiing in Bohemia along with the first championship of the Kingdom of Bohemia in 1896. He attended international ski congresses, representing Bohemia, much to the annoyance of the Austrians, who felt they spoke for the entire Empire.[70] As elsewhere in snow-covered Europe, skiing was started by individuals who had contacts in one way or another with Norwegians: men like Štolba in 1884, reporting on Wergeland's 1865 Norwegian ski history, and Rössler who imported skis from Norway.[71] Much of the early skiing in the Riesengebirge, the mountain country straddling the German Silesian and Austrian Bohemian border, was owed to Graf Harrach, who put his estate personnel on skis. Two ski clubs from Prague, the *Bruslarsky Savodin* and *Cesky Krhonossky Spolek,* made of Jilemmice (later Starkenbach) something of a ski center.[72] Minor incidents such as the felling of a large stag with an iron-tipped pole and using skis to dig out avalanche victims, both reported in Prague's *Kuryr* and analyzed in a 1906 speech, helped to promote skiing.[73] In 1900 the Bohemian Ski Club organized a 10-kilometer race up the Heidelberg, at 1,012 meters, which attracted twenty-seven competitors. By 1909, over a hundred tours had been carried out in the Carpathians.[74] The mountain village of Sławsko, an hour's train ride from Lemberg, became the main skiing center.[75]

On the German side of the Riesengebirge, skis had been used by a few in the 1880s, including playwright Gerhard Hauptmann. More important was a local teacher, Kajetau Baier, and Hauptmann D. O. Vorwerg. Baier made skiing into a required activity for his classes. Vorwerg, who had learned to ski in Norway also found skiing "most valuable for education and recreation." He described and analyzed skiing in *Der Wanderer im Riesengebirge* (The Riesengebirge Tourer), the newspaper of the *Riesengebirge-Verein* (Riesengebirge Association) in 1891. In 1893 he published *Das Schneeschuhlaufen*, an instructional booklet. Those in Hohenelbe objected to what they considered Vorwerg's self-promotion, and it left him an embittered man.[76]

To the west of the Riesengebirge lay the hills of the Erzgebirge—spanning the Czech-German border of the Sudetenland—where reports of skis, "the footboards of the Laplanders," appeared in the 1770s, 1790s, 1824, and 1842, certainly enough odd references to indicate a continuing local use in "Saxony's Siberia," as the 1842 report describes the area.[77] But in the early 1890s, a Norwegian working in the local railway factory was using skis, as were Norwegian students in Dresden and Mittweida, so that *Glück-Auf,* the organ of the *Erzgebirgs-Verein,* could write that "skiing has now got its start" in January 1893, meaning skiing for sport, skiing along Norwegian lines, And, indeed, the first club founded in November 1896 bore the name *Norweger.*[78]

SKIING IN EASTERN EUROPE

The last decade before the turn of the century saw a remarkable and similar development all over Eastern Europe's hilly terrain as well. With the exception of Poland, the development was not supported by the middling classes as it was in Western Europe. This should cause no surprise. The new skisport in the west was associated with men of money, men from countries whose capitalistic economies were producing strong middle classes. In Eastern Europe, wealth remained with the landed gentry, with isolated pockets of middle-class development. Skiing there was largely the domain of the aristocracy and its peasants, along with the military; a few professionals, usually from the major cities, also became interested. Riga, the capital of Latvia, had a shop specializing in ski equipment in 1907. Sofia, Bulgaria's capital, could "practically be called a ski center" in 1918.[79]

Estonian skiing derived from Finland; the country was linked geographically and linguistically. In 1894 the Russian Krasnoyarsk Regiment relocated from Finland to Estonia, where it inspired locals to start skiing. In 1912 the student ski club "Sport" did put on a race around Tartu but it seems to have been one of a kind. Hunters and foresters on skis are reported, but not much else.[80] In Latvia's capital, Scandinavians brought skiing to the townsfolk, who enjoyed themselves skiing in the suburbs and on the river Daugava when it was iced over in 1892 and 1893. Postcards show the continued social attraction of skiing into the Communist period.[81]

Before Lenin's takeover—he enjoyed skiing, found it "indispensable,"

Parade ground unity displayed by the Tsar's ski troops before moving off to fight on the Manchurian front in the Russo-Japanese War, 1905. Their most useful work was as medics. (Author's collection)

partly "because it smells of Russia" in the mountains[82]—skiing had been one of the modes of transport among the many tribes in Siberia and armies from the Middle Ages on. At the turn of the century, Norwegian skis were appearing, but books by Henry Hoek and Anton Fendrich were read mostly by the foreign community. The Russian *Club Polarstern* never amounted to much. In Moscow, an Amateur Ski Club was founded in 1901 with Nansen as patron, but it, too, never came to anything, partly because of the revolutionary unrest in 1905, although Nansen fashion became the most favored ski outfit for the wealthy. Five years later, however, in the 1910–11 season, the first Russian championship was decided over a 30-kilometer course.[83]

To introduce skiing to Hungary, a relay race over 103 kilometers was staged between cyclists and skiers in 1896, creating an immediate interest in the skiers' victory. These racers had time and money for this lark. Foresters and the like had been on skis before this, but only when skiing became a sport did a greater number of people become intrigued. Just as skiing had been promoted in Germany by regional associations, so the Magyar Tourist Association took the lead from 1889. A league of clubs was formed, and nine years later Hungary had its first handbook of skiing.[84] When Zdarsky came to Kronstadt, locals claimed him as their own: "a Hungarian, a Brassoer," trumpeted a Budapest paper.[85] Bilgeri came later. He taught enough adults and children in 1913 to raise a competent, volunteer ski corps in the winter before the war.[86]

Polish hunters and forestry workers were on skis in the late 1880s and 1890s. In 1898, Józefa Schnaidera published *Na nartach Skandynawskich* (On Scandinavian Skis) with forty-one illustrations. This was followed by articles in 1903 and 1905 by Stanisław Barabasz in *Przeglad Zakopiański* (Zakopane Review) and by his book of 1914, *Wspomnienia Narciarza* (Memories of a Skier). Barabasz's skis can be viewed in the Tatra museum in Zakopane. Another venue that received a visit from Zdarsky in 1906 was Lemberg (present-day L'viv in Ukraine), resulting in the *Lwowskie Towarzystwo Karpackie* (Lwow Carpathian Club; L'viv, L'vov, Lvov, Lwów, and Lemberg are names reflecting the history of the same town) in January 1907, while a month later *Zakopiański Odział Narciarzy Towarzystwa Tatrazńskiego* (Zakopane Skiers Section of the Tatra Mountain Club) was founded. This last organization turned itself into an all-Polish association immediately after the war and became the ski section of the Polish Tatra Association in 1923.[87]

Ski contests began in 1907. The 1911 meet at Zakopane achieved international status, crowds, and recognition abroad.[88] These factors would be remembered when Zakopane bid for international races in the 1930s. And, as in other European nations, the military angle was not lacking in Poland. A defense organization of a league of rifle clubs, which included ski training in winter, the *Zwiatzek Strzelecki* (Rifle Association), was founded in 1908. The age divisions—"Eagles," 14–16 year olds; "Audacious," 17–18; and "Marksmen," 19–21—show, again, how the authorities were bringing in youth already trained on skis for possible military duty. In the late 1930s, the organization would boast over 300,000 members.[89]

In Eastern Europe, skiing as a utilitarian pursuit, as one might expect, continued longer than in the more industrialized nations. However, the middle classes in towns and cities began to take a sporting interest in skiing. Zakopane became the center for Polish skiing as early as 1911 and has continued in that prime place right up to this day. The rest of Europe knew that Russians were on skis in the Russo-Japanese War; there had been drawings in such glossy magazines as the *Illustrated London News* and in the 1895 *Universal-Kalender*, besides depiction on postcards. Aristocracy in the west had received skis from Russian cousins.[90] As the Germans threatened, the Russian-French entente had ample opportunity to exchange military ideas; Grand Duke Michael reviewed French troops, and General Joffre watched the Tsar's troops maneuver on the plains of Krasnovar. Both sides were aware of Napoleon's winter problems, and it seems not unlikely that tactics in the snow were discussed; but whether they knew that Russians on skis had harassed Napoleon's retreating men in 1912 is doubtful. The Russians had their Finnish province to rely upon for ski knowledge, the French *Régiment de la Neige* had been under the tutelage of Norwegian advisors. All prepared for war but no one knew what would happen when the tocsin for war sounded.

The Balkan wars made a jittery Europe more nervous, and both the Norwegians and the English had been on skis in that region. Henrik Angell suggested that Montenegrin royalty ski their way free from Turkey, in the same way that his own country had liberated itself from Sweden. He was largely unsuccessful.[91] The English, with no such thoughts, were intent upon gentlemanly-adventuring in this "refreshing oasis of medievalism" as they bedded down with loaded guns by their sides among peasants and their cattle. The Montenegrin minister of war heard of the party's up-country doings and interested himself in the use of skis. Archer Thomson left a Norwegian pair to serve as a model should he decide to equip his troops in the mountain border area.[92]

Political instability in the region, a culture of lawlessness, the machinations of secret societies, and the deviousness of local leaders brought about a situation that the powerful monarchs, brought up as medieval fief holders, yet in charge of modern technological wizardry, could not control. When the heir to the Austrian throne was murdered in Sarajevo by a Bosnian patriot belonging to the Serbian Black Hand, the alliance systems of the great powers ground into action. This Balkan war of 1914, local in June, would be European-wide in August and worldwide in 1917: it became the Great War. Almost exactly one hundred years earlier, Napoleon had fomented the last great war. Without skis, he crossed snow-covered countries and high mountain passes. Now that the major powers had trained troops equipped with skis, would they prove their worth when called to the colors?

CHAPTER 9

The Ladies Ski

*Four things women should learn: to hold the pole correctly, to stay in
the track, keep their distance, and hold their tongues.
—Mathias Zdarsky*

*The rinks attract many women who have not the strength or energy
for the rougher game.—Katherine Furse, 1924*

*It has been urged by some, it really has, that they do not want
a woman to ski well—she is only expected to "look nice" on the
snow.—Olive Hocking, 1914*

Women had used skis since the earliest times. One of Olaus
Magnus's woodcuts shows a woman speeding on skis, hair
streaming out behind her, bow at the ready; another with her
baby on her back sliding along on the way to church. Skis were
utilitarian instruments for everyone. We know little enough
about men's skiing and even less about women's. The Marquis
de Regnard visiting the north in 1681 remarked that women
were equally adroit on their skis when hunting as men were.
Johann Gleditsch, about twenty years later, was also impressed with women's
expertise on skis. These two were westerners, eyes wide for out-of-the-ordinary
experiences. For one who lived in Norway such as the Reverend Wille, however little he may have thought of his female parishioners in 1786, at least
he acknowledged that they could ski.[1] In these centuries when women's roles
were determined by tradition and religion, it is surprising to find such nonchalance in the descriptions of their skiing.

Before World War I the sport of skiing was a male preserve. Of course
some women had taken to it, even been encouraged to enjoy it. The more
independent-minded had formed all-women clubs in Norway, Germany,
Austria, and the United States. But the bundle of Victorian values, dictates
of fashion, medical proscription, and social convention was strong enough to
keep most women away from skiing. Women's functioning role in society as
decorous helpmate, bearer of children, even "exquisite slave,"[2] was not merely
determined by biology and by men but was embraced by the huge majority of
middle-class and upper-class women before World War I.

When bourgeois males in Norway took to skiing in the latter half of the nineteenth century, skiing also appealed to an increasing number of women. Eva Nansen, Fridtjof Nansen's wife, was one of their champions:

> In looking back upon the time when I began to run on skis in my teens, my numerous trips in the Norwegian winter constitute one of the brightest and purest recollections of my life—in them the purest beauty of life and nature is gathered into an indelible, charming picture which has had and always will have an ennobling influence on my mind, and gratefully do I remember them on account of all the health they have conferred on both body and mind. I rejoice when I meet our young girls returning to the city with skis on their shoulders, their ruddy faces beaming with joy and health.
>
> Can anyone seriously assert that the ladies are apt to be demoralized by skirunning, even though they be in the company of gentlemen? [3]

Eva Nansen had embraced some of the *Ski-Idræt* from her husband as she described the purest beauty of life and nature, the ennobling influence, the health of body and mind that skiing confers. She noted how Christiania's bourgeois had taken to ski recreation and how quickly this had occurred.[4] And she questioned the accepted gender relationship, although hardly with feminist vehemence. Still, the fact of women out on skis was enough for the Norwegian newspapers to comment frequently on four women on Kongbakken, skiing by torchlight, or simply that several women were skiing here and there.[5] Outdoor sports were becoming increasingly available to women and skiing's popularity coincided with bicycling, "the most liberating sport" for women, according to Helen Roberts.[6] Arnold Lunn judged that before the bourgeois took to skiing, Christiania women were typical mid-Victorian types with interests only in hearth and family. Today, he wrote after a visit in 1909, the physique of the Christiania women is improved beyond recognition. This resulted in an enlarged mental outlook and active involvement in politics and education. "Skis have played a far larger part than Ibsen in social revolution," he summed up,[7] even though they were still "not welcome in the huts on Sundays or holidays."[8]

We can attribute some of that enthusiasm to Lunn's youth, to propaganda for his own case of inspiring English women to ski, but not all of it by any means. After all, the first all-women's club, Skade, was founded in 1889.[9] Aptly named after the ski goddess, it was unfortunate that the word also means "injury" in Norwegian. Looking at photographs of women, posing formally and caught informally, looking at postcards of women frolicking in the snow, on trips in the woods, and just out and about on skis, one is struck by the fine winter outfits—tight bodice, ankle-length skirt, and wide brimmed hat—obviously not cheap, but equally obviously hardly liberating in any meaningful sense. The first specially designed winter skiing costume was drawn by Andreas Bloch in 1889.[10] For the popular market, girls in traditional dress appeared on postcards, and drawings by Hans Dahl, Fritz Thaulow, Adolph Tidemann, and others, show the simpler dress that the peasant girl wore when out on skis. For church, of course, she might dress up in her silver embroidered costume.[11]

In the rest of Europe, once wealthy men had taken to skiing, their women too joined in to some extent. Hassa Horn, visiting Austria in 1905, noted that skiing was "a rich man's passion."[12] The wealthy women of Vienna were more interested in watching than taking part.[13] Certainly a few of the titled enjoyed themselves on skis. Max Schneider sold skis to one princess, two duchesses (*Herzoginnen*), four princesses (*Fürstinnen*), and eleven countesses (*Gräfinnen*).[14] The British aristocracy delighted in going on holiday to snowy Switzerland. In 1914, of 1,341 women in the Public Schools Alpine Winter Sports Club, 89 held titles.[15] Princess Laetitia de Savoie-Napoléon, Duchess d'Aosta, was patron for the Turin Ski Club's international meet at Bardonec-chia in January 1909; the H.R.H. Infanta Beatriz de Orleans-Borbon claimed to have started skiing around Coburg in 1892 or 1893. The Duquesa de San-tona took to skis with obvious relish at St. Moritz in 1912,[16] one of fifteen titled women, including the crown princess of Germany, who were enjoying the season there.[17]

There was no need for these women to go on expeditions to mountain and col, for there were plenty of areas near the major ski villages where "practise can be had with a *minimum* of fatigue," the *Times* advised in 1910, listing Switzerland's Montana, Villars, Adelboden, Beatenberg, and Wengen[18]—an interesting list that did not mention St. Moritz or Davos.

"A minimum of fatigue": behind that remark lay a number of medical or pseudo-medical proscriptions. That generation of the upper classes that took to skiing in the pre–World War I years was brought up by nurse, governess, and parent imbued with Victorian notions of health. The woman's mission was to produce children, more important in France than anywhere else since the defeat in the 1870–71 war by Germany. Anything that produced healthy women was salutary. There was much discussion about how this was to be achieved. In the Victorian era, a fine pale face was much admired. Any tan not only indicated beauty marred—and a chance to find a husband lost—but was looked upon as an indicator of lower class. Lower classes were rough, coarse,

Around 1900, Norwegian artists, reflecting the growing importance of skiing in the national psyche, painted three classes of skiers. Andreas Bloch's historical soldiers on skis were increasingly popular, while Axel Enders and others painted the well-dressed bourgeois about their skiing enjoyments (left) *and the peasant girl* (right), *wearing her Sunday best.* (Author's collection)

dirty, unmanageable, and probably socialist to boot. But how to keep a face pale in the winter sunshine reflected by snow? The change that sports brought, and particularly the winter sport of skiing, came about only very slowly. Women had to find a way, be allowed to find a way, to enjoy themselves on skis and still remain refined, to use one of the favored words of the day.

And little by little, women took to hiking in the mountains, manning oars, swimming, bicycle riding (perhaps the most questioned sport of all), and riding horses—though mostly sidesaddle. All these summer activities could be done close to home, within sight of all. When the German and English visitors went away to the Alps for winter sporting, they were far away from prying eyes. It was easier there to change social attitudes. The difficulty lay in obtaining recognition and acceptance from peers. "It has been urged by some," wrote Olive Hocking in 1914, "it really has, that they do not want a woman to ski well—she is only expected to 'look nice' on the snow." A cry of disbelief that only shows that the Victorian value system was still around, sometimes more, sometimes less.

Sport for women and girls was to be done in a refined manner. It was all very well for men to struggle, strive, power their way through the snow, for that showed strength. Women, however, should ski aesthetically and most of all with no effort. "Skiing is a really good feminine sport," wrote Lieutenant Gélinet after watching the Club Alpin Français' Third International meet in 1909, "for it does not give the impression of effort, admirable in a man, disgraceful for a woman, but an impression of lightness, grace, speed, and also health"[19]—an impression created by a trim waist above a long skirt billowing out behind her. The health of such a figure wearing the notorious S-shaped corset was questionable and produced a vast literature covering economics, social and moral factors besides the primary concern of health.

ON CORSETS AND TROUSERS

Corset manufacturers of the late nineteenth century quickly perceived that women were getting out and about and provided their clients with different models to suit every occasion: nuptial, ballroom, wet nurse, travel, riding (with an elastic hip), corsets for singing, dancing, swimming, and bicycle riding.[20] A ski corset was on the market in 1911: "Through the Ski-Stay this corset attains a circular lacing, results in a slim figure, is hygienically commendable and unexcelled in elegance."[21]

With a long history, with much change in design, the corset was ripe for reform as the Victorian era ended. Corset reform was part of the general reform for rational dress of the late nineteenth and early twentieth centuries, which was tied to other reforms, especially those concerning women's rights.[22] By 1910, some advanced Edwardian young ladies were replacing the corset with girdle and brassiere,[23] just at the time when they were off to the Alps for a bracing winter sojourn in the snow.

If women could remove their corsets while on holiday on the ski slope— albeit donning them again for the balls and soirées—then skiing resulted not only in a rosy complexion and improved health but, better yet, in a new freedom of movement. However, the corset had been a symbol of moral probity. We still use the expression "strait-laced" to indicate uprightness, puritan attitude, and narrow-mindedness. Valerie Steele suggests that the tango finished off the corset in 1913 and 1914,[24] but I doubt that Badrutt's Palace shook to the tango before World War I. The Bunny Hug and Wiffle Waffle received short shrift in Lenzerheide and Mürren. What did doom the corset in those Alpine

In 1908, "ski-ing will sweep everything before it," and ladies better be costumed to enjoy the cold weather sport. This outfit of silver gray rabbit had a skirt coming well up under the double-breasted bolero, finished with tiny dangling balls of fur. It was lined with white swansdown, which appeared at the edge of the high standup collar, the flared sleeves, and the reverse on the chest. A tiny bow of brilliant cherry velvet gave a delightful color accent at the throat. Off to the slopes! (Country Life, December 26, 1908. Author's collection)

winters was ease of movement without it. "Off with the corset," wrote the Norwegian expert, Laurentius Urdahl in the 1890s. Since everything Norwegians said about skiing was holy writ, this was translated into German and found favor among early Austrian skiers.[25] Karl Pfeiffer, in *Der Ski-Sport*, published by a medical publishing firm in 1911, took it as a matter of fact that "the corset stays, of course, at home."[26]

If the corset was gone, what was to replace it? Undergarments were discussed, usually with reference to how they would show if a fall were taken. Pfeiffer advised dark colors under a foot-free dress, "even so sometimes in a fall [the undergarment] is seen, which causes much laughter."[27] H.R.H. the Infanta of Spain remembered after some seventy years that "some of us had red flannel petticoats which undoubtedly contributed greatly to the spectacular effect of our falls."[28]

Ankle-length dresses, corsets, and petticoats entered the debate over fashion, costume, beauty, and sport. The well-dressed woman was not merely supposed to exhibit the economic status of her husband or father—Veblen's conspicuous consumption—she was expected to take the opportunity to express her own particular look, her style. For sporting activities in which women had been a part for many years, specially designed clothing was available: the riding habit, for example. On the ski slope she wore a dress with a tight-fitting jacket quite similar to a man's. There appeared to be comparatively small room for individual taste. Men and women could agree that the dress length had to be shortened to above the boot. Sensible Beatrix Nickolls, enjoying a holiday with Swedish landowners, sent this note "to womankind who intend to enjoy skidsport in a mountainous country—do not bother about appearances but dress yourself exactly as a Lapman, with skirt *above* your knees."[29] All right perhaps in the north of Sweden, but that would never do in front of the Palace at St. Moritz. But the manufacturers soon discovered that this wealthy clientele would buy all sorts of ski outfits. The ski clothing industry began in the years before World War I.

Women, of course, saw the ease with which men skied in trousers. At the heart of the disagreements over women wearing trousers were three ideas. First, it was simply wrong that the two spheres of male and female should be so similarly dressed. Women's place, for this group, was "the sweet ordering of life," to use Ruskin's phrase, whereas man had to exhibit vigor and responsibility not only at home but also over the entire world. The imperial adventure reached its height around the turn of the century. If much of man's activity was accomplished on horseback, who, then, should wear the breeches? The second contentious objection to women in trousers was a sense of aesthetics.

Women were supposed to look beautiful, and part of the graceful picture was created by the sweep of the dress as the woman skied down the hill—a vision of elegant beauty. A woman in trousers lost the flow to her skiing, she was inelegant, especially when the legs came apart as the skis wandered off track. Last, underlying everything else and only occasionally brought out in the open, was the fear that not only would trousers de-sex women, but that wearing them at all indicated a preference for lesbian liaisons or, at best, bisexual affinities. Thus, when a woman in pants was perceived as an "unaesthetic horror"[30] she not only lacked feminine beauty but was morally suspect:

> Schlimm fällt man auf den bösen Harsch,
> drum sei zur Frau in Hösen barsch.[31]

This untranslatable doggerel's irony lies in the rhyming scheme, but the thrust is obvious: get women in pants off the ski slopes. Outbursts came from religious authorities in the years before the war, "especially . . . women dressing in men's clothes." In Winterberg, a Sauerland ski station, the fashion of wearing trousers was considered "a sort of prostitution," and there was a call to clean the town out. There were laws in Bavaria against trouser-clad women and in France even a prohibition against taking photographs of women in trousers.[32]

But little by little, from 1906 on, more and more women skied in trousers. In 1908, Englishmen raised their eyebrows as they entered the hotel Lebzelter in Zell-am-See to find the place "generally alive with ski runners and skirt-lacking ladies."[33] Influential *Skimeister* Mathias Zdarsky added his imprimatur to women dressing like men for skiing, and others advised women to get rid of their skirts, although one Ski Club of Dresden correspondent in 1909 admitted that she had never seen trousers on women skiers.[34] Some women found a way around all this and skied in trousers and kept a skirt in their knapsack to put on over their trousers when they went into the shops and cafés.[35]

Ski-running became so fashionable that the large shops in London's West End began catering to their clients: the new sporting woman. They supplied "entire costumes of knitted wool," not having the faintest notion of what would happen should its inhabitant fall. A joke making the rounds of one Swiss ski station went like this: "*Mais, ce n'est pas une femme. C'est une boule de neige.*"[36] ("But this isn't a woman, it's a snowball.") It is clear, too, that for some to appear to go skiing was the right thing to do, even if they never tested the snow. Josef Wallner, instructing at Kitzbühel before the war, expected two girls as clients as they were all dressed up with brand-new skis ready every day. But they never came. At the end of the week he couldn't resist asking them why they had never attended his classes. "Oh," one of them replied, "the skis are just part of our costume, we don't really want to go skiing," and off they walked, skis over shoulder.[37]

Women also had to be sartorially prepared for the post-skiing activities, which might include teas, fêtes, parties, dances, and fancy-dress balls. The lady going on holiday, warned the *Times* in 1909, had to take everything she might need "and a little that is unnecessary." By 1913 she might sport a Tyrol costume, bought from Gamages, advertising as the Pioneer of Winter Sports Outfitting.[38] The number of steamer trunks leaving Victoria station on the train to Dover for the ferry crossing to Calais and then on to the Alpine redoubts mounted annually. When many of the Public Schools Alpine Sports Club members took a three or four week winter holiday, the baggage load could resemble that of an imperial expedition.

There was yet another factor in the realm of fashion: color of costume. Color—as the design of clothes themselves—protected against moral dangers. Think of the nurse and nun. In the turn-of-the-century world of wealth there was little question about the color of clothes for men. Dark colors, black or somber gray, gave the tone for seriousness of purpose.[39] Norwegians wore dark blue, but everyone else was warned not to ape the Norwegians unless they could ski as well, and in the years up to 1914, few could make such claim and certainly no woman could. Black, backed by the tradition of Victorian respect-ability, was an unfrivolous color. Besides, it made for the starkest contrast to the virgin whiteness of the snow. Black and gray remained the colors of choice for the serious-minded skier up until the Second World War.

Women tended to follow the male lead, and only little by little did sprigs of color flash here and there before 1914. Accoutered in black with a snappy jacket and trousers, her face topped by a toque, the woman was uniformed to ski. In an era when uniforms gave substance to position, it meant that the woman had not just costumed herself in the role of skier, but she gave notice that she intended to play that part. Whether the right clothes made her ski any better is doubtful.

ENTERTAINMENT OR COMPETITION?

Many of the British women were members of the Public Schools Alpine Sports Club, which, as shown earlier, was not a club in the usual sense of the term at all, even though it permitted members to club together once they were abroad. The real ski clubs admitted women as regular members, but few joined. In the club huts of Nordmarka, above Christiania, women were not welcome on Sundays or holidays. Stockholm's Ski Club had two female members in 1879, the *Schneesportverein* Buntenbock in Lower Saxony had eighteen members of which two were women in 1907. Fifteen women and 316 men made up the Ski Club Vosges in 1910. In Bohemia, the Karpackie Towarzystwo Narciarzy had 181 members in 1911, 28 were women. The Ski Club Schwarzwald, one of the most active early ski clubs, with 564 members in 1897, included 56 women. It drew its membership from the university town of Freiburg, and the Freiburg section of the Ski Club Feldberg (the area where most of the skiing in the Black Forest took place) made efforts to get women to join: "Entrance for women is not only allowed but extremely desirable," read the 1895 protocol. Women even had a hand in founding the Ski Club Arlberg and the Oberharzer Ski Club. Later, particular clubs for women only were founded: Skade (1889) and Goi (1902) in Norway, the Schneerose for Viennese working women (1913), the Damen-Skiclub München (1913), and far away in America's Midwest in 1903, the Nora caused a flurry of excitement which lasted briefly that season.[40] The Munich club called for women who were really interested in skiing—no match-making frivolities for these girls.[41]

Clubs were formed as social units and very quickly took to competition. That was the expected sphere for men, nothing like a race to prove fitness, strength and expertise. But that was not what women were supposed to do at all and, indeed, the Ski Club München refused women entrance: "In the interest of competitiveness, no woman will be admitted."[42]

We must get out of our heads any picture we might have of today's racing, be it downhill, slalom or cross-country. Early races for women were very tame affairs. Mizzi Angerer beat two other competitors in a woman's "downhill" of 600 meters at Mürzzuschlag in 1893. She repeated her victory the next year against four others on a course that had been reduced to 400 meters. At Vienna's Pötzleinsdorf, the course was 300 meters long (the men's race was 1,350 meters). In 1897 only two women entered a race over a 350-meter track, the winner claiming victory in 36 seconds. In 1910, at Montlouis, France, the women's course was only 40 meters. These, then, were hardly strenuous races, but that is exactly the point: women were not supposed to put forth effort.

Yet in other places there was some real competition. At St. Andreasberg in the Harz, the women's race in 1899 was contested over 2,500 meters, which was won in 10 minutes and 13 seconds. Forty-five seconds later came number two, and 1 minute, 45 seconds after her came the last of the three competitors. The women, the report noted, "made in their flowing costume a marvelous impression." And that was what really counted. By 1901 the St. Andreasberg ski fathers had lengthened the course to 3,500 meters, which a Fräulein Kalisch-Turfhaus won in 14 minutes and 12 seconds. The men were racing over a 10-kilometer course that day. At CAF's ski week in 1909, eight women

Mizzi Angerer won the women's events at Mürzzuschlag in 1893 and again in 1894. She is far more a heroine today than she was at a time when women's races were more for male pleasure-gazing than for serious female competition. (The Graphic, January 27, 1893. Author's collection)

"How wonderful and healthy skiing is! I just hope it isn't a passing fad." There were very few women in 1910 who could ski such a telemark turn. (Simplicissimus, *January 10, 1910.* Author's collection)

raced over a 1-kilometer course whereas the men were running 30 kilometers. Mlle. Rose Bally-Salins won in 11 minutes 49 seconds.[43]

Evidently in Mürzzuschlag and the Harz, women on course had become part of the quiet competitive scene. When three women entered the Ski Club Arlberg's race at St. Anton, the editor added in brackets "(*nota bene drei Frauen!*)"[44] All these races were really experimental. There were no rules other than those made up by the organizers who, themselves, often had so little knowledge of skiing that they tended to follow skating or track models. At Innsbruck in 1910 ski poles were permitted for the first time in local races. At Grindelwald's Third Annual Sports Week, the women's ski event "in which elegance of style was as essential as speed," indicated what the organizers deemed most necessary in a refined person. In 1911 five Polish women had 200 vertical meters to descend in their 1,600-meter race in comparison with the men's 800 meters over a 5,200-meter course. At one Chamonix international meet, eight women competed over a 3-kilometer course. Sometimes men and women also raced together. For the Rhône Valley Ski-ing Challenge Cup at Montana-Vermala, Switzerland, open only to the Public Schools Alpine Sports Club membership, Miss Fabling beat Sir Duncan Hay by about 2½ minutes, who was trailed by a Mr. Williams. "A display of magnificent skiing," the *Times* enthused. There were style races for the British ladies, *Kunstläufe* for the Germans, novice races, races with curves in them, and even ski jumping. No one could best the Countess Lemberg, "the floating *Gräfin*," who was reported to have jumped up to 28 meters, really spectacular in comparison to the "plucky efforts of the Misses Marshall, Major, Wasson and Lewis who did between 3 and 4 meters each."[45] But jumping was not recommended for women and it was never really followed up, in spite of the efforts of various Norwegian women that Karin Berg chronicles in her recent book *Hopp, Jenter, Hopp*. In the United States, women's jumping was merely an entre-acte to the "real riding" at the midwestern ski meets of the early days.[46]

But the "New Woman" had made an appearance and begun to shape a different role for herself, in the midst of the male ordering of society. World War I would precipitate many changes such as in women's dress, ski competition, independence to travel, and the freedom to sport on skis. Quite new ways of enjoying a holiday on skis would emerge in the post-war period.

CHAPTER 10 **The Great War**

The ski, a new instrument for war, and just the thing that will
make guerrilla warfare possible on the entire front.
—General Courbebaisse, 1914

The war, the open air, all the activity will certainly exercise a happy
influence on general health.—Club Alpin Français, 1916

The ski battalions must be used like drops of gold.
—Order from Italian High Command, 1917

PREPARING FOR WAR

Armies gave a panache to imperial parades where glittering uniforms were equated with military efficiency. In winter the ski troops of France, Italy, Germany, and Austria provided a thrilling spectacle as they joined in social skisport before the First World War. Yet military skiing should have owed little to the sporting activities. Ski troop leaders ordered forced marches through hilly terrain, which received wide publicity and provided proof of reliance and stamina. But there was a minimum of actual field training.

When the war came in 1914, the mix of sporting skiing imbued with upper-class and nationalistic attitudes combined with the basic training of long marches proved ineffective. The British, for example, imagined themselves in the Hindu Kush "sweeping down on Afridi villages in the winter when the lively occupants are buried in snow up to their necks."[1] Such highly romanticized views of winter warfare played some role in both the Great War and its sequel in 1939–45. At home, in the winter of 1906–07, the Cameron and Seaforth Territorials trained in Scotland, something noted by the Germans and Austrians. The Swiss military were on skis on the Grand St. Bernard Pass as early as 1894 and ran a military ski school out of Andermatt. Georg Bilgeri taught sections of the Turkish army, and in far-flung Japan, Austrian Lieutenant Theodor von Lerch had such a success with his Zdarsky instruction that his memory is kept alive to this day by two statues and a Lerch society.[2]

However, war menaced in Central Europe. The high commands looked to Norway for guidance, yet the Norwegian experience was not necessarily the best model because one vital need for European ski troops did not obtain in

Norway: Europeans first had to be trained to ski. In Norway, universal military service could produce 200,000 men on skis if the reserves were called up. Here there was a connection between civilian skiing and military service, and one knowledgeable observer found it "difficult to separate the task of the Army from that of the [civilian] union."[3] The relationship between officers and men was different too; they worked together. "Officers do not spare themselves," wrote one reporter, but worked, if possible, "even harder than the men." In the rest of Europe, the caste-bound *Junker* of Prussia, the French conservative rightist (monarchist or not), and the upper class of England would find the democracy of such ski trooping difficult and uncongenial.

Norwegian military ski maneuvers were reported in the foreign press with unstilted admiration. The *New York Times* in 1879 commented that skiers were as mobile as cavalry. The *Birmingham Register* titled an appreciative article "The Fastest Army on Earth." The *British Ski Year Book* ran an article on the Norwegian military in its first issue, and the French *Petit Parisien* analyzed Norwegian troop movements in the snow. At home, the Norwegian and Swedish journals were full of reports of winter exercises. Drawings and photographs titillated the enthusiastic. The rest of European militaries concentrated on copying these extraordinary marches: distance covered indicated not only expert technique but also stamina and courage. There was comparatively little field training, so that at the outbreak of war, ski troops were initially thought to be useful only for patrol and courier work.

It comes as a surprise that the Swedes seemed unconcerned about the military application of skiing, given the recent uneasy relationship with Norway to the west and with the Russian province of Finland to the east. It was only in 1892 that the Society for the Development of Skiing (*Skidfrämjandet*) was founded, and in 1901 a permanent military conscription ordered. Even then, only three volunteer military schools practiced skiing with regularity. At the same time, military officers provided the leadership of civilian ski and athletic clubs. Further impetus for ski training came in 1915, and two years later a budget was provided for races among the military. Major help came from a parliamentary subvention to the *Skidfrämjandet* to improve the skiing of youth. Jan Lindroth concludes that it was military defense that gave parliament the push to promote skiing just as the Great War broke out in 1914.[4]

In the rest of Europe only the wealthy had taken to skiing for sport. The major problem facing all the military commands was basic ski training for the recruits who came from mountain peasantry or proletariat. Hence the effort mounted in the schools to get the children out on skis, so they would be ready recruits. The French military actually set up ski schools for civilians in various places.[5] The French *Chasseurs Alpins* were formed to confront the danger from Italy, whose mountainous borders were guarded by the *Alpini*. In November 1902 skis became obligatory for certain units of the *Alpini*.[6] Much of the pressure to form ski troops came from Italian army Lieutenant (later Colonel) Oreste Zavattari, who published a total of eleven books and articles between 1883 and 1909. Concerned with the defense of Italy, he published *Defesa dello stato* in 1884 with no reference to skiing, but soon he became the proselytizer for troops on skis. The ski, he felt was "the bicycle of the snow." The Ministry of Public Instruction, as in other countries, promoted physical education in the schools, since "physical and moral health of the people are the foundations of a good state." It was exactly what Zavattari wanted.[7] By 1905 he had his way, and detachments of fifty men under three lieutenants were deployed on the Austro-Hungarian border.[8] In February 1906, the high command imported Harald Smith from Norway and a Swiss guide, C. Klucher, to train the troops. The first Italian military manual, *Istruzione sull' uso dello ski,* was published in 1908.[9] Once on duty in high Alpine redoubts, the French peasant, now *Chasseur Alpin,* would meet his Italian counterpart, now an *Alpini,* in the Savoy border lands. French and Germans faced each other in the Vosges, Italians and Austrians (both speaking German) in Tyrol. One French weekly talked of how the *Alpini* and *Chasseurs* "fraternize voluntarily on these sovereign heights. They reciprocate their esteem for each other, for they court danger for the same cause." The Italians "guard their frontier, while we guard ours."[10] That was 1902. In 1905 *Le Petit Parisien* ran a front cover depicting soldiers of the "Quinze-neuf" rescuing three Italians lost deep in the snow.[11] An entente was forming.

At CAF's international meet at Mont Genèvre, the *Alpini* met their French counterparts to cement the burgeoning friendship. In the years before the outbreak of hostilities, the *Alpini* numbered about 13,000 men in 128 companies. From each company four men were chosen as skiers. They were complemented by two men on skis from each of the 32 regiments of mountain artillery. In all, then, about 500 men, were singing the skiers' hymn:[12]

Sui lucenti tersi campi
Del nevaio sconfinato
Sorridenti al nostro fato
Noi corriam senza timor.

Over shining cloudless fields so fair
Of everlasting snow,
We go smiling to fate and foe
And run without a fear.

26ᵐᵉ Série   ·1914... Chasseurs alpins Italiens | 1914... Italian alpine light infantry   (E|D)

Although the Italians did not join the war until 1915, they were preparing the Dolomite front in 1914. All men carried snowshoes because some of the defense posts were in rocky terrain and snow where skis were impossible to use. (Author's collection)

The German War Ministry, regarding the *Alpini* ski troops as a model, ordered the training of the same number of men per company for their own field and mountain artillery regiments.[13] In Austria, by the First World War, three-quarters of the ski troops were following the Bilgeri method of skiing rather than that of Zdarsky.[14] Only when Italy joined the war on the side of the allies was there a real need for more ski troops and so more instructors. The Austrian *Alpen-Skiverein* alone supplied sixteen civilian instructors to the army from November 1915 to April 1916.[15] One of them who trained ski troops on the Dolomite front, would in the postwar years become the most respected ski instructor in the whole world, Hannes Schneider.

Switzerland used ski troops to guard its neutrality. Aware of the development of military skiing beyond its borders, an officer on the St. Gotthard pass ordered six pairs of skis in 1893 and 200 pairs the following year. Andermatt and Airolo became centers for the training of volunteers. In 1903, Norwegians Thorleif Bjørnstad, Leif Berg, and the Smith brothers, Harald and Trygve, taught soldiers as well as civilians. The first "Winter Tactics Course with Skis for Gotthard Officers" proved a failure in February 1904; the "older and portly" officers had a difficult time. The younger ones did well though. Five years later, the army authorities reported that there were enough enlisted men who could ski but the officers from the towns still needed instruction.[16]

Swiss skiing was so bound up with wealth and tourism that it "smelled of money," and the authorities did not want to appear to be funding a bourgeois sport. Yet the government was persuaded to fund courses in 1907–08, laying out 20,000 francs for 316 officers and non-coms, and again in 1908–09. Beginners courses followed, and seventeen officers made a Bernese Oberland traverse in 1909. An advanced course for twenty officers was held at Zweisimmen in 1910.[17] Beginning in 1912, a military delegation formed part of the central committee of the Swiss Ski Association.[18] Since there was compulsory enlistment, the military and civilian objectives mixed nicely in the promotion of Swiss skiing for Swiss youth. Should war break out, Switzerland stood prepared to guard the Alpine high passes.

Military races and racers became a source of interest and pride, and the Swiss began to be noted abroad. The Germans, for example in 1914, believed it would be useless to send a team to compete in Pontresina because they had no training in comparison to the Swiss.[19] When Kaiser Wilhelm II visited Switzerland in the autumn of 1912, he inquired of his hosts, "Can your people ski?" and received the reply, "On command, your Majesty, every one!"

While the Swiss budgeted for the military training of their skiing leaders, the Tsar's officers held races carrying their sabers, symbolic, perhaps, of the nature of Russian military skiing. Perhaps. After all, Russian regiments and medics on skis had seen action in Manchuria in the Russo-Japanese war. Yet Russian military skiing—as the entire military itself—was stultified by class organization, just as the whole of Russia floundered under the Tsar's antiquated systems and beliefs.

THE REALITY OF COMBAT

Preparations for war took on a special urgency in 1913 and 1914. During one of the most cloudless summers, civilian Europe seemed determined to forget the world of the assassinated Archduke while the cousins Kaiser and Tsar sent telegrams that finally brought forth the war cries of *"nach Paris"* and *"à Berlin,"* unleashing the "Guns of August."

If there was in France, as Jean-Jacques Becker has clearly shown, not a nationalist fever but more a resolve to defend *la Patrie*,[20] the ski troops stationed on the heights of the Vosges knew they were in the first line of defense, and the best method of defense was to attack. Opposing them were Paulcke's Württembergers. The French officers Gélinet and Lardant, who survived the war, drew the conclusion that military skiers had not produced the expected results.[21] What had actually been expected, however, was not clear. Winter mountain war came to mean attacking until the snow made advance impossible, and then holding the high country. But on the Dolomite front at 10,000 feet amid icy blasts and difficulties of food distribution, defense and patrol work provided much of the winter activity instead of attacking. It was not supposed to be that way.

CAF had immediately put itself at the disposition of the War Ministry.[22] With the war only three months old, Grenoble was designated a special depot for ski soldiers under the command of Henry Duhamel, now a captain in the Chasseurs Alpins. Privately donated skis were sent to Grenoble before a ski factory was opened and CAF's Chalet de Recoin above Uriage was given over to military use. French champion, Alfred Couttet who had been wounded in Alsace, was brought in as instructor. Four centers of instruction were given official status: Briançon, Sarcenas, Huez, and Chartreuse.[23]

However, France's border with Italy was not the important frontier. The Western Front, and particularly the Vosges, was the main theater for early action on skis at the battle with the Germans near St. Dié on December 31, 1914. Norwegian support in the form of an ambulance unit on skis in 1915–16 (an aspect of Norwegian-French cooperation since 1905) was much appreciated.[24] At least one French general thought that the ski would be apt for guerrilla warfare, but that was never the case. Skiers—after all—considered themselves a breed apart; when a German patrol got themselves in difficulties because of wet snow and met some *Chasseurs Alpins*, the French leader advised the Germans on the use of skins and left them with a hand shake and *Ski Heil*. Skiers were a brotherhood and both sides thought that way. In these early days, fraternization in the trenches, particularly at Christmas, worried the opposing staffs on the Western Front. On the other side of the line, the Germans told the same story with a slightly different slant: they had seen the French ski troops but did not fire because "it would have been a shame to shoot a person who skis that well." [25] A month or so later, another meeting was less friendly. Although described as "a contest between skiers," only a few were involved, and the lines remained stable.[26] Prewar ideals and prewar strategy on the ski fronts were no different than on other fronts as the two sides fought to a standstill.

The Vosges remained the region where the French employed their ski troops. In the hilltop firs at Hermannsweiler Kopf, in Alsace, forty Chasseurs fixed bayonets and "dashed down the hill with the speed of an express train into a mass of Germans at the foot" . . . and were all gunned down.[27] *Die Blauen Teufel*, the Blue Devils, as the Germans had nicknamed them, were

Élan vitale *in action in the Vosges: "Again and again the dash and fury of the Blue Devils has won the day." Not this day, though, at Hermannsweiler Kopf in Alsace; all forty were killed.* (The Graphic, April 3, 1915. Author's collection)

not invulnerable. The caption of the graphic drawing describes their "dash and fury of onslaught," and their "dashing bayonet charges," a romanticized form of the French *élan vitale*. More troops were needed. A section of skiers within regiments already stationed there was proposed, but it appears to have been mostly for recreation with the idea that some could help out in winter warfare. When Lieutenant Belmont arrived in Gérardmer in January 1915, he rented a pair of skis to accompany his men on "a march through the forest, magnificent in its whiteness."[28] Nothing about military order, training, tactics— just a continuation of winter recreation which Gérardmer had done so much in the prewar years to promote.

The socialites' ski sport and the needs of war were on both sides intertwined in many ways. In 1915, a "contest between skiers" referred to a firefight, in 1916 a drawing of "the ski artist" improving his marksmanship enlivened a report.[29] A German unit became "the darling of the division" (*Liebling der Division*), another the "sports club." The call-up notice from the Black Forest (*Schwarzwald*), for example, challenged skiing volunteers "to show them [the French] what we've learned." When Eugen Kalkschmidt joined his unit, his "only worry was that the war would end before the ski troops could get into powder snow."[30] The ski troops sang:[31]

Wir sind die Schneeschuhkompagnie,
Der Anzug weiss und glatt die Ski
Wir laufen gen Feind mit Eil
Und unsere Losung heisst: Skiheil!

Of the great ski troops we're all a part,
With whiten shirt and speedy ski
We rush 'gainst foe with gladden heart
And sing "*Skiheil*" with friends we see!

It wasn't all as merry as that, especially on the Dolomite front. The Austro-Hungarians and Italians faced each other on a long, mountainous line. The Austrians, generally, held the high positions. The Italian military commander, General Cordona—portrayed as a skier jumping from summit to summit in 1915—had few options but to try to press the enemy into retreat. Prodigious feats of scaling the Adamello, Ortler, Brenta, and Marmolata, of holding various passes, Comosci, Alto, and Tonale where men destroyed each other with artillery, rifle, and machine gun brought only a stalemate. Avalanches, too, sometimes man-made, tipped the military balance from time to time. On Black Thursday, December 16, 1916, an avalanche on the Marmolata was believed to have killed six thousand Austrian troops.[32]

Some of this fighting has been documented on motion pictures. Photographs, too, portray the endless line of men trudging up into the foothills carrying huge packs; the ingenuity of the men jerry-rigging *telefericas* to haul supplies up and the wounded down. The images of the dark, dank, and bitterly cold caves dynamited into the mountains, which served as patrol headquarters, are particularly chilling. Drawings, paintings, and postcards, on the other hand, romanticized life with the ski troops—as in the case of a poster, "Guarding the Front in Ice and Snow" (*Auf Vorposten in Eis und Schnee*).[33]

Yet there remained some of the camaraderie of the high country among enemies, particularly between the Tyroleans of the Emperor's *Jäger* battalions and the *Alpini*. An Italian paper glorified their own Alpine troops "sweeping down on [the Austrians] and returning victorious, true to their old fame and glory," but added, "they and the Tyrolese, our enemies as they are, are the finest mountaineers in the world."[34] The Italians had captured Bilgeri's manual, translated it and gave due attribution, something that Bilgeri appreciated. In 1916 the high command produced its own *Instruzioni*.[35] Both sides were ski-

Herzliche Weihnachtsgrüße!

These Germans would be in exactly the same Christmas celebration mode in their civilian ski clothes before 1914. Here in wartime, they wave a cheery "Happy Christmas" coming in from patrol. All's well with the ski troops. (Author's collection)

ing in the modern way. According to one of Hannes Schneider's biographers, Austrians and Italians chatted, swapped food and wine, and made the war as gentle as possible. Those enemies, like the French and the Germans in the Vosges, also kept their mountaineers' honor at times. "The sniper is observing us from the crag," wrote Paolo Monelli, "his shot whistles high over our heads. A warning? Honor? Mistake?" Since it was early 1915, it was probably a warning. Then the Germans came to stiffen Austrian resolve.[36] At home in Vienna, the social round continued, provoking the young Kaiser Karl in 1917 to object to the opulent using the railway to Semmering for their continued pleasures.[37]

Although tens of thousands lost their lives in the snow in the Dolomites, although the Russians used ski troops in their advance into Poland, the Turks trained at Erzerum under Austrian instruction, the French ran a military ski school on the Col de Pisoderi to train for the winter warfare in the Balkans, and in far away America there was training in the Midwest and officer cadets were on skis in the East, the war was going to be won or lost not in the mountains but on Europe's Western Front in the mud and blood of Flanders.[38]

World War I ended in November 1918, before the snow-season fighting could begin again. Yet there was still one more action requiring skis: the fight in 1919 against the Bolsheviks in the Murmansk area of northern Russia hard by the Finnish border. Canadians, Italians, Serbians, Russian-Karelians, the French, and even the English provided ski troops. Some nations' men were obviously more trained for this sort of winter warfare than others. One of the most experienced was the Norwegian Henrik Angell, the man who had gone into Montenegro in 1893,[39] who had been on the Western Front as a Foreign Legion officer, and who now found himself in charge of French skiers on the Murmansk front, where he was very badly frostbitten. He died three years later.[40] Angell is among the pantheon of Norwegian skiers, but he seems more an adventurer than anything else. Would Fridtjof Nansen ever have accepted a position as a second lieutenant in the Foreign Legion? Maybe his Montenegrin adventure in 1893 made Angell enough of a hero to be cast in bronze on the pilgrim's trail leading up to Holmenkollen.

The hard and tragic fact was that the ski troops did not prove particularly successful in Carpathians, Dolomites or Vosges. Military skiing was too bound up with sport, and its leaders imbued with romantic prewar ideals that, just as on other fronts, produced a statistical drumbeat of death.

At home, the war wreaked economic havoc on burgeoning ski centers some virtually closing down in France and Switzerland. The total number of visitor days taxed in Chamonix in 1914 was 51,642, which brought in a sum of 10,328 francs. The figures were just about halved in 1915. The 1916 winter season was "virtually nil" according to the report signed by the mayor.[41] If that was an economic disaster, there were also the human casualties. Of 670 men who were mobilized, some 11 percent fell for France. Of 159 guides mobilized, 21 were killed.[42] But Chamonix as a ski center survived because both allied troops and a few neutrals came to winter sport in 1916 and the visitor count rose so that in 1917 and 1918 over 110,000 visitor days brought in between 22,000 and 23,000 francs each year.[43] Meanwhile CAF expelled its German members along with those who supported the German cause, like Swedish explorer Sven Hedin, and Chamonix tried to suppress the German language where skiing was concerned.[44]

The Swiss spent the war guarding the frontiers and playing a somewhat uneasy host to interned prisoners, mostly British and French. Arnold Lunn remained in Switzerland to watch over his father's hotels and took on the job of occupying interned officers and men by taking them skiing, on the whole rather unsuccessfully.[45]

The shooting over, the job of peace making began. France, of course, was diplomatically determined to ensure that Germany did not repeat the attacks of 1870 and 1914, and politically bound to secure the economic future of the country. CAF leadership was fully resolved to help in the planning of postwar skiing, "but the goal will not be exactly the same. . . . We'll have to develop our winter stations, and it will be necessary to make a choice" of venues.[46] This would be extremely difficult yet essential. The TCF lobbied for small hotels and pensions, finding in them the continuation of a mountain way of life with the promise of economic growth.[47] The National Tourist Office, the Ministry of War, railroad companies, and chambers of commerce (*Syndicat d'initiatives*) all interested themselves in the future of tourism in France and the "development of the race by the cult of sport." The same organizations, often run by the very same men, argued over the future of France in almost the same terms as they had in 1914. France had won the war, now France had to "win the peace."[48]

CHAPTER 11

Uneasy Peace—Les Années Folles

It is necessary to send out an alarm call and to point out the
difficulties facing tourism in France. Other countries are doing
well. . . . —"Vite à l'oeuvre," La Montagne, *December 1934*

Down, down, down—schnell, schneller, noch schneller—das ist der
Schrei der Zeit. [Down, down, down—fast, faster, faster yet—this is
the cry of the times.]—Henry Hoek, 1938

Skiing has gone from a glorious frolic, to a sport, to a profession, and
finally to an expression of national efficiency.—A British view, 1938

Recovering from the war meant economic rivalry among
nations in every sphere. For Henry Cuënot, chairman of the
Club Alpin Français' (CAF) Winter Sports Commission, it
meant competition to attract winter sportsmen and -women
to France. The Versailles Treaty was supposed to insure
Germany's lowly status; but even Germany might recover,
especially as the neutrals, Switzerland and the Scandinavian
states, rejected Germany's ostracization from sporting events,
and some monitored what was going on.[1] Even in France there were some
people who were in favor of letting the Germans compete in sports. The majority of public opinion and all the politicians were adamantly opposed. Sport
east of the Rhine was characterized as "murderously preparing the next war
of revenge of which they are already dreaming," as José Germain, chairman
of the French Association of Fighting Writers, told his colleagues.[2] France felt
that it was being left behind in the game of winning the peace. The Germans
"have understood winter sports better than we have. . . . Once again they have
given us the example of their tenacity."[3] "Don't let the foreigners get a real
hold on winter sports and reap the benefits," implored *La Vie au Grand Air*
in 1919. With Austria, no one quite knew what was going to happen since
the vast and ancient Austro-Hungarian Empire had split up. Austria became
a small Alpine country with an enormous ex-imperial capital, Vienna. Italy
seemed to lurch from one chaos to another. Switzerland worried the French
most of all. The country was physically untouched by the war and in pre-1914
days had acquired an envious reputation as the premier land offering winter
sports to an increasing number of visitors.

In the inflationary years after World War I, and particularly in 1923 when the old German mark became worthless, communities printed their own money advertising local delights. These four examples show the joys of the Sauerland, the Harz, and Thuringia. (Author's collection)

CONCERNS OF THE FRENCH

Within France, the desperate search to repopulate the nation began again. The same shrill concerns which had been bandied about prior to 1914 surfaced again: boys should not play with poodles, girls should not ride bicycles, and their parents should swear off absinth.[4] Immediately after the war, state-awarded medals for motherhood, first proposed in 1903, were inaugurated. Ribbons and citations had to do instead of payments. Parliament outlawed birth control in 1920.[5]

After the unprecedented loss of life between 1914 and 1918, the world was visited by an influenza plague that killed more people than had died in the war. Deaths from tuberculosis, too, were a major concern to the government and all those who dealt with tourism in the mountains. In 1926, 12 percent of all deaths in France were from TB, and of that number (about 67,000) nearly 50,000 were between 20 and 55 years old, the age of production and repro-duction.[6] A new ski station like Mégève scrambled to stay contagion-free and attract tourists. Improving water quality, washing walls and corridors, keeping chimneys in excellent condition, and any number of other requirements were forthcoming in the fight against the malady. Hotels were supposed to separate patients from tourists. All tourists were to have a physician-signed certificate that they were tuberculosis-free.[7]

Before the discovery of antibiotics, a variety of TB cures was advocated; sun and hydrotherapy were popular. Both had tendencies toward nudism, sometimes respectable, often voyeuristic and with nothing much to do with hygiene and therapy.[8] Yet the country's health, bound up with recovery from the Great War, with an urgent need for more children and an effort to save those that were afflicted with a disease like TB, made heliotherapy—the sun cure—popular at St. Moritz and Leysin in Switzerland, in northern Jugoslavia and at Briançon in France. "Go winter sporting in the French stations of the Alps and the Jura," PLM posters tempted, and you would remain healthy for the rest of the year. In spite of all the public awareness, as late as 1937, a group from Nancy saw in Mégève "a big room where beasts and people live together, side by side, separated by a balustrade and gutter, the tails of the cows attached to the ceiling."[9] Nevertheless, in the twenty-five years between 1914 and 1939, Mégève grew from three hotels to 66, from 140 beds to 2,400. For the 1938–1939 season, the *Centre Nationale d'Expansion du Tourisme* gave out the following impressive statistics:[10]

LOCATION	STATIONS	BEDS
Savoy	52	11,659
Dauphiné	13	1,055
Briançonnais	17	915
Provence	8	762
Pyrénées	20	2,694
Vosges	8	541
Jura	15	599
Massif Central	9	1,060
Totals	*142*	*19,285*

These sorts of figures seemed evidence enough that France was winning the peace. The ONT studied tourism "as if it were an industrial concern" because tourism had grown into "the big French national industry," with nature providing the capital asset; "the construction of the Eiffel Tower cost 10 million in gold, Mont Blanc costs us nothing!"[11] In spite of the dramatic rise in the number of ski venues, the Savoyard areas were able to retain much of their traditions. There was neither a wholesale sellout to Paris and Lyon money, nor to fashion even if a "strange androgyne, this recent creation blows in at the beginning of each winter . . . to disappear in the spring." The villages could still keep enough of their local identity not to suffer total deculturation. Mégève in 1930 remained very picturesque with its fourteen churches, and women walked the streets in their Haute Savoie folk costume with centuries-old round bonnets. They added a rural charm, an authenticity to the winter experience for the crowd having a cocktail at the icebar.[12] Many in the mountaineering fraternity considered all this development "hurtful to alpinism,"[13] and there remained distrust between diehard mountaineers and skiers right up until the Second World War.

In the first year of peace, the Ministry of War recognized the *Club Alpin Français* with a 10,000-franc subvention as the *Société d'instruction physique et de préparation au service militaire,* continuing to link CAF's civilian status with military preparation as it had in prewar years. In 1921 one million francs was voted for tourism, half the money going to the *Office National de Tourisme* (ONT), and the other half split equally between CAF and the *Touring Club de France* (TCF).[14] "Sport," said Gaston Vidal, the Minister for Sport in 1920, "has become a matter for the state."[15] The "cult of sport" was not just bound up with the future of tourism but also with the future of the French race.[16]

The interest and growth of skiing was sparked by a number of events in the 1920s. Capitalizing on the enthusiasm generated by the Olympic Games at Chamonix, CAF and the TCF created a national exhibition of skiing and winter sports at the Palais de Bois, Paris. The minister of war and the minister of public works were the two honorary presidents. The War Ministry provided an exhibit of *Chasseurs Alpins* equipment.[17] Hoteliers, fashion stores, railroads and *syndicats d'initiative* all aimed at getting a moneyed clientele to the slopes. Skiing became fashionable. President of the Republic Gaston Doumergue opened the CAF-TCF-ONT exhibition at the Palais de Sablons in 1929, certainly an indication of how important France's ski industry and tourist effort had become. The jump on the artificial indoor piste became the high point of shows like this. From mountain lovers came criticisms about how skiing was becoming a circus act.[18]

Many commentators attested to the massive rise in the numbers of Frenchmen taking to skis in the 1930s. "This year again," said CAF's *La Montagne* in 1936, "it is the ski which has gained most adherents," somewhat to the worry, if not disgust of the club's alpinists. Alpine skiing, was *"une grande vogue."* Cross-country races drew fewer and fewer entrants, and there was not one competitor for CAF's 15 km race in 1937. Was France really turning into a

Pre-sci..... volata

One of Coubertin's amusement seekers, this Italian woman entertains little thought of sport and less of health. But the men in the bars of the new resorts of the 1930s won't mind. Fitness was often equated with morality, the two running counter to the social pleasures of après-ski blandishments. (Author's collection) nation of weekending *fêtards*? The number of *téléfériques* rose from two to ten. Though reassuring in economic terms, this development raised deep concern that skiing was becoming so social. True skiers, urged the TCF, flee the worldly stations of over-indulgent and ostentatious salons, chic teas, and blasting jazz where the *jeunesse dorée* in their kaleidoscope of pullovers drink who-knows-what color of cocktail. Better to try elsewhere, like the Vercors where nature remained in its inviolate splendor.[19]

As the fascist threat grew, there was again a hope that the ski might be "very important in the physical and moral upbringing of youth," as was suggested in a letter to the *Revue du Ski*.[20] It all sounded like pre-1914 again, only this time the populace had time for sport; in 1936, the *Front Populaire* brought the work week down to forty hours. "Sport for All," an equivalent of the youth folk programs in Germany and Italy, was supported by the French government too. Although the organization was chaotic, even extending to "disorder, rebellion, depredation and . . . sometimes immorality"—all the Marxists' fault[21]—sport became popular as never before. In 1900 there had been some forty newspapers that could be classified as "sporting"; in 1930 there were 219.[22] France took to skiing perhaps not quite so readily as the Germans and Austrians but with gallic enthusiasm tempered by fears of their fascist neighbors. A war-weary generation of elders hoped skiing would regenerate the race, to face possible threats from Berlin and Rome.

SWISS EFFICIENCY

In the 1920s Switzerland was most heavily competing for tourists with France. The Swiss seemed to have an uncanny understanding of the tourist industry; in 1920, the country's tourist office listed 120 winter resorts at various altitudes so patrons could select the right hotel for the time of year:[23]

ALTITUDE (FEET)	NO. RESORTS	LOCATIONS
above 5,000	15	St. Moritz, Pontresina, Davos, Mürren
4,500–5,000	13	Montana, Lenzerheide, Morgins
4,000–4,500	15	Adelboden, Villars, Wengen, Leysin
3,500–4,000	20	Klosters, Kandersteg, Diablerets
3,000–3,500	22	Grindelwald, Gstaad, Engelberg, Chateau d'Oex
under 3,000	16	Meiringen

As the winter of 1927–28 got underway, hotel interests persuaded the Brig-Visp-Zermatt railway to open the Visp-St. Niklaus section, which, with a sleigh connection, enabled Zermatt to qualify as a winter station even if the slopes were too precipitous for good skiing.[24] What had been one of the great climbing villages for a long time now joined the quest for winter guests, while remaining at the end of the *Haute Route* from Chamonix, pioneered on skis in 1903. The French bemoaned the fact that they had nothing like the statistical evidence the Swiss had collected on tourist movement.[25]

The Swiss tourist industry looked to Great Britain. They did everything they could to make the English visitor's life easy, even to having a warming brazier on the frozen lake for those who flew in to St. Moritz on Imperial Airways. Booklets detailed the railway connections, passport and customs regulations, cost of hotels and boarding houses, availability of sporting equipment. The cost of living "was not higher than elsewhere," prospective travelers were told, with "very moderate hotel prices."[26] During the 1920s "most winter resorts in December and January are almost entirely English," wrote one commentator of the Swiss scene. Another talked about an English season where Swiss were hardly anywhere to be seen; an English dominion, judged the *New York Times*, "where anyone without an Oxford accent was a foreigner."[27]

However, in the Engadine, especially at St. Moritz, about mid-February in came the invading "Teutonic hordes." The orchestras switched from English palm court music to "German jazzes," though smaller hostelries could be patronized in which relative quiet reigned. St. Moritz had built its reputation on attracting wealth and international high society, so much so that would-be resorts were measured against St. Moritz. Full of large hotels, able to supply any amenities and attractions for their guests, St. Moritz also became known as a center for skating and skijoring.[28]

Skijoring, anglicized from the Norwegian *Skikjøring*—skiing behind a horse—was originally employed in carrying army dispatches. Military skiing provided much of the impetus to civilian skiing,[29] and skijoring soon was one of the winter pleasures among the wealthy in Europe at St. Moritz; at Chamonix "it filled the stands" in 1927, and in America at Dartmouth College. Horsemanship was one of aristocracy's remaining differences from the urban masses, so the appeal of skijoring was a natural one. Newsreels, photographs, and drawings in magazines and postcards give some idea of its thrills. Children were pulled by dog and pony, British officers in India tried it behind a yak, Sami behind reindeer, and men from the industrial world behind motorcycle, car, and even airplane.[30]

Skijoring also provided a new form of excitement that seemed so essential

"SWISS, IS HE? HE'S ABOUT THE ONLY FOREIGNER STAYING IN THE HOTEL."

A foreigner in his own land, drawn by Arthur Watts for Punch.
(Punch Almanac for 1934, November 6, 1933. Author's collection)

after the Great War: speed. Its rawest form was the "Flying Kilometer," *Kilo-mètre lancé, fliegende Kilometer*. Conceived by the St. Moritz *Kurdirektor*, Walter Amstutz, as an attraction for the winter crowd, it failed in that respect, but did succeed in setting records. Today often likened to the Californian gold rush miners' races that are portrayed as the foundation of modern speed skiing, the Flying Kilometer had nothing of the mining-camp rivalry. The Flying Kilo-meter was pure speed, and pure speed becomes quite uninteresting to watch. It was, as one Frenchman shrewdly observed, "mathematical observation."[31] Racers came down a prepared steep track absolutely straight, and were timed over the short distance of 150 meters. Some were weighted, others held on to handles mounted on their skis, and the winner in the first race in January 1930 was actually on jumping skis; Guzzi Lantschner was clocked at 105.675 kph (65.44 mph).[32] Later, aerodynamic helmets appeared along with a kind of air-tunnel shroud that enclosed the skier.

This record was broken at Adelboden later in the spring. It was timed over 100 meters at 112.5 kph (69.90 mph), but the conditions were not the same as at St. Moritz, neither was the timed distance, and the notion of equality of con-ditions gave way to realizing that ever faster speeds depended on the steepness of the hill. At St. Moritz, the hill was about 35° where the speed record rose to 135.300 kph and hovered around that figure until World War II. The Flying Kilometer did not cause the crowds to swarm into St. Moritz. It was interest-ing only as a scientific fact. Racers were caught up in the Alpine race circuit, so this was a side issue. Still, the Flying Kilometer was the symbol of speed. When Mont Tremblant was built in the Laurentian Mountains of Quebec, the most daredevil trail was named the Flying Mile.

Speed almost always has something competitive about it. Races in Europe before the war were cross-country. Down-mountain races were experimen-tal. After the war, most had a *Geschmozzel* start, a mass start that made for that folk ingredient of man versus man, or woman for that matter; female competitors often started among the men. As more and more people took to down-mountain racing, it became apparent that *Geschmozzel* starts could be dangerous. There simply was not enough room on a mountainside and certainly not among trees for a mass start. With ski technique becoming more sophisticated, with race meetings reaching national and international levels, rational organization of the skisport was becoming essential. Although it was still true that individuals won events, their trophies now became a matter of national, and in the 1930s, ideological pride. The amateur ideal gave way to economic and ideological logic. The victory by a man who was a product of Nazi training was proof of the superiority of the Nazi way. There were few nay-sayers, often considered quaint amateurs from another world. If Arnold Lunn had not had such tremendous prestige and verbal skill, he would have been considered another old fogy. But he rallied those who had raced and gone down to defeat by the ideologues. "Results are not everything," he wrote to Nathaniel Goodrich, the editor of the *American Ski Annual,* "Your American teams are a very welcome element in these international meetings. . . . The rising tide of national jealousy will perhaps in time ruin competitive skiing, but there are still people who race for the enjoyment of racing and not to prove that one political system is better than another. A cheery team that doesn't take skiing too tragically, and which is in no danger of incurring the displeasure of an indignant dictator if they do badly, is a very valuable element at these meetings."[33]

Back in the 1920s, the Swiss may have claimed that holiday prices were moderate while the Ski Club of Great Britain collected complaints about their Swiss hosts, along with suggestions to better members' holiday experiences. They requested thinning out of trees, removal of fences and other obstacles on favorite runs, and they wanted a structured fee schedule for instruction. They complained about the lack of courtesy on the railways, about faulty ski equipment that had been foisted on them, and objected to exorbitant repair charges and such like matters. Later they fussed about overcrowding on trains, and wanted all hotels equipped with a ski room with repair kits, electric waxing irons, and relief maps. On the slopes there should be a man—or men—with rakes and spades to fill in the holes, construct and keep up small jumps, and mind the slalom poles. They suggested opening up new terrain because there were too many of the Swiss commercial classes who swarmed onto the pistes on weekends and holidays. No one would dream of objecting to the Swiss enjoying their own slopes, but congestion was becoming something of a problem and couldn't something be done to relieve it? The local authorities should be kept "up to the mark."[34] Pressure should be brought on railroad officials to bring down prices or at least, as was offered at Wengen, to sell weekly or monthly passes. Perhaps most irksome were the prices charged for hotel extras: heating and particularly bath water. Switzerland was to be made into what the upper class expected. Comparisons with Sweden and especially Austria brought forth partisan replies. The cartoonists had a field day.

Henry Lunn, the organizer of the aristocracy's pleasures, got around much of this sort of problem by continuing to offer what his Public Schools Alpine Sports Club had provided in the pre-1914 seasons: hotels for club members only. In this way, he not only separated the British from the Swiss, but his club members from those who came with Cook's Tours. Cartoonists made much

Do not mention it at Mürren
For it simply isn't done.

British orthodoxy required serious costume for their Mürren amusements.
The Cooks' tourist is ostracized. (Arkell and Baumer, Winter Sportings, *1929.)*

of the social distinctions in *Punch* and *The Tatler*. With such economic clout, Lunn could almost control entire villages. Mürren was "an outpost of empire," a "sort of Rock of Gibraltar," a place where there was always "British Control" as an announcement in the club yearbook of 1923 put it, and where—written into the constitution and rules—there was to be no gambling, no poker, baccarat or Vingt-et-un—nor any person suffering from TB.[35]

Another aspect of the English invasion of skiing may be seen in the language. Piero Ghighlione, who did so much to promote Italian skiing, found "comfort" connected with Italian inns. Words like "hickory," "gentlemen," "sportsmen," "tea rooms," "dancings" [sic], "weekend," "juniors," "slalom," and "performances" were all interspersed in Italian reports on skiing.[36] Meanwhile the British had anglicized the German *Schuss* by 1932, using it to advertise Jaeger clothes; the French followed suit and sold *Schuss* boots at the 1937 Lyon fair.[37] On the Mürren ski slopes, memorializing the war, were the Hindenburg Line on the Schiltgrat (so-called because it was less formidable than it looked),

Menin Gate, Kitchener's Crash, and Regulars Ramble. Morgins had its Five Bottle Slope. At Maloja there was the Haig, Wengen had its Plum Pudding, and far away in India at Gulmarg, the home-sick (for Mürren) skied into the Punch Bowl, and from Pig Flat to Gadarene or down Lone Tree Slope.[38] There were English chapels, parsons, doctors, not to speak of all the hotels advertising in the Ski Club of Great Britain's *Year Book* as "The leading English Hotel. Class House. Caters entirely for English clientele" at Arosa. Wengen's Regina Hotel was "The Real English Home Abroad"; Mürren's Grand was where "Best English Society" would gather. At Zuoz College, cricket, racquets, and fives were played; it was "A High Class Public School for Boys" in the Engadine. These Englishisms all infected the language of skiing, turned a piece of Swiss property into an English playground, in short, helped in the deculturalization of what had once been Wilhelm Tell's.

With almost imperial certainty, the British were bent on continuing their superior direction of Alpine skiing in the resorts and on the Swiss mountains. They had plenty of support from visiting royalty and continental aristocracy. His Royal Highness the Prince of Wales, England's future king, was at Kitzbühel in 1935, Belgium's King Albert and Queen Elizabeth were at Mégève in 1929, the King of Siam and his family spent six weeks at Morgins in 1936, Prince Umberto of Italy honeymooned on skis and keenly followed the races at Sestrières in 1934. Nicolas of Rumania wrote about ski wax and the Romanian royals frequently took their holidays on skis in the Carpathians. Dutch royalty went to Poland in 1937, while Hollywood royalty, Douglas Fairbanks and Charlie Chaplin, sported at St. Moritz and a bevy of French vedettes were skiing at fashionable resorts in 1939. That year Sir Archibald Sinclair and Lord Hamilton could be found at Chamonix, Sir Kinglsey Wood at St. Gervais, and Sir Hore-Belisha at Hohwald, and the list goes on. The titled and the wealthy gave a social status to skiing. For the Cookies, there was always Cook's Tours, and places such as Lenzerheide in Switzerland became theirs. It suited them and it suited the aristocrats to have them sequestered:

I love to meet those cheery coves
Who always go about in droves,
Who always book
Through Mr. Cook
And love to have their pictures took.[39]

The war had changed much for women. Although upper-class women remained economically dependent, they enjoyed new freedoms now that the Victorian mold had been broken. It was the fashion to be young, and skiing went hand in hand with youthfulness. They took to the new trouser fashion, for it emphasized length and springiness of legs that had been hidden for centuries underneath long skirts. Here was physical freedom. The jacket was cut to minimize the breasts—"man tailored" as an advertisement for Gamage's ski suit had it in 1930.[40] Above all, the bobbed hair. In the Victorian and Edwardian world, long hair had symbolized femininity. As late as 1911, women were instructed to tuck all their hair under the hat, and to leave combs and other impedimenta behind.[41] Although dancer Irene Castle had already cut her hair short before the war, when the young now followed suit it was nothing short of a revolutionary statement. "No one is allowed to be middle aged," sighed lady Troubridge, reflecting the angst of the older generation in the 1920s,[42] as the New Woman reinvented herself by constructing an outward persona to fit the new social relationships she was forming with male and female friends.

The ski villages, wrote Jean Claire-Guyot in *L'Illustration* in 1926, "fill with increasing numbers of people dressed in startlingly colored woolens, pantaloons, and huge studded boots. This masculinity is accentuated by the mode of short hair which is completed by a cigarette, and certain women who seem bent on destroying all their natural charms, have attained the dream of perfection: they completely resemble a man."[43] These were Coubertin's *fêtards*, amusement seekers.

The serious skier was admonished to wear black. Limit your choice to the following, wrote J. B. Ermitage, only half tongue in cheek, "1. Black. 2. Blacker. 3. Blacker still."[44] Grey was still the color at Mürren in the Bernese Oberland:

> Though you walk about in woolies
> That are knit in every hue,
> Though your coat has many colours
> Such as Joseph's never knew,
> Though you're like a human rainbow
> When you're sitting in the sun—
> Do not mention it at Mürren
> For it simply isn't done![45]

Grey or black, "the somber colors of the mountaineer," as one Frenchman put it,[46] were the colors of choice for the upper class. It was not that color per se was unattractive; it was simply that any color appeared garish among the virgin snows of the Allmendhubel, and what was garish was unrefined. Even worse, it might imply a certain sexual availability.

Yet those upper-class notions about color were giving way. The poster advertising Wengen, where the British Downhill Only Club occupied the village and alp in the late 1920s and 1930s, portrayed an easier lifestyle for the younger set of English gentle people who would come to sport with their friends on the Kleine Scheidegg.[47] The gentleman is accoutered to perfection, right down to his British pipe. His Burberry jacket and quasi-military belt give just that touch of discipline to let all understand that control of this foreign piece of land is in safe hands, just as those same hands see to the safety of his lady as he fits her skis. Both symbol of empire and redolent of the fox hunt, the jodhpurs add the right touch of public school or officers mess. The woman's exotic sweater and matching cap catch the holiday mood. The brazen red scarf indicates the length of abandon to which she will allow herself on—and perhaps off—the snow. The success of the poster was not only in attracting a certain class of skiing clientele, but through artistic appeal to the privileged young, it channeled English dreams and excited their desires for enjoyment at Wengen.

Maybe she was a "ski-bunny"—a direct translation of *Skihaserl,* said to originate from the Hassenhorn, near Todtnau in the Black Forest, where women and girls first tried out skiing.[48] Maybe she was an up-and-coming skier, one who would join in a club race or two. As she progressed, she might be among the company of better skiers in the 1920s, women like the Englishwoman, Katherine Furse, or Marie Marvingt who dominated French women's skiing in the period before and after the war.[49] She rallied troops on the Dolomite front, and in the 1920s founded the first ski school for Arabs in Morocco. This *fiancée du danger* was an accomplished aviatrix, and in the early years of the twentieth century, flying and skiing were often associated because of their derring-do.

Marie Marvingt was the only woman to have established a ski school in the 1920s, and maybe it could have only been done in a place like Morocco and for Arabs, people who did not truly count where social skiing was concerned. About the same time, the first teaching book on skiing by a woman was published in Vienna. It was artistic in the sense that the wood-cuts were colored and each part of the instruction was accompanied by a verse. Emma Bormann's *Brieflicher Lehrgang des Skilaufens* (Written Ski Course for Women) was hardly noted.[50] If here and there a woman was involved in founding a club, leading a course, teaching army units, and, after the war, being in charge of excursions for troops on leave, these were the exceptions; there was a very slow acceptance for women as instructors.[51] Instruction in the 1920s was bound up with training and testing the body and soul for skiing in the mountains.

Trainers, as early instructors were often called in the United States, imparted a disciplined approach that they had learned at home in Europe, and discipline was the realm of men. One such Austrian found it easier to instruct women than men "for the reason that the woman has a greater sense of rhythm and a greater capacity for imitation. This follows logically from her experience in dancing. Women seem more willing to surrender to the influence of the instructor than men."[52] In Germany, the *Deutsche Ski-Verein* listed 98 instructors of whom four were women for the 1930–31 season; the next year there were nine out of a total of 122.[53] The *Fédération Française de Ski* exam was opened to women in the 1936–37 season, when Madame Pelletier passed first out of sixty candidates.[54]

The difficulty women had in becoming instructors was nothing to the barriers put up to stop them racing. Those pre–World War I races were hardly exacting tests for women. After the war, particularly among the British, a few women competed with men. Miss Olga Majors was fifth in the British Championship in January 1921, "a fine performance against a field of ten men." But what impressed most was that she skied "beautifully, her skis well together, and her carriage and expression suggesting a good runner out for a pleasant afternoon's run rather than a candidate for a Championship."[55] These comments, almost certainly Arnold Lunn's, exhibit precisely how a woman skier should perform according to the hegemonic masculine view.

The continentals took an even stronger stand against women's races. As the length and difficulty of courses for men increased, it became harder for the older generation to consider these suitable for women. The FIS Congress took up women's racing in 1928. An attempt to draw up special rules was turned down. One delegate then called for a prize for "Elegance." Lunn spoke up for the ladies, reminding everyone that they should have seen Doreen Eliot's fourth place out of a field of seventeen in the Inferno, a race dropping 7,500 feet over 7 or 8 kilometers.[56] The race between English and Swiss women in 1929 brought about the founding of the Swiss Ladies Ski Club.[57]

Voices continued to be raised against women's races in the 1930s. "A sensitive man," wrote a correspondent to one Swiss paper, "cannot watch ladies falling on ski without suffering. Indeed, a ladies race is a *kleine Tortur*." Masculine critics, Lunn chided, "often forget that ladies do not race in order to awaken passionate emotions in the breasts of male spectators. They race because they happen to enjoy racing."[58]

The caliber of women's racing in the 1930s was mixed. In New Zealand, three flags were set far apart for a gentle slalom to ensure a non-falling winner. Only one stick-rider finished without falling. In Europe, Paola Wiesinger won a major championship, partially because her husband-to-be skied ahead of her warning of the tricky spots. There were only mild objections. Betty Woolsey, one of the up-and-coming Americans, related how she was chosen for the U.S. team "more by good luck than ability." No wonder women's events did not earn the spectators' respect as did the men's. Nowhere was this more clear than at the 1932 FIS Championships in Cortina, Italy. Forty-three men competed before the 31 women. Once the men's race was over, the crowd moved off down the wood path that was the women's course, not bothering to stay for the race and, indeed, not a few competitors fell on account of the spectators.[59]

Gradually, as the standard of women's skiing improved, more took to racing. In the 1929 Arlberg-Kandahar, the most prestigious alpine meet, 22 were entered, and by 1937 the number had increased only to 31. These figures are typical and show how slowly attitudes and expertise of women changed. By 1936, some women had become well known: the Norwegian all-rounder, Laila Schou Nilsen; Audrey Sale-Barker and Doreen Eliot from Britain; the Austrian Lantschner sisters, Inge and Hadwig; and Roesli Streiff and Paola Wiesinger from Switzerland and Italy, respectively. None compared with the Belgian born, Swiss citizen turned German, Christel Cranz, who gave Hitler the first gold medal ever awarded in women's Alpine events at the Nazi Olympics in Garmisch-Partenkirchen.

The numbers of women of international standard were low in comparison to the thousands who holidayed on skis in the burgeoning ski centers. The changing fashions they sported reflected both the amount of disposable income and the trends in skiing. At the *Salon des Sports d'Hiver* in 1929, not a word was included about the fashion business of skiing. But at the *Salon's* 1931 exposition, hardly a propitious economic time, "one sees from the fashions exhibited that the woman has adopted the sport of skiing to attract the light, the charm of the sun and of open air and also, why not say it, for the grace of the costumes which show her supple beauty so well."[60] In 1938, Jaeger was advertising bright-colored jackets and a *Vorlage* skirt.[61] (The word *Vorlage* mimicked what the instructor repeated—lean forward). Were women attracted to skiing or to the ever–changing, dazzling ski apparel? Colorful clothing no longer carried a moral price tag. Movie actresses decked out in the latest sporting creations spread across the newspapers and magazines were a constant reminder of the play-world of the wealthy: Michèle Morgan was at Alpe d'Huez, Danielle Darieux at Mégève, and Hollywood stars and starlets graced Sun Valley, already called the "St. Moritz of America" before it opened in December 1936.[62]

The Nazi Olympic Games at Garmisch-Partenkirchen were, of course, politically charged. Women's racing, too, lost some of the amateur quality as the larger events became tests of political success rather than enjoyment of racing. The British and French were drawn into this, however much they disliked it. Racing, even skiing itself, in the years leading up to 1939, lost something of its spirit as the fascist ideologies sullied what was still perceived as a grand amateur sport.

CHAPTER 12 The Winter Olympic Games of Chamonix, St. Moritz, and Lake Placid

Chamonix, 1924: I have explained to Sweden and Norway that they are not Olympic Games. . . . It is absolutely essential that the winter games do not take on the character of Olympic Games.
—Sigfred Edström, Swedish member IOC, 1922

St. Moritz, 1928: The future of these Winter Games seems more than doubtful. The Norwegians were only persuaded with difficulty to enter last winter and will probably enter no more teams . . . in the future.—Arnold Lunn, 1928

Lake Placid, 1932: It has become increasingly apparent to us that you do not fully comprehend the relationship of our organization to the III Winter Olympic Games and the limitations under which we operate as a service organization exclusively.

1)   Handicaps. Clients usually have wealthy infrastructure in place. You don't.

2)   You are geographically remote and just handed us the job.

3)   Great resistance to organize fund raising, and many are really against the indoor ice rink.

4)   Abysmal lack of appreciation that III Olympic Winter Games is a world event.

5)   We started late.

6)   Depression.

—Wayland D. Towner, General Fund Director to Godfrey Dewey, 2 March 1931.

In the forty years before World War II, it was never absolutely clear that skiing would become part of the Olympic Games. Many reasons militated against inclusion. First, there were already two major skiing events, the Holmenkollen competition, held annually outside Oslo and frequently called "The Olympic Games of the North" or some such title, and the *Nordiska Spelen,* run by the Swedes. The Norwegian event had started in 1879 on Huseby Hill and had taken place at Holmenkollen since 1892. The *Nordiska Spelen* ran from 1901 to 1926. Skiing was Nordic only, yet "Alpine skiing," meaning downhill and slalom, was gaining popularity outside Europe, and the *Fédération Internationale de Ski* (FIS) and the International Olympic Committee (IOC) were being badgered to sanction winter events. The Arlberg-Kandahar, the premier downhill race, was already a success by 1930, and Alpine events had their Olympic debut at the Nazi Olympics in Garmisch-Partenkirchen in 1936. Second: The skiing leadership of the Nordic countries, Norway, Sweden and Finland, voiced strong antagonism toward socialites who were amusing themselves with their serious *Ski-Idræt*. Third: The bugbear of professionalism plagued skiing administrators and was particularly difficult to incorporate into Olympism. The concern was over ski teachers. Were they professionals, and if so should they be permitted to race? And if so, in what races? Fourth: The FIS had been granted jurisdiction over ski events, yet the IOC handed down rules that caused much dissension within the FIS. Last: Hanging over all, especially in the 1930s, were the disruptions brought on by fascism's meddling with and finally control of sport. The Nazis wished to insure not only German sport played to their benefit but also Olympic competition. Given international antagonisms, bad weather at St. Moritz in 1928, and, four years later, the expense of traveling to the United States and the maladministration of the skiing events there, it is a little surprising that the Winter Games survived at all.

HOLMENKOLLEN AND *NORDISKA SPELEN*

The Norwegians had created their own national ski tradition. Starting when the lads from Telemark came to Christiania in 1868 and inspired the bourgeois to take up skiing, the leaders of the Christiania Ski Club and the Central Association for the Promotion of Skiing (*Centralforeningen for Utbredelse af Legemsølver*) found that the success of their Huseby tournament required a larger organization devoted solely to skiing. In 1883, the Association for the Promotion of Ski Sports (*Foreningen til Ski-Idrættens Fremme*) was founded, and sponsored local and national competitions, the most important of them on the hills above Christiania, the Holmenkollen meet. The great Fridtjof Nansen had competed in the years before he crossed Greenland on skis, and once Norway had become free from Sweden in 1905, the crown prince jumped in competition and the new king and queen from lowland Denmark and England graced the meet annually and took to skis too, proving their nationality, as it were. Holmenkollen was where the ski culture of Norway was enshrined.

The Holmenkollen meet started as a national festival but soon began attracting foreigners. Swedes, Germans, French, one Englishman, even a lone American competed before the war broke out in 1914. The meet became something of a tourist attraction as well. Foreign glossy magazines like *La Vie au Grand Air, L'Illustration, Illustrierte Zeitung,* and the *Illustrated London News* featured short articles and large drawings of what seemed to them this exotic sport of the North.

Partly because the Holmenkollen lists were open to foreigners, it became the most important competition on the European skiing calendar. Norwegians had the say, naturally, over the rules and regulated the events, how the races and jumps were handled, prizes offered and so on. Skiing at Holmenkollen was all Norwegian. The ski culture of Norway permeated all who came to take part or to watch. The only way to ski was the way Norwegians managed their skis as well as how they administered the skiing events: you could see, hear, and feel how they did things at the annual February gathering. It was *Ski-Idræt* in action.

As more people in Scandinavia as well as in the rest of Europe and in America took to skiing, the Norwegians first broached the idea of calling an international meeting in order to control the sport. It was not by chance that it was scheduled during the Holmenkollen competition of 1910. The delegates, coming to what they already knew to be the cradle of skiing, were awed by the spectacle of this nation on skis.

Meanwhile in neighboring Sweden, "Trumpet of the Fatherland," Viktor Balck organized the *Nordiska Spelen,* first held in 1901 at the time the consulate issue was heating up again. The games were originally intended to keep Norway within the Swedish-dominated pan-Scandinavian bloc. These "exercises on snow" were quickly dubbed Olympic by the French and British press, a winter equivalent of "the Olympic Games of Athens," and "the Olympic Games of the North."[1] Balck planned the games at four-year intervals, as the Olympics were, to take place in the odd years: 1901, 1905, 1909, 1913, and so on. Olympic organizer Pierre de Coubertin viewed them as a "durable institution."[2]

Balck sought to promote his country through sport. He held leadership positions in gymnastic, rowing, and skiing organizations, and had been one of the founding members of his friend Coubertin's International Olympic Committee. He was the driving force behind the successful 1912 Stockholm Summer Olympics. "All I have been able to do, I have done for the love of my country." When he died in 1928, the crown prince gave the eulogy.[3]

The first *Nordiska Spelen* had one effect that was unexpected in 1904. In Styria, Austria, Max Kleinoscheg and Toni Schruf, seeking to promote skiing in the Mürzzuschlag region both for the sport's sake and for economic reasons, decided to hold their own *Nordische Spiele.* The plan was to alternate with the

Swedish games, as well as complement the St. Louis summer Olympics. Held in brilliant sunshine, the competitions attracted huge crowds and seemed set to become a continuing major meeting. The Norwegians took note, especially of their own hero of the meet, Wilhelm Wettergreen, whose form in the jump was unexcelled. He also went off the jump on one ski. Maybe Norwegians were not so pure in their *Idræt* ideal as one might think. It was a crowd thriller.[4] Although there were further games with their Olympic style gold, silver, and bronze medals, to which was added the magic of Nansen's name, these Austrian *Nordische Spiele* were never endorsed by Zdarsky, were criticized by the Graz contingent, and were, perhaps, just not quite social enough for the Viennese Pötzleinsdorf crowd.

In Scandinavia, the 1905 games at Stockholm were crucial; a breakdown in negotiations over the consulate issue, which could easily lead to a war for Norwegian independence, was not by any means an empty threat. The games took place from 4–12 February. Nansen himself had given support to a Norwegian boycott should the consulate negotiations fail—which they did on February 7,[5] so Balck's effort to keep Norway a part of Sweden failed. Sport in this case was not nearly strong enough to assuage nationalistic ardor.

These Northern Games became more Swedish than northern from 1905 through 1909. The London *Times* reported on how the games of 1901 had "attracted the attention of the whole sporting world," whereas the 1909 meet was of "great national importance." The crown prince played a very visible role as acting president of both the Swedish Association for the promotion of Sports as well as the National Federation of Swedish Sports and Gymnastics. The royal family presided on a daily basis.[6]

By 1912, relationships between Norway and Sweden were less strained. Norway had seven years of independence and nothing was going to change that, and the Swedes had that summer pulled off the Olympic Games with verve and efficiency. Successful large-scale sports meets drew tourists, and the Summer Games confirmed the economic boost that tourism could bring. They also confirmed that Coubertin's desire for a culture contest was pretty ridiculous. Twenty-eight artist-contestants vied for honors in architecture, sculpture, music, and literature, four of whom competed in the painting category. The winner was Carlo Pellegrini, a Swiss who is now remembered among skiers for his social winter sports-people depicted on postcards.[7]

But the *Nordiska Spelen* were not without their problems in spite of the efficiency of dealing with Stockholm's lack of snow in 1913—the cross-country skiing events were moved to Ostersund, some 700 kilometers by train to the north. Hundreds of workmen had had to cart in snow for the jump at *Fiskartorpet,* Sweden's answer to Norway's Holmenkollen. It became clear that Stockholm was not the perfect spot for the games by any means.[8] The 1917 games went unnoted because of the Great War. The all-important 1922 Northern Games were almost uniformly criticized within Sweden. Skiers objected to the relay race organization. Worse yet, the sled riders received better prizes than the skiers.

The undercurrent of class antagonism came to the fore. The Northern Games, wrote J. S. Edström to Coubertin, "are now finished. They have not been a success. I much more believe in the up-coming international Games at Chamonix and I am doing my best to persuade the northern countries to take part there." But, he warned, the games must not be called *Olympic.* Call them *International* and the three skiing nations would come.[9]

CONTROLLING THE SKISPORT

Norwegians took note of developments in Austria and they were keenly aware of what was going on in neighboring Sweden. A number of Norwegians, many of them army officers, had been in Austria, Germany, Switzerland, and France. They had felt the pulse of European ski developments that triggered the idea of an International Congress during the Holmenkollen meet in 1910. Invitations were sent not only to the Europeans but also as far away as the United States: Austria, Bohemia, England, France, Germany, Norway, Scotland, Spain, Sweden, and Switzerland accepted. The congress appointed an "international commission" of three who were charged with drawing up rules governing international competition. The original idea was that the three should come from Norway, Sweden, and Central Europe, but there were already disagreements between Austria and Bohemia, part of its empire. Besides, some of the delegates came as representatives of associations rather than as national delegates. Sweden's two, for example, came from the *Svenska Skidlopnings-forbund* (Swedish Ski Association) and the *Foreningen til Skilopningfremjande* (Association for the Propagation of Skiing), one German was a Saxon from the *Schiverband für Sachsen* (Ski Association of Saxony), another represented Imperial Skirunners; he came from the *Skiläufeverrband für das Königreich* (Ski Runners Association for the Kingdom). Russia, Italy, and the United States sent letters of approval but did not attend.[10]

There were so many matters to be discussed: besides the general rules, questions on standards for race courses and jumps, eligibility, and international cooperation. Two topics caused most argument at the congress: prizes, which veered immediately into an amateur-professional debate; and, second, the judging of jumping: how much emphasis should be given to form and how much to distance.

At the next congress, held the following year in Stockholm, the commission was increased to five. The Scandinavians remained firmly in charge. In 1913, the number was up to seven: two Norwegians, two Swedes, one German, one Swiss, and one Austrian. This meeting began the voting by country, but there were still arguments between the Austrians and the Bohemians. Jumping rules had taken up much discussion at all the meetings, but Norwegian rules prevailed and were finally authorized in 1922. The two presidents, Johannes Dahl (1910–14) and Hassa Horn (1914–24) were both Norwegians.

With war looming in 1913, European leaders were worrying more about each other's military plans than about interesting the Scandinavians in holding Winter Olympic Games. Coubertin later claimed that he had tried continually to get winter events included in an Olympic program, but in reality he had not been enthusiastic. There were problems among skaters, speed skaters, ice hockey players, and bobsledders, let alone the arguments over ski jumping and ski races. Skating, particularly, seemed an artificial, urbanized sport whereas skiing, at least, belonged far from the city. Coubertin appreciated skijoring for its military application. Cross-country skiing, too, was useful both for military and civilian communications. Yet Coubertin was not wholly in favor of skiing because it seemed to belong to Norwegians only, and those few who did practice it in the Alps, Coubertin believed, were peasant mountain boys. When tourists took to skiing as a sport, Coubertin considered them *fêtards*—frivolous amusement seekers.[11] Skiing was hardly a sport to uphold his Olympic ideal.

Others had different ideas. Nothing had come of a Czech proposal to hold skiing events as part of the 1900 games.[12] Over the years, there were minor attempts to get a winter Olympic program going, but they always ran up against the adamantly negative Colonel Balck, who saw them as a threat to his *Nordiska Spelen*. Finally, in 1910, there were such harsh words for the colonel that he agreed to bring the issue before the IOC meeting the following year. He had to be reminded to do so, and when pressed, replied simply that it was impossible as the *Nordiska Spelen* were arranged for 1913. The Italian representative, Baron Eugen Brunetta d'Usseaux, then suggested that Balck's *Spelen* be accepted as part of the Vth Olympiad. This produced, according to the minutes, a "very animated" discussion that resulted in a decision a few days later that the *Nordiska Spelen* would not be part of any Olympic program.[13] The Swedes and the Norwegians did not like the idea of their sport being controlled by an international group that had not been brought up with skiing, and believed that Winter Olympic Games would be even more of an extravaganza than the *Nordiska Spelen*. After the 1913 *Nordiska Spelen* were over, the IOC finally allowed cross-country skiing and ski jumping (along with rugby, hockey, archery, polo, ice hockey, and speed skating) as demonstration sports.[14] The Scandinavians, it seemed, were ever more protective of their sport while the IOC sensed a movement to expand winter sports competition.

In the years leading up to World War I, sport was increasingly seen as preparation for military usefulness. Bound up with a nation's fitness, discipline, and nationalism, preparation for the Olympics "is in the best interest of the army itself," wrote the German, Carl Diem, when preparing for the 1916 games which had been awarded to Berlin, the winter competitions to be held in the Black Forest. In a February 1914 *Reichstag* debate, Dr. Müller extolled the Olympic Games as an indicator of the strength of a nation and added ominously that all the training of young people would make them "physically ready for other endeavors as well."[15] By this time, von Hindenburg had mobilized ski detachments, Wilhelm Paulcke had gathered a volunteer corps, and German troops found themselves on skis in the Carpathians, the Dolomites, and the Vosges, facing Russians, Italians, and French.

Meanwhile the call for the regeneration of France had become shrill. Nowhere else in Europe was skiing enjoyed with such desperation. Yet, to the Nordic nations, France's annual Winter Sports Week—always with Scandinavians in attendance—seemed a peculiarly French occasion, as little "Olympic" as their own *Nordiska Spelen*.

In an extraordinary about-face, just before the war, the Norwegians decided to support skiing in an Olympic program.[16] The amazed and horrified Swedes and the surprised Germans were caught off guard. Norwegians seized upon a chance to get out from under Balck's tutelage. Besides, the weather militated against the continuation of the Northern Games in Stockholm. The first Winter Olympic events were scheduled to take place on the Feldberg in the Black Forest. But in 1916, the Great War was the "Great Game."

After the war, the 18th IOC meeting held in August of 1920 was much exercised over the issue of Winter Games. Coubertin penciled in on one protocol, "*Les sports d'hiver sont douteux* [Winter sports are in doubt]."[17] They had become doubtful again because the Norwegians—in yet another extraordinary move—had returned to their old view that the Scandinavians, and really themselves, should control skiing. How could a Europe that had destroyed itself over the four years of war successfully orchestrate such an international competition? Swedish and Norwegian representatives issued a formal statement: "If the Olympic Congress takes this step against our wishes—we announce to the Congress that they may not count on participation from the Nordic countries."[18]

The French continued to pursue their goal in the IOC meeting of May 1921. The Comte de Clary and the Marquis de Polignac were insisting that France—Paris being the chosen venue for the 1924 Olympic Games in summer—be given the right to stage a "Winter Sports Week."[19] Article 53 of the Olympic Charter, however, said that a designated Olympic city could not split its privilege with another. Patently, Paris could not hold winter events. The idea grew in discussion that this hard-and-fast rule could not apply for winter competitions while it was tacitly accepted that any Winter Games should be in the same host country. Therefore when the French IOC members suggested their traditional Winter Sports Week in Chamonix, it was not seen as unreasonable. Since these meets had already international competitors from Italy, Switzerland, and with Norwegian observers too, the proposal was backed by experience. However, by far the most appealing aspect was the immediate acceptance of the proposal by Sweden's Sigfred Edström, who assured the IOC that the Scandinavians would have no objection to a Winter Sports Week. De Clary and de Polignac, however, wanted to tie the Winter Sports Week to the Olympic Games. A formula was worked out whereby the week was called "an international olympic meet of winter sports," a "secondary annex," a "winter prelude" to the Summer Games to be held in Paris.[20]

With much misgiving then, the Scandinavians had decided to compete in Chamonix in 1924. Their next *Nordiska Spelen* were set for 1922. Again they were not a success. When tobogganers received better prizes than skiers, those from Norrland lodged not only a protest but also threatened to resign from the Swedish Ski Association. There was more to it than that. Sledding was sport, skiing remained part of *Idrott*. Sledding was for the leisure class, skiing was manly. This was not the first time that these arguments had been voiced, but in the past there had been criticism of the Northern Games mainly from the political center and center left, from papers such as *Social-Demokraten*. Now they were joined by the liberal *Stockholms Tidning* and *Dagens Nyheter* while others drew a picture of ephemeral salon sports compared with the real ones.[21] Were the *Nordiska Spelen* going to be a social extravaganza or were they going to hark back to true and healthy *Idrott*?

Almost immediately after the contentious *Spelen* ended, Edström wrote to Coubertin, "the Northern Games are now finished. They have not been a success. I much more believe in the coming international games at Chamonix and I am doing my best to persuade the northern countries to take part there." But, he warned the Baron, the games must not be called Olympic. "If they are

called international, then the Norwegians, Swedes and Finns will all come."
When the French National Olympic Committee called for an IOC Congress to
regulate the Winter Games, it appeared to the Scandinavians that the French
were turning their international week into Winter Olympics. "It is essential,"
Edström wrote separately to de Polignac and de Clary, "that the Winter Games
do not take on the character of Olympic Games."[22]

The Scandinavian position obviously had some effect on the Chamonix
organizers. When Frantz Reichel, secretary of the International Winter Sports
Week, showed the Chamonix installation plans to the IOC in Rome in April
1923, he carefully referred to the contests as a "Winter Sports Week" even
though the paper from which he was talking was titled "*Exposé sur la préparation, l'organisation et déroulement des épreuves des Premiers Jeux Olympiques
d'Hiver à Chamonix du 24 janvier au 5 février 1924*" (An overview of the preparation, organization and program of the First Winter Olympic Games at Chamonix from 24 January to 5 February 1924). In reply to a direct question from
Edström, he emphasized that the proposed competitions were not an integral
part of the Olympic Games but were merely under IOC patronage. At this
same meeting, the Dutch, who were to hold the next Olympic Games, pointed
out that it would be impossible to hold the Second Winter Sports Week in
Holland because of lack of snow and suitable terrain.[23] The next set of troubles
obviously lay ahead.

If there was a degree of care within the IOC not to offend the Norwegians
and Swedes, elsewhere the Chamonix "Week" was openly called the Winter
Olympics. Henry Cuënot, president of CAF's Winter Sports Commission, the
organization that had run every Winter Sports Week in France from its incep-
tion in 1907, blatantly announced in the executive committee that "the Olympic Games would be held at Chamonix, 25 January and the following days."
The British referred to "the Olympic Games"; the Americans were thrilled that
the aerial railway would be ready to take them up to the Aiguille du Midi "in
time for the Olympics." "Winter Olympics at Chamonix," headlined the *Miroir
des Sports* in December 1923, and *Neige et Glace* ran a cover of the Chamonix
valley, "the theater of the first Winter Olympics." There were "*eliminatoires
Olympiques*" held at Briançon. The IOC insisted on the visitors' tax, which no
participant to the Summer Games had to pay, to show that this Winter Sports
Week was not like the Summer Olympics. But in the end, participants did not
have to pay the tax. And surely it was not by chance that de Clary asked for and
obtained the Olympic oath at the opening of the Winter Sports Week, something featured on the cover of *L'Illustration,* the middle classes' weekly glossy
par excellence. The more proletarian *Petit Journal* described how "the Olym-

pic Games of 1924 have just begun."[24] Quite evidently just about everybody thought of the Chamonix games as the First Winter Olympics. Nonetheless, Norwegian, Swedes, and Finnish competitors turned up.

Chamonix was a triumph for Norway: gold, silver, and bronze medals in every skiing event except one where they failed to get the bronze. Clean sweeps in the 50-kilometer run, in the special jump, and in the most nurtured of their *Idræt,* the combined event. Thorleif Haug alone won three gold medals. "We Showed the World the Nordic Way," trumpeted the popular Norwegian sports magazine *Sportliv.*[25]

Norway had been showing the world the organizational way for fourteen years as well, and Norwegians got their way at Chamonix with the rules of competition. One vexing problem was the judging of the jump, always the centerpiece of any competition. Norwegians believed that style was more important than distance. Points were assigned to reflect this. Yet many nations' representatives—and jumpers too—were taken by the ever-attractive notion of record-breaking distances. The Americans, for example, at Chamonix had jumped "with fierce determination that was admirable but their style was atrocious."[26] Yet if the jump was the most important of the competitions, the real hero, per Norwegian *Idræt,* was the all-rounder, the man who won the combined event: cross-country running and jumping. He represented both the ideal ski man and *Idrætsmann.* But this ideal did not suit the Europeans who were ill-practiced in the art of jumping, and always well behind in cross-country races.

CONFRONTING PROBLEMS: AMATEURS, ALPINE SKIING, AND NORWEGIANS

When Captain Roll opened the first International Congress in 1910 by saying how fortunate the skisport was to be purely amateur, he added the Norwegian imprimatur to what elites in Europe had been expressing for years. But just who was an amateur and who was a professional? Furthermore, could professionals race? The debate was really over ski teachers. According to Norwegian writ, skiing was not something to be taught at all; it was something you did from the moment you could walk. The last thing you should do was to pay someone else to show you how to ski.

In the amateur world of the elites, especially the British saw no need to draw hard-and-fast lines in statutes governing sports events. There was an understanding no man had to explain: the relationship between mountaineer and guide, athlete and trainer, and on the cricket pitch between "Gentlemen" and "Players." But skiing was different; once in the Alps (and only for a comparatively short length of holiday time), the elite wished to learn how to ski. Consequently, the ski teacher came to play a far larger role in the amateur-professional debate than any other. Of course he received money for his services, and might also obtain better conditions at hotel and ski center because of his ability to attract clientele, all the while being an avid competitor. Matters of professionalism, then, were not so clear on the snows of Switzerland as they were in the London clubs. It came as a surprise to most Europeans that the British came to wield such influence in skiing matters when they were hardly a skiing nation, sending no skier to the 1924 Week nor, indeed, to St. Moritz in 1928. In Arnold Lunn, both *"Enfant terrible"* and "Pope of Skiing," they had a forthright publicist for what came to be called the "Alpine disciplines," exactly that type of skiing that required instruction.

Whether the teaching of skiing was a line of work at all caused much discussion elsewhere too, even prior to 1914, particularly when some military officers taught skiing and took part in races. Class also became increasingly important. If a bricklayer, whose strength was derived from his manual labor, was not allowed to enter Henley's regatta, should an army officer in a ski regiment be allowed to enter ski competitions? The Swedish Sports Federation decided quite clearly in 1906 that "military men on active duty are amateurs." [27] That may have been easy enough for the Swedes, but for the British "all through the history of skiing," wrote a Mr. Howell in 1926, "the best instructors have notoriously in every country come from the 'officer class' rather than from among guides or NCO's." [28] It seemed possible, then, that officers might be dubbed professionals. Since they made up 44 percent of the Ski Club of Great Britain in 1905,[29] this was not an option.

The representatives at the 1912 International Congress decided that each national ski association could treat teachers how it wished, increasing or not "the stringency of rules for its own requirements." This satisfied no one. As was immediately pointed out, a Swiss instructor could compete in Austria, but an Austrian instructor could not compete anywhere.[30] Scandinavians remained firm in their efforts to keep professionalism of any ilk out of international competitions, and most of the delegates to these conferences agreed.

The difficulties multiplied with the beginnings of modern downhill and slalom racing in the 1920s. Both were still anathema to Norwegians, although they delighted in speed, and, of course, the word "slalom," if not the event, was derived from the Norwegian *Slalaam*. Originally, the skills of slalom served to insure that the ski-runner, after a glorious day on the alpine snowfields, could safely wind his way through the woods down to his inn on the valley floor. This sort of skiing, especially the turning part, needed instruction and practice.

Should the man who taught you how to slalom not be permitted to race in sla-loms? Here again is why the instructor in the Alps caused such disagreements among those organizing skiing.

The 1914 International Congress had been testy over rules and regula-tions for the 1916 Olympic Games. The Swedes felt that they would lead to an emphasis on collecting prizes and trophies, and would only injure the sport. The French request to have the minutes distributed also in their language was refused. And the English, enthusiastic that skiing was becoming such a sport, also worried over the military recognition that it received.[31]

The first International Congress after the war met in Stockholm in 1922, just at the time, it will be remembered, when the *Nordiska Spelen* had been such a failure, just at the time when the Chamonix Winter Sports Week was becoming the First Winter Olympic Games in the minds of most people. This congress adopted rules that were identical to those presented by the Norwe-gians. It was becoming obvious, though, that with the growth of the sport, some new governing body was needed. The Czechs proposed an international ski association that became reality as the *Fédération Internationale de Ski* (FIS) at Chamonix on February 2, 1924.[32]

The *Fédération Internationale de Ski,* in spite of its French title, continued to be dominated by Scandinavians. Four Norwegians had been secretaries of the International Ski Congresses held between 1910 and 1924. The FIS elected Sweden's Ivar Holmquist who spoke excellent French, as president, and two Norwegians were vice president and secretary, continuing to drive the Scan-dinavian views of skiing to the fore. It was, then, with some surprise that this new FIS was confronted with the IOC decision in 1925 to turn the Chamonix Winter Sports Week retroactively into the First Winter Olympic Games. At FIS's second meeting in Lahti, Finland, the majority voted in favor of Winter Olympics governed by FIS rules. Norway, Sweden, and Finland voted against it, and the Norwegians actually walked out of the conference.[33] Later, however, the Swedes and Finns came around and voted for holding the next games as Winter Olympics in St. Moritz; but how to bring Norway into the Olympic family? How could a country whose skiers had won every medal save one at the Chamonix week not be part of such an international winter festival as the Olympics?

The new administrative organization had long and bitter arguments with the Norwegian Ski Association and, more publicly, in the newspapers. The debate turned on the question of perverting the Norwegian way of skiing, and on the evils of specialization versus the excellence of all-around sport. The

Norwegian Ski Association's aging board wanted to keep *Ski-Idræt* as pure as they perceived it had always been but, after the spectacular wins in France, the new generation of skiers was eager to compete. Leading the argument to join the Olympics were two military and well-connected officers, Colonel Östgaard, one time mentor (one could never use the term instructor) to Norway's heir to the throne, and Lieutenant Helset, who had dismissed central European record chasing as something that could not harm Norwegian skiing in any case. The vote in the Norwegian Ski Association to join in the St. Moritz Olympics was 29 For, 27 Against.[34] The leadership of the board resigned, and Östgaard and Helset found themselves in charge of Norwegian and—they trusted—international skiing.

The twenty-nine who voted for Norway's participation were amply vindicated. Although the Swedes gained all the medals in the 50-kilometer race, Norwegians made a clean sweep of the 20-kilometer run and the combined, and won gold and silver in the special jump. It really did seem that "unless Norway had taken an active part in the Olympic Winter Games, she would not have been able to regain her position in the FIS and its work. . . . Norway . . . can for the future regard itself as the first ski-ing nation of the world. . . ."[35] High praise coming from a Swede.

Östgaard and Helset may have been riding high on the results of St. Moritz, but now they had to deal with the British proposal for the inclusion of downhill and slalom. It is worth reminding ourselves that downhill and slalom were not at all like the polished performances seen on television today. Racing was a test of inventiveness in differing snow and trail conditions. As late as 1922, for example, a starter of a downhill event in Switzerland advised the "candidates" to adopt stick-riding (straddling their pole hobby-horse style) because of the poor conditions.[36] No wonder the Norwegians believed that Alpine events were "a luxurious sort of skiing for rich people." They looked on the "up-by-rail-down-by-ski" crowd with contempt. A visiting Australian enjoying an Easter ski break at Finse in 1929 noted that Norwegians who did not even ski well considered that nobody but a Norwegian could know anything whatsoever about the art.[37] Even so, the Norwegians voted within their own organization for the downhill and withheld judgment on slalom, both of which were on the agenda for the upcoming FIS meeting in the Norwegian capital. But they were not going into that meeting with any enthusiasm. Östgaard wrote, "Englishmen do not sufficiently appreciate what we consider one of the best things of the ski running: the self-denial during training. The strengthening of character and will, of endurance and of energy which the training produces, is just as valuable from a sporting and human point of view, as the results obtained in the competitions themselves."[38] This could have been Nansen speaking.

Arnold Lunn marshaled support from several well-known and carefully chosen friends of downhill and slalom such as Dr. Karl Rösen, one of the first German supporters of Alpine disciplines, and Rudolf Gomperz, influential member of the Ski Club Arlberg where Hannes Schneider's *Schuss*—the word was already anglicized by 1930—had ousted the Norwegian Telemark turn from the Alps. From the Tirol and the Black Forest came calls for the Alpine disciplines. Even the Swedes seemed inclined to try the new forms of skiing, and from far away Canada came word from the Empire that slalom was "the fairest test of all round ski ability, and should be taken up all over the country." Some Swiss were more blunt: "The Norwegian dictatorship must cease."[39]

Thus the 1930 FIS meeting had high potential for misunderstanding and even anger, or compromise and acceptance. It turned out to be something of an anticlimax because the delegates were much preoccupied over the arrangements for the Winter Olympics to be held at Lake Placid, New York, in 1932. The Alpine disciplines were discussed in a loaded committee with Lieutenant Helset as the lone nay-sayer. On the floor of the full meeting, according to one observer, Östgaard had "seen the handwriting on the wall, and thought he might as well give in graciously as be outvoted." The "Peace of Oslo" was signed at last, and Lunn raised his little Union Jack.[40] But, Östgaard assured his Norwegian audience in ˙*Aftenposten,* it was not to be concluded that the Norwegian Ski Federation had any intention of introducing downhill and slalom races, nor that the country would be represented in those disciplines in foreign meets.[41]

It had taken a full eight years, from 1922 to 1930, for the Norwegians to join the Winter Olympic family as well as to sanction Alpine disciplines, unwilling as they had been and still were. General societal changes, especially after the Great War, bore heavily on their decisions. *Ski-Idræt* was still a strong enough force to garner all but one of the medals at Chamonix and almost as many at St. Moritz, but *Ski-Idræt* was not strong enough to resist the challenge presented by the enthusiasm for downhill and slalom, and the skiing world divided over those that remained "Nordic" and those that became "Alpine." This was not a matter of mere technique; the arguments contained a clash of philosophies. Norwegian *Ski-Idræt* appeared "good," "true," "healthy," and above all "real," something that was peculiarly Norwegian. Alpine skiing was "social," expensive, what detractors called "hotel sport." And it was so unnatural that it required teaching to people who had money to pay for their winter pleasures.

LAKE PLACID 1932

The Scandinavians, who had already expressed doubts that the Swiss could manage the 1928 Olympics, were dismayed to think what Americans might do to their sport.[42] At the FIS conference in Oslo, Fred H. Harris, the American representative, presented all the plans but had to accept a three-man committee to oversee the specific dates of events, a decision to lodge at Lake Placid and not at nearby Saranac Lake, and admission of a special five-man technical committee to ensure satisfactory compliance.[43] Harris questioned this new committee and received a reply that indicated the obvious distrust FIS had of American expertise. The Norwegian representative actually offered his own country as host, should American arrangements prove inadequate. It was humbling for Harris, who spent much of his time defending the expense of the Lake Placid games. The delegates balked at Harris's proposal of per diem expenses, the Swedes wanted to know if Swedish Americans could help, the Germans pleaded poverty, and the Europeans gave serious hope to the rumor that the United States was going to send over a boat to pick them all up. Ever since Harris had arrived, "the matter of expense has been dinned into my ears." There was, he summed up, "a studied attempt to get as much out of us as they can." Even the decision to hold the next congress in the United States was deferred. Harris took this as an attempt "to hold a club over our heads."

If the conversations and discussions in Oslo in 1930 were fractious, they were as nothing compared to those taking place in the United States. Dr. Godfrey Dewey, officially vice president of his father's Lake Placid Club but, de facto, very much in charge of this private and anti-Semitic club, was appointed manager of the U.S. Olympic team at the St. Moritz games. His real reason for going to Europe was to see if it were possible that his private club could hold the next games. He returned full of enthusiasm to find that California, which was to host the 1932 Summer Games in Los Angeles, assumed it should be the venue for the winter sports too. Much argument followed with, in fact, seven venues in the United States proposing themselves as host for the Winter Games. When Lake Placid was picked, California promised rival games, and the state legislature actually appropriated large sums of money so that the state could be "the scene of the 1932 Olympic Winter events."[44] Dewey's frustrations grew.

Dewey ran foul of the American Olympic Association over fund raising and

The 1930 FIS meeting at Oslo that granted the 1932 Olympic Games to Lake Placid, New York, was extremely important for Fred Harris (second right). Since much of the talk was in Norwegian, Harris had brought along Arnulf Poulson (first right) as translator. Arnold Lunn (front left) was very content; this was the meeting that sanctioned his Alpine disciplines. (Courtesy New England Ski Museum)

with its president, Avery Brundage, who felt Dewey's efforts were "doomed to failure;" over the commercialism in a souvenir booklet; and over the deteriorating relationship that Dewey had with the state of New York and particularly with its governor, Franklin Delano Roosevelt mainly over payment for facilities.[45] Dewey seemed unable to get much cooperation. He made efforts to obtain Fridtjof Nansen's endorsement,[46] to bring over Crown Prince Olaf,[47] to have Charles Lindbergh carry the special commemorative mail from Lake Placid,[48] and to have the games opened by President Herbert Hoover.[49] None of these was achieved. There were calls for postponement of the games by the Swedes; the Dutch cried off for financial reasons; and the German hockey team became a doubtful entry. The Spaniards complained over language. Baron Pierre de Coubertin, founder of the modern Olympic Games, took Dewey to task for not keeping in touch with him.[50] Sixty-five nations were invited and sixteen came to the Adirondacks bereft of snow.

After the games were concluded, IOC President Count de Baillet-Latour wrote a congratulatory letter to Dewey that was published in the *Official Report.*

Speaking conservatively, he told Dewey, the Europeans "were more than pleased at the plans made for staging the Games in Lake Placid, facilities for the conduct of the sports, and other arrangements." He thanked the local communities for their share of the burden and wanted Dewey to "know how I feel about the exceptional manner in which this obligation was discharged, a great task masterfully handled."[51]

The Technical Committee of the FIS also tendered its judgment, which, however, was not published in the *Official Report*. "Too big burdens were undoubtedly laid on a few men's shoulders, and those did not manage to perform all that was up to them. They also lacked skilled helpers possessing knowledge and initiative. The arrangements of the skiing contests," the report concluded, "must be termed unsatisfactory due to the fact that management was not entrusted to experts."[52] Two of the thirteen major criticisms were the "necessity of referring questions partly economic, partly technical to Dr. Godfrey Dewey," and that the Lake Placid Club was not a sporting club.[53] Here were the core problems around which all others circulated, some enormous, others as miniscule as when Norwegian jumpers refused to jump because the Lake Placid Club professional was doing the tramping of the snow.[54] Resolution of any problem could only be handled by Dewey, hence he was required here, there, and everywhere, and all the time.

The Lake Placid Club was a private club owned by Godfrey Dewey's father, Melvil, inventor of the librarians' Dewey Decimal System and proponent of "Simplified Spelling." Members of his club came mostly from Eastern moneyed families, white and Christian, people who enjoyed Yuletide festivals and skijoring on the golf course, where collegiate competitions were designated "amusements."[55] Only a small part of society was prepared not to smoke, flaunt their jewelry, or indulge in "rekless skiing"—any one of which could mean expulsion from the club.[56] The Technical Committee fully realized that this was no ski club that was running the show. Dewey's stubbornness won the Lake Placid Club its 1932 Olympics. It was the last games that were Nordic only, the last games in which there were no ski events for women, and the last games to be run under private auspices. These third Winter Games brought an era to an end. Already in 1931, the IOC had awarded the 1936 games to Germany for the summer in Berlin, and for the winter in the small Bavarian ski towns of Garmisch and Partenkirchen, and already swastikas flew at ski meets; already the Nazis were on the march.

CHAPTER 13

Europeans Abroad in the East

Japan: *Now the Alpine method of skiing is the method of skiing in Japan. The growth of skiing is enormous. All middle and high school students in snow areas have ski clubs. Many ski books are translated, and papers report on ski activities. In the past 15 years, Japan has really taken to skis; it is a real folk sport.*—Leopold von Winkler, 1925

India: *At Gulmarg, winter sports may be enjoyed in conditions which even Switzerland or Austria could not better. The skiing slopes are many and varied, the place is accessible, and the weather better than Europe.*—Illustrated London News, 1935

In the nineteenth century only a very few Central Europeans were on skis. They gained their knowledge, and often their equipment, from Scandinavia, especially from Norway. Norway was a poor country, and there was an exodus of educated and would-be educated, particularly missionaries, engineers, and students, to central Europe, to North and South America, to Africa and the East. The height of this emigration occurred when skiing was becoming a sport, taken up by the bourgeois. Skiing in Norway at the turn of the century was a mix of the old utilitarian business of getting about the countryside and a leisure activity for town and city people. When Norwegians individually or en masse emigrated to foreign snowy parts, it is not surprising that they used skis as a means of getting about in winter, and often skied for fun and sport. The majority (they are few in number) of Norwegians who traveled to China, Japan, New Zealand, and Australia, and found themselves contending with winter conditions, naturally took to their skis.[1] This may be a most interesting piece of historical recognition but, as this analysis will show, the early Norse skiers who first laid western tracks in the East had virtually no effect on the development of skiing in China, Japan, or New Zealand. In Australia it was slightly different, and British imperial officers on leave gave a start to skiing in India.

Jakob Vaage's *Norske ski erobrer verden*, published in 1952, and his subsequent *Skienes verden* along with a number of other publications, virtually list who, when, and where Norwegians laid their tracks.[2] Vaage thought in terms of Norwegian skis "conquering" the world, yet in China, Japan, and New Zealand, Norwegians hardly left a trace. It would be Germans in China, Austrians in Japan, and Englishmen in New Zealand who played the main roles. Vaage had nothing to say about India and Afghanistan. One of the great sadnesses about Vaage's work is that he never documented his material properly. *Norske ski erobrer verden* merely lists those with whom he either talked or had correspondence. He was free with his knowledge, yet when any attempt was made to show him incorrect, or even that there were other factors involved, he became aggressively defensive. He remained feisty to the end.[3] There are, therefore, difficulties in evaluating his work. Used judiciously, it can and has added an immense store to our knowledge.

CHINA: NO CONVERTS HERE

Various indigenous people over the vast area of China were on skis for centuries before any Westerner came. Eighteen-year-old Arthur Hertzberg, a missionary from Norway, arrived in 1899.[4] He had been assigned to Laohokow, about 500 kilometers from Hanchow. When snow came, he ordered some skis as any good *Idrætsmann* would. Whether Hertzberg expected the ideas behind *Idræt* to be passed to the Chinese is highly questionable, but many of them melded well with a healthy, Christian outlook. The snow lasted only a few days and Hertzberg returned to Norway.

He was back again in 1903, to the province of Hunan, this time bringing a pair of skis with him. It is not clear if he used them. His son, Gerhard Hertzberg, remembered a deep snow in 1913 or 1914 but could not recall any particular use of skis. Thus it was, according to Vaage, that Norwegian skis "conquered" China. There is nothing to indicate that the Chinese took to Nordic skiing. However, in Jilin province the ancient ways of skiing continued into the 1940s, according to the recent *History of Skiing in China*.[5]

On his return from the Russo-Japanese war, Alfred Rustad received a pair of skis from his sister in Oslo and used them around Tientsin, China, in the winter of 1905–06 in connection with his work for the Great Northern Telegraph Company. He was photographed on skis in Hetamen Street, Peking. Later, in the northern region around Kalgan, he gave his skis to a Danish Dr. Krebs to use on his rounds.[6] But nothing more is known and the Chinese emulated neither Rustad nor Krebs.

The next we hear of Westerners in China is in the mid–1920s when two Germans had their photos taken skiing by the Great Wall near Peking.[7] J. S. von Dewall's account of skiing behind coolies in a type of skijoring never before attempted, obviously appealed to the exotic in Carl Luther, longtime editor of *Der Winter*, whose search for ski "firsts" was often uppermost in his endeavors.

MANCHURIA—GRAPH . FEBRUARY 1939 . VOL.VII NO. 2

満洲グラフ

55

When Japan had attacked Manchuria in 1931, folk skiing was age-old in the province of Jilin. But here it is obvious that Hannes Schneider's downhill technique was well established by 1939. That can only have been picked up from the military, to whom Schneider had demonstrated and lectured when he was invited to visit Japan in 1930. (Manchuria-Graph, *February 1939.* Author's collection)

Von Dewall and his friend Fritz Mühlenweg had a grand time, stopping traffic, showing off to the expatriate colonies. At the Great Wall, they dismissed their coolies and found perfect powder snow hour after hour, up and down in grand form and marvelous weather. Yet nothing became of this Western skiing in China, even though the foreign community continued to ski in the 1930s.[8] The Peking Chinese did not take to skiing and the locals in the hilly areas continued in their age-old ways—until the Japanese invasion of Manchuria.

JAPAN FOLLOWS EUROPE'S LEAD

Traditional skiing had its own indigenous quirks in Japan and among related tribes like the Ainu. In the twelfth century, the Japanese Sato reported on the use of skis but I have not been able to trace this reference.[9] The researches of Leopold von Schrenck conducted on his two-year Amur region trip in the mid 1850s provided the first secure knowledge of the fishing culture of the Giljaken. In winter, these people used two types of skis: small (4.5 feet long), called *Lakk*, and larger, called *Eng*.[10] They were used as outriggers when sitting astride a sled.[11] Both types of skis were held by a withy construction that could be tightened around the heel, thus keeping the foot more or less securely in place. A long pole with a wheel-basket at one end and a rectangular, spade-like blade at the other was carried. Drawings in Yamamoto's *Karafuto Ainu Jukyo to Mingo* show the longer pair obviously used while hunting, and the shorter pair for sled riding. There is a better illustration of the latter in von Schrenk's *Reisen,* along with other drawings of skis.[12]

The well-known Swedish explorer Baron Carl Nordenskjöld also traveled the region a generation later and wrote a book that he illustrated with the now well-known depiction of an Ainu being drawn by a reindeer. This he took from a Japanese book published in 1804.[13] From this and other sparse evidence, the conclusion is inevitable: peoples who used skis before the arrival of the Europeans did so in their age-old ways. The military would change all that. Western culture invaded Japan. Children singing the civilization bell song counted the advantages of Western civilization: beef and cameras, lightning conductors and watches, steamers and umbrellas.[14] Japan's military and naval chiefs embraced Western materials and methods too, so it is no surprise that the military became interested not only in the formation of ski troops but also in having ski instruction in the schools for a pool of recruits should the country call.

As a result of the deaths of 199 soldiers (most reports vary from 400 to 1,000) caught during blizzards on a 40-kilometer march from Aomori to Hakkota-San (Hokkaido), the Japanese High Command decided to equip some detachments with skis. In Western accounts the date of the storm is variously given as 1897, 1901, or is not given at all.[15] Whether, as Vaage suggests, this disaster prompted Norwegian consul Peter Ottesen to send for Hagen skis and instruct the Japanese how to use them in 1902, is not clear. Carl Luther, who believed that the storm took place in 1897, and Wilhelm Paulcke, who did not say, both believed that this disaster made the Japanese army command think about ski troops. If, indeed, the army chiefs were advised to institute a ski regiment, nothing whatsoever came of it, even after a military commission recommended obtaining more equipment for further winter troop movements on snow.[16]

During the Russo-Japanese war, the Russians successfully employed ski troops, and according to a German report this prompted the Japanese to order skis from Norway and Switzerland at very short notice.[17] When trials were made in Japan, they proved inconclusive, and the equipping of troops with skiing gear was again postponed.[18] After the war a British embassy official brought skis with him and presented them to a Japanese officer, but "the gift remained only as an ornament."[19]

Although there were occasional Westerners on skis in Japan after the Russo-Japanese war,[20] it was not until the military again became interested that skiing really began in Japan. Besides the Japanese officer who took a course in Norway in 1910 and returned with half a dozen pairs of skis, the major impetus came from two Austrians, both of whom arrived in Japan about the same time in 1910.

For the foreign community in Nokohama, Egon Edler von Kratzer from Vienna gave instruction in 1910–11. Word soon got out and the following winter he was invited to teach in Kosaka, twenty hours by train north of Tokyo. He was instrumental in founding the Alpine Ski Club of Japan in 1913 and received much publicity in both local and Tokyo papers.[21]

This all coincided with the exchange visit of Oberleutnant Theodor von Lerch. Von Lerch had eight years of skiing experience and was an ardent follower of Mathias Zdarsky and his Lilienfeld method. He had brought two pairs of skis in his luggage. At Takata in the snowy foothills of the Japanese Alps, he proposed skiing and gave instruction to a receptive group of officers in 1911, and ten pairs of skis were made locally in a few days. One who later became the "leading protector" of skiing in Japan, Lieutenant Horiuchi, had the instructions translated into French. Von Lerch also undertook high-country touring and, with von Kratzer, was responsible for the founding of the Japanese Alpine Club.[22]

The numbers of Japanese who took to skiing increased enormously in the

央給金田谷山二於テ

婦人ノスキー練習

These Japanese women must have learned their one-pole technique from Theodor von Lerch, who had come to Japan as a military attaché and immediately gave lessons to troops on skis as well as to civilians, especially to physical education instructors. Like some Europeans, the Japanese military high command was already planning to train recruits for ski units. (Author's collection)

period up and into the First World War. This was due to three factors. Officers, whom von Lerch had taught, returned to their own regiments to instruct others how to ski. By 1913 there was already a questioning of the Lilienfeld technique because Japanese officers received other instructional books such as Bilgeri's.[23] Second, both von Lerch and von Kratzer also gave instruction to civilians. The local and national press took this up and a film crew actually came up to Hokkaido to record these snowy goings-on in 1913. The media spread the gospel of skiing. Last, and most important, army officers also taught school physical education instructors, who then made skiing part of the winter physical education requirement in their school curricula.[24]

The Japanese realized von Lerch's importance for the civilian skiers and would-be skiers; they put his picture on chocolate boxes. *Lerch-ame* was one of the favorites, and they could still be bought locally twenty years later.[25] Today, there are two statues of von Lerch, one on Mt. Kanaya and the other in the town of Kucchan, as well as a flourishing von Lerch society.

In 1912, the Ski Club Echigo and the members of the University of Sapporo's ski club appeared more interested in making a tour of Mt. Fuji than in mastering the intricacies of the kind of skiing that appealed to the Europeans who stayed in the lowlands for their skiing pleasures. Those who wanted serious ski mountaineering joined von Kratzer's and von Lerch's Alpine Ski Club of Japan, a European-driven club with few Japanese members. Japanese ski mountaineering really only started in the early 1920s.[26] After von Kratzer left for the United States, another Austrian, Leopold von Winkler, offered courses to university groups. Some of the more wealthy students traveled to the Alps and others studied in the United States.[27] Some read and translated a number of the ski books that came from the European presses in ever increasing numbers in the late 1920s and early 1930s. Between 1923 and 1931, five skiing venues opened in Fukui prefecture and the railroads seized on a new clientele, allowing skis to be carried free of charge, offering discounts, and generally advertising skiing in much the same way as the PLM had done in France. Photos appeared in the papers, snow reports were given, and reports of postal and forestry workers on skis made good copy.[28] Japan's crown prince became involved in skiing, and Prince Chichibu was a favorite among the English in Switzerland. He was elected to the prestigious Kandahar Ski Club and donated a challenge cup.[29] Finally, in 1926, the National Ski Association of Japan was founded.[30]

Two years later Japanese skiers began competing internationally in Europe. A 50-kilometer race won by a Finn in 3 hours, 25 minutes, and 38 seconds, found three Japanese at the end of the pack, an hour and an hour and a half behind the Finn.[31] This was hardly a startling entry in the field of international competition, but it was an entry in an event that, for example, the British consistently refused to join.

That same year three Norwegian ski instructors left for Japan, the result of success at the Olympic Games at St. Moritz; Snersrud had won a bronze in the combined event, and Kolterud was a member of the gold-winning military patrol.[32] They came to Sapporo to teach university students as well as those attracted to ski touring by the local tourist bureau. They visited the burgeoning ski factories of Hokkaido, the largest producing ten thousand pairs of skis in one season. At the end of their stay, Lieutenant Helset was invited to instruct the 7th Japanese Division and made tours with the men and officers.[33] But the trio, though they stayed two months, had little effect because of the developing interest in Alpine skiing. In spite of the conditions militating against Alpine skiing (although not at Sapporo), most Japanese resorts like Akkakura were at low altitude, and many could hardly boast of excellent conditions. Half the resorts described in a Nippon Yesen Kaisha Steamship brochure, "Where to Skate and Ski in Japan," advertised the snow as "soft, damp and sticky"—not exactly a catchy phrase to attract those for whom Alpine powder was the delight. Still, the Japanese and especially the young seemed to enjoy frolicking about in the snow with a quite un-European enthusiasm: "*Schuss . . . Punkt!*" exclaimed a Swiss paper. In Japan, newspapers regularly carried articles and photos of skiing in the winter months. "Every urchin" in the mountain villages, it appeared to a visiting Englishman, had a pair of skis, often made of bamboo; the large department stores carried all necessary equipment (although taller men were warned to take their own gear). Good ski shops could be found in Tokyo and Kobe, as well as at Takata, von Lerch's old stomping ground, where runs with Swiss and Austrian names delighted both Japanese and their European visitors.[34]

Above all it was the youth who attracted the attention of one British holidaymaker. Three hundred on the slopes, the great majority school boys and students wearing "neat blue jackets with gild buttons and peaked student caps." A dozen girls in breeches must have seemed "strange to the few men of the older generation present."[35] These youths learned any sort of skiing they were offered.

And then Skimeister Hannes Schneider himself was invited from Austria.[36] His films had preceded him and may have been the reason he was asked to come. *Der weisse Rausch* had been shown all over Japan between 1932 and 1935 to much acclaim.[37] His Arlberg technique, defended by his St. Anton Ski School with zealousness bordering on religious idolatry, swept the remaining Norwegian style Telemark turns off the Alps and replaced them with the downhill *Schuss*. Schneider came to Japan to teach the army and interested civilians the Arlberg style of skiing. It was to the Okura *Hutte* (sic) that a Japanese tourist bureau brochure invited the foreigners, in English, extolling the delights of the Okura *Schanze,* the jump.[38] While the social aspects and amenities were all described in English, the language of skiing was German in the Japanese Alps. Asoh Takeharu was the first to pass the Austrian ski teaching exam under Schneider in 1936.[39] By that date the Nazi press claimed that ally Japan could boast five million skiers.[40] Whether the figure is accurate is not important. By 1936, Japan had become a nation of skiers, one that could produce a seventh place in the jumping event at the 1936 Olympic Games at Garmisch-Partenkirchen. Skiing in Japan was "already a folk-sport as it is with us," enthused a German reporter.[41]

As politics encroached more and more on international sport, as Japan's imperialist moves rubbed up against English-speaking Asia, the National Ski Association of Japan was replaced by the *Zen Nippon Ski Renmei* in 1938, an obvious reflection of nationalism.[42] Japan had escaped the tutelage of the West.

Sapporo received the Winter Olympic Games for 1940, albeit under very curious conditions; but the Second World War put an end to fun and games on snow.

RUSTIC SKI LIFE IN NEW ZEALAND

China and Japan were the "Far East," an exotic adventure for Western Europeans. New Zealand and Australia, as English colonies, provided a different type of adventure. According to Jakob Vaage, Carl Christian Torstensen Bjerknes, adventuring gold miner in California, Australia, and New Zealand, first put on skis on New Zealand's South Island in 1855.[43] Twenty years later, Norwegian miners in the Serpentine goldfields in central Otago (S. Island) used skis on a regular basis and certainly inspired one lad of ten to have a lot of fun.[44] The Naseby Historical Museum displays an 1895 New Zealander's homemade ski of Norwegian pattern, but nothing seems to be known of ski activity during the turn of the century. Again, the Norwegian import was never capitalized upon. Nansen's *First Crossing of Greenland* was read by G. E. Mannering and Marmaduke Dixon, who then used reaper "fans," with no need to do much shaping for they were similar to skis described by Nansen. In November 1893 they provided a means for the safe crossing of covered crevasses and questionable snow bridges while on mountaineering excursions in the New Zealand Alps.[45]

Although there were others who used these homemade contraptions, skiing developed only when it became part of tourism. Captain Bernard Head, a visiting Englishman, and L. M. Earle, who had European experience, based themselves at the hotel, the Hermitage at Mount Cook in 1909 to explore nearby glaciers. Part of Head's diary has been published and gives a good idea of the primitive beginnings of a tourist sport.[46] Up on the Müller glacier where they pitched camp, "ski-poles and climbing ropes were used to fix the tents" (October 9). "Upper part of the running was good, but lower down the snow was insufficient. Left ski one hour from camp" (October 10). "Packed five pairs of skis on to pack-horse and left for Ball Hut. Left Hermitage 12, arrived hut 5.15, about 13 miles" (October 16). "Practised on glacier. Good snow but rather hard. In afternoon went up glacier about three miles and enjoyed a splendid run home on very fast snow" (October 18). "Bad weather so gave up" (October 20, 21, 22, 23, 24).

In December they were using Australian made mountain ash skis with a number of grooves on the underside. There was a single strap for a foothold, which Head and Earle found wanting, so they constructed their own devices for keeping their feet more secure on the skis.

This exploratory skiing on primitive equipment paved the way for ski tourism. In 1910, the year after Head and Earle's adventuring, fifty pairs of Norwegian skis were imported. It would be "pioneer work," wrote Head to an acquaintance. "The people think me rather mad on it at present, but when they have started they will think otherwise." [47]

At the Hermitage, the most well known guide, Pete Graham, and others, were taking to skis as adjuncts of their mountaineering.[48] To begin with, skiing parties were not all that welcome since the guides had to tow the guests' skis up the glacier for them to attempt the run down. In 1910 a fillip was given to the Hermitage when some members of Scott's expedition came for a little practice. Tryggve Gran, Scott's Norwegian skiing instructor, was not among the group, but on his return from that ill-prepared expedition, Graham took him up Mount Cook.[49] In 1912 the Mount Cook Motor Company began running a service from Christchurch that included "a motor sledge. . . . Last year the experimental machine carried six passengers at 20 to 25 mph."[50] Norwegian skis were on view at the tourist office and were available for hire. Sensing an expanding tourist market, the Hermitage stayed open well into the winter of 1914 and "kinematograph pictures [were] taken of skiing on the Müller glacier," for Graham to take to Australia to drum up business. He was off to see if Kosciuskio's winter carnival could serve as a model for the opening of the newly constructed Müller hut.[51] But the Great War intervened.

Right at the end of that war, the Norwegian consul at Melbourne came for a visit and displayed his breathtaking skiing expertise. But from the Department of Tourist and Health Resorts, orders came down for the word "skee" be used in preference to the Norwegian "ski." "'Skee,'" the instruction noted, "is the English form of the word."[52] Skiing may have been a Norwegian import but it was becoming anglicized in the colony.

C. C. Richardson's *The Ski Runner* had given practical advice to two North Island ski adventurers in the Mt. Ruapehu region who explored the area on equipment imported from Switzerland. Their enthusiasm led them to found the Mount Ruapehu Ski Club in 1913.[53] The club was part of a larger organization, which came to be known as the Federated Mountain Clubs of New Zealand, composed of those who skied, climbed, and tramped. Skiing then came under the jurisdiction of a seven-member New Zealand Ski Council, which established, copied, and controlled the ski tests à la Ski Club of Great Britain. It then oversaw provincial and national championships, selected teams, and generally managed all facets of organized skiing in the colony.[54]

The standard of skiing was extremely low well into the 1930s. Rules for a 1923 race, for example, included the requirement that skis had to be worn throughout the entire race. If a competitor dropped a stick, he had to recover it and finish the race with all his equipment. Men like H. H. Elworthy, member of the elite Kandahar Ski Club and with Swiss experience, did well in the early races. All looked forward to the Australian Tom Mitchell's skiing in 1932. "No one was sufficiently optimistic to imagine that any . . . runners would be able to lower his colours, but all were keen to see such an expert in action." They were not disappointed. The slalom course, however, was "far too difficult for the average New Zealand runner which proves that our standard is really quite low as yet."[55]

Photographs show how important the building of club huts was, how long a trek in before any hill could be enjoyed, and, perhaps most of all, how expensive the importing of skis was; hence many people simply made their own into the 1920s. During that decade, club races became popular, often run with no poles. When a good skier did appear, locals were awed. The Norwegian guide Olaf Pedersen could certainly ski but "has no idea of teaching and doesn't try!"[56] A well-known British skier, and instructor, Barry Caulfeild, traveled out at the invitation of the Mount Cook Tourist Company in 1934,[57] but it was not until one of Hannes Schneider's instructors, Ernst Skardarasy, taught the Arlberg technique in 1938 that New Zealanders could be said to have begun to ski in modern fashion. That same year a rope tow was built bringing high hopes of much more skiing, but it broke down after a few hours and never saw service again.[58] At Arthur's Pass a local hut owner bought the entire stock of Norwegian skis to be found in Christchurch and Dunedin, some eight pairs, in 1927. He expected a tourist boom, but that did not happen until the Swiss Oscar Coberger arrived the next year after guiding and instructing at Mount Cook.[59]

Although Norwegians may have been the first on skis in New Zealand, their influence can hardly be counted. In the 1920s, New Zealanders floundered about in the snow, and although the Ruapehu Ski Club did have the Norwegian Pedersen, it was his jumping exhibitions that attracted spectators, not his teaching of skiers. Naturally a few Britons found their way to England's nether outpost of empire where they reenacted what their own Ski Club devised at home. Just as British skiing came to embrace the Arlberg technique in the 1930s, so too did the technique take hold among the colonials under the same tutelage of Hannes Schneider and his world-renowned ski schooling.

AUSTRALIA: ABOVE WORRY LEVEL

Ski developments in Australia took a different turn. The mix of immigrant skiing in mining camps combined with colonial club activity, both receiving a boost from government and railroad interests, turned Australian skiing into a sport by 1910.

Jakob Vaage claims that Carl Bjerknes, having been in California during the early gold rush, left for Australia and New Zealand and was first on skis in the Kiandra district in 1855.[60] It seems unlikely. Gold was not discovered until 1858 or 1859, and the rush began in October 1859.[61] A character called Bumpstone, an unlikely name for a Swede, is also credited with being first on skis, but it is difficult to find supporting evidence for this, too. Arnold Lunn's claim that skis were used in the 1830s by hunting parties in Tasmania has never received confirmation. He describes the skis as three feet long and turned up at both ends.[62]

With newspaper reports of skiing, beginning in the winter of 1861, we are on firmer ground. From the *Monaro Mercury*'s correspondent came descriptions that the "heaven pointing, snow clad mountains afford . . . some pleasure. Scores of young people are frequently engaged climbing the lofty summits with snow shoes, and then sliding down with a volancy that would do credit to some of our railway trains." After ten feet of snow had fallen, the *Yass Courier* reported that young men were not moping over the fire any more but making themselves "Lapland shoes, and taking a long stick in each hand, move about. On the worst of days they amuse themselves with sliding, and some have come down in right grand style."[63]

This was mining-camp skiing that had about it a rough-and-ready character whether in the making of skis or in the carnival races, with one day set aside for the Chinese labor to compete.[64] The records of the Kiandra Ski Club, and of Charles Kerry, were lost in a fire, so the beginnings of organized skiing are difficult to evaluate. From about 1895 on there is more material, including a run of photographs taken by Kerry. He was the perennial president of a loose organization known as the New South Wales Alpine Club in Sydney. He took parties into the Australian Alps, to Kiandra. It was an exhausting experience both for Kerry and his clients. First came the rail trip to Cooma, then by stage to Adaminaby. The following day a further stage to the snow line, and the final eight or so miles had to be done on skis. "Novices were expected to get along tolerably well after the first few hundred yards." And with luggage on their backs.[65]

Once the exhausted party reached Kiandra, they found the inhabitants on skis. These instruments were mostly of their own making. The Kiandra ski— examples can be seen in the Ski Club of Great Britain in Wimbledon, and at the Norwegian Ski Museum situated under Holmenkollen's jump—had "butter pat" grooves, one deep cut, or no grooves at all. The tips were turned up to quite an extent (similar to the "traveling" skis of the California gold rush era), heels rounded, and a footplate of rubber or linoleum was nailed on. Either a strap or a laced, wider piece of leather held the boot in place.[66] These Kiandra skis were in use into the 1930s, even though a Norwegian had made more sophisticated types following the Norwegian pattern in the 1870s. Others had fixed up more secure bindings, and even a few Norwegian models had been imported.[67] This conservatism was remarkably similar to mining-camp skiing in California.[68]

Races—open to men, women, and youths (boys or girls), as well as to Chinese labor—were also more or less the same as in the western American gold fields. Competitors raced down a short course of about 400 yards or less at speeds of up to 50 mph.[69]

The Sydney paper in 1901 made much of the arrival of Borre Winther, portraying him in "true Norwegian fashion" as skiing in a low crouch. This was actually the exact opposite of the stylish upright stance of Norwegian skiers. The race, too, was not at all like those in Norway. Winther was pitted against "one of the most daring and clever riders of the Snow Mountains," William Pattinson, who showed Winther the heels of his skis at the start. Winther, however, shot past him in a crouch, but as the two approached the finish it was neck and neck and both fell and scrambled for the line. Winther got there first but was disqualified, as both feet had to be in the shoes. He later redeemed himself by winning the jump.[70] The race description matches the free-for-all type of races of California miners rather than the controlled skisport run by the Norwegian Ski Association. This sort of racing was not for Charles Kerry's guests. Besides, as the ores ran thin, the population decreased, and Kiandra seemed increasingly isolated. The last races were held in 1911.

By that date, Kosciusko, about 80 kilometers away, had already become the center of Australian skiing, thanks to the Tourist Bureau which opened a 100-room hotel in 1909. The New South Wales Railway ensured good connections and advertised heavily. The journey was made by rail to Cooma, then by taxi to within 15 kilometers of the hotel and the final leg was by truck. Australian-made skis and other equipment was available for hire, and wax—Moko (from the Chinese *Makee-go*)—was at hand.[71]

The Great War put Australian skiing—as elsewhere—on hold. In the 1920s the Kosciusko Alpine Club provided the impetus for organized skiing, but it remained regional. The Ski Club of Australia was founded in the interests of touring and exploration with an impressive board of directors; Governor-Generals Lords Foster and Stonehaven were patrons. A committee of eight,

Though looking like a copy of British skiing, in fact Australia had its own tradition of gold-rush skiing before economic interests turned it into the fashionable sport portrayed here in 1931. Various governmental agencies had successfully promoted skiing, and when Austrians came down under to teach in the early 1930s, they found skiers ready to listen to their Arlberg explanations. (The Illustrated London News, *June 20, 1931.* Author's collection)

representing Victoria, South Australia, Queensland, Western Australia, and Tasmania (in the early 1930s), soon took on the role of the governing organization for the whole country. Following the Ski Club of Great Britain, to which it affiliated in 1926, it conducted tests, gave instruction, and held meets along British lines. It added its voice in persuading the government to build the Munion Hotel in the Australian Alps. It selected and ran provincial and national championships, and also international competitions.[72] Australian skiing owed much to Stewart Jamieson, the driving force behind consolidating the organization. It required much "dissipation of inter-state suspicion and jealousy," which was Jamieson's contribution, and the club came to speak for all-Australian skiing.[73]

In the late 1920s, modern Alpine skiing came to Australia via some Austrians. First to arrive was Alois Mock in 1927 whose "swings were the sensation."[74] Well they might have been; the Kosciusko Alpine Club had introduced a "Turning championship" only two years before that promised to become an important event even though few could turn.[75] More influential yet, the Victorian Railways Commission hired Franz Skardarasy from Hannes Schneider's Ski School in 1936. His brother, Ernst, returned with him in 1937 and 1938. In 1939 more Austrians—Leopold Fiedler, Toni Walch, Richard Werle, and Friedl Pfeifer—brought the Arlberg technique to Kosciusko, Hotham, and Buffalo. The Victorian Railways Commission also installed "an endless ropeway" of some 120 yards in length at Buffalo. The Commission controlled the hotel called The Chalet too.[76]

Thus, just before World War II, skiing with all its social ramifications became part of Australia's winter sport offerings. You could go to Tasmania "where men are men, and skiers wear shin pads," or some place where your skiing holiday would put you "thousands of feet above worry level."[77]

RECREATING MÜRREN IN INDIA

Although a Swiss party was first to ski in the Himalayas, mountaineers and military officers from Britain were the two types who showed an interest in promoting skiing in India. As early as 1902, a Swiss threesome, hiring 250 porters (coolies in those days), spent close to three months on the glaciers of Baltoro and Goodwin-Austin using skis to explore up to heights of 6,000 meters.[78] English mountaineers, mindful of the weight and bulk of equipment to be carried, also considered skis as possibilities, not so much for actually going up mountains as for excursions from the high mountain camps.[79] Behind these thoughts, as the well-respected Arctic explorer Captain Frederick Jackson expressed to the annual meeting of the Ski Club of Great Britain in 1904, was the idea that troops on skis might be useful for patrol work on the North West Frontier, although some military men questioned the value of ski detachments defending such a hazardous area (for skiing) as the Hindu Kush.[80]

Part of the army's interest was in keeping communication lines open in the more mountainous areas. Skis were proposed for Kashmir's telegraph operations in the Gilgit region to secure the 250-mile stretch to Srinagar in the winter of 1907–08. In spite of the twenty pairs of skis available, the service never got off the ground, largely because the natives did not stay long enough to learn the rudiments of skiing.[81] The Srinagar-Gilgit route involved the crossing of two passes at about 12,000 and 13,500 feet, not impossible heights by any means.

The first time one hears about skiing for recreation is in 1904 and 1905. Lieutenant C. Fitzpatrick, with Swiss experience, crossed the Margan Pass in Kashmir, and when posted to Chitral in 1907 enjoyed himself, alone, on skis.[82] Very few individuals took to skiing in the days prior to the Great War.[83] Kenneth Mason, surveying in Kashmir between 1911 and 1913, had skis and Caulfeild's How to Ski and How Not To, sent out from London's well known sporting goods store Lillywhites. Only after the war, with Mürren experiences behind them, did officers found the Ski Club of India in 1926, with Gulmarg as a base. Well known as a summer resort with golf, polo, fishing, bungalows and a hotel, Gulmarg was a long day from Rawalpindi—the Aldershot of India. Actually the road stopped at Tangmarg, where villagers then transported visitors and their baggage up to Gulmarg—Meadow of Roses—called India's St. Moritz as early as 1927.[84]

A retired English Major Kenneth Hadow owned a chalet and spent some time on skis in Gulmarg. As more officers came to enjoy the slopes, the Ski Club of India was founded in 1926. Difficulties were immense: no quarters were heated, not even Nedou's Hotel; catering was nonexistent; and there was no ski equipment. A brochure for the 1932–33 season warned visitors that Gulmarg, although becoming a resort like a Swiss center, should not be measured by the same standard. There was no central heating and guests were advised to bring as much bedding as possible.[85] A gunner, Captain C. G. Curteis, spent his summer leave showing a Kashmiri mistri how to make skis and initiated a blacksmith and leatherworker into the mysteries of bindings. The army's marching boot served as a ski boot.[86] Garrison alerts due to Ghandi's peregrinations and the more local worry of Abdul Gafur's Redshirts made for canceled

Evoking imperial power on skis while advertising Simla, the most important of British India's high mountain leave stations, this luggage label is an enticement to the ruling officer class. In fact, Gulmarg, where skiing was developing, was 350 miles as the crow flies northwest of Simla. (Author's collection)

leaves. Even so, the number of people coming to Gulmarg increased and the club received the benediction of the Viceroy, Lord Willingdon, who presented a cup, as did Lillywhite's. Soon, skiers started their races on Lone Tree Slope and dropped into the Punch Bowl: they might have been at Mürren.

In March 1930, teams from the Services competed for a trophy given specifically to make senior officers in India realize that the sporting world was not circumscribed only by tiger shoots, pig sticking, and polo. Skiing, thanks to the inter-regimental competition, became part of the morale boosting so vital to keeping imperial officers content; the latter created their own sporting world in Kashmir—a remake of that other outpost of empire in Switzerland, Arnold Lunn's Mürren. A small shelter was built, then a large one that was destroyed by avalanche, and finally a specially designed roof covered a larger establishment in which there were bunkrooms for gentlemen and ladies. The cook had separate quarters.

The garrison at Chitral was only some two or three days away from the Russian stations on the other side of the Pamirs. The North West frontier was more an area of nomadic tribes than a well-defined line separating red

British India from the brown of that mysterious place called Afghanistan in every school child's atlas. Folk in the high Pamirs bound "woven snowplates to their feet to get about in the winter snows," according to anthropologist Georg Buschan. Other observers remarked on local tribesmen riding branches down to the valleys below, while yet others sat on a thick piece of wood about one and a half feet long by a foot wide with some sort of grips at the side, a primitive form of toboggan.[87]

Members of the British legation in Kabul in 1925 most likely introduced skiing to Afghanistan. A few of the younger Afghan nobility gave the sport a try but there was no real enthusiasm. Still, the British community was able to set up a slalom in 1934 at Dar-ul-Fanum, near ex-king Amanullah's deserted capital. About 15 miles out of Kabul lay the 8,000-foot-high expanse of Argandeh Pass. When the Germans arrived two years later they wrote home of "a ski paradise in Afghanistan."[88] Hardly.

The same class of men who had organized skiing along British lines in Europe, and particularly in Switzerland, repeated their experience of alp and col on *himal* (mountain) and *la* (pass) when they found themselves posted there. They continued the traditions of the Ski Club of Great Britain. At Chitral, G. B. S. Hindley, Royal Artillery, signed himself as the official representative of the Ski Club of Great Britain.[89] The men who made this little sporting world for themselves in the Meadow of Roses would soon have to face the mobs whipped to frenzy by Il Duce and Der Führer, the forces of Japan that raped Nanking, and who knew what unimaginable horrors Stalin was concocting? Better take that last run on Lone Tree Slope.

CHAPTER 14 Europeans Abroad in the Americas

U.S.A.: Grand Lake, Colorado, a sparkling Snow Norse mecca—
a St. Moritz right in Denver's back yard.—Denver Post, 1931

Canada: Canada has extraordinary ski-ing potentialities and the
general standard of ski-ing among all classes, more especially the non-
wealthy and non-leisured classes is impressive.—Alan d'Egville, 1931

South America: Los gringos locos se van a la nieve. [The crazy
foreigners go up to the snow.]—Santiago, Chile, locals, 1926

U.S.A.

"Skiing is one of our foreign importations which is absolutely unobjectionable," *Leslie's Weekly* informed America's middle-class readers in the winter of 1893.[1] Scandinavians, particularly Norwegians, had been the first on skis in the continental United States in 1841. From a midwestern base, they dominated American skiing with their *Idræt* culture until well into the 1920s.[2] Having used skis as a means of locomotion for centuries, Scandinavians made a game and a sport of it. In the new country immigrant interest in racing across the countryside continued, but, increasingly, jumping from constructed towers became the centerpiece of most competitions. Urbanites were to take to ski, and *Ski-Idræt*—skisport—became part of the national winter ambiance.

In the 1920s and increasingly in the decade before the Second World War, a second group of Europeans with a different ski culture that we now call "Alpine," emigrated to eastern America, to wooded and hilly New England. A social spirit of skiing with its attendant economic spin-offs of inns, tows, fashion, and equipment appealed to urban groups. Skiing in the Midwest had been available to anyone who cared to try it whereas in the East it was the preserve of the wealthy for quite some time. Especially at well-to-do eastern colleges and later at ski clubs dominated by college graduates, skiing was promoted as a leisure pursuit, something to be learned rather than a thing belonging to one's heritage, and as such it was to spread to the city office worker in the following decade. The Austrian "Arlberg crouch" came to symbolize the new style as German jargon took over from the Norwegian, as cross-country and jumping were superseded by downhill and slalom, and as *Idræt* was replaced by amusement. In short, the culture of the skisport in the United States gave way to civilized social skiing.[3]

Gold Rush Skiers

There is one aside that needs discussion in any attempt to analyze the development of American skiing. Introduced by immigrants to the high mountain mining camps of gold rush California from 1853 on, long, wide boards became the only means of travel for whole communities covered in deep Sierra powder snow for which the webbed snowshoe simply did not suffice.[4] The term "ski" was not in use, so to distinguish them from Native American and Canadian snowshoes, they were variously called "Norwegian snow-shoes," "Norway skates," or "Norwegian Snow Skates"; however, the term for skiing remained "snowshoeing" well into the 1930s.

The most consistent reporting of "snowshoeing" concerns two activities: mail delivery and racing. Hero status was conferred on John A. Thompson (originally from Tinn, Norway) because in 1856 he made winter communication between the Great Basin of Utah and the Pacific Coast efficient for the first time. "Snowshoe" Thompson's 90-mile crossing from Genoa to Placerville over snowed-in mountain ranges was an instant success.[5] Gradually skiing mailmen, Norwegians and others, became ubiquitous in the high country and were much appreciated.[6] In isolated communities, delivery of mail and holding school were the two main indicators of civilization, thus the respect shown for the skiing mailman, whether in the purple prose of a local editor who hailed "our snow shoe heeled Mercury . . . a stunner, a velocipede," or in the more sober tone of another who noted "the fidelity . . . of Thos. Brown . . . at all times, through drifting snows and blinding storms commendable dispatch has been the rule."[7]

There was a time, usually February and early March, when the snows made mining impossible. Racing was, to quote the president of the Alturas Snow Shoe Club, "to fill in the time during the long, tedious winters when everybody is idle, affording an innocent amusement and healthy-giving exercise, thereby keeping the muscles in tune for the labors of the summer."[8] High-sounding words. The races were really a midwinter carnival that pitted individuals from several rival camps against each other for large sums of money. The boys raced straight down prepared tracks anywhere from 900 to 2,000 feet long, two to six abreast. The fastest "dope," as wax was called, a most carefully guarded secret, frequently won the race, and the success of "Greased Lightning" or "old Black" received comment. Prizes at the big tournaments were often $100, a not inconsiderable sum when a miner's wage was between $2 and $3 a day.[9]

Women's racing was also popular though more as a change of pace during the carnival meeting. The freedom permitted women by men in enjoying the sport was born out of necessity and general liberality of frontier community life. As long as the proper sort of dresses were worn, men did not object to women indulging in skiing, one of the "manly sports."[10] Boys raced, girls raced, Chinese laborers raced, and there was much gambling, drinking, dancing, and horseplay.

This Californian snowshoeing had no effect on the rest of the country. In spite of all the evidence of organized, modern sport: rules and regulations, timers, starters, course layers, clubs, uniforms, record keeping, champions, etc., it was merely a thing of the moment to pass the winter away in companionable—for the most part—and competitive enjoyment. In a region and in an era of extraordinary superlatives, why not "let the world and the balance of creation . . . know that a challenge for a snow-shoe race is accepted" and that your club will "furnish a man to compete . . . for any sum of money from $1000 to $100,000."[11] But when Californians inquired about the Midwestern National Ski Association's tournament, the Norwegians simply did not bother to reply, so no Californian skiing was tested in the larger American arena.[12]

Midwestern Immigrants: Beating the Record

How different from this Sierra Nevada razzmatazz was the Scandinavian immigrant way of life in the agricultural, logging, and mining communities of the Midwest where church, school, library, and club kept the ties from the old country firm and gave an ethnic cohesiveness to village and town. The sports in those communities were generally imported from England, but skiing was a Norwegian preserve, hence *Ski-Idræt* became the principal foundation for organized skiing. A man like immigrant Axel Holter, longtime secretary of the National Ski Association, urged his readers to consider that "of all Winter Sports, there is none so healthy, none so invigorating, none quite so pleasant and enjoyable as the skisport." "Why?" he asked rhetorically. "Because one is constantly in touch with the beautiful Nature of God, inhaling the pure, fresh air in abundance. . . . It will improve your mind as well as your muscle and make you better fitted to perform your everyday duties. In Norway," he told his American audience, "you see hundreds off on skis, just like a great big healthy family commingling in the purest of harmony."[13] This was the imported *Ski-Idræt* of a generation of immigrants.

Norwegians dominated early skiing in the United States. They fostered the belief—and it was remarkably widespread—that really and truly only Norwegians *could* ski. But as more and more different nationals arrived in the areas

The Scandinavian Woman and Home

Kvinden og Hjemmet

JANUARY 1916

CEDAR RAPIDS, IOWA   VOLUME XXIX. No. 1

SKI SPORT
IN SCANDINAVIA

In Iowa, U.S.A., in 1916, Woman and Home *helped to keep alive the skiing traditions brought from the old country. Scandinavian immigrants to cities quickly became assimilated, but those who settled in rural areas, while striving for the American bourgeois dream, clung to their own language, founded churches, created libraries and societies, and, witness the magazine, continued the sport they had enjoyed back home. (Kvinden og Hjemmet, January 1916. Author's collection)* where Scandinavians had settled, as Norwegians themselves became accultur-ated in America, many of the leading organizers of the skisport felt their duty lay both in guarding the *Idræt* ideals and in passing them on to the rest of America.

The skisport comprised two activities: cross-country and jumping. The utilitarian locomotion was the base for competitive racing, but immigrants tired quickly of the sweat and lack of heroics a cross-country run demanded. Jumping became ever more important as leaps neared the magic 100-foot mark and drew large crowds of spectators. The meets required organization. In the 1880s clubs had been formed out of the need to represent communi-ties at local carnivals. With the advent of easy railroad communication, clubs hosted much larger meets, and more permanent organizations emerged. In 1905, five clubs founded the National Ski Association of America. Two years later there were twenty-seven, all but one in the Midwest.[14]

The Association's journal, *The Skisport,* an obvious translation of *Ski-Idræt,* was a means of holding on to *Idræt* as well as propagating the ideals for which it stood. Articles were written in Norwegian, an odd poem appeared in that language, there was a regular column "Fra Christiania" (From Christiania, as Oslo was then called), and once, when there was discussion about changing the rules for jumping, the editor simply published verbatim the rules in Nor-wegian and added, in English, that they were to be followed.[15] However keen the immigrants were to make skiing an American sport, they were equally determined to guard its Norwegian purity.

But money entered into all this. A good tournament—which very quickly came to mean a good jumping competition—brought thousands of spectators into town. This economic lift to a small community prompted the business sector to recruit well-known jumpers from Norway by promising employment. The attraction of the competition was the voyeuristic appeal of record length attained in the leap. This became a problem because the *Idræt* ideal called not merely for distance but also for style. Yet, however fervently the National Ski Association's leadership clung to *Idræt,* both spectators and jumpers delighted in record lengths. By building jumps ever higher, towns created the possibil-ity, probability, certainty even, of one of the experts stretching his jump to the magic mark of 100 feet, which became almost standard advertising.

An example from Duluth illustrates exactly the importance that business interests gave to record jumping in 1908. After a new record of 122 feet had been established at a neighboring city, the organizers of the Duluth tourna-ment changed the position of the "take-off" to give the competitors more of a chance at a longer flight in the air. But the goal of the tournament—breaking

Torger Hemmetsveit, one of the brothers who made their skiing mark in Norway before emigrating to the United States, displays magnificent form. The aesthetic success of the "upright" jumping style, such a crowd pleaser in 1893, replaced the "squat" style in competitions. It also made for greater length, and soon the quest for record jumps replaced the wish for perfection of style. (Frank Leslie's Illustrated Weekly, *February 2, 1893.* Author's collection)

the record—was not accomplished. The city immediately decided to hold another competition a week later "being intent on beating the record." Many jumpers came near the old mark, but two Duluth men (both born in Norway) were the heroes: professional John Evenson beat the record by 9 feet and Arnold Olsen established an amateur record. It was exactly as the city had hoped: "Duluth thus established what it had been looking for, two American records by two Duluth skiers on a Duluth hill." [16]

This endless striving for records, this sensationalism—"tumble-jumping" it was called—produced reaction from the European homelands. [17] Holter, who had spent his life passing on his cultural heritage to the new land, now felt he had to defend the American way the skisport was taking. "The nature of our people is such that it demands first place in all athletic events, and they will support anything in which there is a question of new records." Later he wrote: "We refuse to take a back seat," and went on belligerently, "if records are what will bring us to the front, we are going after them and we will get them by the horns. Sure!" [18] In a span of one generation the melting pot had replaced the Norwegian with an American.

The excitement of the jumping competitions popularized skiing in the United States. Movies were first made in 1911, rotogravure sections of national papers featured ski jumping, magazines like *Harper's* and *Leslie's* gave skiing, often illustrated with a jump, a wide readership. [19] These illustrated weeklies lay on the coffee tables of the richer sector of society for whom money making had become a sort of malaise and who longed for a release from the oppression of overheated radiators. The skisport provided an appealing possibility.

New England College Men Catch On

In the early years of the twentieth century, skiing's appeal took hold in two specific places in eastern America, and they both remained influential right up to the Second World War: the Lake Placid Club in the Adirondack Mountains of New York, and Dartmouth College in the Granite State of New Hampshire. In 1905 the discriminatory Lake Placid Club remained open in winter for the silk stocking set to enjoy skating, skiing, and skijoring. Social competitions, woodland walks, ski jumping on the undulations of the golf course were combined with Yuletide festivities, a college week, and, in the 1920s, "international" competitions. In reality this meant that one or two (usually) Norwegian instructors, a few Canadians among American collegians, raced and jumped to the plaudits of the social crowd. It was all enough, evidently, to persuade the International Olympic Committee to award the 1932 Winter Games to the club, much to the outrage of some Californians who contemplated holding

*Not for the fainthearted! One manual advised the skier to let go once the airplane actually left the ground. The scene plays on the Lake Placid, New York, golf course. This photograph was sufficiently titillating to be published in a 1927 French weekly. (*L'Illustration, March 5, 1927. *Author's collection)*

rival games.[20] The Lake Placid Club, wealthy and far from immigrant tradition, received great criticism—mostly deserved—for the way the Olympic skiing events were mishandled. Even so, it signaled a major shift in American ski development: from Norwegian dominated midwestern *Idræt* sport to wealthy, social, eastern skiing.

Dartmouth College, also located in the East, put skiing on an organized basis with the founding of the Outing Club in 1909.[21] Other colleges followed quickly, and Dartmouth became the fulcrum around which eastern America learned to ski. Their initiation came from nearby immigrant Norwegian loggers in Berlin, New Hampshire, home of one of the two Nansen Ski Clubs in the country, and also from books, particularly British ones (no one could read Norwegian), that expounded upon skiing in the Alps in an upper-class ambiance very different from the culture of *Idræt*. When Fred Harris, founder of the Dartmouth Outing Club, wrote an article in the 1920 *National Geographic*, freshman admissions to the college rose 300 percent.[22] Wealthy white America, perhaps out to rid itself of the unease induced by industrial society, certainly determined to put the horrors of World War I behind it, took to the trail as "a skyway leading through grandeurs of winter scenery in the solemnity of nature's cathedral trees," as the caption of one photograph has it. Faculty statistics showed that scholarship profited from ski excursions. *Mens sana in corpore sano:* that old classical, Renaissance and then Romantic ideal, close enough to *Idræt* to be indistinguishable from it in a collegiate setting, paved the way for cross-country racing, jumping, expeditions, carnivals, and attempts to climb mountains on skis.

When those men—students were always called men in those days—graduated, they joined or founded clubs to continue their skiing pleasures: the Appalachian Mountain Club in the East, the Sierra Club in the West, or the Dartmouth Outing Club of Boston: nearly all had a collegiate ethos.

Alpine Ski Fever

One of the new clubs was the Ski Club Hochgebirge, founded in 1930; another was the Schussverein. There was also the Skidreiverein, and Denver was the headquarters of the Colorado Arlberg Ski Club. The Germanic influence was evident all over New England and making its way across the country. Why? In the 1920s, eastern skiers found that the Nordic, Midwest-based National Ski Association was simply of little help, so seven clubs founded the United States Eastern Amateur Ski Association (USEASA) in 1922. By 1934, there were 112 member clubs; by 1940, the number was up to 181.[23] These clubs were interested in Alpine skiing, brought back from Europe by the wealthy who pilgrimaged to two particular venues: Mürren in Switzerland, where Arnold Lunn, "high priest of skiing" and "king of the ski world," as he was described by two Americans, held court; and to St. Anton am Arlberg in Austria, where Hannes Schneider, "idol of skiers the world over," disciplined the wealthy in his Arlberg technique. When Americans returned home they recreated the Arlberg style of skiing along with British social enjoyment in the Green and White Mountains north of New York and Boston.

Those who took up Alpine skiing almost automatically began to race. If speed and dash were what this Anglo-Arlberg sport was all about, the testing came in club races, state championships, and national competitions. In 1934, the first *Ski Annual,* written and published by eastern Alpine skiers, devoted 31 of its 168 pages solely to the results of competitions, covering the junior intraclub competition of the Lebanon (New Hampshire) Outing Club with the same statistical detail as the United States National Championship. In 1935, the editor of the annual regretted that the printing was so costly that he had to cut out all but the very important results. The nine pages included the winners of eight major European meets.[24] It shows how important the European skiing scene was to Americans as they took up modern skiing.

A comparatively few superior skiers—many from Dartmouth College (four were on the 1936 Olympic team)—dominated ski racing. As the technology of ski construction improved—lamination, steel edges, Amstutz springs—the speed that racers could achieve increased. This was exciting and challenging for the Class A racer, but often the not-so-good, hurtling themselves after the best, took serious falls and the increase in accidents alarmed responsible leaders in USEASA and the clubs. There were calls—following the British—for "no fall" races and for a giant slalom. "This is not sport any more," wrote one of the most respected instructors, Otto Schniebs, "but peaceful war," as he left his coaching job at Dartmouth College to form his own ski school "in the interest of sound skiing."[25]

The standard of women's skiing was extremely low. One woman found herself on the Olympic squad because she had won a couple of races "more by good luck than ability."[26] Even so, the teams for the 1935 FIS World Championships and the 1936 Olympics were made up of America's best: a few expatriates living in Europe and a number of wealthy young women who made an annual trip to the Alps. But the Europeans were far superior. "I don't honestly think it was a bad last," wrote one team member.[27]

If the women's team was characterized as "too good looking to know how to ski," the men's team was "frankly a pickup affair." In 1937 advertisements were placed in the Paris edition of the *New York Tribune* in the hopes of raising a team.[28] Yet they were the stars, and when they returned home the names of Durrance, Livermore, and Bright recur over and over again among the names of immigrants like Prager, Pfeifer, and Matt. They all migrated from racing to teaching.

"Bend ze Kneez"

The political conditions in Europe made it increasingly attractive for ski instructors to come to the United States, and any ski school worth its name had to have a European on its staff: superb technique, accent, pipe, *Lederhosen*, and the indefatigable chasing of the *Skihaserl* became the image that America enjoyed as being part of the social ski scene.[29] These social matters still ran up against the inherited Norse tradition, and for a number of years each instructor defended his own system. When just about anyone who could ski at all was able to pass himself off as an instructor, the leadership of the Eastern United States Amateur Ski Association decided to institute professional examination. There was much argument over what exactly was to be taught, the stringency of the requirements, and how to make sure that certification would be honored. Americans, it was believed, would not accept the Austrian insistence on the perfection of a turn before learning the next step, yet those Arlberg disciples of Schneider already in the United States thought of themselves as guardians of holy writ. Benno Rybizka, as the poster said quite plainly, was in charge of the "American Branch of the Hannes Schneider Ski School" at Jackson and Mount Cranmore. But there were Swiss instructors, some Norwegian experts, and sundry others all with slight variations of technique and teaching methods: the "battle of the ski schools" was on. Finally a committee of the USEASA decided that instructors should have "sufficient English," be over 18 and under 55, and be able to demonstrate and analyze various turns, Arlberg and Telemark among them, and diagnose errors. First aid and emergency treatment of fractures, sprains, and frostbite were also required knowledge. Seventeen took the first exam in February 1938; seven passed. But the old ways died hard. Lowell Thomas, America's prime wireless broadcaster, exhorted all those involved not to "permit international bickering and national jealousies to thrive on anything so splendid as skiing." He urged that we "learn what we can from our cousins across the water, so long as they don't make the learning process a chore."[30] When Hannes Schneider was sprung from Nazi house arrest in 1939 to make his home in New Hampshire, it seemed that the Arlberg system of skiing and teaching would remain entrenched, and eastern dominance in skiing would continue forever.

Mechanization for a New Clientele

In New England the popularity of skiing was given an enormous boost by "the mechanization of skiing." The wealthy owned cars by the 1920s and 1930s, and the New Hampshire state government and business leadership realized that winter tourism would increase revenue. By 1927, the two major passes in ski country were kept open in winter; snow ploughs had replaced snow rollers.

More important was the snow train. Some 197 people (mostly from the wealthy clubs) entrained from Boston's North station on January 11, 1931, for the small village of Warner.[31] By 1940 trains were leaving all large cities in the East for New Hampshire and Vermont, from New York to the Poconos of Pennsylvania, from Chicago to the Cascades, from San Francisco to the Sierra, and from Los Angeles and New York to Sun Valley, Idaho. But it was the Boston "Snow Train" that captured the imagination of a new clientele, secretaries and factory workers, bank employees and shop assistants. Growled an old Dartmouth ski team captain, "It was like Coney Island."[32] These new-to-skiing people were not the healthy outdoor types, left-over muscular Christians, but people who wanted a day or maybe a weekend of fun and amusement that, if combined with a spring suntan, would insure you were special back at work on Monday morning. "You'll have a Glorious Sun-Day," promised a superlatively healthy girl from a Boston and Maine Railroad poster.[33]

These folk needed places to ski. President Franklin Roosevelt had been elected to office because he seemed to promise leadership in Depression-era America. Wealthy skiers applied for and obtained Civilian Conservation Corps labor—one of Roosevelt's innovations to put young men to work—to cut ski trails in the heavily forested hills and mountains of New England. These leaders had often skied and raced in Europe with the British. The ideal of a down mountain race, "taking it straight," redolent of the fox hunt, provided the model for the initial slits through the woods. When complaints were heard, wider, intermediate and then novice slopes were cleared for these new skiers to enjoy their sport.[34]

In 1938 the National Ski Patrol System came into official existence. The vast increase in the numbers of people on skis caused more accidents, although the real fillip for the creation of the NSPS was the death of a wealthy socialite in a race.[35] The same group of organizers, members of the patrician Amateur Ski Club of New York, the Ski Club Hochgebirge, and the Appalachian Mountain Club, promoted snow trains and trail development, professional instruction and the National Ski Patrol.

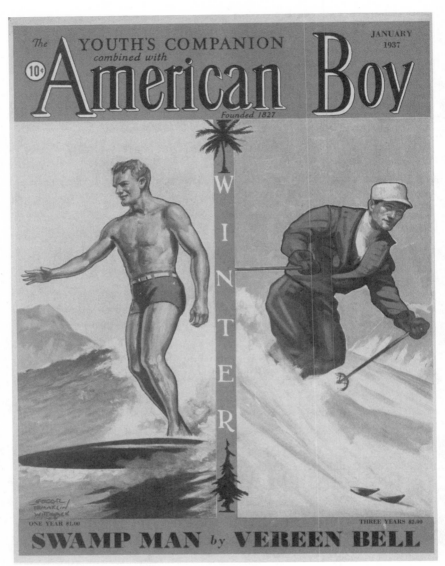

As the depression eased, there was a choice for a winter vacation for those with disposable wealth. Both offered an athletic and healthy lifestyle to the American boy in 1937. (American Boy, January 1937. Author's collection)

More and more people were skiing on the same trails because more and more lifts provided comparatively easy uphill transportation. The rope tow, cheap to put up, hardly ever really efficient, did the main duty from 1935 on.[36] The more sophisticated J-bar appeared, then the social T-bar, known in the early years as the "he-and-she-stick." The world's first chairlift was working in December 1936 at Sun Valley, Idaho, and finally the ride of all rides, an aerial tram at Cannon Mountain in New Hampshire, "The Sky Route to Ski Fun," as the advertisement had it, was the direct result of wealthy Americans who had been using funiculars and cog railways in Austria.[37]

In the 1930s cheap transportation brought city people to skiing venues. Once there, they found that the mechanized lifts had removed the really sweaty effort of climbing. For people who had only limited free time, the new opportunities for fun and frolic in the snow far away from home held tremendous appeal. They were the city office workers, a very different type of person from the muscular collegian. Remote villages provided mechanized skiing, farm houses turned into cozy inns, restaurants offered Alpine specialties. Ski teachers were available, ski shops repaired damaged equipment, and one valley even had the first "ski doctor," the well-respected Dr. Shedd, to repair the bones of the unfortunate.

Finally there was a market incentive for ski manufacturing in all its varieties. This had not always been so. As early as 1905, the Theo. Johnsen Company in Maine had manufactured high quality skis. But they had failed to sell, simply because the market was then not large enough in the eastern United States, and they were not able to break into midwestern territory where Strand and Lund were turning out thousands of pairs each year.[38]

Once skiing became social, fashion houses, taking their cue from Europe, began a brisk business. New skiers had to be taught about apparel and equipment, and ski instructors, especially those with accents, easily found an off-season job in a ski shop in late fall. Some of the expensive shops even had an indoor slide. The old guard loved the jokes: "Where did you learn your skiing, my dear?" asks one bright young thing of another. "At Saks, Fifth Avenue."

Films—"Sun Valley Serenade" is still shown nightly at that winter resort—especially the films of Fanck and Schneider, but also Pathé News, regular newspaper columns, radio announcements, popular magazines, and specialist ski publications all spread the word. Photographs of Hollywood celebrities, of princesses of Rumania, of Count this and the Marchioness of that, vied with the grins of Amy Smith of Worcester, Massachusetts. The snob appeal of skiing found new levels.

Both Claudette Colbert and Amy Smith had an endless choice of ski equipment from Washington on the Pacific Coast to Maine on the Atlantic seaboard, from a tiny shop in Craftsbury Common, Vermont to famous Groswolds in Denver. Skis made from cheap varieties of wood as well as expensive ridge-topped hickories were steel-edged in the 1930s. Poles were nearly always of bamboo, but already steel shafts made their appearance. Ski boots with a groove around the heel to hold the binding were available from manufacturers, although all skiers longed for the made-to-order Limmer, the aristocrat of boots with a price to match.

Two ski shops dominated, both in Boston: Asa Osborn and Oscar Hambro. "Shop" is not quite the right word. As one Boston reporter put it: "A major portion of Asa's clientele has always regarded the shop more as a club than a store."[39] This was where the elite met to ponder the weather, fix the next snow train destination, scrutinize new equipment, discuss safety, admire race results, talk of Europe and, as the war loomed, increasingly of the Rocky Mountains of Colorado, of Sun Valley, the Californian Sierra, and the Northwest's peaks, Mts. Hood and Rainier.

The Lure of the West

As in California in the nineteenth century, gold and silver had been discovered in Colorado, and mining camps had sprung up at elevations above snow line. The well-known resort of Aspen, for example, got its start with the discovery of silver at 8,000 feet. For getting about in winter, for mail delivery, carnival race meetings, and general enjoyment, the use of skis was part of Colorado mining culture too, but it does not appear to have been carried on at such a frenetic or competitive rate as in gold rush California.[40] Early Colorado skiing seemed to take on more of a recreational aspect. A 1912 Steamboat Springs paper was reporting on skiing as if it were the society column: "An overland skiing party was made up in town [Hot Sulphur Springs] on Wednesday morning: C. Howelsen, A. Schmidt, John Peyer, Mrs. H. B. Fuller and Miss Pansy Perry. The tour included a distance of 10 or 12 miles among the timbered hills southwest of town. A delightful time was had."[41] Howelsen was Karl Hovelsen, winner of the King's Medal at the Holmenkollen jump in 1903, a.k.a. the intrepid "Captain Howelsen" of Barnum and Bailey's Circus doing his famous ski-jumping act; and in 1912 Steamboat Springs had found in him its skiing mentor.[42]

Paradoxically it was jumping that brought Colorado to be noticed across the nation, and the first time a national meet was held outside the Midwest was in Denver in 1920. This western turn was caused by a number of leading midwestern jumpers going to Steamboat Springs and accomplishing astounding lengths, nearing world-record distance. Then Ragnar Omtvedt jumped 192 feet and 9 inches and immediately promised over 200 feet the next season: a new world record for Colorado.[43]

Others had taken long trips into the mountains and over ranges where one snowfield after another gave way to endless vistas of pristine snow, untracked powder, and incomparable springtime corn.[44] With some poor snow winters in the eastern United States and the lack of openslope skiing, the West appeared increasingly attractive. As early as 1920, National Ski Association President G. C. Torguson had predicted that the Rocky Mountain states "will undoubtedly become the center of ski activities in America."[45] It was quite an admission for the Norse midwesterner.

Influential easterners traveled west in the 1930s to see for themselves and reported, in strikingly similar terms, that they had found better slopes and more perfect snow than in Europe. In Colorado, near Aspen, plans were laid for a resort larger than Zermatt. In Oregon, the Roosevelt recovery program built Timberline Lodge. California gave a boost to Yosemite by constructing both a tunnel into the National Park and the magnificent Ahawahnee hotel. Yet, however superlative these developments were, they were all measured against Averell Harriman's Sun Valley, called America's St. Moritz even before it opened in December 1936 with its novel up-ski, the world's first chairlift.

Harriman was president of the Union Pacific Railroad. He hired Count Schaffgotsch, "not much of a skier but he knew resorts," to find a spot close to the Union Pacific's track in order to boost winter business. The Count traveled the West and, off what had looked like an unlikely railroad spur at Ketchum, Idaho, spent three days exploring the Sawtooth Range. Harriman bought the land for just over $10 an acre. As improbable as all this sounds, he next hired the advertising genius who had turned a sand spit near Miami, Florida, into a mecca for the wealthy called Miami Beach. He managed the same transformation with the isolated, snowed-in mountains of Idaho. "This burg," publicist Steve Hannigan memoed of the old cowpuncher's ranch, "must be one place where roughing it must be a luxury."[46]

This was the formula for success, and Harriman constructed magnificent log buildings—luxurious accommodation in rustic style. Cocktails would be served in the outdoor heated swimming pool. There was a hut in the backcountry in which Groucho Marx wished to be married. An antelope and a St. Bernard rubbed noses in the snow. German chefs, French waiters, and Austrian *Skilehrers* waited on a Hollywood clientele: the snowed-in backcountry mountains of Idaho had become "Sun Valley," America's own European resort. The famous advertisement of a handsome, shirtless young man rubbing the sweat off his face was in reality a vaselined model photographed in a New York studio, but it did the trick.

Sun Valley, however, was not only a playpen for the glamorous. It also had fine skiing, which, combined with the chairlift, made it a regular venue on the racing circuit for European visiting teams and top U.S. skiers. Dick Durrance, the United States' best Alpine skier in the 1930s, retired the Harriman Cup in 1940.

Each of the major western resorts advertised their delights, proclaiming that America had its own Europe right at home. The West's appeal lay in

> Four miles of downhill running, carefree and as happy as the winds that flew with us. Gone and far behind—the noise and clamor of the city. Forgotten all the sordid things that ever surround one in this greedy rush to exist among the smoke stacks of the city, for here, in the cover of the towering, unchanging mountains, for a few brief days, we *lived*.[47]

The technical, financial, and sporting foundation for a new phase of skiing had been laid in the West as the United States prepared for the Second World War. All the various facets that make up today's sport of skiing were present by 1940, some more developed than others. There were resorts (now destination resorts) that catered to the vacationer and the day skier, for the top economic bracket and the not so wealthy. There was a transportation system that closed the gap between city and ski slope, even a local air service out of Boston with the "Snow Plane" taking its cue from the Snow Train, and, for the wealthy, flights from East to West and to Canada were also a choice.[48]

Equipment was available for all budgets, and a fashion industry broke new records annually.[49] As war loomed in Europe, easterners realized the promise of the Rocky Mountains without a thought that their own playground would be eclipsed. The Second World War put the entire sport and ski business on hold, and modern skiing in the United States is a post-1945 phenomenon. The original Aspen project to build a resort complex larger than Zermatt died with Billy Fiske when he was shot down flying a Hurricane with 601 Squadron, R.A.F., in the Battle of Britain.[50] After the war, 10th Mountain veteran Friedl Pfeifer, one-time immigrant from Austria, created the new Aspen. Let that stand as a symbol of the connections among ethnicity, economics, and enthusiasm that underpinned the promise and development of American skiing in its first hundred years, from 1840 until 1940.

Much like American skiers, early skiers in Canada were either immigrants like the Gjerdrum brothers from Norway, or had some experience like the Governor General Lord Frederick Hamilton who had skied while on a tour of duty in Russia. The years when the ski tracks first appeared were the 1870s and 1880s.[51] The two main areas were in and around Montreal, and out in the Canadian West.

Montreal, built around its Mount Royal, was a natural landscape for the sport of skiing taken up in the 1880s by McGill University professors and students. A club was formed in 1904. Fifty percent of the skis were Finnish made, perhaps because a Finn became the group's mentor before he moved away to become president of the Finnish College in the midwestern United States.[52]

There was no wholesale defection to skiing. Snowshoeing was already part of Canadian winter culture, and well-established clubs with rituals and feasts played major roles in the annual winter carnivals. Only from about 1910 did skiing become a recognized winter sport; that year the Montreal Carnival directors brought in a Norwegian immigrant from Minneapolis, John Rudd, to show off his somersaulting on skis.[53]

"He wants to travel a mile a minute on skis," headlined the Revelstoke paper. Olaus Jeldnes was already the skiing star of the area in 1897. He was not afraid of speed, but he judged Red Mountain a little too steep as he planned to use his pole as a drag. This was mining-camp winter fun. Immigrants made their own skis, the power company cut a 100-foot lineway that doubled as race course, cleared brush, built a jump, and organized a carnival in which ski racing and jumping vied with hockey, curling bonspiels, snowshoe racing, and coasting contests.[54]

By the late 1890s, in spite of continued home-manufacture, skis became available on a commercial basis. The Hingston Smith Arms Company of Winnipeg was careful to point out that skis "could be used in place of snowshoes" in its 1897 advertisement.[55] At the beginning of the season it was supplying two lengths of skis, 6-foot and 8-foot. In March, it was marketing to boys, ladies, and men in 6-, 7-, and 8-foot lengths. By 1911, skis made from aspen and pine, fixed with imported Huitfeld bindings, were available.[56] The market had evidently grown sufficiently to make the importing of equipment a good economic prospect.

As in the American Midwest, the ski jump was the crowd pleaser. Immigrants did not have to be told that length was only one part of the jump. What marked a good jumper was his style; yet the immigrant boys were all for length, and to begin with, 3 feet was added to the length if a jumper did not fall.[57] Olaus Jeldnes won the 1900 Canadian Championship with jumps of just over 28 and 26 feet. These jumps were a little like the old country's *Hoplaam* in which the racer came down a course and took a jump. In this case, competitors skied down one street and leaped off a 6-foot bluff of snow.[58] In 1915, the Canadian Championship's new rules stipulated 20 points for style, along with 1 point per foot jumped. Deductions were taken for falls, touching with one or both hands.[59] These rules were in line with Norwegian regulations. The somewhat free-for-all attitudes were giving way to organization.

But not too much organization. The heroes of the meets were the jumpers. When Torgal Noren made 84 feet, the crowd roared its appreciation. It was the best jump in Canada in 1905. Two years later, business interests provided the Sullivan-Seagram Trophy "to an amateur breaking 84 feet." Noren won it, by springing "so high in the air that . . . he was skiing in the clouds."[60] The exaggerations of newspaper reporting were part of the fun of the fair. The trophy was to be awarded to an amateur. At this meet, there were also five professional jumpers competing, but Torgal Noren beat them all with a jump of about 90 feet[61] (the reporter for the *Manitoba Morning Free Press* wasn't sure of the exact length, and it hardly mattered since the 84 feet had been beaten). But Noren was not as pure as all that. The following year he demanded $75 in coin or a watch and chain of the same value just to compete. The organizers refused, and the tournament went ahead without him to hail a winner who managed 80.5 feet. Four days later, Noren jumped 101 feet 4 inches.[62] These amateur-professional shenanigans plagued skiing in Canada as they did in the United States. Here, the organizers remained determined not to be browbeaten into anything. If a fellow wanted to be a professional, that was well and good, but he shouldn't do so at the expense of the amateur organizers.

At the 1908 meet, the ladies raced. Over the years, there had been strong Catholic resistance to women's participation in winter sports. In 1886, Bishop Fabre's circular considered tobogganing and snowshoeing "near paths of sin." Besides, snowshoeing was invented by the Indians as necessity and was never intended for civilized women. Ladies winter sporting costumes were unbecoming.[63] There had been some liberalization over the next twenty years, but still, only three entries were taken for the race, which ran down one street. The winning time was one minute, and both first- and second-place ladies fell down. No mention was made of the third. Eight years later, there were four contestants, and it was only after the Great War when two events for women were scheduled: a 2-mile race and a Ladies Ski Run.[64]

If there were few ladies, the only men who indulged in the skisport appeared to be Norwegians. In 1915, the Phoenix Ski Club made a determined effort "to make itself more representative of the town because presently all members are Scandinavians."[65] This ethnic exclusiveness born of the perceived inbred Norwegianness of skiing, of an immigrant need to preserve social cohesion in a strange land, gave way after two generations. Second-generation Norwegians thought of themselves as Canadian-Norwegians and were wanting to pass on their sport to the enjoyment of all. Meanwhile, back in Montreal, organizers had realized that non-Norwegians would never have a chance of winning the jump, so in 1907 and 1908 they began one competition for a "Norwegian class" and another for a "Canadian class."[66]

Revelstoke and the mining camps were not the only venues where skiing was popular in the West. In fact, a rather different sort of skiing, European in attitude and actuality, could be found at Banff. When the Canadian Pacific Railway kept their Banff Tourist Hotel open for the winter of 1910, it meant that "America is to have her first Davos." Seven years before, Swiss guide Edward Feuz had been hired and had initiated alpine touring. It was, indeed, as if Switzerland had been transported to the Canadian Rockies. Austrian mountain guides arrived in 1910, and Conrad Klein founded the Banff Ski Club a year later.[67] This early social skiing continued with major hotel, railway, and lift development. With its Canadian Pacific Railway connection, its stunning vistas, majestic hotels, and marvelous snowfields, Banff did seem to be the Mürren of the Rockies.[68]

A second, quite different development also occurred in Canada: it advertised the wilderness of the Rockies, and of skiing in isolation at a Matterhorn look-alike, Mount Assiniboine. Two days ski march in, and one would be greeted by the Marquis d'Albizzi and Erling Strom. In 1928, a party of Appalachian Mountain Club members joined Albizzi for a month. He had gone ahead with a Swiss guide and a maid, "two luxurious appurtances for smoothing out life's details." After climbing for over an hour, the group watched Strom and Albizzi whiz down the slope in two minutes. Evenings were spent listening to Albizzi's World War I yarns in between guitar strumming and singing Russian and Italian songs. The fun stopped promptly at 9 p.m.; there was the next day's skiing to consider.[69] Here was both cultural and natural Europe in Canada for those who could afford the luxury of travel, time, guide, and maid.

Eastern Skiing Mechanizes

Emil Cochand from Switzerland's Jura was hired by the Laurentian Mountain Association to offer ski instruction in the Ste. Agathe area in 1910. He was the first such person actually paid to come over from Europe for this purpose.

He built Chalet Cochand and ran it for many years. His lodge became almost a destination lodge—the term "resort" is inappropriate—for wealthy Americans from Boston and New York. Traveling north by train to Montreal and then catching a connection up to the Laurentians could be done overnight. The trip had an attractive foreign quality to it; *Québecois* accent and *Habitant* soup provided the après-ski delights after a good day's touring in the wooded hills. Advertisements and photographs of Cochand in the *New York Times* in the 1920s promoted the Laurentians. Prominent New England skier John Holden wrote in 1928 that the Laurentians provided ski conditions "far beyond the fondest hopes of anyone who has confined his activities to New England and the Adirondacks."[70]

Those woods were being cleared of brush for trail skiing by Hermann Smith-Johannsen, later known as Chief Jack Rabbit, more usually, Jack Rabbit Johannsen, a mercurial Norwegian immigrant and Canada's most well known skier. He was hired by the Laurentian Mountain Association to cut the brush, make the trails. Over the years, they have become Jack Rabbit's trail system. Few realize today that he got his start thanks to Emil Cochand and the Laurentian Mountain Association.[71]

But in those interwar years, the Arlberg *Schuss* was sweeping Nordic skiing off the hills of Europe at the same time that mountain railroads were eliminating the hours of sweat required for the ascent. As in the United States, new immigrants from the Alps brought the techniques of modern downhill and slalom skiing to Canada. At the same time, the rope tow began twisting its way up the hill at Shawbridge, already well known for its skiing terrain. Foster's Folly, Alex Foster's jerry-built tow, inaugurated the tow era in North America in 1931–32 season. For $1 a day and tickets made out for Gents Only, skiers had the chance for downhill skiing as much as their arm muscles could take. "Gents Only": there was a belief that the soaked hawser would be too much for the ladies.[72] Venues with tows where the undulations of the Laurentian foothills gave way to steeper slopes became the places to ski. New England skiers' *Ski Bulletin* advertised Grey Rocks at Ste. Jovite seven times and the next season thirteen times, along with Val Morin and Ste. Agathe.[73] Downhill skiing, with an emphasis on the Arlberg technique, had come to Canada. It was a mark of acceptance when the British Kandahar Club presented the "Quebec Kandahar Cup" for an annual run starting in 1932. The first race was held on Mt. Tremblant, and the well-known skiers George Jost and Harry Pangman came in first and second. Jost went on to win the Roberts of Kandahar in 1933 (albeit with a much-disputed toboggan style of skiing), while Pangman represented Canada at the Lake Placid and Garmisch Partenkirchen Olympic Games.

Fast downhill courses needed for race training could be found in several places in the Laurentians, but Mont Tremblant became the area's most well known venue. Multimillionaire Joe Ryan first came in February 1938, bought the area, broke ground in October, and four months later the Mont Tremblant Lodge was open with a 4,500-foot chairlift in operation. Combining modern efficiency with Habitant charm, the Laurentians had a resort to compete with America's Sun Valley and the growing ski centers of New England.[74]

Canada continued cross-country skiing as race and recreation in the 1930s while it was almost done away with in the United States. For Americans, Canada provided a foreignness that, considering the ease of access, made the Laurentians and the Rockies appealing in an era when an Atlantic crossing took a week. As war threatened in Europe, the neighbor to the north offered to those with disposable wealth ski vacations with a special flair.

SOUTH AMERICA

At home in Norway on December 2, 1889, K. J. Johansen saw an advertisement in *Verdens Gang* for fifteen strong men, aged of 20–30, to work in the Andes Mountains of South America. After a thirty-seven day voyage, he left for Mendoza, Argentina and began work as a letter carrier over the Andes chain to Portillo in Chile—later to become the "St. Moritz of Chile." In fact, the advertisement was for young males who could ski, to build the high-altitude tunnel for the Transandine railway.[75] No skiing developed from the Norwegians who came for the work except an occasional utilitarian use, such as the Norwegian employee of the Braden copper mine who checked the water supply in the hills in the winters before the Great War. When the Chilean consul to Norway, Fernando Valdivieso, returned with four pairs of skis and four poles, no skiing developed in spite of his initial enthusiasm.[76] In 1915 a youngster returned from Europe bringing twelve pairs of skis with him, and he and his friends had a merry time. Norwegians Eilert Sundt and friend Thorleif Bache skied part way up Anaconda.[77] But nothing developed from these early adventures.

The skisport only took off when the Chilean Ski Club was founded in 1922[78] and, more especially, when Agustín Edwards took a hand in promoting the sport. It was not easy; in the early days, locals, like so many before them in Europe, looked upon skiers as *gringos locos*—nutty foreigners who went off looking for snow.[79]

Agustín Edwards was a wealthy Chilean, educated at Eton and Oxford,

Agustín Edwards, scion of a wealthy Santiago, Chile, family, organized ski clubs and ski developments, hosted foreign stars and racers, sent teams abroad, and brought South America into the world of skiing in the 1930s. (Courtesy New England Ski Museum)

member of the Ski Club of Great Britain and the Kandahar, a man equally at home discussing cricket at Lords or the price of beer at Mürren. He owned Santiago's largest daily newspaper, *El Mercurio,* the city's main bank, *Banco Edwards,* and had business interests in tramways, gasworks, and breweries.[80] It is remarkable how many wealthy men decided to spend their time and money helping the cause of skiing while holding other positions: Roland Palmedo in the United States, Walter Amstutz in Switzerland, Henry Duhamel in France. Agustín Edwards fits right in with this type of promoter of skiing. He hosted prominent skiers from abroad, helped out with American teams, and supported Chilean racers coming to the United States.

Skiing in a semimodern form began about 1930 among a number of clubs, some expatriate. At one time, the Ski Club of Chile held a membership of fourteen nationalities, a Dane as president, with Englishmen and Italians on the board. A German excursion club, the *Deutsche und Österreichische Ausflugs-verein,* was affiliated with the home organization, and did much skiing in the winter.[81]

The outstanding fact of Chilean and Argentinean skiing was the difficulty of travel to the ski fields and accommodation once there. In spite of good and cheap railways, connections with narrow-gauge lines and roads, most areas where skiing was practiced required a further 3 to 8 miles by mule or on foot. Club huts there were, but often with minimal modern conveniences. An occasional one might supply food, but most did not. For an out of town skier, it was essential to have introductions, since the huts belonged to the clubs.

The largest club was the Ski Club of Chile, with two hundred members in 1936 who did most of their skiing at Cerro Colorado. From Santiago a road led up 27 miles to 5,700 feet. The club hut, sleeping thirty, was 6 miles further on. A larger hut with baths and food was in the planning stage.[82]

The only place with a hotel was at Portillo on the Transandine Railway line. The train from Santiago took three hours to Los Andes (one and a half by car). Then came another smaller train track fitted with cars—*autocarril*—which took a further three and a half hours to get up to Portillo at 9,500 feet. The simple, clean hotel with accommodation for thirty had two bathrooms and was booked up a year in advance.[83] This was certainly not Switzerland.

But what marvelous skiing: vast touring possibilities with runs of 5 to 10 miles downhill in a number of places on the Cordillera chain. It was just a matter of getting there. From Portillo, a wonderful run, dropping 3,000 feet to Juncal was possible, and if the timing was right, you could catch the next *autocarril* up again. "The first part is over perfect open fields, the latter part is slalom work among rocks," Edwards warned, "very amusing but requiring a knowledge of turns."[84] Agustín Edwards's description has an authentic ring to it, concerning both the type of skiing available and the standard expected of a South American skier of the 1930s.[85] But this was the 1930s and the Ski Club of Chile had taken to racing downhill and slalom. Cross-country was found uninteresting, but a relay race was substituted. The club was fortunate to have inspiration from a couple of Swiss lads.[86] At Bariloche, in Argentina, the knowledge of turns was available from Hans Nöble of Innsbruck and Sestrières, under contract for five years to the National Parks to instruct and advise on ski resort management.[87]

Skiing development in South America was in a primitive state compared to that in the North, but not everyone minded. Building roads to make access to the high mountains and club huts was not always appreciated by the members. Some preferred the mules, "otherwise we'll get day trippers." How true that had become in North America where a healthy outdoor experience was turning into another Coney Island on the hills, another day when the parking lot was full, the line for the rope tow paralleled the one you joined earlier in the day to obtain your snow train ticket, and an extra rope tow was put up to handle "rush hour."[88] There was none of this in South America, but it was so far away. When the American ski team went south, they did so thanks to a nineteen-day voyage on a Grace Line boat . . . while one member flew from Miami in only four hours. The future of a ski tourist trade was in the making.

CHAPTER 15

Skiing under Siege

La formidable tralala.
—*The 1936 Winter Olympic Games*

Wenn die Olympiade vorbei
Schlagen wir die Juden zu Brei!

When it's over, this Olympic bash,
We'll beat the Jews all to hash.
—*S.A. slogan, 1936*

The aristocracy of Europe delighted in skiing, perhaps to escape the horrifying thought of another war brewing. They might even meet Hjalmar Schacht or Albert Speer, two of Hitler's top henchmen, on the slopes. Not the Führer though; he found skiing frivolous and dangerous.[1] The nearest he got to it was opening the Garmisch-Partenkirchen Olympic Games of 1936 and having a photo op with locals on skis around Berchtesgaden. On the other hand, they might meet up with Mussolini, who liked to make everyone believe that he could ski well even though he never got the hang of putting his hands through the loops of his ski poles correctly. His "torso of bronze," on display in the springtime snow proved his fitness,[2] and he was keen on sport as a means to better the health of the nation.

Italian skiing had had a slow start in comparison with the neighboring snow countries. Only the Alpini had made an impact on the public's imagination, but there had been such a debacle in the mountains at the end of the Great War that Italy, in spite of being on the victors' side, was left in economic and political chaos so that mere existence took people's entire energy. In 1921, there were only seven ski clubs in the Val d'Aosta; but a summer race on the Italian side of the Théodul attracted a crowd of five hundred the next season. The Ski Club of Turin published ski tour itineraries in 1920, but they looked back to the prewar years. In 1926, Piero Ghiglione, who had done much to popularize skiing, judged that Italy had two ski stations worthy of the name: Clavières, the site of the first women's national championship in 1922, and Cortina d'Ampezzo.[3] Compared to Germany, Austria, and France, few Italians

The park in Milan provided the ski grounds for the 300 members of the city's ski club in 1924.
(La Domenica del Corriere, *January 20, 1924.* Author's collection)

took to skiing. Mussolini changed that; by 1936, an estimated 600,000 of his people were on skis.[4]

Government sponsored *Dopolavoro* (after-work) excursions brought city folk out into the countryside. It is not too much to say that the success of Terminillo (2,213 m) was due to Mussolini's initiative. He had been told about the mountain, took the old mule path up, and ordered a road built. An instant resort with hotel and restaurants quickly materialized about two and a half hours from Rome. A little further away, Gran Sasso d'Italia's (2,914 m) *téléférique* took skiers up to 2,100 meters. Hotel, restaurant, bar with dancing, and ski rentals were booming.[5] Both were excellent venues for bus trips from Rome, just right for *Opera Nazionale Dopolavoro* pleasures. The numbers of participants (not just skiers) rose steadily from an initial 280,000 in 1926 to 1,445,000 in 1929, to 2,785,000 in 1936, and 3,832,000 in 1939.[6] These impressive statistics were not lost on the French, who sent a reporter to inspect "the black uniforms on the white snow." The correct positioning of the skis "affirmed the artistic attraction of repetition." Skiers were being choreographed, just like the whole nation. More and more, people were becoming anonymous and interchangeable parts of the fascists' social organism.[7]

Mussolini wanted fit youth for Italy's armies, which were going to turn the Mediterranean Sea into Mare Nostrum. He was able to control the sports associations by infiltrating them with fascist members, taking them over, and abolishing some. Through the *Opera Nazionale Balilla* (ONB), children were brought up from birth under fascist programs. The Duce ordered that Italian women were not to be Americanized, by which he meant that the honor and prizes attached with winning interfered with the "modesty, meditation or docility of bride or mother."[8] In order to produce strong babies, Mussolini excluded women from the more vigorous sports but allowed "tennis, archery, skating, dressage, swimming, skiing, alpinism and rowing," provided they were not practiced to excess, for fear that might cause damage to their "fundamental mission in life."[9] The Roman Catholic Church remained adamantly against "kindling eroticism," as it termed these activities but, in fact, had little power to stop them. Girls and women welcomed the *Dopolavoro* trips.[10]

Cortina d'Ampezzo was Italy's most venerable ski station,[11] but for Mussolini building something new was better than venerating something old. With a good population base in the northern industrial cities of Milan, Turin, and Genoa, the lure of Monte Cervinia (Matterhorn) created interest in a new station on its Italian side, Breuil-Cervinia. With sound economic backing, the

Marveling at the artistic harmony brought about by repetition of these Italian youngsters and entranced by the stark black of the uniforms against the white of the snow, the French commentator was much concerned that the modern collective mentality was effacing individuals, making each anonymous and interchangeable. (L'Illustration, *Feburary 24, 1934.* Author's collection)

first stage of a *téléférique* rose from Breuil to Plan Maison in 1936, and two years later extended to the Plateau Rosa. Breuil-Cervinia, with a long snow season, was served by an all-weather road, fourteen hotels, a *téléski*, instructors, and good publicity. In the 1938–39 season, 16,286 Italians came to enjoy winter and summer sports, but only 2,099 foreigners.[12]

Bigger projects were in view. Sestrières, a high-altitude hamlet near the French border, was the place chosen by the Fiat magnate and senator Giovanni Agnelli for the first destination resort in the Alps: two hours by car from Turin and five from Milan, situated at a pass joining two valleys. Agnelli built two extraordinary circular hotels as well as two cable cars. The futuristic modernism epitomized Mussolini's new Italy, "the triumph of the most up-to-date technical rationalization applied to the organization of a skiing center."[13] Guido Tonella's guide, published in 1934 in English,[14] listed 74 ski runs, 20 of which required no climbing at all thanks to the lifts. The one-time hamlet now included a bank, shops, smaller inns, post, telephone, laundry, hairdresser and water works.[15] Old-time charm was supplied by the very few local women who continued to wear their traditional costumes.[16]

The cylindrical hotels became the symbol of Sestrières; "man has merely put the finishing touches to nature's handiwork," exclaimed Tonella.[17] Actually, man had done exactly the opposite: the wealthy clientele invaded the most pristine high-country solitude. There, at the very top of Italy's white world, were the two towers rising phallic-like from the virgin snows. There was nothing, it seemed, that Mussolini's Italy could not do.

Except win races. What had in the 1920s been sporting competition among like-minded amateurs now became a matter of political victory or defeat. Given the fascists' use of all sports to create the new men and women, victories proved the strength of the political system. Speed became marketable as victories boosted economies as well. Yet skiing was still such an individual matter, and in the 1930s, victors of races and professional instructors gave the feeling that it was indeed endorsing individual endeavor. This would clash with the fascist dictatorships that relied on the power of the masses to proclaim only one individual to be leader, the specially named Duce or Führer.

ANTI-SEMITISM IN AUSTRIA AND GERMANY

The Germans did very well at the Garmisch-Partenkirchen Winter Olympics in 1936. Twenty-eight nations had sent 775 competitors (at Lake Placid, seventeen nations had fielded 300 competitors). Franz Pfnur won gold in the men's Alpine events, and Christel Cranz gold for the women. The Nazis had made the Garmisch area pseudo-free of anti-Semitic slogans, posters, and ambience, but it was never really hidden.[18] How could it be? Not only was it central to Nazi ideology, but anti-Semitism had an age-old history in all of Europe and had become one of the great issues in the late nineteenth century when Hitler was growing up in Linz and Vienna. Particularly appealing in the universities to faculty and students, anti-Semitism also found many adherents in gymnastic, Alpine, and ski clubs. Combining anti-Jewish social, political, and economic programs, many of the associations wanted a unity of all German tribes, as they liked to think of themselves. The German and Austrian Alpine Clubs had merged in 1872.[19] Some Austrians hoped that skiing would develop in Austria as it had in Germany "for the good of the German soul, the German mind, and German strength."[20] In 1905 the Austrian Ski Association, the Österreichische Ski Verband—ÖSV, had actually been founded in Germany. After the war, the Treaty of St. Germain outraged Austrians and they blamed their representatives at the conference led by Otto Bauer, a Jew, for failing to accomplish Austria's desired *Anschluss* with Germany.[21]

In the 1920s, the Styrian Land Association (*Steirische Landesverband*) suggested to the Austrian Ski Association that they put an "Aryan-only" clause into their statutes. The German Folk Ski Association (*Deutschvölkischer Skiverband*) also pressured the ÖSV, and in 1923 the so-called "*Arierparagraph*" was included. It required that members be of Aryan descent and of German ethnic background. The Austrian Touring Club excluded Jews that year too.[22] Other clubs excluded members who were married to Jews, while the Christian-German Gymnastic Association (*Christlich-deutsche Turnerschaft*) boycotted Jewish businesses and were generally antagonistic to the "Jewish spirit."[23]

The Austrian Ski Association, with its forty-six clubs and 2,435 members in 1927,[24] became increasingly racial by "cultivating and encouraging German racial consciousness."[25] This was too much for some club members who left the ÖSV because they felt skiing and politics did not mix. Some formed a new association, claiming skiing was absolutely apolitical and circumvented the *Arierparagraph* by welcoming the unwanted as "guests." The Kitzbühel Sports Club was founded in 1924 by two Austrian counts and a well-known English major and was run by the Ski Club of Great Britain's representative. The club, wrote Count Franz Schlik, "has no political or national tendencies." For those who wanted an Aryan-only experience, the Kitzbühel Winter Sports Association remained available.[26] The Ski Club Arlberg left the ÖSV in 1924 too. When FIS was founded a joint delegation represented Austria, one organization allowing Jews, the other excluding them.[27] In spite of all the disruptions, membership in the ÖSV was up to 12,482 for the 1931–32 season.[28]

These were small figures compared to Germany: 76,185 members which, however, included Dutch, Germans in Czechoslovakia, and even the 135 members of the German Ski Club of New York. If the 36,717 youth members were included, the total rose to 142,549.[29] The youth sections were going to be important; here were the future fit young men for the Nazi military schemes. As early as 1919, the German Ski Association (*Deutscher Ski Verband;* DSV) asked that all skis from demobilized troops be given to children.[30] School kids were on skis, new ski clubs proliferated, ski scenes were pictured on the *Notgeld* of about twenty villages, and ski weather reporting began on the *Süddeutscher Rundfunk* thanks to the initiative of the *Schwäbische Schneelaufverband*. Skiing began to be presented as highly social too.[31] If society was being tempted into skiing again, worker organizations were strong enough to hold the first Worker Wintersports Olympics, the *Arbeiterwintersport-Olympiade,* in Schreiberhau in the Riesengebirge in 1925: cross-country and jumping competitions were held, and also a *Hindernislauf,* a run with the kind of obstacles that any touring skier might encounter. The next Worker Winter Games were held in Mürzzuschlag in 1931.[32] Skiing was becoming a major outdoor activity in a recovering Germany, with local authorities realizing the economic advantages it could bring in winter.

And then the Nazis gained power.

THE "CRUSADE FOR THE SKI" IN FRANCE

"Finally France is waking up," wrote Gabriel Hanot, one of the most respected sports journalists, writing of the developing ski infrastructure in the Pyrenees in 1921.[33] Why did the foreign world not know of France's superior ski venues?[34] Lack of advertising would seem to be the answer, but the French were also peculiarly insular. Even ten years later, another journalist who kept a sharp eye on ski developments, E.-G. Drigny, complained that not enough had been done and therefore French ski towns were being neglected.[35] But this was not really true. As before the War, fervent concern was voiced not only over the economic struggles but also over the Germans; they were on the move again.

So the French hired Norwegian trainers, and the Ministry of Public Instruction encouraged local physical education classes to be followed by skiing. Eighty boys and girls put on a good show at Chamonix.[36] Things were looking up in 1929, but then came the Wall Street crash, the resulting political chaos in Germany, and the coming to power of the Nazis. France's fears were justified.

With the number of skiers rising, the French ski manufacturers tried to move into a market dominated by Scandinavians, Austrians, Germans, and Swiss. Even the Norwegians manufactured a special Alpine ski.[37] Abel Rossignol of Rossignol Skis was put in charge of a TCF-called meeting of ski manufacturers to lay out a plan for making and marketing French skis.[38] They could rely on the prewar establishments of Rossignol, Gleize, and Connink; and then came Chrétien at Gérardmer to serve the Vosges market, Amoudroz of Chamonix, and Duret at Habère-Lullin. They were joined by Norwegian expatriate Thor Tangvald at Courbevoie, Manufacture Franco-Suisse at Grenoble, Saint-Chamond's Societé Française du Ski et Canoe, the Lacroix brothers at Les Rousses for the Jura region, and a whole raft of smaller concerns, thirteen of them by 1936. In Nancy, skis with bakelite bottoms were manufactured.[39] There were calls for government protection, especially from import taxes on hickory wood, all of which came from the United States.[40]

France was economically on the move, yet competition kept on coming from abroad—sometimes with some rather novel ideas. Skis with aluminum and copper covering the wood were tried in Switzerland; duraluminum was found too dangerous, folding skis with heavy hinges impractical. There were laminated skis from Canada, the Gabrac metal-soled ski found favor among the Alpini, the Swedes experimented with aluminum and also with teak, the British tried steel, skis with "rear ends able to move . . . much like rudders" proved disastrous, and, for summer practice, roller skis appeared on the market. After two seasons of testing, an adjustable replacement tip was marketed by the well-respected London firm of Lillywhites.[41]

The senator from Savoy, Antoine Borrel, weighed in. Since so many French skiers went abroad, they had to be enticed to stay at home by a *"programme ensemble"* requiring full collaboration of transport, ski centers, and hoteliers. France must become a nation organized for winter sports.[42] *"Vite à l'oeuvre"* (let's get to work quickly), urged *La Montagne*.[43] Snow removal competitions were organized.[44] The Briançon-Grenoble route over the col de Lauteret was inaugurated by André Citroën leading the secretary of state for tourism and other politicians. They made it over the pass with chains on their wheels, and the whole escapade was viewed as a national triumph.[45]

There was no triumph on the race course. "Why did we do so poorly?" asked journalist Saint-Jacques after the 1928 St. Moritz Olympic Games. Underlying the poor selection process and unsound training, the fundamental reason was that *montagnards* were simply not open to the notion of sport and their parochialism made them indifferent to competition and particularly to international competition. Since the Norwegian boys who won just about everything at Chamonix (and again at St. Moritz) were working lads and woodsmen, the call had gone out in France to get skis to the mountain folk; but it would take many years of training to reach international competence. Among the urban clientele in the period between the Chamonix and St. Moritz games, the sport of downhill skiing had gained momentum over ski touring. The idea grew that city children might take ski vacations, that schools might include skiing in the physical education program, and that university students might benefit from this winter sport. *L'Illustration* felt it had to explain that putting the students from Grenoble Academy through their paces on skis "is, of course, for health and is good training for physical vigor." The department of Isère was the first to arrange a universities ski meet. It was the bourgeois rather than the mountain peasants who got intrigued by skiing and competing. This is not to say that Norwegians went out of style; it was always a coup to have Norwegians at French competitions. Martial Payot may have been France's national champion in 1928, but five Norwegians running *hors concours* "obviously win everything."[46]

There were some hopeful signs, with one name coming up repeatedly: Émile Allais—a mountain lad who had taken to Alpine skiing at Mégève. With all France's Olympic hopes pinned upon him in 1936, he was outdone by the Germans—he did get a bronze but that was not enough in the national battle—but he recouped and won the Arlberg-Kandahar in 1937 as well as the World Championship. James Couttet continued this golden run in 1938. Besides these two, the names of so many Austrians and Germans (and after the *Anschluss* it made little difference) dominated the race results and the sports magazines.

The year of Allais' triumph, the *École Nationale de Ski Français*—ENSF—was approved by the *Fédération de Ski Français*—FFS—on September 26, 1937, and received 300,000 francs from the government. Up until that time "it did not matter who could teach, nor where, nor how." [47] A French method of skiing, and particularly ski teaching, was needed. Schneider's Arlberg system had removed the telemark from the Alps and dominated the French-, English-, and German-speaking countries. *Das Wunder des Schneeschuhs* had been translated in 1930 as *Merveilles du Ski*. With the Austrian ambassador in attendance, Schneider was brought to Paris in November 1937 to talk on the present state of skiing. [48] Already ten years earlier in Switzerland, canton Graubünden had distinguished between guides and ski teachers. The first ski school was founded in 1929 at St. Moritz, and an instructors course was given in 1932. An instructors association, 500 members strong, affiliated with 54 ski schools was formed two years later. Swiss ski schools operated even in Strasbourg, Paris, Nice, and Amsterdam in 1935. [49]

Instructors may well have been the stars of the ski world, but those who won races were identified with a style of skiing hence, in the economic race to attract holiday makers, winning races became a matter of national concern. Herein lies the real importance of Allais' and Couttet's victories in 1937 and 1938; finally the French had a winner. It is unclear just what was being taught in French ski centers in the earlier 1930s. There were plenty of German texts available but "without doubt, . . . we follow a method we can call French." Georges Bargillat could not say what it was because it did not have exact rules; it came from experience "conforming to the genius of our race which wants simplicity, clarity and moderation." [50] Meanwhile Superbagnère was advertising its Arlberg method with teachers imported from Austria, the Stem-Club of Lyon had just been founded, Mégève had taken to the Arlberg, Kurt Wick from St. Anton wrote a primer (*École Arlberg*), and the Skimeister himself judged candidate-instructors at Mont Revard in 1936. "France now swears by the Arlberg," Gabriel Hanot told his readers in *L'Illustration*. [51]

But maybe for not much longer. In the face of the almost ubiquitous acceptance of the Arlberg system, what was it about the French method that proved attractive enough to lure Frenchman, at least, away from Schneider's system?

Allais had been, like many others, impressed by Austrian Toni Seelos's speed in the turns. He kept his feet together and seemed to achieve a seamless run by weight shifting and forward lean. Allais explained this new technique of missing the stages of stem turn and stem christiania, both staples of the Arlberg. Stiffer, steel-edged skis and bindings that fixed the boot tightly to the ski helped to reach this goal.[52] In 1937 he published *Ski Français*, the first major work to challenge Schneider's Arlberg technique. The "French declaration of independence" was how the influential Roland Palmedo reviewed it for an American audience.[53]

Émile Allais was France's first Alpine champion, expert in downhill and superb in slalom. In the world of ski racing there was little discussion about downhill, and much argument about slalom. Its Norwegian name and background played no part in the modern race. The slalom's modern form was Lunn-inspired and Lunn-ruled.[54] By the 1930s, the idea of slalom being a test simulating tree running had given way to its being a race between gates for speed only; style was immaterial. Some men had actually trimmed their skis down to about 190 centimeters to avoid catching the poles. Of course, that was deemed unfair. The New England Ski Museum holds one pair of skis with a dab of white paint on the tips. Splashed on by an official at the start of the 1937 downhill, it insured that the competitor would use the same pair in the slalom.[55]

Also there was still much argument about professionalism in the 1920s and 1930s. One way to solve the problem, as the Swiss did in 1932, was to have five different classes on race day: 1) Golden, 2) Guides and Teachers, 3) Amateurs, 4) Servants, and 5) Visitors.[56] That may have been acceptable on a local level obviously geared to include the tourists, but for large meets, especially international ones, the ski teacher was considered a professional. Instructor and *Slalommeister* Seelos, for example, never was named to the Austrian Olympic team.

The other way to give instructors the opportunity to race was to open the world competitions under FIS management to them.[57] These had begun in Mürren in 1931 under stormy conditions and one event was cancelled; in Cortina in 1932 the lack of snow exposed stumps and rocks, slalom poles made of stout wood were broken, and the crowd moved off down the same path on which the ladies were racing. Clearly FIS meets were not well organized. The Austrians in 1933 decided that something much better would be forthcoming. The 1933 FIS competition was held outside Innsbruck and the authorities determined to capitalize on the event; it became the first big-time organized ski meet: practice jumps and a 25,000-seat stadium at Bergisel were constructed. Special trains from northern Germany were announced, and for these visitors a whole program of activities was advertised: photo and winter clothing exhibitions, international boxing, bridge, and dancing competitions, various receptions, fireworks, and Tirol evenings and receptions. An FIS ball and prize giving ended the festivities. The skiing conditions were just passable. Lunn reported that the downhill, run on a 12-foot wide ribbon of snow, contained a glade where a succession of bumps were "nicely calculated to hurl the ski-runner . . . on to tree stumps." Heavy downpours of sleet and drizzle during the meet made everything more difficult. The Austrians entered about a hundred competitors, all the other nations about half a dozen. FIS actually had a rule on the books limiting the number of competitors to six per nation, so the Austrians simply described the race as "unofficial" and were not called on it. In spite of the difficulties, the Innsbruck organizers carried the meet off.

Innsbruck again hosted the 1936 FIS meet just after the Nazi Olympics. In a way it was supposed to show up the Germans because at the FIS meets, instructors were allowed to race and Austria had the top men. But the meet was a fiasco. The downhill was described as resembling a five-turn toboggan run that was completely iced over. Willy Steuri, "blood streaming from his face hit the stumps" and was carried off on a stretcher. It "was murder," said the American Norman Reid, a remark echoed by all the best skiers. One English racer mowed down some spectators, so did Rolande Zanni, the Italian, and Rudi Matt crashed after "an involuntary leap into the spectators." "I shan't race again at Innsbruck," said the conqueror of the Matterhorn's North Face, Hermann Steuri, "without my ice axe." Sigmund Ruud, the Norwegian jumper sliding sideways at speed, fell, and men counted five somersaults as he bounded off stumps and rocks. The crowd became hysterical. He survived. Standing at the bottom of the course, FIS President N. R. Østgaard of Norway must have wondered why he had ever allowed such ski goings-on as this to be sanctioned by his organization. He didn't say a word, not wanting to interfere with the downhill experts. A Swiss was not so silent: "The organizers ought to be hanged." The problem was that there was no one individual or committee absolutely in charge, although in Alpine matters everyone bowed to Arnold Lunn, and Lunn only postponed the start. After it was over, "we all agreed that the straight race should have been cancelled," he wrote as well he might; out of 54 competitors, 17 were too seriously injured to finish. René Levainville, writing in *Neige et Glace*, blamed the emphasis on the drive for tourist business for the fiasco. The fact that the piste itself was not policed made it more than just dangerous for the spectators, and, indeed, there were three stretcher cases and

One of Troyer's impressive posters advertised the FIS championships in Innsbruck in 1933, here in postcard form. The Austrian government realized that philately, too, might bring note to the event. (Author's collection)

one broken leg among those watching. Postponement was not an option as the Swiss and the French had to leave right away to ready themselves for their own championships. There were many lessons to be learned.

In Norway, meanwhile, the Norwegian ski fathers remained adamantly opposed to the Arlberg technique and any other Alpine method and competitions. They had forbidden their students to enter the downhill and slalom competitions at the Universities' World Championship at Cortina in 1928, and refused to send a team to the FIS Innsbruck meeting in 1933, although some Norwegians competed. Norwegian ski businesses offered to cover the expenses, but to the conservative clique running the Norwegian Ski Association that smacked of professionals racing. Besides, the team would also be racing against Alpine ski instructors and that proved a blatant acceptance of professional racing. The Norwegian racers themselves, and the press, all wanted to go to Austria but, opined *Der Winter,* "Dementis is of course possible."[58] Carl Luther's parting shot was part of a long simmering confrontation over Norwegian acceptance of Alpine skiing. There had been a belief that Norwegians had boycotted both the film and the book in the case of Fanck and Schneider's *Wunder des Schneeschuhs.* The book had sold 1,100 copies in Japan, not a copy in Norway. Norwegians were simply not interested in that sort of skiing.[59] The Europeans felt the Norwegian overlordship of the ski sport was heavy handed. They had simply had enough of Norwegian snootiness, and there were enough good skiers in the Alps who could show skill, speed, enjoyment, and the new technique to any Norwegian if he (or she) cared to join in.

UP-SKI REVOLUTION

The numbers of good Alpine skiers increased because they were able to ski so much more with ski lifts. Alpine Europe had many mountain railways, the funicular at Mont Revard dating from 1892. In the 1930s trams became common especially in France and Switzerland. One might think that the 1,000–2,000 materiel lifts built on the Dolomite front might have provided ideas and experience for peacetime skisport use. But no; it was not until 1934 that Ernst Constam's first *téléski* rose 300 meters up a 60-meter vertical at Davos to provide 62,000 skiers that first season with a simple, easy and cheap ride to the top. The next season St. Moritz had one, and in 1937 five more were built in Switzerland. All the lifts increased the number of downhill runs. The *téléférique,* said the *Revue du Ski,* "has created downhill skiing in France," and added that France was better equipped than other countries in Europe, for there were nine working in 1937.[60] Cable lifts of various sorts—*montes pentes*—numbered seventeen that year.[61] The *Syndicat National des Téléfériques* et *Téléskis de France*—SNTF—was founded in 1938. Following the success of the American invention of the chair lift, which debuted in the new resort of Sun Valley in December 1936, Europe's first was at Pustevny in Czechoslovakia in 1939.[62] All over Europe skiing was becoming so easy and skiers liked it that way. The effort of the climb to the top, once part of a winter culture, was eliminated by technology.

NAZI POLITICS AND NAZI OLYMPICS

Winter culture in Germany and increasingly in Austria was co-opted by the Nazis. The swastika had already flown at the FIS conference in Oberhof, Thuringia, in 1931,[63] and the Nazis were titillated by a *Hakenkreuz* found on old snowshoes from Ingermanland, Sweden.[64] *Der Winter,* long respected under Carl Luther's editorship, turned toward the Nazis as the 1934–35 season got underway. The header for October's issue was still social, November's depicted Aryan arrogance.[65] Already in 1933, photos of top Nazis inspecting ski facilities in the Harz had been published.[66] The Aryan clause became more prominent, and new clubs such as the Lauscha Winter Sports Association made it quite clear who could join: those 18 and over with no police record and who could prove Aryan descent.[67]

The German Ski Association was abolished in 1937. Josef Maier, who had been in charge of the DSV, became the leader of the new organization,[68] the *Fachamt Skilauf,* which took its place as part of the *Deutsche Reichsverband für Leibesübungen.* The *Anschluss* with Austria brought on a flood of Germanising: "*Gross-Deutschland:* the World's Strongest Winter Sport Nation!" Euphoria over Austria was equaled when parts of Czechoslovakia were brought into the Nazi fold. *Der Winter* headlined "Sudeten German Ski Lands Come Home to the *Reich.*"[69] Photographs of the Nazi elite at ski meets, of Himmler shaking hands with an SS patrol, and of other officers inspecting jumps appeared in the papers. Hitler, too, can be seen on the covers of the *Ski-Sport,* the *Fachamt Skilauf's* official magazine not just at the opening of the 1936 Winter Olympics, but also at the first National Socialist Meet. Yet Hitler had let it be known among his court that if he had his way he would "forbid these sports with all the accidents people have doing them," as Albert Speer recorded. Still, the Führer realized that "the mountain troops draw their recruits from such fools."[70]

Other matters weighed heavily on the Nazis supporting the skisport. It may have started as a folk sport, but patently by the 1930s it was a winter amusement for those with means. It may have made people healthy, but it also seemed to value individual performance rather than the *Gemeinschaft* the Nazis were building. Germany had been granted the Olympic Games before Hitler took over and of course Hitler could have canceled them, but he decided that the philosophical costs of mounting a winter spectacle in Garmisch-Partenkirchen followed by a summer extravaganza in Berlin far outweighed any concern he had about the embourgeoisement of the German people. To the contrary, here was a chance to show off the new German man . . . and woman. Women's events of downhill and slalom were on the Olympic program for the first time thanks to the close vote of 9 to 8 in the IOC.[71]

In the run-up to the Winter Games in February 1936, Nazi anti-Semitic policies created a furor among liberals in the Western world. The Olympic Committee had been assured that non-Aryans could participate.[72] IOC President Count Baillet-Latour and U.S. member General Charles Sherrill each called for and received assurances that anti-Semitic signs would be removed. A boycott was threatened if the Nazis failed to keep their word. The British ambassador had memoed his Foreign Office of the enormous importance the Nazis were attaching to the games; they were going to impress everyone on "the capacity and solidity of the Nazi regime."[73] Hitler had decided that the 775 competitors from twenty-eight nations should be impressed with the new Germany, and had ordered the contentious anti-Jewish slogans, placards, and posters removed from the roadsides leading from Munich to Garmisch-Partenkirchen and within the town itself.

This boycott was no mere threat. As early as August 1935, the American Commission on Fair Play, too, had called attention to the rife anti-Semitism, and Hitler had promised to have the posters taken down. That was enough for Avery Brundage, president of the American Olympic Committee and committed friend of the new Germany. Political maneuvering had "no significance in the world of sport," he pronounced, whether this was within Germany's borders or outside, "political policy . . . has no bearing." In speaking to a crowd of 20,000 at the German Day rally called by the American-German *Bund*, a pro-Nazi organization, he proclaimed, "No country since ancient Greece has displayed a more public interest in the Olympic spirit in general than you find in Germany." That audience ended by singing *Deutschland über alles* and the *Horst Wessel* song. Meanwhile he wanted his American teams selected on the basis of good character, unquestionable sportsmanship besides athletic performance.[74]

The movement for a major boycott was strongest in the United States, and it would have been a sporting disaster if their fifty-five team members were not present. There was also a movement in Britain where Arnold Lunn was trying to organize top churchmen—somewhat unsuccessfully.[75] France might well follow suit. But the boycott failed, Brundage prevailed, and the games of

Garmisch were opened by Hitler on February 6 just as the snow began to fall. After a dry spell, it was another of the Führer's miracles.[76]

> Que la neige soit!
> Et la neige vint.
> Skieurs, ayez foi
> / ans l'ordre divin.

> Let there be snow!
> And the snow fell fine.
> Skiers' faith was a-glow
> In the order divine.

Nazi opposition lost heart, according to Dr. Karl Rösen, when "English aristocrats, the very people who set such store by civilized standards, were prepared to accept the hospitality by thugs like Göring." He wondered if any of the Germany of Goethe would survive Goebbels. It would have been far better to have gone through with the boycott, he wrote to Lunn. Happily he kept Lunn's reply in which he expressed admiration for Rösen's anti-Nazi stand. Later, when he was captured by U.S. forces in Garmisch, he produced the letter and was immediately given a municipal position.[77]

The games were a golden triumph for Germany in the Alpine skiing events: Franz Pfnur for the men, and the remarkable Christel Cranz whose astonishing seven-second lead in the slalom pulled her into first place after a fall in the downhill. It seemed to prove that the Aryan man and woman were supreme.

The other European fascist power did not fare so well. Finding fantastic excuses, euphemisms of bad luck for poor performance, Italy's day was saved by a close win in the ski patrol race over the Finns. The win could not have been more fortuitous; the victory on the Garmisch cross-country course was instantly equated with military victory in the parched highlands of Ethiopia. "The glorious Alpine Soldiers come out at Garmisch as being the best soldiers in the world, proving the efficiency of the Army in every field," headlined *La Littorale*. (The Norwegians had not sent a team.) It was "the most important victory of the Fourth Winter Olympic Games," trumpeted *Neve e Ghiaccio*. (Not bad for a demonstration event). It was, said *Lo sport fascista*, "a warning to the whole world." The motto of the Central Military School of Alpinism at Aosta, "Dare and Believe," was made manifest to the Italian public.[78]

From start to finish, the Garmisch games were a controlled festival. The party rallies at Nuremberg had given the Nazis the know-how of event organizing, crowd control, spectacular showmanship: all were applicable to the world's Winter Olympic Games. "Immense," was the word journalist Jacques Dieterlen used in trying to capture the essence of Garmisch: "all is immense, exaggerated, nearly disproportionate"—the *Reichsarbeitsdienst* (Reich Labor Service) numbered 6,000. Later: "all is immense and all is singularly grave, posed, without any surprises, without any joy, no overflow of youthful gaiety." One sensed somehow that in Germany "one doesn't amuse oneself, one reconstructs and one hasn't the time to laugh."[79]

The youth of the white world may have been called to compete, but the Nazis co-opted them for their own purposes. The *New York Times* correspondent took a different view: tourists will go home "averring that Germany is the most peace-loving, unmilitaristic, hospitable and tolerant country in Europe."[80] The Nazi propaganda machine worked wondrously. All was quiet for some days after the games; then Hitler ordered his men into the Rhineland. Some believed that the games and the Rhineland occupation had been coordinated.[81]

Christel Cranz was the skiing star of the games, Sonja Henie was the skating star of the games. Women made their mark at Garmisch-Partenkirchen. Yet, in the fascist world, there was much ambiguity about elite sportswomen. The destiny of the Nazi woman was motherhood. Swimming, folk dancing, and gymnastics would foster grace in a woman. Strenuous sports endangered fertility.[82]

There was little discussion about children skiing. The *Hitler Jugend* (Hitler Youth) and the girls' *Bund Deutscher Mädel* (German Girls Alliance) and (for older girls) *Glaube und Schönheit* (Faith and Beauty), prepared boys for the tough world of Nazi expansion and the girls for Aryan motherhood. *Kraft durch Freude,* or "Strength through Joy," cadres were taught by specially trained instructors. The *Fachamt Skilauf* had 33,000 pairs of skis available for 35 Reichsmark a pair to those who joined the ski courses in the winter of 1935–36. Compared to the 900,000 enrolled in swimming activities, the number of skiers was small, but the well-trained youngsters formed the core of the Nazi *Jägerbattalione* of the Second World War.

The Hitler Youth's first ski meet took place at Marktneukirchen in Saxony on January 26–27, 1934. Seven hundred would take part in the next year's competition at Bad Reichenhall. Inspecting and giving prestige to the event, leader of the *Hitler Jugend* Baldur von Schirach, as well as that *alte Kämpfer* now Reichssportführer Hans von Tschammer und Osten, were on hand. Fifteen hundred were competing in skating and skiing events, and in 1939, the

"One Week of Winter Sports Insures a Year of Health" was probably France's most influential advertising phrase of the 1930s promoting skiing. The Paris-Lyon-Méditerranée (PLM) railway used it to entice passengers to skiing venues located along its lines. (L'Illustration, December 8, 1934. Author's collection)

high point was the inauguration of the *Führerwettkämpfe*—the Führer's competition,[83] a special race honoring Hitler himself, attesting to the importance the Nazis gave to skiing as they prepared for war.

Much enthusiasm was generated at the Hitler Youth ski school at Nesselwang, with its own special Adolf Hitler Ski Village. Ski instruction, race trials, and orienteering comprised the curriculum. "The ski school stands as a symbol of the bodily and world-view upbringing of the new German youth, the youth of the Führer and our Chancellor, Adolf Hitler." One hundred thousand boys were signed up to ski. Community living and song fests produced fit youth bound to the leader. And gas masks were available in January 1939.[84] So . . . it wasn't going to be just fun and games after all.

The French did not think so either. Hitler's success in marching into the Rhineland, his sweep into Austria unopposed, and his takeover of Czechoslovakia caused increasing worry about the fitness of their nation, especially the young, the pool of would-be recruits. At the Congress of the French Ski Federation (FFS), held in Marseilles late in September 1936, the president of the Provence Federation, Jean Vizern, exhorted delegates:[85]

> It is by skiing we must win back our youth, it is through the ski we must rekindle in youth the flame of faith which is disappearing. Those who are in charge of French skiing are the engineers and doctors. They know better than anyone else this need of the ski to recreate the body and soul, to renew the moral atmosphere where one can remake our people into a healthy race, enthusiastic, valiant. The ski is the path . . . the tonic . . . magic . . . miracle which will bring about the rebirth of healthy energies of the race, the resurrection of the flesh and the wakening of the heart.

Well might President Vizern have been worried as well as the delegates who had traveled south on the Paris-Lyon-Méditerranée train, leaving Paris and the northern cities with the slogan blazoned on the PLM posters: Eight Days of Skiing would Bring One Year of Health. In the winter of 1936, a hundred thousand Hitler Youth were gathering for ski training and orienteering. Could "one week of skiing for one year of health" compete?

CHAPTER 16 The Schneider Phenomenon

So macht man es. [This is how you do it.]
—*Hannes Schneider explaining how to ski, 1907*

I will put speed into everyone's skiing. It is speed that is the lure, not touring.—*Hannes Schneider, 1908*

$$MR^2 \frac{d\beta}{dt} + mr^2 \frac{da}{dt} = 0$$

$$da = d\beta \frac{MR^2}{mr^2}$$

—*French explanation of a Christiania turn, 1928*

In the early morning hours of March 12, 1938, Austria's most famous Alpine skier was ordered out of his home in St. Anton am Arlberg, leaving his wife and two children behind. He was taken with five others to the school and then to prison in Landeck. He remained there for twenty-five days before being permitted to go to Garmisch-Partenkirchen under a form of house arrest in the care of an old skiing competitor and friend, now lawyer, Dr. Karl Rösen. He was eventually allowed to leave Germany. The family was reunited in Munich before they took the train to Paris. At Le Havre they boarded the *Queen Mary* for the crossing to New York. The Schneiders arrived on February 9, 1939, and were taken to North Conway, New Hampshire, in the ski region of New England, where the Skimeister remained until he died in 1955. Behind these bare facts lay a mix of politics and sport the likes of which were never seen before or after. Since Hannes Schneider was the Alpine winter world's most well known and respected skier in the 1920s and 1930s, this was not the expulsion of a mere sportsman who transgressed Nazi policy nor, indeed, of a top competitor, though he had made a name for himself in the early years. In those days the stars of the skiing world were the instructors, not the best racers, and of all the instructors Schneider was the most renowned, a man whose ski technique and influence reached every corner of Alpine skiing's experience.

Schneider had taken ski lessons with Viktor Sohm—an adherent of the Norwegian technique—in the winter of 1903–04. In 1907, he recounted, "I received my call to St. Anton am Arlberg . . . as ski teacher."[1] Teaching in those days was demonstrating. Only Mathias Zdarsky had given thought to explaining the hows and whys of turns, and Schneider found Zdarsky's skiing labored. Still, Zdarsky's Lilienfeld method, along with his strong personality, attracted over a thousand to his classes in 1904.[2] Other instructors were also demonstrating only: Reinhard Spielmann in Semmering, Sebastian Monitzer at Kitzbühel, and Alois Skazel at Mürzzuschlag. Schneider, then, was not Austria's first professional instructor by any means. Besides, compared to Zdarsky he had so few pupils in 1907–08 that he spent much of his time experimenting with technique. Out of his lone experience came the snowplow, the stem turn, and the stem-Christiania, which he linked together to make possible a fairly fast, safe descent. Speedy and safe skiing became his mark, and the lean-forward and crouch positions marked a Schneider student. At the start, no one was around to share his enthusiasm. In fact, others, similarly insular, were trying out more or less the same manner of skiing: Eduard Capiti in Switzerland, and a Norwegian, Jakobsen, in Kitzbühel.

As Schneider put more emphasis on the stem-Christiania, he neglected the Telemark turn. Two factors indicated that this new technique was a success. In 1910, Schneider competed well in Switzerland, and he had excellent results with his teaching. He began to be noted abroad.[3]

That season proved exceptional in another way. Schneider now had so many pupils that he divided them up according to ability, taking "beginners" for two hours, "intermediates" for two hours, and "advanced" for two hours. Soon he was unable to teach everybody who came, so he recruited and trained some local lads as instructors for the following winter. When Walter Bernays, a regular St. Anton visitor, filled out his application to join the Ski Club of Great Britain in 1912, after listing his accomplishments of stem, and stem-Christiania turns, he added, "Did my last Telemark in 1912. Hope I shall die before I do another."[4] However gratuitous the remark, it shows just how effective Schneider's technique had become.

During the war, Schneider met an old student of his, Paul Passini, now *Leutnant* Passini, who immediately arranged for him to be seconded to the Italian front. Passini and Schneider first took 120 men between them. Then they selected the best, turned them into instructors, and received a new batch of men for ski training every four weeks. Although there were Austrian military manuals available,[5] and although Zdarsky's method was generally preferred by the top military command, Passini gave Schneider free rein. Since these were military courses, Schneider ordered and the men obeyed. He would carry this discipline into his civilian courses in the 1920s and 1930s.

SCHNEIDER AND FANCK: THE WONDERS OF SKIING

After the war came the films. *Das Wunder des Schneeschuhs* premiered in the Paulussaal (Paulus hall) in Freiburg im Breisgau in the autumn of 1920 to enormous enthusiasm. Next winter *Eine Fuchsjagd im Engadin* was a marvelous success. Dr. Arnold Fanck had found a new genre for his mountain films and Schneider showed the world what his ski technique could do. "Without him," Fanck wrote generously in his autobiography, "all my photographic knowledge . . . would not have come to much."[6] These films were shown worldwide and in a way were responsible for removing the Telemark turn from the Alps and converting the public to what was being called "Alpine skiing."

Films depicting skiing had been made before the war, in Europe, Japan and in the United States.[7] Arnold Fanck was fortunate in having Sepp Allgeier do much of the early filming. Allgeier had three excellent qualifications: he was an accomplished Schwarzwald skier, he had knowledge of filmmaking (having worked for Express Films of Freiburg), and he had made the 1913 Monte Rosa film in which Fanck and two others had taken part.[8] Fanck trained other cameramen; Hans Schneeburger became prominent. He found the perfect star in Hannes Schneider, and the men of his ski school made powder skiing in the Alps look fascinating, entrancing, dare-devilish, and heroic. One excellent skier was Luis Trenker, who went on to make his own films. Another was Otto Lang, who later made films in Hollywood.

Schneider starred in twelve films. Besides the two already mentioned, two others were particularly well received: *Die weisse Hölle vom Piz Palü* and *Der weisse Rausch* made in 1930. Fanck required men to chase the "fox," and Schneider's ski school provided the pack. Audiences thrilled to see the best skiers chasing the master in the most glorious Alpine settings.

Fanck needed a female lead. Leni Riefenstahl, contracted to play in *Der heilige Berg* in 1925, persuaded Luis Trenker to show her how to ski. She improved further under Walter Prager's guidance. By 1929, for *Die weisse Hölle vom Piz Palü*, she was accomplished enough on skis to play opposite him. Luggi Foeger doubled for her when truly expert skiing was required. She was actually selected to train for the German Olympic team,[9] but does not appear to have taken that seriously.

The films were superb propaganda for Schneider's ski school. During the Great War, slow-motion filming had been developed to help in the understand-

Nummer 1704 Illustrierter 13. Jahrgang 1931
Film-Kurier

Der weisse Rausch
(NEUE WUNDER DES SCHNEESCHUHS)
REGIE: DR. ARNOLD FANCK

Arnold Fanck and Hannes Schneider's most popular film, White Ecstasy, played to audiences around the world—except in Norway. Schneider, with Leni Riefenstahl in tow, while escaping a posse of his instructors, showed the world the poetry that his ski technique could accomplish in the pristine mountain powder. (Film Kurier, January 13, 1931. Author's collection)

ing of the curve and mass of a projectile. "The memory," wrote Fanck later, "of a shell as if it were floating in the air . . . boring itself leisurely, as it were, before my eyes through the thick armor-plating never left me." He bought one of these new "wonder instruments" weighing some 500 kilograms (1,100 lbs), lugged it up to 3,000 meters, and had instant success with the results.[10] The slo-mo shots still captivate today. At the time, one perceptive critic wrote that Fanck's films "have cultural values of the greatest importance." But what sort of culture? Was it that he made the natural world of rock, ice, and avalanche into living characters, as Béla Balazs wondered about *Stürme über Montblanc?* Or was it forceful propaganda for the culture of the noble, white, human elite, as Axel Eggebrecht warned in 1927?[11] The films also had a heroic quality to them, something that film historian Siegfried Kracauer believed was symptomatic of the toughened folk, men who struggled with rock, glacier, and snow, the sort of manhood upon which the Nazis could depend.[12] Susan Sontag, writing more of mountaineering than of skiing, saw Fanck's work as "beautiful and terrifying," an unlimited effort toward some mystical goal, in the same way that later was to be made both visible and actual in the worship of the Führer.[13]

Some of these analyses come, of course, with hindsight. Schneider, who was invariably pictured as an unspoiled villager, who ate simple meals, worked hard, and who skied magnificently, had none of these thoughts. But it was, to use Schneider's words, "the huge success of these films . . . which carried my technique out into the world." Many of the shots from *Das Wunder des Schneeschuhs* were used in the substantial instructional book of the same title.[14]

SKIMEISTER TO THE WORLD

In 1924 Schneider's method of teaching skiing was prescribed by the Land Tyrol for the entire region. Leading German instructors came to St. Anton and returned home committed to the Arlberg technique. The Tyrolean Ski Association and the Association of Tyrolean Professional Ski Teachers conducted the first ski instructors examination in February 1925, and the Germans in Allgäu and Bavaria followed suit. They conferred on Schneider the title *Ehrenlehrwart*—Honorary Instructor—and made him *Ehrenförderer*—Honorary Patron of the German Ski Association. School physical education teachers in the Tyrol were also required, by a 1928 law, to be skiers as well as proficient teachers of skiing—all following Schneider's system, by this time known as the Arlberg technique. No wonder the Swiss objected to "the canonization of Hannes Schneider."[15]

The objections were partially theoretical ones of technique, but these were comparatively unimportant outside of Scandinavia. What mattered in the

1920s was that each country should "win the peace," as the French had termed the economic competition for tourists after the Great War. If Schneider's Arlberg method of skiing and teaching became the Austrian and German way too, the Swiss were determined to find their own economic freedom outside of the Arlberg. In a long chapter in Roland Palmedo's book *Skiing: the International Sport,* published in 1937, Christian Rubi, head of the Wengen ski school, wrote of ski instruction in Switzerland without a mention of Schneider and the Arlberg technique. Arosa skiers found Schneider's method "ugly and unnecessarily strenuous."[16] The French who lagged behind the other Alpine countries, once they realized that the folk sport of cross-country running, so well exhibited by the Norwegians at the 1924 Chamonix Week, was not appealing to the moneyed crowd, simply imported Arlbergers to teach them how to schuss down their own alps.[17] An Austrian ski school was set up in London, and other Arlberg exponents began finding their way to the United States (Otto Schniebs) and later in the 1930s to Australia and New Zealand (the Skardarasy brothers and Friedl Pfeifer).[18]

Schneider's ski school was immensely successful, both in attracting tourists to St. Anton as well as spreading the Arlberg technique. His method, noted the London *Times* in 1935, "has come to be regarded as something with which it would be a sort of sacrilege to tamper." Hannes found himself invited to places as far away as the United States and Japan. The world—an upper-class and wealthy bourgeois world—came to the Tyrol to learn the master's technique. Kings of Rumania and Belgium shared classes with actors and actresses from Hollywood and Berlin, industrialists from England stemmed with financial men from Boston. Thousands of the more well-to-do of Europe, especially the Germans, were there "not so much to ski as with the set purpose of *learning* to ski." In January 1930 Schneider had eighteen salaried instructors and fourteen probationers on his staff. "One almost expects to hear a military bugle call," as classes were divided and promotions took place. The determination to learn was intense; "it oozes at every pore."[19] This sort of ski teaching is difficult for us to understand today. It found its critics when imported to the United States, but Schneider came from a world where discipline produced results and that was the way it worked.

Schneider and St. Anton got a further boost through the introduction of the Arlberg-Kandahar race, first held in 1928. Suggested by Arnold Lunn with the backing of his Kandahar Club, organized by Schneider and the Ski Club Arlberg, the first A-K turned out to be an international meet with 45 entries and 300 spectators. Two years later, 140 men and 28 women were entered, and the crowd swelled to 2,000.[20]

In fact, Schneider was not even present at this third running of the A-K; he was instructing in Japan.[21] This A-K had produced such a field of experts that it had obviously become the premier Alpine event of the world. 1930 was the same year that the FIS accepted downhill and—with much misgiving—slalom, for international competitions. Both disciplines would make their Olympic appearance in the 1936 Winter Games at Garmisch-Partenkirchen.

The A-K continued to prosper and results were weighed against other races. The Swiss "whose prestige had somewhat suffered as a result of the FIS [races]," were more than pleased when their man, Willy Steuri won both the "straight race," as downhill was called, and the slalom in 1935. It was the Arlbergers turn in 1936 with Friedl Pfeifer winning the slalom and taking a third in the downhill to get the combined.[22]

POLITICAL DISRUPTIONS ON THE RACE COURSE

Ominous, politically inspired hooliganism was fomented by the Nazis. The 1934 A-K course at St. Anton had been guarded day and night for the 116 men and 24 women competitors.[23] At Kitzbühel in 1933 and again in 1934, the Hahnenkamm race had to be canceled. At Hall, just before the last event of the Land Tyrol championships, "*Deutschland über alles*" took over the proceedings and competitors and spectators sang the Nazis'"Horst Wessel" with Hitler salutes.[24] Austria had to abandon many races that season because of Nazi disruption, and there was no FIS representative to which they could complain. Small beer, perhaps, compared to the unremitting, virulent Nazi radio campaign, the nazification of the *Heimwehr* and the attempted assassination of Chancellor Engelbert Dollfuss. Still, it was something to contemplate, especially when in July Chancellor Dollfuss was killed and the care of Austria was given to Kurt von Schuschnigg. He was eventually browbeaten by Hitler and his cohorts into pardoning Austrian Nazis and taking certain Nazis into his cabinet. Economic pressure was applied when the Nazis levied a 1,000 Reichsmark tax per German crossing the border from June 1, 1933. This crippled many ski villages, but some, like Kitzbühel, were able to make up for the loss of German custom by appealing to the French and English, the high point being the visit of the Prince of Wales in February 1935. Under interrogation at the Nuremberg trials, Franz von Papen candidly described the border tax as the "first step toward preparation for *Anschluss*." There was general relief when it was lifted after three years.[25]

Schneider had been attacked in the socialist newspaper *Der Rote Adler*, and later in the *Schwarze Korps* he was described as "a ravenous Jew" and "devourer of Nazis" (*Nazifresser*). On the other side, Arnold Lunn extolled Schneider's

Hannes Schneider (right) hobnobbing with the chancellor of Austria, Kurt von Schuschnigg (left), the man who had taken over after the Nazis had murdered Dollfuss and who would be brow-beaten by Hitler into taking Nazis into his cabinet. On March 11, 1938, he resigned. The German army moved into Austria the next day. (Courtesy Herbert Schneider and New England Ski Museum)

"granite-like integrity which is unaffected by the vacillations of political fashion." He was referring to Schneider's support of one-time president and benefactor of the Ski Club Arlberg, apostate Jew Rudolf Gomperz. He had been director of tourism for many years in St. Anton, and had been responsible, irony of all ironies, for arranging for Germans to take a special course with Schneider in the winter of 1926–27. Between 1927 and 1932 about two thousand Germans came to St. Anton annually, characterized as a "pre-*Anschluss*" takeover by one French critic. The Austrian Nazis were particularly incensed that Schneider maintained ties to his old friend Gomperz.[26] He had also had run-ins with Leni Riefenstahl while filming. At the time they were merely arguments, but after Riefenstahl's monumental success with her ideological films of the party rallies and the 1936 Berlin Olympics, *"la grande dictatrice du cinéma allemand"* had influence at the highest levels. After the difficulties she had had with Schneider, she was spitefully content to see him imprisoned.[27]

The 1937 A-K was held in Mürren, Switzerland—Lunn's seat of empire—with Willy Walch from the Arlberg winning the straight race. He was beaten for the combined by the French ace, Émile Allais. Christel Cranz dominated the women's events as expected.[28] Politics seemed not to enter into this occasion on neutral ground.

ANSCHLUSS

When the *Rote Adler* launched an attack on the "the two clever dicks" (*beiden Schlaumeier*) of St. Anton, Schuler and Schneider, and went on to characterize Schneider's economic control as "shop satrapy" (*Geschäftssatrapie*),[29] twenty-four of his full-time instructors signed a statement refuting the allegations. One did not. Even though Schneider did not ask for his resignation, Karl Moser fled to Nazi Germany for protection.[30] This incident, according to Hans Thöni, a biographer of Schneider, became enough of an affair to help Dollfuss defeat the Socialists.[31] The Nazi press (discounting the articles portraying Schneider as a pro-Jewish, anti-German economic exploiter) certainly knew him as a pro Dolfuss-Austria man, whom the chancellor had named "Austrian Sport Consul"—and which Schneider had refused.[32] No matter, the Ski Club Arlberg was struck from the rolls of the German Ski Association in May. If the Nazis could not cripple the capitalist Schneider by criticism, then they could by causing economic hardship: the 1,000 Reichsmark border tax made life difficult for many folk in the village, but the ski school survived, thanks, in part, to Rudolf Gomperz' efforts.[33] Schneider's prestige continued to spread as a number of his instructors left to found "The American Branch of the Hannes Schneider Ski School" in the eastern United States, while Schneider himself performed at the ski shows in Boston and New York in 1936.[34]

But in 1938, in the night and morning of March 11 and 12, Hitler's *Anschluss* began. Schneider and five others were taken in the early hours first to the school, and then to Landeck jail.[35]

That day Alice Wolfe, a wealthy American who had made St. Anton a second home since the 1920s, and who had become an organizer, sponsor, coach, and confidante of American women skiers and women's teams, called Arnold Lunn, who happened to be in Rome. Lunn, who had, in fact, already received the news, immediately caught the train north to St. Anton and convened a meeting of the Kandahar Club. It was a foregone conclusion that the A-K race, scheduled for the following week, would be canceled. Four members made up

A typical advertisement in the
United States for Arnold Fanck's
film Der weisse Rausch, *now called*
The Ski Chase. *The only name that
matters is Hannes Schneider; Fanck
is not even mentioned. When the
German editions of* Wunder des
Schneeschuhs *were published,
the authors were always Fanck and
Schneider. In the English translation,
they were listed as Schneider and
Fanck. (Boston Evening Transcript,
1936. Author's collection)*

a subcommittee and drafted a letter to the Ski Club Arlberg explaining how impossible it would be to run the A-K without Hannes since "he enjoys the affectionate respect of all those who have helped to organize or who have competed in this event." It would be, the letter went on, "an unthinkable dereliction if we were to hold the race under these tragic circumstances."[36]

Lunn then tackled Karl Moser, the Schneider instructor who refused to disavow the 1934 *Rote Adler* article and who had now returned as Nazi mayor of St. Anton. He told him that the traditional A-K simply would not be held. The name Kandahar was not to be used. Moser became flustered and decided to go to higher authority. Dr. Martin in Vienna, one time Austrian FIS representative, discovered that he too could make no decision. Lunn telegraphed one-time SA lynch-gang leader,[37] now *Reichssportführer,* Hans von Tschammer und Osten, who immediately saw a way out. Well and good, if it was not going to be the Arlberg-Kandahar, let it be the first Arlberg race. But Lunn did not have it all his own way. An irate member of the Ski Club Arlberg scolded him for canceling the race, "mixing up sport and politics." Lunn, never at a loss for a bon mot, inquired icily if Schneider had been imprisoned because he skied badly.[38] The Germans were not about to bow to pressure from a bunch of Anglo-Saxon ski racers led by an irascible old Englishman who did not even ski particularly well. The race did take place though boycotted by the British, Americans, French, and Swiss. Baron Peter le Fort from the *German Ski-fachamt* praised the sixty men and fifteen women for making the First Arlberg Race such a success.[39]

Meanwhile, Mrs. Wolfe was doing something eminently practical for Schneider and his fellow prisoners. By bribing the jailers, she had regular meals brought in to the prisoners on a daily basis. She also started casting around for influential help. Austrian state secretary Schmid was contacted, and her local hunting guide made state minister Esser aware of Schneider's difficulties. He promised help if needed.[40] Pressure came from other quarters. The Colorado Arlberg Ski Club, headquartered in Denver, "all Aryans, incidentally," telegraphed Hitler unanimously protesting the recent persecution and incarceration of Schneider and urged Hitler "to use influence, if any, to obtain his amnesty." The club threatened a boycott of German ski resorts and competitions. The more influential Amateur Ski Club of New York sent wires; the Orange Mountain Ski Club, of Orange, New Jersey, wondered how it could entertain a visiting German team for an upcoming race.[41] But more than telegrams and threats were needed.

Help came from two very different men. And here the tale takes a further political turn.[42] Attorney Dr. Karl Rösen of Garmisch-Partenkirchen, longtime friend of downhill and slalom, had been appointed by the Bavarian High Court as legal counsel for Hitler in his defense at the Beer Hall Putsch trial in February-March 1924. Although Hitler conducted his own defense, the Nazis appear not to have forgotten Rösen's service. There is, however, not a word about Rösen as public defender in the three books of documents I have looked at, one of which was *Der Hitler-Prozess vor dem Volksgericht in München*, a verbatim report published immediately after the trial. There is not a word on Rösen in Ernst Deuerlein's Bavarian documents, nor in Lothar Gruchmann and Reinhard Weber's four volumes, *Der Hitler-Prozess 1924*. Hanns Hubert Hoffmann's *Der Hitlerputsch, Krisenjahre deutscher Geschichte 1920–1924*, generally acknowledged the best book on the Putsch, also makes no mention of Rösen. The documentary evidence, then, is entirely lacking. In fact, the only piece of written evidence remotely associated is that Alice Wolfe wrote that she met secretly in Innsbruck with a lawyer who had done work for the Nazis.[43] Whether this was Rösen or not one cannot say. Yet Otto Lang, one of Schneider's close associates and a man to whom he wrote fairly regularly when he first arrived in the United States, said that it was common knowledge that Hitler owed Rösen a favor.[44] Rösen, a man who had refused to be bribed with an important party position, was never a member of the NSDAP;[45] however he was able to make connections through a regular St. Anton visitor, *Oberleutnant* Betzold, who worked in Göring's adjutant's office in the *Reichsluftfahrtministerium* under *Ministerialrat* Drabe and made it possible for Rösen to speak to Drabe. He must have been effective; Drabe, apparently on his own initiative, then brought the Schneider case to Göring's notice. A Rösen memorandum detailing Schneider's importance for Arlberg tourism also impressed the Nazi elite.[46] Göring had already been lobbied by Edith, Lady Londonderry, one of a coterie of English aristocrats who felt that the way to deal with Hitler was to befriend him. She was particularly exercised by the fact that Schneider was supposed to have taken a part at Obergurgl in the third annual Londonderry Snow Eagle race for which she had presented a cup. She and her husband had also entertained the Ribbentrops and had been entertained by the Görings. They were on such a personal level that she liked to think of the *Reichsmarschall* as "my Siegfried." Göring had replied that he would look into the Schneider matter.[47] Rösen was given powers to manage the Schneider case, thus bypassing the local Innsbruck Gestapo office.[48]

Dr. Fritz Todt had also made occasional visits to St. Anton and he knew Schneider superficially, so here Rösen contacted his friend Wörner who had once employed Dr. Todt to argue for Schneider's release. Wörner also informed Hermann Esser, state secretary in the tourist department of the Reich's Propaganda Ministry, who promised help if needed.

With Rösen, Schneider went to see *Ministerialrat* Drabe, who immediately wanted to know if Rösen was acting as Schneider's lawyer but was told he was merely a friend. Schneider stated his case factually, with no nastiness or vengeful attitude. He left an excellent impression. Although Rösen maintained his "friend" status, it was observed that the "handling of all the negotiations does not lack the know-how which any savvy lawyer would use in such affairs." Rösen had opened up a Schneider file and it was full of documents.

THE AMERICAN CONNECTION

After twenty-five days in Landeck prison, Schneider was permitted to take the train to Garmisch-Partenkirchen to be under Rösen's eye. He may have actually stayed with Rösen for a while; later he lodged at the Gasthof Melber. Rösen's house remained his address for official mail. Schneider had no idea how long this comparatively liberal form of house arrest in Garmisch-Partenkirchen would last. He felt hopeful; he was offered the directorship of the ski school there, but this was later rescinded;[49] obviously German Nazis tried to capitalize on the Skimeister's fame. The Austrian Nazis remained antagonistic, even hatched a plan to "capture" Schneider from Garmisch, and took out their spite on his family back in St. Anton.

In mid November 1938, Schneider sent a typed, six-page, single-spaced letter with much accompanying documentation to *Reichsführer* of the SS, Heinrich Himmler. It was an item-by-item evaluation, rejection, and commentary on the many accusations brought up over the previous four years. The careful organization, the logical and clear responses, the not-quite-legalese of the document give the impression that behind the writer was a legal mind. Hannes Schneider, after all, left formal schooling at fourteen. Rösen must have outlined the arguments, talked them over with Schneider before finalizing the request; there isn't a spelling mistake in the six pages. It was supported by many other documents and presented an excellent case for permitting Schneider to leave Germany. It ended by requesting a "personal interview with a specialist from the *Reichsführer's* office."[50] The letter has a dual quality to it. It is obviously a personal refutation that Schneider is making, and yet the manner in which it is written is almost abrupt. It pulls few punches. "Moser gave orders that I was not to be greeted." "I was visited in Garmisch-Partenkirchen by people from St. Anton, even Nazis." "My situation was demolished by influences from St. Anton, maybe Innsbruck." "I am pure Aryan." "I was never in a concentration camp." And so on. One of the supporting documents, and there were five of them, was "My Behavior Towards Herrn Bürgermeister Moser:" six pages long (one page is missing), written in non-legalese, with occasional spelling mistakes, it is the personal details that give it authenticity—very different from Schneider's letter to Himmler.

It appears, then, that Rösen sent Schneider to Berlin when it was probable that the Austrian Nazis might kidnap him, and he had been very cordially received in Berlin.[51] Himmler had signed the papers. Hannes's refusal to explain any of these things played against him from time to time.

Besides the offer of heading up the ski schools at Garmisch-Partenkirchen, he had received offers from St. Moritz, from Lake Placid, site of the 1932 Olympic Games, and from Canada; but the most attractive was from a Harvey Gibson of North Conway, in ski country New Hampshire, from where real help emerged. Gibson proposed a five-year contract for room and board in a fully furnished house with a cook, plus $3,000 for each four-month long winter season. As long as nothing interfered with the development of North Conway as a ski center, Hannes could consult, fish, hunt, and travel.[52] How and why was this man, relatively unknown to the ski world, willing to present such an offer?

Benno Rybizka, one of Schneider's St. Anton instructors, had been hired to run "The American Branch of the Hannes Schneider Ski School" at North Conway. Rybizka had the ear of Harvey Gibson, a native of the town, part owner of the ski development, and on the boards of many local institutions. Gibson was well known as president of the Manufacturers Trust Company of New York, a large merchant bank. In this matter, however, he was far more influential as the chairman of the American Committee for the Short-Term Creditors of Germany.

Gibson had already had many dealings with Hjalmar Schacht, the Special Currency commissioner of the newly opened Rentenbank in 1924. Schacht received his appointment only a week after Hitler's abortive Beer Hall Putsch of November 8–11, 1923. His was a herculean task: to convert the worthless paper into a currency based on the value of land and industry in Germany. Schacht, Hitler's "financial wizard," to use William Shirer's well-known characterization, had been sent to Washington immediately after Franklin Roosevelt's election in 1933. In 1938, actually on the day after the Arlberg-Kandahar race should have taken place, Schacht, as president of the Reichsbank and Minister without Portfolio in Hitler's cabinet, addressed the Austrian bank in Vienna and extolled the *Anschluss,* now a week old, as "a communion of German will and German thought." Patently, Schneider was not part of this communion. In Gibson's autobiography, he only hints at what went on in the year of negotiation. Schacht, he wrote, was "anxious to do me favors, and very kindly interested himself in the matter" of Schneider's release. Schacht had taken lessons at St. Anton,[53] and one cannot help wondering whether memories of those Arlberg days in the snow played a role. Probably not; money was what counted. How much money was passed over by Gibson's representative, or what changes in the German debt structure were negotiated in exchange, one cannot say based on the available evidence. On his side, Schneider would be free to leave Germany with his family on one condition: he was never to talk about his experience.

The official line was that he was leaving for contracted employment, but the details of his contract with Harvey Gibson were not public knowledge. In fact, Gibson had trouble with his Board of Directors in North Conway, since some did not wish to give Schneider a five-year contract.[54] Gibson had to buy them out. It was a disadvantage that Schneider was not to talk of his troubles; he was accused of harboring Nazi sympathies. To exchange prison for the comforts of Rösen's home and the Gasthof Melber could easily be misinterpreted.

Gibson's representatives met the family in Paris and saw them through to Cherbourg and aboard the *Queen Mary* for the Atlantic crossing to New York. Only a few people knew of Schneider's expected arrival in New York. It was publicly announced two days before the *Queen Mary* docked. There was immediate jubilation in New England's ski community. Expectations soared: Schneider would repeat the phenomenal success of his St. Anton Ski School in North Conway. When a small group of people met him it included a few reporters. He was immediately asked about his difficulties with the Nazis. He "had nothing to say about it,"[55] and that was that because the press had agreed not to press the question.

What do we make of this mix of politics and sport in the late 1930s?

Schneider's removal was accomplished by Austrian Nazis acting out, vendetta fashion, to settle old grievances. Karl Moser had left the ski school in 1934 after the abortive Nazi coup vowing vengeance on his return. Having removed Schneider, the Austrian Nazis discovered that their masters, the German Nazis, had an international problem on their hands. The very fact that Schneider was offered the job of coordinating the ski schools at Garmisch-Partenkirchen, tantalizingly close to St. Anton, must have been as much of a temptation to him as it would have been a sporting and propaganda coup for the German Nazis. But Schneider was the sort of Austrian who would not go along with the post-*Anschluss* hurrahs of "Two souls with one mind" ("*Zwei Seelen, ein Gedanke.*")

That he ended up in the United States is not so surprising; not a few of his instructors—and other Austrians too—were already there and in charge of ski schools. There were four from St. Anton in North Conway alone. Benno Rybizka, the director of the ski school, knew that he would lose his job the moment Schneider arrived. He did, in fact, become assistant director.

The financial finagling between the representatives of Gibson and Schacht was crucial in bringing Schneider to the United States, and more particularly to North Conway. Pressure came from many skiers, men of the stature of Lunn and Palmedo. Rösen found the letters and petitions, particularly from foreigners of help in making his case.[56] After the success of the *Anschluss* and the comparatively minor political fallout it engendered, the canceling of the A-K was awkward for the Nazis but that was about it.

Besides, all this soon faded. Schneider arrived in the United States on February 9, 1939. September 1 was less than seven months away.

CHAPTER 17 The Russo-Finnish War

"WHITE BATS on Skis"
—Headline in the London Times, *December 11, 1939*

*They are so many, and our country is so small. Where shall we
bury them?—Popular saying during the war*

 The *Années Folles* had really ended with the fascist domination
of central Europe. For some, the Rome-Berlin axis provided a
comforting barrier to any communist Soviet expansion. The
appeasing West saw itself beset by ideologies of the far right
and the far left, and America, isolationist anyway, was so far
away.

BEFORE THE WAR

Hitler and Stalin teamed up in August of 1939 to the amazement of peoples
and politicians alike. The fear for Poland consumed the British and the French.
Negotiating with the Russians too, the Allies had taken note that the Russians
still were thinking of Finland as part of the long-standing Tsarist bloc of Baltic
states, whereas for Western negotiators, Finland was part of Scandinavia. But
they gave little or no thought to any Russian intentions to demand territory
from Finland.

Immediately after the Nazi-Soviet Pact came the dreaded September 1 attack
on Poland. The Germans overwhelmed the Poles, and Europe and the world
was astonished. Where would the next blow fall? No one knew; it was eerily
quiet. On September 17, Soviet troops invaded Poland; on the 29th Estonia
granted Russian demands for naval and air bases; a week later Latvia gave similar concessions; five days after that, Lithuania concluded a fifteen-year mutual
assistance pact. On November 26 the Finns rejected all Russian requests. Four
days later, the Soviets attacked them on three fronts.

SOVIET INVASION

The Russians expected a quick victory as a matter of course since they had
overwhelming advantages of manpower and industrial capacity. But winter—
"General Winter," Napoleon had called it—was on the side of the Finns.
Ski-running was a regular seasonal activity, "an instinctive skill," the *Times*

Evoking the biblical David and Goliath story, cartoonist Leslie Illingworth asks, "Who aids?"
(Punch, *February 21, 1940.* Author's collection)

assured British readers.[1] For the invading Soviet troops, a *Russian Manual of Ski-Fighting* had quickly been printed in October and November, more useful for tourist than for soldier. Finns were scathing about its many elementary errors.[2]

The Finnish army of 200,000, many operating in small ski sections, faced forty-five Russian divisions. In this most bitter of winters, the Russian armor and artillery were halted, surrounded, and dispatched by men camouflaged in white, soldiers who, phantom-like, appeared from the woods and slipped away almost unseen. Even when the Russians sent in experienced ski men, the Finns caught them crossing the ice and annihilated them.[3] No one heard of Finnish disasters because they never let any correspondent witness a defeat. No photos were allowed of the dead. Until the end of the war the news that got out, wrote American reporter Carl Mydans, was of an "unbroken series of Finnish successes."[4] The Finns were so successful in their ski actions that they believed it was only a matter of time before help would arrive from abroad.[5]

In France, Britain, and America, Finland had been held in deep regard before the Soviet invasion. The country seemed a bastion of democracy even with the difficulties of sharing a long border with the communist behemoth to the east. Finland had also continued to repay its debt throughout the Depression, the only country to do so, something particularly impressive to the Americans.

When the Soviets attacked, the Finns seemed to stand up so well for democracy, justice, freedom—the very objects France and England were supposedly fighting for. Here was "a little people," reminiscent of Belgium in the First World War, putting up such a valiant resistance while the so-called phony war was preoccupying the major powers. "Finland" became a cause that one could support wholeheartedly without breaking one's normal life routine. "For three months Paris and the Côte d'Azur staged galas for Finland. If you wanted to fill the Opera or the Cannes Carleton this would do it," wrote Alfred Fabre-Luce in his perceptive journal. "Would you like to see a few beautiful girls parade by in the latest fashion while having your tea? Finland would serve as the pretext."[6] Arthur Koestler, in a concentration camp in France at the time, was even more biting; each Finnish victory was welcomed as if it were France's own. The Frenchman was like "a voyeur who gets his thrills and satisfaction out of watching other people's virile exploits, which he is unable to imitate."[7] The journalists' descriptions of phantom soldiers in their white cloaks, of bursting incendiaries among the great freeze of winter, and of flashing displays of the northern lights thrilled the French public, who saw the Mannerheim line as a northern Maginot Line defended by winter sportsmen.[8] For the political right, the Finnish war seemed the successful beginning of the crusade against Bolshevism. It was action, sporting and manly, in comparison to the *Sitz-Krieg* on the Western Front.

Volunteers from the Fifth Scots Guards began ski training in Chamonix. Much welcomed by the locals and the Chasseurs Alpins,[9] they were part of an International Volunteer force under the command of Teddy Roosevelt's son, Kermit.[10]

Finland inspired the same sort of romantic attachment that the Spanish

Finnish immigrants parade in St. Paul, Minnesota, U.S.A., before leaving to join the international brigade on the Karelian front in the Russo-Finnish War. They arrived after the conflict had ended. (Author's collection)

Civil War had commanded (bringing together like-minded American leftists who formed the Abraham Lincoln Brigade). Now the Russo-Finnish War attracted some 350 men to the Finnish-American Legion, as part of the 11,500 foreign volunteers recruited from thirty nations.[11] They came from the Finnish immigrant communities of the midwestern United States.[12] Quite suddenly American skiers' sport had a new purpose, and they subscribed willingly to the Finnish Relief organization while they reveled in learning that one patrol had covered 350 kilometers in twelve days to blow up a railroad line.[13] Photos of the phantom Finns—this description recurs time and again—appeared in the ski magazines. The Finnish skiing troops impressed the American army leadership to some extent, although they had "no intention of creating an army on skis." But it might see action in Alaska or some other northern front, so experiments were to take place during the winter of 1940–41 in the snow belt regions of the country.[14] David Bradley, a Dartmouth College skier and would-be Olympic team member for 1940, was sent to Finland to observe and report. He arrived the day after the armistice was signed.

I talked to David Bradley while he looked over the treasured scrapbook of his days in Finland. A midwesterner, with expertise in all facets of skiing,

Who could doubt, with drawings like this, that doughty little Finland was bringing the behemoth Soviet communist state to its knees? (La Domenica del Corriere, June 14, 1940. Author's collection)

he was an experienced cross-country runner; but when he tried skiing with the *pieksu*, the boots with the turned up toes pushed under a simple leather strap, he had trouble controlling the skis. This simple binding was precisely what made it possible for the Finnish troops to get into and out of their skis so quickly, though not all the ski troops had such type of equipment. When the biggest factory to produce skis with release bindings was bombed by the Russians,[15] the *Touring Club de France,* along with the *Club Alpin Français* and the *Ski Club de Paris,* began a collection of skis.[16] "I was not impressed by the skis of the leisured classes," commented John Langdon-Davis.[17] Many, even

Donations of skis piled up in France in 1940 may look impressive to the uninitiated, but they were the wrong kind of equipment and too late anyway to aid in the defense of Finland against the Soviet Union. (L'Illustration, *March 2, 1940.* Author's collection)

most, were downhill skis with fixed bindings requiring a special boot, all more suitable to Font Remeu than Finland.

Editorializing, Dr. Sandoz, who wrote frequently for the French ski publication, *Neige et Glace,* praised the Finns for having given "the most magnificent proof of services rendered by the practical sports of a people . . . its athletes have been the best in the world"—he was thinking of the ski racer Niemi who had distinguished himself at the longer distances—"and it is these athletes that are the most zealous defenders of their country." He likened the Finnish heroes to the Greek resistance to Artaxerxes' hordes, to the opposition of the Swiss peasantry to the Holy Roman Emperor. He finished by congratulating them on a job well done, one that "can be imitated."[18] There had been a hope—there were so many hopes in France in 1940—that the "courage and wisdom of the peasant people of Finland would find a ready echo in our own people."[19] The idea that it would be the best of the nation, the unsophisticated, unspoiled, un-urbanized mountain country boy who would come to the rescue of an unnerved France was as attractive as it was illogical.

The London *Times* took a different view. The editor was struck by the combination of premodern and modern in this war. "While Helsinki suffers or expects all the latest devilries of aerial bombardment, the snowbound regions of the north are attacked and defended in a world of reindeer transport and skis."[20] But modern power did eventually win, and all the West would do was wrap their failures in poems about "Finland Snow":

Hide her away, we dare not look upon her
Who bore the Christian banner for her own
And held that stale anachronism, Honour,
Sacred, and strove to keep it so, alone.[21]

For all the modernization that had gone on over the almost six thousand years of ski activity, it is an odd coincidence that this process was brought to a symbolic end by the return to the practical use of skis that would have been recognized thousands of years before. Fridtjof Nansen's use of skis to cross Greenland spawned the sport of skiing that from then on until the Second World War developed into its modern form. Yet, at the very end, the Finns relied on the ancient type of equipment to see them through a modern war in the snow. They could not win the war alone and had to sue for peace. But the spectacle of the iron and steel monsters of Soviet military might opposed by those ancient and well-tried, even homemade, traditional skis, is one of the astounding images of skiing's long history.

Epilogue

The whole subject requires, of course, far fuller and more systematic treatment. . . . It is strange that this has not been done hitherto, but such is the case, notwithstanding the really important part which "ski" . . . have evidently played in the history of civilization.
—Fridtjof Nansen, 1890

It is possible to attach too much significance to the history of a sport, but it is also possible to under-estimate the social reactions of sport on national life.—Arnold Lunn, 1927

 Looking over skiing's six-thousand-year history, I am struck by the immense time span during which skis were purely of utilitarian value. They were an essential part of the folk culture of snowy lands. The bog skis and their modern counterparts used right up into the 1930s by an occasional outdoorsman hunting deer or fox, were instruments of necessity, as were those of the Finnish troops who dealt death to the Soviet forces frozen in the Finnish woods. Skis over the millennia changed shape only slightly, and the single pole remained in use into the twentieth century. Bindings varied according to usage, locale, and available material but remained more or less the same up to the time of the Finnish war.

If the tools for skiing hardly changed, industrialism brought about a profound change in their use. A new urban sector of society took to skiing as leisure-time enjoyment, as winter sport. Toward the end of the nineteenth century, the wealthy and urban bourgeois acquired their skiing skills from the folk skiers. Sondre Norheim and his fellow skiers from the remote Telemark valley displayed their expertise to the Christiania bourgeois, who were so enthusiastic that they even joined a ski school run by these peasants. Norwegian immigrants working as loggers in the mill town of Berlin, New Hampshire, showed the wealthy university men of nearby Dartmouth College how to jump.

The bourgeois of Christiania also did something else—as did the university students in America—which is characteristic of modernization: they created a special skiing venue, Huseby; and when that proved unsatisfactory because of its inconsistent snow depth, they moved to Holmenkollen, and there, at the annual competition, Norwegian nationalism came to be put on view. Four thousand miles across the Atlantic, one student founded an entirely new club—the Dartmouth Outing Club—from which winter sports, but especially skiing, spread to the nearby universities, then to the entire region. It made of one particular high mountain spot, Tuckerman Ravine, backed by a 900-foot headwall, a spring pilgrimage destination—which it remains to this day.

For over five thousand years the imperative for putting on skis was necessity: food, fuel, visiting, trading, and war. There was little change. The mention of a few names such as Arnljot, Trysil Knud, Lemminkainen, the Birkebeiner rescue, we owe mostly to nineteenth-century romantic idealists. But as skiing became a sport, names of people who influenced the development of skiing (many of which have found their way into the present book) can literally fill up pages. From Norway: Angell, Huitfeld, Nansen, Nielsen (Bjarne), Norheim, Østgaard, Qual, Roll, Samson; from neighboring Sweden: Balck, Nordenskiold; from Austria: von Arlt, Bilgeri, Kleinoscheg, Resch, Schadek, Schneider (Hannes), Schollmeyer, Schruf, Sohm, and Zdarsky. The Czech Rössler-Orovsky, Poles Barabasz, Marusarz, and Zaruski and the Slovenian Badjura played leading roles. The Swiss Amstutz, Badrutt, Iselin, and Straumann and the Italians Ghiglione, Hess, and Zavattari would join the French contingent of Allais, Clerc, Cuënot, Duhamel, and Mlle. Marvingt. The Germans Frl. Cranz, Hoek, Luther, Paulcke, Rickmers, Rotter, and Schneider (Max) and the Englishmen Caulfeild, Lunn, and Richardson would also be on the list. Immigrants to the United States like the Hemmetsveits, Hovelsen, Schniebs, Tellefsen, and Thompson joined by the Americans Harris, Mrs. Kiaer (the former Mrs. Pennington and Mrs. Wolfe), and Palmedo were influential. Johansen in Canada, von Lerch in Japan, and Edwards in Chile would also be among this group.

This might not be your list. All and more were extremely important in their own spheres, but three dominate in the creation of modern skiing: Fridtjof Nansen, Arnold Lunn, and Hannes Schneider. All three would have been disheartened at the turns that post–World War II skiing has taken. In their own lives, Nansen, who died in 1930, and Lunn, who passed on in 1974, both complained bitterly about modern developments. Schneider survived for only ten years after the end of the war, and it was not clear by 1955, especially in the New England region of the United States where he had settled, that his method of teaching and of skiing would be eclipsed, even though New England had already lost its premier status in America to the Rocky Mountain states, and American instruction was far beyond the "bend-ze-kneez" stage.

These men were not experimenting in a vacuum. Nansen had a long history of utilitarian use for skis behind him. Nordenskiold had ventured into the arctic world and the Austrian Peyer had returned to Vienna with skis. However, there were two quite unexpected results of Nansen's skiing: it pushed him to the forefront of the Norwegian political stage during the most crucial years leading to independence, and, as unlikely as it sounds, his ski exploits were the base for his role as world-ambassador at large.

The second result was equally a surprise: out of his ski exploits came the sport of skiing in its modern guise. No other man who did such physical feats as successfully crossing Greenland on skis and failing so adventurously to reach the North Pole on skis, ever achieved such immediate and long-lasting heroic status. Initially, these ski exploits were done far from the public gaze. Only on his return was the hero acclaimed, first on a personal level and then, when his own version of his trials was published in *Paa Ski over Grønland* followed by his many, many lectures all over the world, an aftereffect of hero status was confirmed time and again.

This second effect was due to the instantaneous translations into English and particularly German of his Greenland book. "Nansen fever," which spread over the German-speaking middle and upper classes immediately on publication in 1890, says more about the predilections of the wealthy than it does about Nansen. Only one in a million might actually sally forth on something as otherworldly as Nansen had essayed. The bourgeois and upper classes took to the cult of the individual, seen as the true ideal of a man, one who would rescue the country from the socialist rabble and rebuild a nation from its glorious past. If these were German ideas, they were very easily applied to a figure like Nansen. He embodied Nietzsche's superman: reliant on individualism, bravery, and instinct, appearing out of the icy wastes of the North. Part of the German Junker ethos prior to the First World War was bound up with the military officer corps. It is no coincidence that the military in Germany and Austria-Hungary took to skiing as part social covenant, part proof that men should strive to be like Nansen—heroic. In France there was no Nansen fever, but the military establishment, the spiritual home of right-leaning nationalism so enmeshed in anti-Prussianism since 1871, took to skiing to regenerate the nation.

Nansen's skiing escapades were carried on in the name of utility, and of science; yet when the aristocracies of Europe took to skiing, though they gave a nod to the use of skis for forester, farmer, and postman, they thought of skis as instruments of amusement . . . of sport. On the whole, Nansen does not seem to have been a very amusing man. Studiously serious, desperately hard working, always interested in testing the limits of human endeavor, he was not prepared to understand that skiing could be great fun. As Norway's *Idrætsmann,*

082/200

Fridtjof Nansen drew this self-portrait in 1930, the year he died. He looks calm and detached, settled into a handsome old age. But it was not so; he remained to the end a driven man, one who had done so much yet felt somehow unsatisfied. (Author's collection)

he upheld that ideal in a ski world that was far more ready to indulge in an amusing weekend than in bettering body and soul in the great outdoors. His son, Odd, has a telling remark about his father when they were on a ski tour in 1925. "It was as if as long as he lived, all his ski tours—even if they were only around his home . . . were still taking place on the Greenland ice cap . . . or on the pack ice of the polar sea."[1] Here is the paradox: the very enthusiasm that his lonely expeditions to the nether parts of the icy world provided the tales from which his contemporaries created the sport of social skiing.

Arnold Lunn was an unlikely champion of modern skiing. This precocious son of a self-made father whose ecumenical concerns first made the winter tourist business feasible, thereby providing his son with a living among the Alps, had two abiding preoccupations: to find religious truth, and a love of mountains (especially Swiss ones), the two not necessarily always separate. As the clever jester, he survived public school; and as he went on to Oxford and to mountaineering and skiing, the humorist in him was never suppressed and could be produced at will. His love of mountains, first as mountaineer, then as skier, then as prolific writer on both subjects, set the pattern for his life. He reveled in leaving foggy London, the Dover-Calais ferry was his charger across to France, and the approach to the Alps thrilled him just as much in his eighties as it had in his twenties. Thanks to his father's business, he could spend every winter in Grindelwald, Montana, or Mürren. Once on skis, he ran up against two problems: mountaineers, and Norwegians with their dogmatic insistence on cross-country running.

Mountaineers were comparatively easily won over to the use of skis. Climbing aids had always been questionable adjuncts to what was perceived as a pure sport. By 1900, however, ropes, crampons, and ice axes had become acceptable. However, skis were attached to the feet and the feet were supposed to do the work, deliberately, one step after another. What finally brought the mountaineering fraternity around to the use of skis was the enormous amount of time saved in the descent so that more peaks could be captured. And the descent came to be the nearest thing to flying. Having acquired the technique to manage the swift downward rush in differing snow conditions, the downhill portion opened up a new world of sport and fun.

Norwegians were not nearly so easily won over. Their preoccupation with their style of skiing has been analyzed extensively. Here I merely want to underline that Lunn, and Schneider for that matter, never wanted to do away with the Telemark if that was what folks up north considered a religious rite. What Lunn objected to so strenuously was Norwegian insistence that the

Skiing's man-for-all-seasons Arnold Lunn invented modern downhill and slalom competitions, cofounded the most prestigious Alpine race in the 1930s, the Arlberg-Kandahar, was editor of the Year Book of the Ski Club of Great Britain *from 1920 until his death in 1974, was England's representative to the FIS—and he still had time to ski and write about fifty books.* (*Mitchell,* Downhill Ski-Racing, *1931*)

Alpine disciplines were not true skiing, merely tourist amusement. Which is, of course, exactly what they were. The clash between the upholders of *Ski-Idræt* and Lunn, the upper class controversialist with impeccable logic, never deteriorated into the near diplomatic incident spawned by Mathias Zdarsky. Lunn gathered increasing support during the 1920s for his versions of downhill running and slalom racing. Of course, he was persuading, cajoling, and preaching to the like-minded in the Ski Club of Great Britain and the Public Schools Alpine Sports Club. Norwegians, who had been in charge of the international racing program since before the First World War, eventually gave ground and, however unwillingly, acknowledged the new Alpine disciplines. The Norwegian ski fathers were not quite sure how to take the successes of their men and women in the downhill events at the 1936 Winter Olympic Games. Both Birger Ruud and Laila Schou Nilson won the downhills by over 4 seconds, and three Norwegian men placed in the first ten. This was an impressive showing by a team that only three years before had been forbidden by the Norwegian ski authorities to compete in Alpine events.[2]

Slalom was the more difficult of the two disciplines to define. A good skier who made numerous turns could be called a "slalomist," but by the end of the 1920s the slalom came to mean the race through a flagged course. Lunn had difficulties with changes in rules, with skiing styles, and with deteriorating course conditions during each race. When equality of conditions was one of the marks of fairness of the race, the use of the same course defied this prime requirement. Over the years, Lunn argued annually in the *Year Book* of the Ski Club of Great Britain and wrote tirelessly to French, German, and Swiss magazines and journals. He became the arbiter of Alpine matters of skiing.

Lunn abhorred what was happening to competition that he liked to think of as enjoyment. His Alps were despoiled by the ideological nationalism of the 1930s. As the Nazis used sport for their own ends, Lunn found himself increasingly the spokesman for the once carefree upper-class world of skiing pleasures that were sliding away from his grasp.

Lunn had a great ally in Hannes Schneider. Coming from a totally different background, this village lad who left school at fourteen to become a cheese maker was an unlikely candidate to become Skimeister to the world. Schneider's recognition of speed as the vital ingredient of the attraction of skiing set him apart. He knew intuitively what Friedrich Nietzsche realized, that the true man wanted two things: danger and play. After much trial, Schneider experienced the thrill of speed on the edge of danger. His lifework was teaching others how to obtain this same thrill. "I will make it safe," he had said; but when you see the film *Der weisse Rausch*, the White Ecstasy is not only the untouched miles of whiteness but also the beauty that is captured in the speed and danger as the skier schusses the virgin snows in a vast mountain world.

Schneider's teaching method embraced a step-by-step process by which the student learned to handle the skis in different snows at different speeds. Once up to the Christiania Swing, she or he could tackle any mountain. It was then up to the skier to decide just how fast a descent would be made. In an era in which industrialization had produced comfort, the ski mountains gave an opportunity to free a man from the mollycoddling urban world, and under Schneider's guidance he would fly through the pristine snows as free as a bird. Otto Lang, one of Schneider's best instructors, wrote that "we should all look on skiing as an art akin to ballet—dancing to imaginary music. It is not only 'exercise,' or merely 'sport,' but revelation for body and soul."[3]

The majority of skiers never attained such aesthetic heights. In providing

Teacher of royalty and aristocracy Hannes Schneider is taking his lunch of bread and cheese at a mountain hut. These images were important in keeping the ideal of a true skier in the public eye as skiing became a moneyed social phenomenon. (Courtesy Herbert Schneider and New England Ski Museum)

a livelihood, in protecting a nation, in espousing an ideology, in competing on alp and alm, skiers brought meaning to their lives. Throughout skiing's six-thousand year history, man has felt a sense of beauty and other-worldliness with the glissade of the ski, the wind in his face, at one with nature, however much of a necessity it was. This exhilaration survived as the ski culture became one of civilization's sports.

NOTES

PREFACE

1. Ronald G. Popperwell, *Norway* (New York: Praeger, 1972), 20 n. 2. The first time the name Christiania was used to designate a particular type of ski turn was in 1901 in Norway, according to Erwin Mehl, "Entwicklung des Abfahrts-Unterrichtes," *Jahrbuch des Deutschen Alpenvereins* (1940): 17 n. 3. The verb "to chrisitiania," shortened to "to christie," was used in the Arlberg technique and is often believed to be an invention of Hannes Schneider.

INTRODUCTION

1. A play on the final verse of Verlaine's *Art Poétique* (1874; first published 1882): "Que ton vers soit la bonne aventure / Eparse au vent crispé du matin / Qui va fleurant la menthe et le thym . . . / Et tout le reste est littérature."

2. Roberta Park, "A Decade of the Body: Researching and Writing about Health, Fitness, Exercise, and Sport, 1983–1993," *Journal of Sport History* 21 (1994): 59–82.

3. Gertrude Himmelfarb, "Telling It As You Like It," *Times Literary Supplement*, 16 October 1992.

CHAPTER I. ARCHEOLOGY AND MYTH

1. Arne Klausen, "The Torch Relay," in *Olympic Games as Performance and Public Event: The Case of the XVII Winter Olympic Games in Norway*, ed. Arne Klausen (New York: Berghahn Books, 1999), 77, 79, 83.

2. Jan Vilkuna, "Why Do We Find Ancient Skis?" in *3rd FIS Ski History Conference*, ed. Winter Sports Museum (Mürzzuschlag: Winter Sports Museum, 2004), 58. For a dating report from 1986, see Naturhistoriska Riksmuseet, laboratoriet för isotopgeologi, Stockholm, 14 October 1987.

3. K. B. Wiklund, "Några tankar om snöskors och skidors upprinnelse," *På Skidor* (1926): 1–18; "Mera om skidans historia," ibid. (1929): 252–279; "Den nordiska skidan, den södra och den arktiska," ibid. (1931): 5–50; "Ett par gamla notiser om finnarnas skidor," ibid. (1932): 331–332. See also his obituary by Carl Nordensen in ibid. (1935): 404–407. Toivo I. Itkonen, "Finlands fornskidor," ibid. (1937): 71–89. See also Nülo Valonen, "Varhaisia lappalais-suomalaisia kosketuksia," *Ethnologia Fennica* (1980): 21–96. My thanks to Merja Heiskanen for this reference and for translations of sections of Finnish materials. Nils Lid, *Ski fundet frå Furnes* (Oslo: Noregs Boklag i Umbod, 1938); *Skifundet frå Øvrebø* (Oslo: Brøggers, 1932); "Til Norsk Skihistorie," *Aarbok* (1931):

71–79; *On the History of Norwegian Skis* (Oslo: Foreningen til Skiidrætens Fremme, 1937). For an overview, in English, see Artur Zettersten, "The Origins of Skiing," in *Skiing: The International Sport,* ed. Roland Palmedo (New York: Derrydale Press, 1937), 3–19; be warned, however, that the author has written "Baltic," for example on page 15, when it should read "Gulf of Bothnia," and in five other places it should read "Bothnic." Letter, Zettersten to Gründer, Stockholm, 5 November 1939, in Zettersten archive, Swedish Ski Museum (Svenska Skidmuseet), Umeå, Sweden.

4. Gösta Berg, *Finds of Skis from Prehistoric Time in Swedish Bogs* (Stockholm: Generalstabens Litografiska Anstalts Förlag, 1950).

5. G. Mary-Rousselière, "A Few Problems Elucidated . . . and New Questions Raised by Recent Finds in the North Baffin Islands Region," *Arctic* 32 (March 1979): 28. For the Ostyak ski, see photo in *På Skidor* (1931): 34.

6. Vilkuna, "The Binding of the Prehistoric Ski from Mänttä," in *History of Skiing Conference, Holmenkollen, Oslo, 16–18.9.1998* (Oslo: Skiforeningen, 1998), 70–74.

7. M. Schiponskij, in *Fysik Kultur och Sport* 1, no. 2 (1936), is the earliest analysis. See Zettersten, "Urskidans historia," *På Skidor* (1937): 397. Gregoriy M. Burov, "Some Mesolithic Wooden Artifacts from the Site of Vis I in the European North East of the U.S.S.R.," in *The Mesolithic in Europe: Papers Presented at the Third International Symposium, Edinburgh, 1985,* ed. Clive Bonsall (Edinburgh: John Donald [1985?]), 391–401, especially 392–395. Burov, "The Prehistoric Skis of North Eastern Europe (Russia)," in *3rd FIS Ski History Conference,* 21. Moose are called elk in Europe. Another Russian find of a meter-long piece of ash surfaced in 1985 in the Pskor region near the Dnepr River in northwest Russia, but I have been unable to find whether the proposed date of c. 4000 BC has been confirmed. *Aftenbladet* (Stockholm), 25 January 1985; *Svenska Dagbladet,* 25 January 1985; and *Västerbottens Kurieren,* 26 January 1985, reported the find with slightly varying details.

8. Wiklund, "Mera om skidans historia," *På Skidor* (1929): 278. Zettersten in Palmedo, *Skiing: The International Sport,* 14–16. Linguistic research reveals that the groove was not ubiquitous until the mid-nineteenth century. Arnold Dalen, "Scandinavian Ski Terminology, "*History of Skiing Conference,* 52–53. This was a shortened version of his article "Les origines et la terminologie du ski en Scandinavie," *Proxima Thulé* 3 (Printemps 1998): 49–77.

9. In the United States, one commentator wrote in 1900, "Those who consider themselves expert in running [skiing] disdain such a precaution as grooved skis." H. H. Lewis, "Ski Running," *Munsey's Magazine* 22 (February 1900): 666. There is a grooving machine on display at the museum in Quincy, California. See also David C. Mills, "California Pioneers on Skis," *American Ski Annual* (1938–39): 42.

10. All the ski museums display poles, but the most remarkable collection is at Oslo's Holmenkollen Ski Museum. Berg, *Finds of Skis,* 54.

11. Josef Marquart, "Ein arabischer Bericht über die arktischen (uralischen) Länder aus dem 10. Jahrhundert," *Ungarische Jahrbücher* IV (1924): 261. See also Erwin Mehl, *Grundriss der Weltgeschichte des Schifahrens* (Schorndorf bei Stuttgart: Karl Hofmann, 1964), 31.

12. Guttorm Gjessing, *Nordenfjelske ristinger av malinger av den arktiske gruppe* (Oslo: Aschehoug, 1936), 9–10. Ernst Manker, *Die lappische Zaubertrommel* (Stockholm: Hugo Gebers, 1950), 2:18. Karin Berg, *Ski i Norge* (Oslo: Aventura, 1993), 79. For the 1850 date, see Schwed in an unnamed academic review from St. Petersburg, in Mehl, *Grundriss*, 47. W. J. Raudonikas, *Les gravures rupestres des bords du lac Onéga et de la mer Blanche*, 2 vols. (Moskow, Leningrad: 1936, 1938). See also the commentaries by Gösta Berg in *På Skidor* (1940): 346–349; Kenneth Åström, "En hällristning vid Vita Havet," *Acta Bothnesia Occidentalis* 2 (1986): 156–161; and most recently by Steinar Sørensen, "Helleristininger som historisk kilde," *Adorenten* (1997): 25–32.

13. Miklos Erdy, "The Survival of Shaman Tradition in Siberian Rock Art—a Hunnic Relic," in *Siberian Rock Art—Archeology, Interpretation and Conservation,* ed. D. Seglie (Pinerolo, Italy: Cesmar, 1999): 32–61, with photos of the skiers on pp. 28, 29. My thanks to Miklos Erdy. The find is 25 miles northeast of Shira, called Khakassia on some maps.

14. Åström and Ove Norberg, "Förhistoriska och medeltida skidor," *Västerbotten* 2 (1984): 85. Manker, "Fennoskandias fornskidor," *Fornvännen* (1971): 77–91. Itkonen, "Finlands fornskidor," *På Skidor* (1937): 86–87. For the Böksta stone, see Otto v. Friesen, "Vår första skidlöparbild," *På Skidor* (1925): v–xi; Mehl, *Grundriss*, 78.

15. Xinhua News Agency in *People's Daily Online,* January 23, 2006. My thanks to Nils Larsen for this reference.

16. Heimskringsla III, 293, cited in Mehl, *Grundriss*, 78.

17. Maria Leach, ed., *Dictionary of Folklore, Myth and Legend*, 2 vols. (New York: Funk and Wagnall, 1950), 2:1158. Ivar Lindquist, "Gudar på skidor," *På Skidor* (1929): 8–15.

18. Jan de Vries, *Germanische Religionsgeschichte*, 1957, cited in Mehl, *Grundriss*, 84. See also Helge Refsum, "Some Aspects of Norway's Contribution to Ski History," *British Ski Year Book* (1937): 8. [Hereafter *BSYB*.]

19. Dalen, "Scandinavian Ski Terminology," *History of Skiing Conference*, 50.

20. *Fläto-Buche.* Kristiania, 1860, 1:219, cited in Mehl, *Grundriss*, 72. Lindquist, "Guden på skidor," *På Skidor* (1929): 8–15. Gebhardt Kiene, "Ull und Skadi," *Der Winter* 6 (December 22, 1911): 137. Rune Flaten, "Hvem var skiguden Ull?" *Årbok* (1999): 38–53, and "Skigudinnen Skade," ibid. (2000): 58–71. See also Leach, *Dictionary,* 1158; Bergen Evans, *Dictionary of Mythology, mainly Classical* (Lincoln: Centennial Press, 1970), 226, 229–230, 251. Gertrude Jobes, *Dictionary of Mythology, Folklore and Symbols* (New York: Scarecrow Press, 1962), 2:1622.

21. Karl Müllenhoff, *Deutsche Altertumskunde* (Berlin: Weidmannsche Buchhand-lung, 1887), 2:359. There is, however, only one map from 1086 or 1124 showing Scandinavia as an island. Leonid S. Chetkin, "Mappa Mundi and Scandinavia," *Scandinavian Studies* 65 (1993): 491. Scandinavia may be derived from Skåne, called Sconia by Adam of Bremen in 1070. Ibid., 493.

22. Jobes, *Dictionary*, 1:780, 2:1622. Frau Holle is most well known via Grimms' tales. Brüder Grimm, "Frau Holle," in *Die Märchen der Brüder Grimm* (Leipzig: Insel-Verlag, 1924), 1:121–122.

23. Fridtjof Nansen, *Paa Ski over Grønland* (Kristiania: Aschehoug, 1890), 78.

24. Dalen, "Scandinavian Ski Terminology," *Ski History Conference*, 50–53.

25. Berg, *Ski i Norge*, 10–12.

26. Åke Svahn, "Idrott und Sport. Eine semantische Studie zu zwei schwedischen Fachtermini," *Stadion* V (1979): 20–41.

27. "Feast of Ager, or Quarrel of Lok," *Icelandic Poetry or the Edda of Saemund*, trans. A. S. Cottle (Bristol: N. Biggs, 1797), 175–176.

28. Information from Leif Torgersen.

29. Nansen, *Paa Ski over Grønland*, 94–100.

30. Itkonen, "Finlands fornskidor," *På Skidor* (1937): 72–3.

31. John Geipel, *The Europeans* (New York: Pegasus, 1970).

32. Wiklund, "Några tankar om snöskors," *På Skidor* (1926): 2. J. Marshall, cited in, "A Note on the History of Skiing," *BSYB* (1909): 63. See also Fritz Flor, *Beitrag zu den Problemen der arktischen Kulturgliederung* (Wien: Anthropologische Gesellschaft, 1933), 53–59. On extended hunting expeditions, some tribes hired interpreters who knew the language of the "Siberian foreigners." The movement of peoples increased in the seventeenth century as Russian expansion to the Amur and northeastern Siberia was encouraged. In this way, words traveled with the traders. Oleg V. Bychkov, "In the Seventeenth Century: Lifestyle and Economy," *Arctic Anthropology* 31 (1994): 77–78.

33. M. D. Teben'kov, *Atlas of the Northwest Coasts of America from the Bering Straits to Cape Corrientes and the Aleutian Islands with Several Sheets on the Northeast Coast of Asia*, compiled by Teben'kov when he was Governor of Russian Alaska and published in 1852, cited in Dave Brann, "Russian Skiers: The First to Make Tracks in North America," in *International Ski History Congress 2002: Collected Papers*, ed. E. John B. Allen (New Hartford: ISHA, 2002), 15–16.

34. Diego de Rosales, *Historia de el reyno de Chile*, 3 vols. (Valparaiso: 1674–1678), 1:198. See also John M. Cooper, "Aboriginal South American Snowshoes in Primitive Man," Washington XVII (1945). Martin Gusinde, *Die Feuerland-Indianer*, 3 vols. (Wien: Verlag der Internationalen Zeitschrift "Anthropos," 1931), 1:215.

35. Henry Hoek, "Von alten Ski in Graubünden," *Der Schnee-Hase* 2, no. 6 (1932): 156, 160, 162. *New York Times*, 15 March 1888.

1. The seminal work in English is O. T. Mason, *Primitive Travel and Transport*. Report of the U.S. National Museum for 1894 (Washington, D.C.: GPO, 1896), 381–410. D. S. Davidson, "Snowshoes," *Memoirs of the American Philosophical Society* 6 (1937): 21–207. Davidson has also analyzed snowshoes in Korea and Japan in *Ethnos* 18 (1953): 45–72. Snowshoes are surprisingly not generally associated with Europe, but they have a long history in places as far removed from each other as the Basque country of Spain and the Carpathian mountains in Eastern Europe. Artur Zettersten, "Snöskor användas av baskernia i norra Spanien," *På Skidor* (1932): 336. Bela Gunda, "Snöskorna hos Karpaternas Folk," ibid., (1940): 229–237. For Swiss snowshoes, see Karl Meuli, "Scythica Vergiliana: Ethnographisches, Archäologisches und Mythologisches zu Virgils Georgica," *Schweizerisches Archiv für Volkskunde* 56 (1960): 112–113.

2. John R. Gillis, "Tunnels of the Pacific Railroad," *Transactions of the American Society of Civil Engineers* (1874): 114. For similar observations, see *Charles Kellogg, the Nature Singer, His Book,* cited in Dr. Clarence W. Kellogg, Diary, 85–86. TMS in Plumas County Museum, Quincy, Calif. William H. Brewer, *Up and Down in California in 1860–1864,* ed. Francis P. Farquhar (New Haven: Yale University Press, 1930), 435. Letter, William E. Mills to D. Mills, Norwell, Mass., December 17, 1924, reprinted in *The Skisport* (1924–25): 35.

3. Film, "Legends of American Skiing." Keystone Films, dir. Richard Moulton, 1982. Boris Orel, "Ljudske smuci na Bloski planoti, v Vidovskih hribih in v njih Sosesčini," *Slovenski Etnograf* 9 (1956): 86, 89. [Summary in English, 85–89]

4. "The Wooden-Board People" is the name given in Chinese history to the Tujue, first noted on skis in the Song dynasty (960–1279). Liu Quilu and Liu Yueye, "Sports on Ice and Snow in Ancient China," in *Winter Games, Warm Traditions,* ed. Matti Goksøyr et al. (Oslo: Norwegian Society of Sport History, 1994), 71.

5. Ibid., 70–71. The article is based on Shang Caizhen et al., eds., *The History of Skiing in China* (Wuhan: Chinese Ski Association and the Cultural and Historical Working Association of the State Sports Association, 1993), in Chinese.

6. An earlier translation reads: "Afraid of falling into holes in the snow, people would ride on sliding wood which would stop when touching anything." The translator explained that the "sliding wood" was "a board or toboggan carried uphill by people and used for sliding downhill." The carrying of skis uphill appears in an account of the Baximis folk. Li Di, "Some Records about the Arctic in Early Chinese Books," *Earth Sciences History* 10 (1991): 220–221.

7. Caizhen et al. *A History of Chinese Skiing.* I am indebted to my colleague, Dr. Xiaoxiong Li for translation, as well as for insights into Chinese history and social activity. See also Wilhelm Schott, *Über die Ächten Kirgisen* (Berlin: Akademie der Wissenschaften, 1865), 435–448, 470.

8. Carl J. Luther, "Geschichte des Schnee- und Eissports," in G. A. E. Bogeng, *Geschichte des Sports aller Völker und Zeiten* (Leipzig: E. A. Seeman, 1926), 2:502. Charles M. Dudley, *Sixty Centuries of Skiing* (Brattleboro: Stephen Daye, 1935), 32. Yves Ballu, *L'épopée du ski* (Paris: Arthaud, 1981), 31–32.

9. Procopius, *History of the Wars: the Gothic War*, Book 6, xv, 16, in *Procopius* with an English translation by H. B. Dewing (Cambridge: Harvard University Press, 1961), 3:410. Paulus Diaconus, *Historia Langobardorum* in *Monumenta Germanica Historica* I, 5, cited in Konrad Maurer, "Das Schneeschuhlaufen in Norwegen," *Zeitschrift des Vereins für Volkskunde* 2 (1892): 307–308, although he mistranslated *skrida* as "jump" rather than "slide." *Gesta Hamburg* 4, 31, cited in Meuli, "Scythia Vergiliana," 115–116, n. 93. Karl Müllenhoff, *Deutsche Altertumskunde* (Berlin: Weidmannsche Buchhandlung, 1887), 2:41 and 44 mentions a variety of spellings: Scretefennae, Scritifinnae, Scrithifinnae, Scritobini, Scritovini and Scridifrinorum.

10. Snorri Sturluson, *Younger Edda*, cited in Luther, "History and Development of Ski Racing," in Roland Palmedo, *Skiing: The International Sport* (New York: Derrydale, 1938), 183. It is surprising that this "remark" is not included in Jakob Vaage's lists. See, for example, Jakob Vaage, "Milepeler og merkedager gjennom 4000 år," *Norske Skiløpere: Østlandet Nord* (Oslo: Ranheim, 1955), 9–42, which appears again, with minor changes, in his *Skienes verden* (Oslo: Hjemmenes, 1979), 250–266.

11. Snorri Sturluson, *Heimskringla: the Olaf Sagas*, trans. Samuel Lang (London: Dent, 1915; reprinted 1930), 10. Vaage, "Milepeler," *Norske Skiløpere*, 10.

12. Sturluson, *Heimskringla*, 193. Snorri Sturluson, *The Stories of the Kings of Norway called The Round World* (*Heimskringla*), done into English from the Icelandic by William Morris and Eiríkr Magnússon (London: Bernard Quaritch, 1894), 4:156.

13. Sturluson, *Stories of the Kings of Norway* 4:22.

14. Saxo Grammaticus, *The First Nine Books of the Danish History of Saxo*, trans. Oliver Elton, Publications of the Folklore Society, no. 33 (1893), reprinted Nendeln: Kraus, 1967, 327. See also the epigraph from *The King's Mirror*, trans. Laurence M. Larson (New York: Twayne, 1917), 103.

15. Saxo Grammaticus, *The First Nine Books*, 373.

16. K. B. Wiklund, "Den nordiska skidan," *På Skidor* (1931): 10. R. G. Latham, *Norway and the Norwegians*, 2 vols. (London: Bentley, 1840), 1:265, explained the difficulty for his English readers: "A Fin in England, means a native of Finland. A Fin in Norway, means a man from Finmark, i.e. a Laplander. The true Finlanders call themselves Cwains. The native I met in Kristiania said he was not a Lapp but a Fin. In his own tongue a Sami." Forty years later, Sophus Tromholt, *Under the Rays of the Aurora Borealis* (London: Sampson Low, Marston, Searle and Rivington, 1885), 2:101, explained that "the Swedes call the Lapps *Lappar* (Lapps), but by the Norwegians they are called *Finner* (Finns), while the Finns call them *Lappalaiset*. They call themselves *Sabmeladschak*. The

Finns, on the other hand, call themselves *Suomalaiset* or *Landalaiset,* but the Norwegians call them *Kvæner* (*Kvæns*), while the Swedes call them *Finnar* (Finns), and the Lapps *Laddeladschak.*" This information comes from one who knows; Tromholt was part of an international polar research expedition to northern Scandinavia in 1882–1883.

17. Cited, with no source, in Ballu, *L'épopée du ski,* 35, n.21.

18. Laurentius Urdahl, *Haandbog i Skiløbning* (Kristiania: Hjalmar Bigler, 1893; reprinted Oslo: Aschehoug, 1993), 41. Johan Bååth, "Några drag ur skidløpnings historia," *På Skidor* (1900–1901): 96.

19. B. I. Bergmann, *Lyschniji Sport Moskau* (Moskow: Staatsverlag für Leibesübungen, 1940), and C. Lehrberg, "Untersuchungen zur Erläuterung der alten Geschichte Russlands," Petersburg, 1816, both cited in Erwin Mehl, *Grundriss der Weltgeschichte des Schifahrens* (Schorndorf bei Stuttgart: Karl Hofmann, 1964), 87. There is a very early reference to skiers in the Kiev area in the twelfth century. See Meuli, "Scythia Vergiliana," *Schweizerisches Archiv für Volkskunde* 56 (1960): 116, n.93.

20. Sigismund von Herberstein, *Rerum Moscoviticarum commentarii,* published in Vienna in 1549 and in German in 1557. The Italian version, published by G. B. Prezzano in 1550, cited in Mario Cereghini, "Le ski dans la littérature et l'iconographie italienne du 16è siècle," *Les Alpes* (March 1950): 115.

21. Oleg V. Ovsyannikov, "Medieval Skis in Northern Russia," paper circulated at History of Skiing Conference, Oslo, 16–18 September 1998, TMS, 21–27.

22. *The Kalevala: the Epic Poem of Finland,* trans. J. M. Crawford (New York: Columbian, 1891), 1:177. I prefer this translation's more romantic, and therefore more contemporaneous, slant to that of E. P. Magoun, *The Kalevala or Poems of the Kaleval District,* comp. Elias Lönnrot (Cambridge: Harvard University Press, 1963), poem 13.

23. Kaarle Krohn, "Der Hansakaufmann in der finnischen Volksdichtung," *Finnisch-ugarische Forschungen* 16 (1923–24): 125–143. Krohn has also written other articles on the *Kalevala;* see Mehl, *Grundriss,* 102–107.

24. Knut Gjerset, *History of the Norwegian People* [1914], reprinted from 1932 edition (New York: AMS Press, 1969), 2:56–60. Gustav Storm, "Et brev til pave Nicolaus den 5[te] om Norges beligeenhed og undre," Introduction to *Det norsk geografiske selskab Aarbok,* 210, Oslo, cited in Kurt Johannesson, *The Renaissance of the Goths in Sixteenth-Century Sweden,* trans. and ed. James Larson (Berkeley: University of California Press, 1992), 172.

25. Elfriede R. Knauer, *Die Carta Marina des Olaus Magnus von 1539* (Göttingen: Gratia, 1981), 28. See also John Granlund, "The *Carta Marina* of Olaus Magnus," *Imago Mundi* 8 (1951): 35–43.

26. Johannesson, *Renaissance of the Goths,* 173–185.

27. Ibid., 180. Revelation 3:11.

28. Olaus Magnus, *A Compendious History of the Goths, Swedes and Vandals* (London:

1635), and excerpt in *Sierra Club Bulletin* 23 (April 1938): 101. In 1996, an English translation of the complete 1555 version was published by the Hakluyt Society. *Olaus Magnus, Historia de Gentibus Septentrionalibus, Romæ 1555*, trans. Peter Fisher and Humphrey Higgins; ed. Peter Foote (London: Hakluyt Society, 1996), especially 22–23. The translation is somewhat different from the 1635 one given in the text.

29. Johannesson, *Renaissance of the Goths*, xix.

30. Hans Hildebrand, "Olaus Magnus och hans Historia," *Historisk Tidskrift* 4 (1884): 340–342. Knauer's careful analysis of the *Carta Marina*, especially detailed on animals and monsters, is remarkable for its lack of any attempt to discuss the so prominently displayed skis.

31. Virgilio Ricci, "Lo sci nei suo precedenti storici é nel suo sviluppo in Italia," *Rivista Mensile de Club Italiano Alpino* 46, no. 2 (1937): 58. See also the picture in Luther, "Der erste Schwung in der Literatur," *Der Winter* 13 (April 1938): 200.

32. John Schefferus, *The History of Lapland* ([Oxford]: At the Theater in Oxon, 1674), 100.

33. Torquato Tasso, *Jerusalem Delivered*, Canto XIV, 34. There was, of course, no Italian word for ski. Tasso's "lunghi stricsi," however, makes it clear that he was talking about long skis.

34. Giovanni Guagnini, *Sarmatiae Europeae descriptio* (Crakow, 1578). The woodcut has been reproduced many times. For one example, see Mario Cereghini, *5000 Years of Winter-Sports* (Milano: Edizione del Milione, 1955), 35.

35. Johannesson, *Renaissance of the Goths*, 206.

36. Vaage, *Skienes Verden*, 251. For how the Birkebeiner race was initiated in 1932, see Lars Høgvold, "Birkebeiner-rennet," *Norske Skiløpere: Østlandet Nord*, 207–209.

37. Vaage, *Skienes Verden*, 251. Maurer, "Das Schneeschuhlaufen in Norwegen," *Zeitschrift des Vereins für Volkskunde* 2 (1892): 309.

38. Vaage, *Skienes Verden*, 251.

39. Karen Larsen, *A History of Norway* (Princeton: Princeton University Press, for the American-Scandinavian Foundation, 1948), 171–172.

40. Hugo Rich Sandberg, *Den Finske Skidan i Arbetets och Idrottens Tjanst*, trans. from Finnish by Ossian Reuter (Helsingfors: Söderström, 1893), 88–90.

41. L. Wolf, *Norvegia Illustrata*, 1651. O. Wergeland, *Skiløbning, dens historie og krigsanvendelse* (Kristiania: Christian Schibsted, 1865), 56–57. Fridtjof Nansen, *Paa Ski over Grønland* (Kristiania: Aschehoug, 1890), 91–92. Luther, in *Der Winter* 9 (1914–1915): 35 and 16 (1922–1923): 165. Mehl, *Grundriss*, 94–96.

42. Jens Henrik Emahusen, "Exercises von einer Compagnie Schii-Leuffers auf denen Schiihen," in *Der Winter* 29 (January 1936): 90–93. As an aside, Emahusen's use of *Schii* in 1735, introduces the word into the German language.

43. Vaage, *Skienes Verden*, 254.

44. Tor Hjelm, "En hærordning-forendring offentlig premiering av skiløpning, og opprinnelsen til den moderne skisport for 200 år siden," *Hærmuseet Akershus, Oslo Årbok* (1965): 1–37.

45. Olav Christiansen, *Skiidret för Sondre. Vinterveien til et norsk selvbilde* (Oslo: Gyldendal, 1993). Kristen Mo, "The Development of the Sport of Skiing," *Winter Games, Warm Traditions,* 182–191.

46. Zettersten, "Huru begagnades skidan under vårt sista vinterkrieg på svensk botten," *På Skidor* (1903–4): 1–18.

47. In the course of his critiquing Olaus Magnus' woodcuts, Schefferus had drawn attention to the ski in the Wormius museum. For a picture of the ski on display, see *På Skidor* (1931): 406.

48. For Martinière, see *The Travels of Monsieur Maupertius and his Associates of the Royal Academy of Sciences made by the Order of the French King to Determine the Figure of the Earth at the Polar Circle,* in *A Curious Collection of Travels, Selected from the Writers of all Nations,* 10 vols. (London: Newberry, 1761), 10:136. See also page 167 for a different type of ski used by the Samoyeds. For Regnard, see L. Le Bondidier, "Note sur le ski au XVIIè siècle," *La Montagne* 181 (April 1925): 107–108. Ballu, *L'épopée du ski,* 52. For Negri, see Håkan Tjerneld, "Francesco Negri," *På Skidor* (1943): 310–313. A porcelain plate made in Italy in the seventeenth century shows a typically Scandinavian scene. *Der Winter* 4 (November 1934): 57. For Brand, see Adam Brand, *Neu-vermehrte Beschreibung seiner grossen chinesischen Reise* (Lübeck, 1734), 82–83. (His trip was from 1692–95.) For Gleditsch, see Joh. Ludwig Gleditsch, *Historische Reise* (Leipzig: 1699). HMS in Deutscher Skiverband, Carl Luther Archiv 7, Box: Large Unnamed, in Planegg, Germany. [Hereafter DSV L-A.] Johan Scheller, *Reise-Beschreibung von Lappland und Bothnien* (Jena: 1713), 81, in Zettersten Archive, Umeå, HMS, 455. These wonders never penetrated the Iberian peninsula, where Norway remained, in the seventeenth and eighteenth centuries, a land of darkness, *"la Noruega oscura"* (17th century), "the perpetual night of Norway," (17th century), nor in Brazil, "a land which never sees the sun" (18th century). M. Castro, "Noruega," *Revista de filología española* 6 (1919): 185; Leo Spitzer note in ibid., 9 (1922): 316–317.

49. Vaage, *Skienes Verden,* 52–53, besides the above mentioned (except Gleditsch), Vaage only manages to find four references in the seventeenth century.

50. Harald Beyer, *A History of Norwegian Literature,* ed. and trans. Einar Haugen (New York: New York University Press, for the American-Scandinavian Foundation, 1956), 7–9.

51. Martin Absalon, trained in Wittenberg, cited in ibid., 82.

52. The exception is von Herberstein who was born at Vipava, Slovenia. Johann Weichhard Frhr. von Valvasor, *Die Ehre des Herzogtums Krain* (Laibach: 1689). E. H. Schollmeyer, *Auf Schneeschuhen: ein Handbuch für Forstleute, Jäger und Touristen*

(Klagenfurt: Joh. Leon, sen., 1893), 20. An even wider public knew of Valvasor with the book's mention in the *Österreichische Touristen-Zeitung* (1893): 23. For the exhibition in Vienna, see *Der Winter* 8 (October 20, 1913): 21.

53. Borut Batagelj, "Snežke," *Kronika* 50 (2002): 50. My thanks to Aleš Guček and Borut Batagelj for conversations and insights about Bloke skiing as well as translations.

54. Schollmeyer, *Auf Schneeschuhen*, 20. J. Šavlj and M. Bor, *Unsere Vorfahren die Veneter* (Wien: 1988), and most recently, Aleš Guček, *Po smučinah od pradavnine* (Ljubljana: Magnolija, 1998), particularly 18–24.

55. Zěcevič Ljubisà, "Bloke Schifahren—Autochton oder Import?" *Cerknica & Postoina* (September 1988): 60.

56. Batagelj, "Discovering Bloke Skiing and Its Mythical Dimension," in *3rd FIS Ski History Conference*, ed. Wintersportmuseum (Mürzzuschlag: Wintersportmuseum, 2004), 23–29.

57. The major source for Bloke skiing is Boris Orel, *Bloški smuci: Vprašanje Njihovanje nastanka in Rasvoja* (Ljubljana: Institut za slovensko narodopisje, 1964). Summary in English, see p. 180. "Divieto dell'attività sciatoria civile," and "Obbligato di consegna degli sci," *Bollettino Ufficiale per la provincia di Lugiana*, 8 February 1942 and 19 July 1942, signed by Emilio Grazioli, Italian High Commissioner for Ljubljana. My thanks to Borut Batagelj for sending me copies. See also Batagelj, "Udarce smučarstvu med drugo vojno" (A Blow to Skiing during World War II), *Sport* 48 (2000): 44–45. A recent article by Dolfe Rajtmajer, "The Slovenian Origins of European Skiing," *International Journal of the History of Sport* 11 (April 1994): 97–101, does not add to our knowledge.

58. G. U. A. Vieth, *Versuch einer Enzyklopädie der Leibesübungen* (Berlin: Hartmann, 1794), 3:376. Kaiser-Franz Akten, Vienna State Archives, cited in Orel, *Bloški smuci*, 45, 179.

59. Josef Berk in *Novice*, cited in Ulaga Drago, "300 Jahre der Niederschrift (Verschreibung) Valvasors über Bloke Schilaufen," *Cerknica & Postoina* (1989): 9–10. Luther, "Ein Besuch im Lande der Smuči," 4, TMS in DSV L-A, envelope cil: Besuch im Lande der Smuči.

CHAPTER 3. THE NORWEGIAN THRUST

1. For bear, see M. R. Bernard, *Sport in Norway, and Where to Find It* (London: Chapman and Hall, 1864), 181. Lord Frederic Hamilton, *Vanished Pomp of Yesterday* (London: Hodder and Stoughton, 1937), 123. For wolves, see Johan Turi, *Turi's Book of Lappland*, ed. and trans. into Danish by E. D. Hatt; done from the Danish by E. Gee Nash (Oosterhout, N.B.: The Netherlands Anthropological Publications, 1966), 110–111. There is a portrait of Turi when he was 70, drawn in 1910, in *Svenska Turistföreningens Årsskrift* (1929): 110. See also *Skidlöpnings Främjande* (1896–97): 177; *På Skidor* (1897–98):

92–95, and (1900–1901): 225. For boar, see *Neige et Glace* 8 (October 1930): 10. For fox, see *Revue Alpine*, Sect. Lyonnaise 21, no. 1 (1920): 68.

2. F. Hedges Butler hired a Swedish guide and "Johann Thurri, the well-known Lapp and wolf hunter." F. Hedges Butler, "Through Lapland with Skis and Reindeer," *British Ski Year Book* (1913): 271.

3. Svenska Skidmuseet, Document File No. 787. See also E. John B. Allen, "Early Canadian Skis: Notes from Europe," *Canadian Journal of History of Sport* 17 (May 1986): 88–90. In France, in 1929, one prize for a cross-country race was a sculpted Stone Age hunter with a wolf tied to a massive pole carried across one shoulder. The ideal of the utility of skis in nature's battleground authenticated the winner in this so civilized race. Deutscher Skiverband, Carl Luther Archiv [hereafter DSV L-A.], in Planegg, Germany. Envelope: Jagd auf Skiern.

4. E. G. Ravenstein, *The Russians on the Amur, its Discovery, Conquest, and Colonization* (London: Trübner, 1861), 94. Frederick George Jackson, *The Great Frozen Land: Narrative of a Winter Journey across the Tundra and a Sojourn among the Samoyeds,* ed. from his journals by Arthur Montefiore (London: Macmillan, 1895), 69.

5. Sten Bergman, *Through Kamchatka by Dog-Sled and Skis* (Philadelphia: Lippincott, 1927), 61–62. G. H. von Langsdorff, *Bemerkungen auf einer Reise um die Welt in den Jahren 1803 bis 1807* (Frankfort am Mayn: Wilmans, 1812), 2:290–291.

6. John Bachelor, *The Ainu of Japan* (London: Religious Tract Society, 1892), 186–187. Georges Montandon, *La civilization Aïnou* (Paris: Payot, 1937), 120. Letter, Professor Emiko Ohnuki-Tierney to author, Madison, Wisconsin, 3 October 1978.

7. George F. Wright, *Asiatic Russia*, 2 vols. (New York: McLure, Phillips, 1902), 1:257–263.

8. Sverker Sörlin, "Nature, Skiing and Swedish Nationalism," *The International Journal of the History of Sport* 12 (August 1995): 147–163.

9. Letter, Cecil Spring-Rice to Lady Helen Ferguson, Stockholm, 31 March 1909, in *The Letters and Friendships of Sir Cecil Spring Rice: A Record,* ed. Stephen Gwynn, 2 vols. (Boston: Houghton Mifflin, 1929), 2:134–135.

10. *Skilling-Magasin* 32 (1841), cited in Olav Bø, *Skiing Throughout History,* trans. W. Edson Richmond (Oslo: Norske Samlaget, 1993), 37.

11. Harald Beyer, *A History of Norwegian Literature,* ed. and trans. Einar Haugen (New York: New York University Press, for the American-Scandinavian Foundation, 1956), 83.

12. Ibid., 110.

13. For a brief analysis of language and nationalism, see E. J. Hobsbawm, *Nations and Nationalism since 1780: Programme, Myth, Reality* (Cambridge: Cambridge University Press, 1990), 51–63.

14. Einar Sunde, "Oscar Wergeland: An Apostle for Skiing," in *International Ski His-*

tory Congress 2002: Collected Papers, ed. E. John B. Allen (New Hartford: ISHA, 2002), 207–212.

15. The analysis by the Swede, Åke Svahn, "Idrott und Sport. Eine semantische Studie zu zwei schwedischen Fachtermini," *Stadion* 5, no. 1 (1979): 20–41, stood alone for twenty years. Now, Tor Bomann-Larsen, *Den evige sne* (Oslo: Cappelens, 1993) provides the best extended overview.

16. It was probably not as clear as I am making it out to be because snow as a symbol of purity and morality is strong in the Christian canon. Psalms 51:7 and Isaiah 1:18.

17. *Verdens Gang*, 3 March 1893. Interestingly, this was reproduced almost immediately in a Minneapolis, Minn. (where there were many Scandinavian immigrants) newspaper. *The North*, 29 March 1893. Eva Nansen was a singer, specializing in romanticizing the old Norse songs. She was well connected. Her father was Professor Sars, the pioneering marine biologist and later, professor of zoology, her brother was a prominent historian, her uncle was Johan Welhaven.

18. G. U. A. Vieth, *Versuch einer Enzyklopädie der Leibesübungen* (Berlin: Hartmann, 1794), I, 3, 371–376. *Mineralogische Geschichte des sächsischen Erzgebirges*, cited in Fritz Benk, "Die Geschichte des Skilaufs und seine wirtschaftliche Bedeutung," Ph.D. diss., Leopold-Franzen University (1953), 16. Karl August Engel, *Erdbeschreibung von Sachsen*, cited in *Der Winter* 7 (January 1933): 106. Erwin Mehl, *Grundriss der Weltgeschichte des Schifahrens* (Schorndorf bei Stuttgart: Karl Hofmann, 1964), 28–29. Saxon miners had worked in the mines in southern Norway in the sixteenth century. Information from Leif Torgersen.

19. Joh. Conr. Friedr. GutsMuths, *Gymnastik für Jugend enthaltend eine praktische Anweisung zu Leibesübungen. Ein Beytrag* (Schnepfental: 1804), 386–391. *Philanthropinum Karl Wassmannsdorf Jahrbücher der deutschen Turnkunst* (1884), 403, cited in Mehl, *Grundriss*, 138–139. No one seems to have noted the harassment of Napoleon's retreating armies by Russian peasants on skis. Igor M. Boutine, *Lyzhnyi Sport* [The Sport of Skiing] (Moskow: Akademia, 2000). Thanks to Harold Leich for translations.

20. Possibly reported in the *Magdeburgischen Zeitung*, "Der Harz," 10 February 1909, 54. The trip was probably made in 1884.

21. *Allgemeine Sport-Zeitung*, 23 February 1892, 183.

22. Letter, Josef Wallner to Erwin Mehl, Semmering, 14 January 1952, TMS. Nachlass Mehl, Wintersportmuseum, Mürzzuschlag. Carl Egger, "England und Amerika," *Ski* [Swiss] 5 (1909): 145.

23. *Aarbok* (1895–96): 118–123 reprints the German report of Holmenkollen from the *Allgemeine Sport-Zeitung*. G. Mikusch, "Christiania," *Aarbok* (1906): 93. Letter, Wilhelm Paulcke to Ski Club Todtnau, Baden Baden, 25 November 1892. HMS in Todtnau Ski Club Archives, privately held.

24. Letter, Nicolay Noodt to Max Kleinoscheg, Trondheim, 11 December 1890. HMS in Mürzzuschlag Archives.

25. *Österreichische Touristen-Zeitung*, 15 December 1892, 290.

26. One might be tempted to see this as lower class–upper class skiing open to all, but Samson went on to become a member of the Storting, so he was hardly a typical baker's boy.

27. *Allgemeine Sport-Zeitung*, 22 March 1896, 247, and 29 March 1896, 269. Hassa Horn, "Skitur in Østerrigste Alpen," *Aarbok* (1905): 47.

28. *Allgemeine Sport-Zeitung*, 2 February 1913, 114.

29. *Österreichische Touristen-Zeitung*, 1 January 1911, 5.

30. "Jagd," ibid., 22 February 1891, 194. *Der Schneeschuh*, 16 March 1894, 39. D. Ritter von Poschinger, "Entstehung des Schneeschuhlaufens im Böhmerwald," *Der Bayerwald* 4 (1912): 108. See also catalogs in Luther Archive: DSV L-A.

31. *Der Schneeschuh*, 16 November 1894, 3.

32. Berecz & Löbl *Catalog*, Vienna, n.d. [1895?]. "Der Harz," TMS in DSV L-A 1.4: Ein Gutachten, Braunlage, 1909–52. Cil [Carl J. Luther], "Erste Ereignisse im deutschen Skilauf," *Der Winter* 24 (1930–31): 5. *Allgemeine Sport-Zeitung*, 21 January 1894, 61. *Deutsche Turn-Zeitung* (1894): 114, 132. Myrtle Simpson, "*Skisters*": *The Story of Scottish Skiing* (Carrbridge: Landmark, 1982), 22. Hans Althaus, ed., *Erinnerungen aus fünfzig Jahren Skisport* (Bern: Büchler, 1950), 17. *Der Naturfreund* 12 (1908): 279. Josef Wallner, TMS in Wintersportmuseum, Mürzzuschlag, 2.

33. *Allgemeine Sport-Zeitung*, 20 February 1910, 181. C. Egger, "Wann kam der erste Ski nach der Schweiz?" *Ski* [Swiss] 10 (February 1905): 148–149. "Geschichtliches," ibid., 5 (1909): 82. *Les sports d'hiver en Suisse 1906–97*, 76. Drawings appeared in *Gartenlaube*, *Über Land und Meer*, *Illustrierte Zeitung*, *Das Buch für Alle* and others.

34. Letter, Dr. Otto Absagen in *The Times*, 20 March 1937. The Swiss had already run a course for guides in 1902. *Allgemeine Sport-Zeitung*, 16 February 1902, 156. Wilhelm Paulcke, "Auf Skiern im Hochgebirge," *Zeitschrift des Deutschen und Österreichischen Alpenvereins* 2 (1902): 183, *Deutsche Alpenzeitung*, 15 January 1902, 25, and 2 March 1902, 24.

35. Wilhelm Munack, "Wintersport in Dänemark," *Der Winter* 7 (December 1911): 248. *Ski Notes & Queries* 11 (April 1948): 20. Jörn Hansen, "Come to Norway my Friend—Danish Winter Sport as Tourism," in *Winter Games, Warm Traditions*, ed. Matti Goksøyr et al. (Oslo: Norwegian Society of Sport History, 1994), 46. For Russia, J. F. Baddeley, *Russia in the 'Eighties'* (London: Longmans, Green, 1921), 253–254. See also the marvelous drawing in the Ski Club of Great Britain, Wimbledon in which there is much information.

36. *L'Illustration*, 17 February 1912, 135.

37. *Tromsø Tidende,* 4 April 1843, cited in Bø, *Skiing Throughout History,* 67, and 80. L. F. K. von Thiele, "The Norwegian Olympic Games," *Wide World Magazine* 9 (1902): 466. Pierre Minelle, "Rapport: FIS 1930," *Revue du Ski,* 1 May 1930, 5.

38. Torbjørn Støverud, *Milestones of Norwegian Literature* (Oslo: Grundt, 1967), 89. Oscar J. Falnes, *National Romanticism in Norway* (New York: Columbia University Press, 1933; reprint, New York: AMS Press, 1968), 65–66. R. G. Latham, *Norway and the Norwegians,* 2 vols. (London: Bentley, 1840), 2:120. See also ibid., 1:50.

39. *Neu Helsingborg Post,* 2 August 1836, and *Dagens Nyheter,* 24 August 1867, cited in Svahn, "Idrott und Sport," *Stadion* 5 (1979): 26.

40. F. Wedel Jarlsberg, *Reisen gjennem livet* (Oslo: Gyldendal, 1932), 111. Vice versa: Gladstone visited Norway twice, and, on the second visit in 1885, he decided to fight for Home Rule for Ireland. Philip Magnus, *Gladstone: A Biography* (London: John Murray, 1963), 332. See also W. E. Gladstone, *The Gladstone Diaries,* vol. 11 (July 1883–December 1886), ed. H. C. G. Mathews (Oxford: Clarendon, 1990), 385–387.

41. Anthony D. Smith, *Theories of Nationalism* (London: Duckworth, 1983), 271.

42. Jacob Aull in *Morgenbladet,* no. 14 (1849), cited by Falnes, *National Romanticism in Norway,* 68.

43. See particularly John R. Gillis, "Memory and Identity: the History of a Relationship," and David Lowenthal, "Identity, Heritage, and History," in *Commemorations: the Politics of National Identity,* ed. John R. Gillis (Princeton: Princeton University Press, 1994), 3–24, 41–57.

44. Marcus Jacob Monrad (1816–97) in Falnes, *National Romanticism in Norway,* 75. Dahl and Bull quoted in Karen Larsen, *A History of Norway* (Princeton: Princeton University Press, for the American-Scandinavian Foundation, 1948), 416, 443.

45. Beyer, *History of Norwegian Literature,* 119.

46. Larsen, *History of Norway,* 479–480. See also Frank Edgar Farley, *Scandinavian Influences in the English Romantic Movement,* vol. 9, *Studies and Notes in Philology and Literature* (Boston: Ginn, 1903), 91, 189, 196–197, 203.

47. P. C. Asbjørnsen and Jørgen Moe, *Norske Folke-eventyr* (1851–52), lxi–lxii, cited in Falnes, *National Romanticism in Norway,* 229.

48. Beyer, *History of Norwegian Literature,* 151.

49. Explained to an American audience as early as 1902 as "the birthplace of the ski." Henry Thomas Chinton, "Winter Sports," *Cosmopolitan* 32 (January 1902): 237.

50. Cited in Jakob Vaage, "Milepeler og merkedager gjennom 4000 år," *Norske Skiløpere: Østlandet Nord* (Oslo: Ranheim, 1955), 9–42, which appears again, with minor changes, in his *Skienes verden* (Oslo: Hjemmenes, 1979), 17.

51. Vaage, *Skienes Verden,* 255.

52. Cited in Vaage, "Milepeler," 18–19.

53. Aasmund Olavsson Vinje in *Drammens Tidende,* in Vaage, *Skienes Verden,* 255. Olav Christensen, *Skiidrett før Sondre. Vinterveien til et nasjonalt selvbilde* (Ad Notam Gyldendal, 1993), 124.

54. Snorri Sturluson, *The Stories of the Kings of Norway Called the Round World* (*Heimskringla*), trans. from Icelandic by William Morris and Eiríkr Magnússon (London: Bernard Quaritch, 1894), 2:299.

55. As literary critic Dr. Georg Brandes told Mrs. Tweedie. Mrs. Alec Tweedie, *A Winter Jaunt in Norway* (London: Bliss, Sands, and Foster, 1894), 270–271.

56. Bomann-Larsen, *Den evige sne,* 1993. Fridtjof Nansen, *Paa Ski over Grønland* (Kristiania: Aschehoug, 1890), 78.

57. Giovanni Bach, "Swedish literature," in *The History of Scandinavian Literatures,* Bach et al. (New York: Dial Press, 1938; reprint, Port Washington: Kennikat, 1965), 106–107. Elias Bredsdorf, Brita Mortensen, Ronald Popperwell, *An Introduction to Scandinavian Literature from the Earliest Times to Our Day* (Copenhagen: Einar Munksgaard, 1951; reprint, Westport, Conn.: Greenwood Press, 1976), 30–36.

CHAPTER 4. FRIDTJOF NANSEN

1. The only major critic was Knut Hamsun.

2. Karin Berg, *Fridtjof Nansen og hans kvinnen* (Oslo: Shibsted, 2004).

3. *The Bystander* 10, no. 130 (May 30, 1906), 423.

4. Cited in Roland Huntford, *Nansen: The Hero as Explorer* (New York: Barnes and Noble, 1998), 513.

5. Ibid., 535.

6. Karen Larsen, *A History of Norway* (Princeton: Princeton University Press, for the American-Scandinavian Foundation, 1948), 233.

7. Ibid., 336–337.

8. Oscar J. Falnes, *National Romanticism in Norway* (New York: Columbia University Press, 1933; reprint, New York: AMS Press, 1968), 359.

9. *New York Times,* 4 June 1884, 2.

10. "In June of this year [1888], Conservator Nansen makes a big imaginative 'far jump' across Greenland. Last seats in the ice stadium." Reprinted in *Der Winter* 23 (December 1929): 281. "Return tickets not required" was a caption to another joke. Exhibited in Musée Dauphinois, Grenoble, France, July 1996. Several English papers criticized the proposed expedition. Fridtjof Nansen, *Paa Ski over Grønland* (Kristiania: Aschehoug, 1890), 17.

11. Ibid., 7–8. Huntford, *Nansen,* 68, 131.

12. F. Wedel Jarlsberg, *Reisen gjennem livet* (Oslo: Gyldendal, 1932), 109.

13. *The Times* (London), 16 November 1888, 10.

14. Carl J. Luther, "Braunlage 1909," 16. Printed article found in Deutscher Skiverband, Carl Luther Archiv [DSV L-A.], in Planegg, Germany. 1.4 envelope: Braunlage 1909.

15. Vaage, Jakob Vaage, "Milepeler og merkedager gjennom 4000 år," *Norske Skiløpere: Østlandet Nord* (Oslo: Ranheim, 1955), 9–42, which appears again, with minor changes, in his *Skienes verden* (Oslo: Hjemmenes, 1979), 29–30. Henrik Angell, about whom we will hear later, had already made this trip a couple of months before Nansen.

16. Nansen, *Paa Ski over Grønland*, 9. See also "Frithof Nansens ledsgere," *Skilling-Magazin* (1888): 342, with illustration. He had refused to take Henrik Angell, because he was educated. Nansen was looking for peasants, natural folk, and attempted to attract Mikkel Hemmetsveit, the jumper who, after some years, emigrated to the United States. For Mikkel Hemmetsveit in the U.S., see Helen M. White, *The Tale of a Comet and Other Stories* (St. Paul: Minnesota Historical Society Press, 1984), 128–151.

17. Nansen, *Paa Ski over Grønland*, 112.

18. Professor of Greek, Emil Smith, cited in Tor Bomann-Larsen, *Den evige sne* (Oslo: Cappelens, 1993), 63.

19. Fridtjof Nansen, *Farthest North* (New York: Harper, 1898), 34.

20. Ibid., 10, 277.

21. Ibid., 202–203, 362.

22. Ibid., 406–407, 433, 462.

23. Ibid., 570–573. *Illustrated London News*, 12 September 1896, front cover and p. 335. The full conversation is reported in Huntford, *Nansen*, 341.

24. Jacob B. Bull, *Fridtjof Nansen*, trans. Mordaunt R. Bernard (Boston: Heath, 1903), 131. See also Bomann-Larsen, *Den evige sne*, 20.

25. Cited in Bomann-Larsen, *Den evige sne*, 75

26. Alexander Kielland to Bjørnson, cited in ibid., 88. Huntford, *Nansen*, 359–360.

27. Bomann-Larsen, *Den evige sne*, 92.

28. Anton Fendrich, *Der Skiläufer: Ein Lehr- und Wanderbuch* (Stuttgart: Franck'sche Verlagshandlung, n.d.), 11. Theodor Herzog, *Aus der Frühzeit des Skilaufs in Deutschland* (Munich: ASC, 1961), 1. Georg Blab, *Anleitung zur Erlernung des Schneeschuhlaufens* (Munich: 1895), 5. Nansen, Letter to Ski Club Todtnau, Lysaker, 5 January 1892. TMS in SC Todtnau Archives. Max Schneider paraphrased some of Nansen in his magazine *Der Tourist* from 1890 on. See also his *Schneeschuh und Schlitten für Sport, Jagd u. Verkehr* (Berlin: Fontane, 1905), 26.

29. Alexander Bronische et al., *Hahnenkamm. The Chronicle of a Myth: 100 Years of the Kitzbühel Ski Club* (Munich: Kitzbühel Ski Club, 2003), 18–19. *Allgemeine Sport-Zeitung*, 4 February 1900, 108. Mathias Zdarsky, "Unsere Lehrwarte," *Der Schnee* 10 (1906): 15. Josef Müller, "Vor zwanzig Jahren," *Zwanzig Jahre Österreichischer Ski-Verein* (Wien: Österreichischer Ski-Verein, 1912), 6.

30. Letter, Nicolay Noodt to Max Kleinoscheg, Trondheim, 11 December 1890, TMS. Wintersportmuseum Mürzzuschlag Archives. For the cycling connection, see A. Rödling, "Zur Geschichte des Österreichischen Ski-Verbandes," *Der Skilauf in Österreich* (Wien: Österreichischer Ski-Verband, 1927), 18. Hans Heidinger, "Der Beitrag Mürzzuschlags zur Entwicklung des Skilaufs," *Sport: Sinn und Wahn* (Mürzzuschlag: Steirische Landesausstellung, 1991), 155.

31. On Kleinoscheg and Schruf, see *Allgemeine Sport-Zeitung*, 12 February 1893, 149. On Nansen Hut, see ibid., 3 January 1897, 12–13. See also letter, Josef Müller to Nansen, Wien, 28 November 1896. HMS in Oslo University Library: MS fol. 1924: 14b Österrike. For the races and exhibition in 1894, see *Österreichische Touristen-Zeitung*, 1 November 1893, 260; 1 January 1894, 4–5; 15 January 1894, 18. *Allgemeine Sport-Zeitung*, 14 January 1894, 40. *Deutsche Turn-Zeitung* (1894): 82.

32. *Katalog der Wintersport-Ausstellung (5. bis 10. Jänner 1894 in Mürzzuschlag a. S*, in Wintersportmuseum, Mürzzuschlag Archives. *Allgemeine Sport-Zeitung*, 15 November 1903, 1491, and 26 January 1913, 86. *Allgemeines Korrespondenzblatt*, 16 February 1906, 171.

33. Letter, Schruf to Nansen, Mürzzuschlag, 6 February 1923, and 8 June 1928; Kleinoscheg to Nansen, Graz, New Year 1930. HMSS in Oslo University Library, MS fol.1924: 14b Østerrike.

34. Karl Roll, "Norske skiløbere i Wien og skirendene den 5. og 6. Januar 1896," *Aarbog* (1895–96): 126–138. Roll, "Ein Norweger über Wien," *Allgemeine Sport-Zeitung*, 22 March 1896, 12, and 29 March 1896, 247, 269.

35. Leif Berg in a Norwegian sports magazine (1905), cited in Tim Ashburner, *The History of Ski Jumping* (Shrewsbury: Quiller Press, 2003), 50.

36. Müller, "Vor zwanzig Jahren," *Zwanzig Jahre Österreichischer Ski-Verein*, 9. E. C. Richardson, "Early Days," *British Ski Year Book* (1920): 10. [Hereafter *BSYB*.]

37. Letter, Otto Lutter to Theodor Hüttenegger, Graz, 1930. TMS, Wintersportmuseum Mürzzuschlag Archives. File: Fach-Beiträge Sect. L. *Aftenbladet*, 12 January 1881, 4.

38. Lutz Eichenberger, "Fridtjof Nansen: The Originator of Skiing in Switzerland?" in *Winter Games, Warm Traditions*, ed. Matti Goksøyr et al. (Oslo: Norwegian Society of Sport History, 1994), 275–283.

39. Letter, Nansen to Kleinoscheg, Lysaker, 12 February 1904. TMS in Wintersportmuseum Mürzzuschlag Archives. Nachlass Mehl No. 19.

40. *Brown Bulletin* 10 (February 1929): 3. *New York Times*, 3 February 1929, 8.

41. *La Montagne*, 20 April 1906, 189, and 20 October 1908, 200. Letter, Edouard Seltzer to H. Archer Thomson, Souma, Boufarik, Algeria, received 9 November 1908, in *BSYB* (1920), 51. *Allgemeine Sport-Zeitung*, 27 March 1910, 318. Vaage, *Skienes Verden*, 263. For South Africa, see *Cape Times*, 8 and 15 July 1929, 9, 11. For an overview see,

R. F. Windrain, "Ski-ing in S. Africa," *BSYB* (1930): 499–502. I am indebted to Floris van der Merwe of Stellenbosch University for obtaining copies of the *Cape Times*.

42. Jakob Vaage, *Norske ski erobrer verden* (Oslo: Gyldendal, 1952), 216–217. *Deutsche Alpenzeitung* 2 (January 1903): 193. *Sport Universel*, 23 March 1902, 45. E. C. Richardson, "Ski Riding in Australia," *BSYB* (1906): 23. Letter, G. Long to *The Times* (London), 1 March 1939.

43. G. E. Mannering, "An Early Use of Ski in the New Zealand Alps," *Australia and New Zealand Ski Year Book* (1938): 52–53. A. Warburton, "Early New Zealand Ski-ing," ibid. (1936): 121. Photographs in the Museum at the Hermitage, Mt. Cook, New Zealand. *The Press* (Christchurch, NZ), 22 May 1912, 2.

44 Wedel Jarlsberg, *Reisen*, 110. For Nansen's dress in Oslo, see Robert Ferguson, *Enigma: The Life of Knut Hamsun* (New York: Farrar, Strauss and Giroux, 1987), 108. Nansen caused a stir in Picadilly and Regent Street according to the *Pall Mall Gazette*. Huntford, *Nansen*, 25, 130, 132. Dr. Gustav Jaeger's "Sanitary Woolen Clothing" allowed the "evaporation of noxious emanations." For Jaeger as part of the German nature movement, see Giselher Spitzer, *Der deutsche Naturismus. Idee und Entwicklung einer volkerzieherischen Bewegung im Schnittfeld von Lebensreform, Sport und Politik* (Ahrensburg: Czwalina, 1983), 23.

CHAPTER 5. CREATING THE SKISPORT

1. Allen Guttmann, *From Ritual to Record: The Nature of Modern Sports* (New York: Columbia University Press, 1978).

2. Jakob Vaage, *Skienes verden* (Oslo: Hjemmenes, 1979), 57, 261. *Norsk Idrætsblad*, 29 January 1896, 24. On the glue, see Roland Huntford, *Nansen: The Hero as Explorer* (New York: Barnes and Noble, 1998), 229.

3. Letter, Henry Duhamel to Louis Arnaud. HMS printed in *Ski Français 1934–1949: XXXe Anniversaire de la Fédération Française de Ski* (Lyon: Durand-Girard [1949]), 5–6. See also Louis Helly, *Cent ans de ski français* (Grenoble: Cahiers de l'Alpe, 1966), 19–22.

4. Heinz Polednik, *Stolze Erinnerungen: Die Geschichte des Wintersportes in den Sudentenländern* (München: Buch- und Kunstdruckerei, n.d. [1971?]), 21. Vaage, *Skienes Verden*, 260.

5. *Deutsche Turn-Zeitung* (1893): 933.

6. Klaus C. Wildte, *Daten zur Sportgeschichte*, 4 vols. (Schorndorff bei Stuttgart, Karl Hoffmann, 1970–1980), 2:113. Letter, Max Schneider to Cil [Carl J. Luther], Rostock, 13 July 1930. HMS in Deutscher Skiverband, Carl Luther Archiv [DSV L-A.], in Planegg, Germany.

7. *British Ski Year Book* (1910): 95. [Hereafter *BSYB.*] See also the advertisement for John M. Livie, "Britain's Premier Ski Maker," in E. C. Richardson, *'Shilling' Ski Runner* (London: Richardson and Wroughton, [1910]), n.p.

8. *Katalog* [of Winter Exhibition], 5–10 January 1894, Mürzzuschlag, n.p.

9. *Allgemeine Sport-Zeitung*, 27 January 1895, 89.

10. Ibid., 6 March 1902, 267.

11. *Allgemeines Korrespondenzblatt*, 31 January 1907, 149.

12. Richard Staub, "Internationale Ausstellung in Kristiania," *Ski* [Swiss] 7 (January 1907): 78–79, and 8 (February 1907): 93.

13. Ibid., 10 (March 1907): 105.

14. The easiest place to see this in skiing is on postcards of the time.

15. According to the exhibit in Nordiska Museet, Stockholm, 1998.

16. Staub, "Internationale Ausstellung," *Ski* 10 (March 1907): 105. Although iron sidings had been used in Romerike in the 1820s and toe bindings were available in Numedal and Trondheim fifty years later, Fritz Huitfeldt's bindings, patented in 1894, were the most successful. See also Olav Bø, *Skiing Throughout History* (Oslo: Det Norske Samlaget, 1993), 85.

17. German safety binding, see *Ski* [U.S.] (December 1955): 61. *La Montagne*, 20 April 1908, 59–60; 20 December 1908, 239–241.

18. Capitaine Bernard, "Étude sur le ski," ibid., 3 March 1906, 10. R. Gélinet, "Nouvelles attaches: Nouveaux skis," ibid., 20 November 1911, 635–637. Louis Falisse, "A propos des fixations de ski," ibid., 2 February 1913, 84–89. See also J. Sessely-Richardson, *Une lumière sur la question des attaches* (Genève: Forelsen [1911?]), 6–7.

19. *Gérardmer-Saison* 219 (1909): 60, and 269 (1910): 7.

20. K. Coman, "Skiing in the Guadarrama," *Home Progress* 5 (December 1915): 162–163. For the history of early skiing in Spain, see M. G. Aróstegui y J. L. Gilabert, *El gran circo blanco: Historia del esqui alpino* (Valladolid: Miñón, 1980), 37–42.

21. *Allgemeine Sport-Zeitung*, 5 February 1893, 127–128. In fact only eight of the thirty-four hours were spent actually skiing.

22. In *Norsk Idrætsblad*, translated as "Ein Norweger über Wien," *Allgemeine Sport-Zeitung*, 22 March 1896, 247. Examples of skis following Norwegian patterns in the 1890s include Julius Kahne (Benneckenstein, Hochharz), Julius Henel (Breslau), Richard Bulch (Dresden), Kohn Brothers (Vienna), Thonet Brothers (Vienna), Kindl (Graz). Catalogs in Luther Collection and advertisements in newspapers, DSV L-A.

23. *Ashland News*, 16 December 1905; 27 November 1906; 17 December 1906; 4 January 1907. *Ashland Daily Press*, 9 and 23 December 1907. *Iron Ore*, 7 December 1904; 10 February 1906. Ingeborg Burnside (Holter's daughter), interviewed by author, Ashland, Wisconsin, 26 January 1984. See also E. John B. Allen, *From Skisport to Skiing: One Hundred Years of an American Sport, 1840–1940* (Amherst: University of Massachusetts Press, 1993), 70–74, for early ski manufacturing in the United States.

24. Theo. A. Johnsen, *The Winter Sport of Skeeing* (Portland, Maine: Theo. A. Johnsen, 1905), 6–7, 42–45, 57.

25. A. H. Gibson, *Osborne Reynolds and his Work in Hydraulics and Hydrodynamics* (London: The British Council, 1946), 4–7. Michel Braquins maintains the date is 1886; see his "Une histoire du ski des origines au milieu du XXe siècle," *Revue du Palais de la Découverte* 20 (January 1991): 26–27.

26. Letter, Max Schneider to Cil, Rostock, 21 October 1924. HMS in Luther Collection, DSV L-A. Schneider had a collection of over a hundred catalogs at one time. There are presently about thirty in the museum at Planegg.

27. Catalogs in the Luther Collection, DSV L-A. See the skis of Godet and Nicole-Farnier, two artisans making skis by 1907, on exhibit in Le Grand Tétra, Les Rousses. G. Flusin, "Ski-Club Dauphinois," *Le Moniteur Dauphinois,* 25 January 1896, n.p. Letter, René Vilmain to *La Montagne* 297 (April 1938): 122–123. H. Martin, "Du ski moyen de transport au ski jurassien," *Le Jura Français* 106 (1965): 499, cited in Yves Moralès, "Exercises corporals et les sports dans les Jura (1870–1914)." Mémoire de D. E. A. 1989–1990, Université de Franche-Compté, U. F. R. des Sciences du Language, de l'Homme et de la Société. TMS, 217–218, 225. The Abbé Blot of Besse in the Auvergne had the same experience. Pierre-André Chauvet, *Musée du Ski,* n.d., n.p. [2000?]. Letter, Max Schneider to Cil, Rostock, 1932 in Luther Collection, DSV L-A.

28. Catalogs in the Luther Collection, DSV L-A. Marcellin Bérot, *L'Épopée du ski aux Pyrénées* (Toulouse, Milan, Tarbes: Randonnées Pyrénées, 1991), 15, 18, 26. A.S.-J., "Bibliothèque au ski," *Le Ski* (April–July 1946): 372.

29. *Catalog Hagen,* Krisitiania, probably 1895, DSV L-A collection.

30. Polednik, *Stolze Erinnerungen,* 24. *Deutsche Alpenzeitung* 42-43 (2nd March issue 1902): 24.

31. Willi Romberg, "Der Wintersport auf der Internationalen Ausstellung für Sport und Spiel zu Frankfurt a.M.," *Ski-Chronik* 2 (1909–10): 17–18.

32. Capitaine Nerlinger, "Le ski court," *La Montagne,* 20 December 1910, 702–703. *Revue des Alpes Dauphinoises,* 15 August 1909, back cover. Jakob Vaage, "Milepeler og merkedager gjennom 4000 år," *Norske Skiløpere: Østlandet Nord* (Oslo: Ranheim, 1955), 28.

33. F. F. Roget, "Ski-running in the High Alps," *BYSB* II, 7 (1911): 17–18.

34. Touring Club de France, *Ski Utilitaire,* 1. See also M.V., "Fabrication d'un ski," *La Vie au Grand Air,* 9 January 1908, 25, and *Revue Alpine* (Sect. Lyonnais) 13 (March 1907): 132.

35. *La Montagne,* 20 January 1909, 41. A.S.-J., "Bibliothèque du skieur," *Le Ski* (April–July 1946): 372.

36. Max Schneider, "Die Einführung des Schneeschuhlaufs in Deutschland," *Der Winter* 17 (August 1924): 243–244.

37. *La Montagne,* 20 March 1908, 130.

38. A. L. [Arnold Lunn], "Kandahar Story," TMS in box 6, folder 3, Lunn Papers, Georgetown University, Washington, D.C.

39. Advertisement in *BSYB* (1907), (1908), (1909): n.p.; (1911): vii; (1912): xi. *Public Schools Alpine Sports Club Year Book* (1912): iv. Letter to *Winter Sports Review* (1911–12): 38.

40. *L'Hiver en Suisse* (Berne: Chemins de fer fédéraux, 1912), 9–58.

41. *La Montagne,* 20 December 1907, 596; 20 November 1909, 670. Bernard Janin, "Le Tourisme dans les Grandes Alpes Italiennes: Breuil-Cervinia et Valtournanche," *Revue Géographique Alpine* 52 (1964): 217.

42. Dr. Esmont in *Gazette Médicale,* cited in *Alpinismus und Wintersport,* 16 October 1907, n.p.

43. J. B., "L'Hiver aux Pyrénées," *La Vie au Grand Air,* 29 February 1908, 141. See also where the "social atmosphere of peculiar energy and hilarity which is now threatening the sunny social resorts of the South of France with a new and formidable rivalry." Harold Spender, "Winter at Beatenberg," *Public Schools Alpine Sports Club Year Book* (1912): 69.

44. "Mountaineering—the Alpine Club," *Blackwood's Magazine* 86 (October 1859): 460.

45. Jean Miège, "La vie touristique en Savoie," *Revue Géographique Alpine* 21 (1933): 756–757, 771–773.

46. Lunn, "The Pioneers," *BSYB* (1927): 191.

47. Michel Payot, "Les skis . . . au Col de Balme (12 February 1902)," *Bulletin Mensuel* (Sect. Vosgiennes) (April 1902): 106–108. Payot, "Le passage du Col du Géant en skis," *Annuaire du Club Alpin Français* 28 (1902): 3–9. Payot, "De Chamonix à Zermatt en skis," *Revue Alpine* 9, no. 9 (1903): 269–284.

48. *Revue Mensuel* (April 1902): 100. *La Montagne,* 20 December 1908, 242. By 1914 there were large hotels, three with 500 beds, one with 250, and the total of available beds was 2,700. See Miège, "Vie touristique en Savoie," *Revue Géographique Alpine* 21 (1933): 785.

49. For one example, from the Vosges, see *Gérardmer-Saison,* 30 March 1909, 9.

50. *La Montagne,* 20 January 1908, 9. S., "Le concours international de Chamonix," *Revue Alpine* (Sect. Lyonnais) 14 (February 1908): 47. A brochure of 1908–9 proclaimed the hyphenated title of "Chamonix-Mt. Blanc." It is the earliest that I have noticed. Seen in Fonds Payot, Conservatoire d'Art et d'Histoire de Haute Savoie, Annecy.

51. TMS signed by mayor, box 8M 58, file: Classement des hotels 1920–1936, in Archives de la Mairie, Chamonix.

52. Marcel Violette, "Chamonix, station d'hiver," *La Vie au Grand Air,* 11 January 1908, 35–37.

53. Winter visitors for 1911–12 season: 11,725, for 1912–13: 12,975, for 1913–14: 15,895. *La Montagne*, 4 April 1914, 223.

54. *Excelsior*, 6 February 1912, in Album Memento AR 1502, CAF archives, Paris. *Aftenposten*, 20 December 1911, *Lettura Sportiva*, 17 February 1912. See also *La Montagne*, 1 January 1912, 40; 3 March 1912, 154. For an account of the meet, see P. Alloix, "VIe concours international de ski," ibid., 144.

55. *BSYB* (1913): x. Meeting of Committee, 9 April 1914, in File: SI 1912–1928: Registre des délibérations. HMS, Marie Archive, Chamonix.

56. All in *Illustrierte Zeitung*, 24 December 1908. It is of interest, too, that this Leipzig based paper contained nine full pages of advertisements: six for Germany, one for Austria, one for Switzerland, and one for a variety of goods. Note that France did not advertise. This was not because of any anti-German sentiment; the French were simply late starters in the economic rush for clientele.

57. Judith Williamson, *Decoding Advertisements: Ideology and Meaning in Advertising* (London: Boyars, 1978), see especially 24–36.

58. Ulf Hamilton, "The Concours d'art in OS 1912," in *Memory and Beauty*, ed. Agnieszka Majkowska et al. (Warsaw: Foundation of the Olympic Education Centre and the Museum of Sports and Tourism in Warsaw, 2002), 99–106.

59. Letter, Max Schneider to Cil, Berlin, 22 November 1908. HMS in L-A DSV.

60. *Allgemeine Sport-Zeitung*, 5 April 1896, 297.

61. *Österreichische Touristen-Zeitung*, 1 December 1909, 283.

62. F. F. Roget, *Hints on Alpine Sports* (London: Burberry's, [1912]).

63. *Wintersport-Kalender für Sachsen, Thüringen und Harz 1913–1914* (Leipzig: Werner Dietsch, 1913).

64. Auguste Robin, "Le ski et le tobogganning," *Les Sports Modernes Illustrés* (Paris: Larousse, 1905).

65. *Neige et Glace*, 16 October 1932, 23. *Les Sports d'Hiver* was published between 1908 and 1924 but treated skiing only from time to time although more frequently after World War I. It became *Les Sports d'Hiver et Alpinisme*.

66. *Allgemeine Sport-Zeitung*, 4 December 1904, 1508. *Deutsche Turn-Zeitung*, 10 February 1896, 54. *Chronik 1907–8 Ski Club Winterberg* (Westdeutschland Skiverband. Skiklub Winterberg) [1966], 25. *BSYB* (1912): 98. *The Times*, 4 January 1910, 19.

67. *Chronik 1907–8 Ski Club Winterberg*, 25.

68. *Gérardmer-Saison*, 24 April and 8 May 1910, 1–2.

69. Abbé Blot in April 1908 and February 1911 in Chauvet, *Musée du Ski*, n.p. Skis continued to be given to local curés instrumental in getting particularly local youth on skis up until about 1930. See, for example, *Circulaire trimestrielle*, Sect. d'Isère du CAF 3 (January 1928): 8.

70. *Norsk Idrætsblad*, 25 February 1888, 36. See also ibid., 1 December 1888, 188. The

expense of carrying skis had already received publicity the season before: 0.75 Kr for skis, 0.40 Kr. for skier from Christiania to Sandviken. "Jernbanerne og skiløberene," ibid., 27 February 1887, 44. Kristin Moe, *Snø og ski i Norsk malerkunst 1847–1924* (Oslo: Skiforeningen, 1999), 36.

71. *La Montagne* 4, no. 11 (1908): 444. Bérot, *Épopée Pyrénées*, 31–35.

72. C. Janot, "Sports d'hiver en Auvergne," *Revue d'Auvergne* 92, no. 1 (1978): 441.

73. *La Montagne* 10, no. 7 (July 1914): 402. *Jungfrau Railway of Switzerland* (Zürich: Fretz, n.d.) is a good technical, visual and descriptive pamphlet.

74. *L'Hiver en Suisse* (Genève et Bellegarde, 1912).

75. Miège, "Vie touristique en Savoie," *Revue Géographique Alpine* 21 (1933): 750, n. 1.

76. Letter, Journal et liste des étrangers du Bas-Valais, Montreux, to mayor, Chamonix, 24 September 1908. TMS, File: Tourisme, Correspondence divers 1890 à 1910. Mairie archives, Chamonix.

77. "Le dernier concours de ski à Chamonix," *Lectures pour tous* (1908), 449.

78. *Allgemeine Sport-Zeitung*, 12 November 1899, 1385; 5 November 1904, 1396. "Skier auf der Strassenbahn," *Der Schnee*, 24 December 1909, 2.

79. Mathias Zdarsky, "Ein Zopf," *Allgemeine Sport-Zeitung*, 11 March 1900, 212. *Der Schnee*, 19 January 1906, 2; 21 October 1908, 5–6. *Österreichische Touristen-Zeitung*, 1 February 1906, 30–31.

80. *Allgemeine Sport-Zeitung*, 11 March 1900, 212. *Der Schnee*, 19 January 1906; 21 October 1908, 5–6. *Österreichische Touristen-Zeitung*, 1 February 1906, 30–31.

81. *Der Winter* 21 (March 1909): 227. See also *Allgemeine Sport-Zeitung*, 2 October 1910, 1321.

82. *Der Schnee*, 20 February 1909, 1. For a statistical overview, see Wolfgang Meixner, "Zur Entwicklung des Tourismus in Tirol und Vorarlberg," in *Internationale Konferenz: Hannes Schneider—Pionier des Skisports*, ed. Christof Thoeny (St. Anton am Arlberg, 8–10 April 2005), n.p. TMS.

83. *50 Jahre SC Garmisch*, 10. Carl J. Luther, ed., *50 Jahre Bayerischer Skiverband*, n.p.

84. *Chronik 1907–8 Ski Club Winterberg*, 25. *Der Winter* 6 (December 1911): 146. For an account of traveling from London to St. Moritz in the early 1890s—one left the train at Chur and took horse sleighs—see Letter, W. J. M. to *The Times*, 12 January 1939, 11. E. C. Richardson, "British Skiing at Home and Abroad," *Aarbok* (1913): 123. Gordon Selfridge, "ein fanatischer Sportler," of the well-known fashion emporium in London, Selfridges, had such a weekend in 1914. *Der Winter* 8 (March 1914): 492.

85. *The Times*, 18 December 1913, 13.

86. Anita Lee-Bapty, "British Skiers and the Development of Swiss Ski Resorts, 1880–1914," 4. TMS unpublished paper. Tirol had such a society in the 1870s. Meixner, "Zur Entwicklung des Tourismus in Tirol und Vorarlberg," in Thoeny, *Internationale Konferenz—Hannes Schneider*, n.p., TMS.

87. Joseph Vaillot, "Un project conçu en 1835 pour monter en chemin de fer au sommet du Mont Blanc," *La Montagne*, 20 March 1908, 106–117. Mme. Maige-Lefournier, *Le ski, le soleil et la neige–Le Mont Revard* (Chambéry: Dardel, 1912), 37.

88. Interview with Klaus Winterhalter, Schollach, 11 September 2001. Winterhalter's lift dates vary from 1903 to 1908. The patent was granted for 1908–9. My thanks to Martin Schwer for introductions and translation. German television has made a documentary of the lift. The lift is being restored and will be in working condition in its original place.

89. Alfred Rüsch and Hugo Rhomberg, "Sprunghügelanlagen auf dem Bödele bei Dornbirn," *Der Winter* (1908/09): 29. *BSYB* (1910): 70. Paul Zimmermann, "Der erste Skilift der Welt," *Die Gebirgstruppe* 2 (April 1994): 38–40. See also Wolfgang Allgeuer, "History of Vorarlberg's cable cars and ski lifts," in Wolfgang Allgeuer, Peter Strauss and Christoph Volaucnik, *Centenary of Skiing Vorarlberg*. Bregenz: Vorarlberg State Tourist Board, 1986, 9.

90. Dartmouth Outing Club minutes, 5 February 1915. HMS, Baker Library, Dartmouth College, Hanover, N.H. For early tows in the United States, see Allen, *From Skisport to Skiing*, 109–110.

91. Bishop Wilkinson consecrated the Anglican church at Chateau d'Oex in 1899, bringing the total number of English churches in the Alps to seventy. My thanks to Clive Atkinson of St. Peter's, Chateau d'Oex. Jim Ring, *How the English Made the Alps* (London: John Murray, 2000), 172–174.

CHAPTER 6. THE ENGLISH PLAY

1. "She," *T. P's Weekly*, 12 February 1904, 226. *Alpine Journal* 31 (August 1903): 497. *Yorkshire Post*, 2 March 1939, quoted in *Ski Notes & Queries* 68 (May 1939): 119. [*SN&Q.*]

2. Herbert Asquith, Prime Minister and member of the Public Schools Alpine Sports Club cited in *British Ski Year Book* (1938): 432. [*BSYB.*]

3. "Some Memories 1905–26," *Public Schools Alpine Sports Club Year Book* (1927): 113.

4. Allen Guttmann, *Games and Empires: Modern Sports and Cultural Imperialism* (New York: Columbia University Press, 1994); see especially chap. 9: "Cultural Imperialism?" 172–188. For the British particularly, see Richard Holt, *Sport and the British: A Modern History* (Oxford: Oxford University Press, 1989), chap. 4: "Empire and Nation," 203–279.

5. *BSYB* (1905): 44–46. In a discussion on the merits of pronouncing "ski" or "she," one reverend thought it inadvisable that he should chat with his slum parishioners about "she-ing." *SN&Q* 6 (December 1931): 282.

6. *BSYB* (1905): 44–46.

7. Arnold Henry Moore Lunn, *Come What May* (Boston: Little Brown, 1941), 74.

8. *The Times*, 10 February 1906, 6, and 14 January 1908, 12.

9. John Premble, *The Mediterranean Passion* (Oxford: Oxford University Press, 1987), 246. For the Goms valley assessment, see Letter, Lunn to Mother, Mürren, 15 February 1916. TMS copy in box 1, folder 1, The Sir Arnold Lunn papers, Special collections, Lauinger Library, Georgetown University, Washington D.C.

10. Premble, *Mediterranean Passion*, 246.

11. Margaret Symonds, *Out of the Past* (1925), 298, cited in ibid., 254.

12. Figures are based on Murray's *Handbook* (1892), and the Swiss historian, Fueter, cited in J. A. R. Pimlott, *The Englishman's Holiday: A Social History* (Hassocks: Harvester Press, 1976), 209. *Country Life*, 23 November 1912, 19.

13. Cited in Pimlott, *Englishman's Holiday*, 209.

14. Premble, *Mediterranean Passion*, 246. Norwegian visitors numbered 13,000 in 1886, 20,000 in 1902. Ronald G. Popperwell, *Norway* (New York: Praeger, 1972), 39.

15. For example, the funicular at Chantarella above St. Moritz was built primarily for convalescents but was used instantly by skiers. *The Times*, 25 February 1912, 11.

16. *BSYB* (1913): viii. The Jura advertisement is 1973/497 in ski box 3, folder: Grafik. Schweizerisches Sportmuseum, Basel, Switzerland.

17. *The Times*, 28 December 1909, 15. Charles W. Domville-Fife, *Things Seen in Switzerland in Winter* (London: Seeley, Service, 1926), 24.

18. *The Times*, 17 February 1912, 15.

19. Arnold Lunn, *Ski-ing* (London: Eveleigh Nash, 1913), 109.

20. "Some Memories," *Public Schools Alpine Sports Club Year Book* (1927): 110–112.

21. Ibid., (1914): 100–101.

22. Ibid., (1914): 130–208.

23. Ibid., (1914): 113.

24. Ibid., (1914): 91–92. See also letter, Lynx Eye to *Winter Sports Review* (1912–1913): 271. Lunn, *Come What May*, 80.

25. *Illustrated London News*, 13 February 1909, 230–231.

26. W. R. Rickmers, "The Alpine Skee and Mountaineering," *Alpine Journal* 21 (August 1903): 454. E. C. Richardson, "English Ski-running," *Aarbok* (1907): 121–122.

27. Domville-Fife, *Things Seen in Switzerland*, 48.

28. Cecil Slingsby, "Round the Horungtinder in Winter," *Den Norske Turist Forenings Aarbog* (1880): 91, 103, 107. See also his book, *Norway the Northern Playground: Sketches of Climbing and Mountain Exploration in Norway between 1872 and 1903* (Edinburgh: David Douglas, 1904), 200, and in *Winter Sports Review* (1911–1912): 238, where he says that his suggestion was "the earliest known recommendation to mountain lovers to take a run on ski over the wildest mountain region of their country." It would be interesting to know if Fridtjof Nansen read Slingsby.

29. Although one of the most articulate mountaineer-writers, David Roberts, main-

tains that the love of nature had little to do with their interest in mountaineering. Elite mountaineers are "uncheerful about hiking, impatient with the weather, insensitive to the subtleties of landscape." "Patey Agonistes: A Look at Climbing Autobiographies," *Ascent* (1974), reprinted in David Roberts, *Moments of Doubt and Other Mountaineering Writings* (Seattle: Mountaineers, 1986), 187.

30. Dr. Engel, *La littérature alpestre en France et en Angleterre aux XVIIè et XVIIIè siècles*, cited in Lunn, "Mountain Mystique," 14, TMS in box 7, folder 5, Lunn Papers. I take much of this from the above ms., 13–17, and from Lunn, "The Swiss and Their Mountains," 1–14, TMS copy, in box 7, folder 5, Lunn Papers. See also Adalbert Elschenbroich, "Nachwort," in Haller's poems published in Stuttgart (Walter Rost, 1956), 104. "Die Alpen" is on pp. 3–22. Richard Strauss composed "An Alpine Symphony" in 1888. There was a general cultural acceptance of the Alps as a romantic notion.

31. Henry H. Hoek, "Von alten Ski in Graubünden," *Der Schnee-Hase* 2, no. 6 (1932): 157, 160–162. Hoek, *Ma bella Engadina: Ski und Schnee im Engadin* (Hamburg: Enoch, 1933), 29, 37–38.

32. Raymond Flower, *The Story of Ski-ing and Other Winter Sports* (London: Angus and Robertson, 1976), 36.

33. *The Times,* 29 March 1910.

34. Letter, W. A. B. Coolidge to Lunn, Grindelwald, 12 November 1918. TMS in box 1, folder 28, Lunn Papers. See also Lunn, Diary "Visit to Coolidge," 8 September 1918. TMS copy in box 9, folder 40, Lunn Papers.

35. In box 9, folder 50, Lunn Papers.

36. *Bulletin* (Section Vosgienne) (May–June 1904): 35–36; *Allgemeine Sport-Zeitung,* 6 March 1904, 239; *Norsk Idrætsblad* 22 (1904): 113.

37. *La Montagne,* 20 October 1907, 459.

38. Josef Müller, "Vor zwanzig Jahren," *Zwanzig Jahre Österreichischer Ski-Verein. Festschrift anlässlich des zwanzigjährigen Bestandes. Herausgegeben vom österreichischen Ski-Verein gegründet 8. Nov. 1892* (Wien: Österreichischer Ski-Verein, 1912), 8.

39. *SN&Q* (May 1929): 98; and ibid. (October 1929): 136.

40. J. W. und Fr. Scheibert, *Der Wintersport* (Leipzig: Grethlein, 1905), 107.

41. A. Conan Doyle, "An Alpine Pass on 'Ski'," *Strand Magazine* (December 1894): 657–661. In America, it was published in *McClure's Magazine*. See also Conan Doyle, *Memories and Adventures* (London: Hodder and Stoughton, 1924), 291–293.

42. *Public Schools Alpine Sports Club Year Book* (1914): 168. See also Jerome K. Jerome, *My Life and Times* (London: John Murray, 1926; reprinted 1983), 170–175.

43. Karl Egger, "Geschichtliches," *Ski* [Swiss] 5 (1909): 93. Jakob Vaage, *Skienes Verden* (Oslo: Hjemmenes, 1979), 227, has a different version of the story. There is a magnificent 1913 poster done for the Montigny-Orsières railway by Albert Muret of the monks streaming down from the hospice.

44. *Winterthurer Tagblatt* cited in Eduard Naeff, "Erinnerungen eines Skiveteranen," *Die Alpen* 5 (1929): 41. Alexander von Steiger, "Pragel und Schild im Winter 1892/93," *Ski* [Swiss] 24-25 (1929): 53–58. There is a curious entry in *Ski* 28 (1892): 497, which notes that Kjelsberg crossed the Pragel in January 1892. This appears to be an error. See also letter, Charles King to *The Times*, 22 March 1937, 8.

45. *Allgemeine Sport-Zeitung*, 20 March 1892, 188. The Mürzzuschlag Wintersport-museum holds a film reenacting the climb.

46. Albert von Planta, *75 Jahre Ski Club Alpina St. Moritz: 1903–1978* (St. Moritz: S.C. Alpina [1978?]), 5 (Fuorcla Surlej); ibid 16 (Longhin); Wilhelm Lohmüller, "Eroberung des Berner Oberlandes durch den Ski," *Die Alpen* 7 (1931): 202 (Grimsel), 203 (Ober-alpstock); Offermann; "Anfangen," 36 (Luckmanier). Wilhelm Lehner, "Die ersten Ski-Dreitausender," *Winter Schönheit* (1949/50): 6 (Hoher Sonnblick).

47. *L'Echo des Alpes* 35 (January 1899): 29–30.

48. Wilhelm Paulcke, "Eine Winterfahrt auf Schneeschuhen quer durch das Berner Oberland (18. bis 23. Jänner 1897)," *Österreichische Alpen-Zeitung*, 13 May 1897, 117–123; 27 May 1897, 129–135; 10 June 1897, 141–146. See also Paulcke, "Auf Skiern im Hochgebirge," *Zeitschrift des Deutschen und Österreichischen Alpen-Vereins* 33 (1902): 170–186, especially 175. He summed up the years 1896–1900 as not only important in the history of alpinism but as opening up "a new phase in winter expedition possibilities." Paulcke, "Zur Entwicklung des alpinen Skilaufs in den Jahren 1896–1900," ibid., 23 (2 May 1901): 116–17. Paulcke continued to write about it, in "Der Triumph des Skis im Hochgebirge," *Der Winter* 20 (1926–27): 132–136.

49. Hugo Mylius, the conquerer of Mont Blanc, received a long write up in *The Times*, 4 March 1904, 9.

50. Letter, de Linde to Editor, Hythe, 2 September 1936, *BSYB* (1939): 207.

51. *L'Echo des Alpes* 41 (March 1905): 111–112. The continuing discussion may be followed in ibid. (April 1905): 148; *Ski* [Swiss] 3 (1905): 147; ibid. 5 (1905): 114.

52. Paulcke, "Auf Skiern im Hochgebirge," *Zeitschrift des Deutschen u. Österreichischen Alpen-Vereins* 33 (1902): 173–175, for Paulcke's own account. For an analysis, see Lohmüller, "Die erste Sommer-Ski-Hochtur," *Der Winter* 26 (November 1932): 37–40.

53. *Gazette de Lausanne* in Lunn Scrapbook in box 12, folder 3, Lunn Papers. *The Times*, 9 January 1908, 3.

54. Lunn Scrapbook in box 12, folders 2 and 3. For Roget, see Lunn, Diary, 27 March 1918. TMS copy in box 9, folder 50, Lunn Papers.

55. Letter, Lunn to Marcel Kurz, 7 June 1917. TMS copy in box 1, folder 10, Lunn Papers.

56. Letter, Kurz to Lunn, Goeschenen, 21 June 1917. HMS in ibid.

57. Lunn, *Ski-ing*, 188–191. Lunn, *Come What May*, 171.

58. *Allgemeine Sport-Zeitung*, 2 February 1908, 99.

59. Lunn, *A History of Ski-ing* (London: Oxford University Press, 1927), 216–217. *BSYB* (1912): 152. No one knows why Lord Roberts of Kandahar lent his prestigious name to this race. He had no interest in skiing and had never been to the Alps in winter. Arnold Lunn speculated that his father asked Lord Lytton to approach him. Lunn, *'Unkilled for So Long'* (London: Allen and Unwin, 1968), 40.

60. "Roberts of Kandahar," *Public Schools Alpine Sports Club Year Book* (1912): 33

61. Arnold Lunn has not yet attracted a biographer. Richard Holt, "An Englishman in the Alps: Arnold Lunn, Amateurism and the Invention of Alpine Ski Racing," *International Journal of the History of Sport* 9 (December 1992): 421–432, is not, in spite of its title, really about skiing, but the author analyzed how his background, manners, social connections, and ideology affected his role. See especially ibid., 422.

62. Alan d'Egville, *Adventures in Safety* (London: Sampson Low and Marston, n.d.), 288.

63. Georges Blanchon, "Images de Murren," *Neige et Glace* 15 (May 1937): 328–329.

64. Names of races varied from district to district in Norway and Sweden. Einar Stoltenberg, cited in Olav Bø, *Skiing Throughout History* (Oslo: Det Norske Samlaget, 1993), 53–54. Artur Zettersten, HMS, 29–31 in Svenska Skidmuseet, Umeå. More readily available is John Weinstock, "Sondre Norheim: Folk Hero to Immigrant," *Norwegian-American Studies* 29 (1983): 347–348.

65. *Fædrelandet* no. 20 (1879), cited by Vaage, *Skienes Verden,* 132.

66. "Holmenkollen races," *BSYB* (1906): 31.

67. *Allgemeine Sport-Zeitung,* 19 March 1911, 305; 2 February 1913, 114. Willi Romberg, *Mit Ski und Rodel. Taschenbuch für Wintersportlustige,* 2nd ed. (Leipzig: Leiner, 1910 [?]), 97–98. Letter, Commander J. H. W. Shirley, Oxshott, 15 January 1956, to editor, *BSYB* (1956): 103.

68. F. Klute, "Kunst- oder Hindernislauf?" *Der Winter* 5 (April 1911): 342–343. See also ibid. (June 1911): 357.

69. For what follows on Zdarsky and his *Torlauf,* see Letter, Mathias Zdarsky to Mehl, Marktl im Traisentale, 3 February 1932, Zdarsky-Archiv, Lilienfeld, Austria. Erwin Mehl, "Mathias Zdarsky (1856–1940) in Lilienfeld-Marktl: Lilienfeld als Wiege der alpinen Schifahrtechnik und des Torlaufes. Hier erfand Zdarsky sein lebensrettendes Zelt," in *Heimatkunde des Bezirkes Lilienfeld,* vol. 2 (1963), reprinted with additions by Franz Klaus, 1985, in Zdarsky-Archiv. Letters, Otto Lutter to Theodor Hüttenegger, Graz, 28 April 1950, and Lutter to Richard Guttmann, Graz, May 1951. TMSS in Fach-Beiträge Skigeschichte Wertvoll, sect. L, Wintersportmuseum Mürzzuschlag. Wolf Kitterle, *75 Jahre Torlauf* (Wien: Kitterle, 1979), has reprinted the original *Wettfahr-Urkunde ausgestellt für die Wettfahrer, Starter, Wegrichter und Zielrichter, welche sich an dem Ski Wettfahren in Lilienfeld am 19. März 1905 beteiligten,* 4–23. For Zdarsky's challenge to the Norwegians, see *Alpiner Winter Sport* 2 (January 1905): 153–154. See

also C. N. Schwerdtner, "Meine Reise nach Christiania," *Allgemeines Korrespondenz-blatt* II (February 1905): 109–III. W. Fleischmann und E. Steinbrüchel, *Lilienfelder oder Norweger? Zur Aufklärung in einem alten Sportstreit! Ein historischer Rückblick aus den Aktenstücken* (Diessen: Huber, 1910), particularly 61–85. There were other challenges, see *Allgemeine Sport-Zeitung*, 26 April 1903, 471; 5 and 12 February 1899, 138, 165. A challenge came almost a century later, in 1993, at a meeting of sports museum directors held at the Olympic Museum, Lausanne, 3 September 1993, when the director of the Swiss Sports Museum, Dr. Max Triet, was challenged over his interpretation of the beginning of slalom by Franz Klaus, the director of the Zdarsky Archive. Following the incident, there was a flurry of correspondence in various newsletters.

70. Josef Wallner TMS, 4. Wintersportmuseum Mürzzuschlag.

71. Zdarsky, "Nicht primitives Wettfahren," *Allgemeine Sport-Zeitung*, 4 February 1900, 108. Letter, Zdarsky to Mehl, 3 February 1932. Zdarsky-Archiv.

72. Lunn cited by Erwin Mehl, *Zdarsky: Festschrift zum 80. Geburtstag des Begründers der alpinen Schifahrweise 25. Februar 1936* (Wien: Deutscher Verlag für Jugend und Volk, 1936), 95.

73. The Kandahar Ski Club was founded as a racing club with the secondary object of securing international recognition for downhill racing. *Kandahar Review* 3 (November 1934): 10.

74. *BSYB* (1923): 121.

75. E. C. Richardson, *The Ski-Runner* (London: Cecil Palmer, 1924), 223–224.

76. *Aftenposten*, trans. Mrs. Krefting and published in *BSYB* (1932): 566.

77. For example, in the *Bulletin Pyrénéen* (January–March 1928) and Letter, Arnold Lunn to Tauern, 27 April 1926, S. C. Freiburg K 2/30, Nr. 23, Stadtarchiv der Stadt Freiburg i. B., cited by Vera Martinelli, *Frauen in den Anfängen des Skisportes: Das Beispiel Schwarzwald*, masters thesis, Albert-Ludwigs-Universität Freiburg i. Breisgau (2004), 26.

78. Lunn, *History of Ski-ing*, 229.

79. *Adam* (December 1931).

80. *BSYB* (1926).

81. *Ski Survey* 1, no. 7 (1974): 382–383.

CHAPTER 7. THE FRENCH WORRY

1. Henry Cuënot, "Le ski, ses origines en France et le rôle du C. A. F. dans son développement," *La Montagne* 231 (March–April 1931): 98. Cuënot, "Le role de la Fédération Française de Ski," *Les Sports de Neige et Glace*, 16 January 1926, 133.

2. Archives de Département d'Isère, Grenoble: Hygiène et Santé Publique, 1902, in Série 113M/8 (1898–1903).

3. *La Montagne* (1906): 397, (1908): 200–201, (1910): 610.

4. Ibid. (1913): 642–644.

5. Maurice Allotte de Fuy, *Ascensions d'hiver du Pic de la Croix de Belledone* (Grenoble: Vallier, 1891), 15.

6. *Annuaire de l'Observatoire* (1884), cited in M. Maige-Lefournier, *Le ski, le soleil et la neige* (Mont Revard conference, 1910–11), 15.

7. Ibid., 17.

8. Henri Clerc, "Rapport des expériences de skis exécutées dans les environs de Briançon par le 159me. Reg. D'Inf. Au cours des hivers 1900–1901 et 1901–1902." Copy HMS in Musée Dauphinois. A great number of conscripts were shorter than 1.54 meters (5 ft. 1/2 in.). André Palluel-Guillard, "Problèmes sanitaires et physiologiques de la Savoie au XIXe siècle," *Mosaïques d'Histoire en Savoie* 88 (1983): 71.

9. *Revue Alpine* (1903–4), cited in Yves Ballu, *L'hiver de glisse et de glace* (Evreux: Gallimard, 1991), 18–19. Guy Thuillier, "Pour une histoire de l'hygiène corporelle," *Revue d'histoire économique et sociale* 46 (1968): 233–34, 243.

10. "Pâques à Val d'Isère," CAF Section Vosgiènne, *Revue* 14 (Hiver 1937–38): 16.

11. Françoise Brochet, *Le goitre et le cretinisme en Savoie: aspect historique*, Ph.D. thesis, Faculté de Pharmacie, Université Claude Bernard, Lyon (1986), 2. Marcel Guillamo et al., *Vie militaire et débuts du ski dans le Briançonnais (1890–1910)* (Gap: Louis-Jean, 1989), 32, 48.

12. Veyret-Vernier, "Tourisme au secours de la montagne," *Revue de Géographie Alpine* 44 (1956): 29–30.

13. *New York Times*, 3 February 1920.

14. Dr. Chevrot, *Recherches sur la dépopulation des campagnes et moyens de la combattre* (Lons-le-Saunier, 1906), cited in Yves Moralès, "Les exercises corporels et les sports dans le Jura (1870–1914)." Mémoire de D.E.A. 1989–1990, Université de Franche-Compté, U.F.R. des Sciences du Language, de l'Homme et de la Société. TMS, 57. For problems in the Pyrenees, see F. Viard, "Considérations sur le goitre endémique de Savoie . . . et autres lieux," *Concours Médicale* 80 (1962): 4633–40.

15. Document 30 in Archives de la Bibliothèque Municipale, Briançon. Moralès notes that the most popular sporting societies in the Jura in the years 1870–1914 were shooting (with 105), then gymnastics (75), those giving military instruction (36), touring (32), and, a long way behind, ski clubs (8). Moralès, "Les exercises corporels," 86–98. When war did come, there was little enthusiasm for the conflict and no strong nationalistic feeling among those called to the colors. Jean-Jacques Becker, *1914: Comment les Français sont entrés dans la guerre* (Paris: Fondation Nationale des Sciences Politiques, 1977), esp. 269–291.

16. Rapport de l'Inspecteur d'Académie des Hautes Alpes au Préfet des Hautes Alpes, Gap, 9 October 1908. HMS copy, Document 16, Arch. Dép. 4M 322, Bibliothèque Municipale, Briançon.

17. Cuënot, "Role de la Fédération Française de Ski," *Neige et Glace,* 16 January 1926, 133–134.

18. A. Fouillé, *Psychologie du peuple français* (Paris: 1899), a book that was in its eighth edition in 1927, cited by Joseph J. Spengler, *France Faces Depopulation* (Durham: Duke University Press, 1938), 135. P. Tissié, *La fatigue et l'entrainement physique* (Paris: Alcans, 1897), 84, cited in Yves Moralès, "Le Jura régénérant ou la valeur hygiénique des sports d'hiver," in *Sport et santé dans l'histoire,* ed. Thierry Terret (Sankt Augustin: ISHPES, 1999), 316.

19. *The Times,* 16 January 1883.

20. Philip E. Ogden and Marie-Monique Huss, "Demography and Pronatalism in France in the Nineteenth and Twentieth Centuries," *Journal of Historical Geography* 8, no. 3 (1982): 291–292. Richard Tomlinson et al., "France in Peril," *History Today* 35 (1985): 24–31.

21. Max Nordau, *Degeneration,* trans. from 2nd ed. of the German work (Lincoln: University of Nebraska Press, 1993), 2. He is talking more of the upper echelons of French society, something that *Der Wintersport,* the official paper of the Austrian Winter Sport Clubs in Vienna recognized. Noggler, "Wintersport-Klassen-Rassenpolitik," *Der Wintersport,* 2 March 1912, 149.

22. Spengler, *France Faces Depopulation,* 122–130. Tomlinson, "France in Peril," *History Today* 35 (April 1985): 24–31. Camille Mauclair, cited in Priscilla Robertson, *An Experience of Women: Pattern and Change in 19th Century Europe* (Philadelphia: Temple University Press, 1982), 221. See also Karen Offen, "Exploring the Sexual Politics of Republican Nationalism," in *Nationhood and Nationalism in France: From Boulangism to the Great War 1889–1918,* ed. R. Tombs (London: HarperCollins Academic, 1991), 196–203.

23. Cuënot, "Role de la Fédération Française de Ski," *Neige et Glace,* 16 January 1926, 133–134. Henry Spont, "Le ski," *La Vie au Grand Air,* 29 December 1905, 1105. *Forez-Auvergne* (February 1911), quoted in M. Achard, *Histoire du ski et des sports d'hiver dans le massif du Pilat (Loire-Forez) de 1892 à nos jours* (Le Bessat-St. Etienne: Achard, 1989), 76.

24. Charles Grandmougin, "Au Club Alpin," *Journal le Petit Comtois,* 17 December 1884, reprinted in Moralès, "Les exercises corporals," 135–136.

25. *La Montagne,* 20 October 1906, 472.

26. For what follows on the 1907 meet, see Roger Merle, *Histoire du ski dans le Briançonnais* (Gap: Ophrys/Alpes et Midi, 1989), 48. *Le Monde Illustré,* 23 February 1907. *La Montagne,* 20 March 1907, 136–138. For a Norwegian view, see H. Durban Hansen, "Fra frankrige første internationale Skiløb," *Aarbok* (1907): 107–108.

27. For the attendance figures, see F. R., "Le concours international de ski au Mont Genèvre (11–12 février 1907)," *Revue Alpine* 13, no. 3 (March 1907): 112. *La Montagne,* 20 March 1907, 136.

28. *La Montagne*, 20 April 1907, 172–176.

29. Grazioli Lanti, "Ski-ing in Italy," *British Ski Year Book* (1907): 34.

30. *Le Paysan Briançonnais* (14 February 1907) cited in Merle, *Histoire du ski dans le Briançonnais*, 47.

31. *La Montagne*, 2 February 1914, 105. *The Times*, 6 February 1914. *New York Times*, 21 January, and 5, 6 February 1914. F.-A. Weel, "Les experiences de traîneaux automobiles," *La Vie au Grand Air*, 4 April 1908, 211.

32. *La Vie au Grand Air*, 11 April 1908, II.

33. *7è CAF International à Gérardmer*, n.p.

34. Letter, CAF to Mayor of Chamonix, 1908, in archives de la Mairie, Chamonix. TMS in File: Tourisme, Corr. Div. 1890–1910.

35. *La Montagne* 6 (February 1910): 122.

36. Ibid., 5 (January 1909): 41.

37. *L'Union Républicaine*, 27 February 1909.

38. Achard, *Histoire du ski du Pilat*, 45.

39. Auguste Schorderet, "Impressions d'un spectateur," *La Montagne* 6 (February 1910): 92.

40. Capitaine François, "Organisation défensive d'Italie dans les Alpes Maritimes et Ligurienne," (1898). HMS in Musée des Troupes Alpines, Grenoble, France. This "absolutely confidential" work had nothing on winter defense. Both France and Italy kept frontier zones off limits to civilians. *Revue Alpine* 7 (June 1901): 174. S. Valot, *Des marches et manoeuvres en pays de montagne* (Paris: Librairie militaire de L. Beaudoin, 1892), 10. Lt. Rochefrette, "La poste de Fréjus: Hivernage de 1893–1894," HMS. Archives départementales de la Savoie, Chambéry, J 133.

41. Widmann, "Travail d'hiver," analyzed in Capitaine Lestien (d'après les souvenirs du Dr. Minelle), "Les débuts du ski en France," *Cahiers d'information des Troupes de Montagne* 23 (May–June 1953): 32. Auguste Monnier, "Le ski," *L'Illustration*, 8 March 1902, 154–155. For Thouverez, see Louis Helly, *100 ans de ski français* (Grenoble: Cahiers de l'Alpe, 1966), 24–25. For an excellent contemporary overview of the Chasseurs Alpins, see Julien Bregeault, "Les Chasseurs Alpins," *Annuaire du Club Alpin Français* 25 (1898): 34–82.

42. Lestien, "Débuts de ski en France," *Les Cahiers des Troupes de Montagne* 23 (May–June 1953): 32. For Widmann's exploits, see *Mémorial de la Loire* (1897), in Achard, *Histoire du ski du Pilat*, 21.

43. Bregeault, "Les Chasseurs Alpins," *Annuaire du Club Alpin Français* 25 (1898): 70.

44. "Expériences de ski." HMS in Salle d'Honneur, 159ème Régiment, Briançon.

45. Marcel Guillamo, "Clerc, Henri," 3. TMS in folder in Salle d'Honneur, 159ème Régiment, Briançon.

46. Henrik Angell, "Ça va bien, mon Capitaine," first appeared in Angell's report

from Briançon dated 10 February 1903 as "Paa Ski in den franke Alper," *Morgenbladet*, 27 March 1903. See also "Bore Skiløbere i Frankrige," ibid., 17 March 1903, and F. Q. [Finn Qual], "Fra skiskolen i Briançon," *Aarbok* (1903): 51. This was later translated and published in Switzerland as "L'École de ski à Briançon," *Ski* [Swiss], 13 January 1905, 93–94. The Norwegian rucksack was discussed in O. N. [O. Nool], "Sac du Capitaine Roll ou sac Bergen," *La Montagne* 9 (October 1913): 563.

47. *Le Petit Journal*, 20 February 1901, and *La Vie au Grand Air*, 9 March 1902, and see also p. 148.

48. Commandant De Bonnival, *Étude sur les marches et manoeuvres dans la haute montagne pendant l'hiver* (Paris: Charles-Lavauzelle, 1903), 17–18.

49. Oreste Zavattari, *Gli Ski nella Guerra d'Invierno sulle Nostri Alpi* (Roma: Bogera, 1900). Zavattari, "Alpinismo militare III: gli skie i nostri Alpini," *Rivista Mensile* 21 (February 1902): 40–48. Lt. Roiti's article in *Esercito Italiano*, 12 March 1897, translated and reprinted in *Le Moniteur Dauphinois*, 20 March 1897.

50. Jean Pourroy, "Le ski dans l'Armée," *La Vie au Grand Air*, 10 March 1904, 191.

51. Ibid., 190–191. For other deaths, see *La Montagne* 1 (June 1905): 325.

52. Capitaine Rivas, *Petit manuel du skieur* (Briançon: Paul Vollaire, 1906). What follows comes from this short book and page references will not be footnoted.

53. Lestien, "Les débuts de ski en France," *Cahiers des Troupes de Montagne* (1953), 35 says the skis only cost between 8 and 10 francs. My figure of 15 is derived from Rivas's between 14 and 18 francs. Clerc, "Rapport," 19, 47.

54. *Allgemeines Korrespondenzblatt*, 2 February 1906, 150–151.

55. *La Durrance*, 18 March 1906, cited in Merle, *Histoire du ski dans le Briançonnais*, 16. *La Montagne* 2 (December 1906): 593–594.

56. *The Times*, 24 July 1908. *La Montagne* 3 (December 1907): 573–574.

57. K. Vilh. Amundsen, "Fra frankriges Internationale Skistaverne," *Aarbok* (1908): 65. J. D., "Concours international de ski à Chamonix," *La Montagne*, 20 February 1908, 78–79, 82.

58. F. Q. [Finn Qual], "Fra Skirende i Grenoble, Albertville, Chamonix og Morez i 1909," *Aarbok* (1909): 50.

59. *La Vie au Grand Air*, 11 January 1908, cover. See also the cartoon in the same paper of two women, one with "Italia" on her skirt, the other with "RF." "Bonjour, ma soeur!" The ski was becoming the means of union between the two nations, commented the paper.

60. Gerd Kumreich, "Joan of Arc between Right and Left," in Tombs, *Nationhood and Nationalism in France*, 63–71.

61. *La Montagne* 7 (December 1911): 711–712, 9 (April 1913): 224. *Gérardmer-Saison*, 30 March 1913, 10.

62. Maige-Lefournier, *Ski, soleil et neige*, 10.

63. Georges Rozet, "Les Brevets sportifs," *Éclair* (January 1913) in Album Memento, AR 1503, CAF Archives, Paris.

64. *La Montagne* 9 (April 1913): 240. For a critical view, see Rozet, "Les sports. Officiers et soldats sportifs: le ski," *L'Opinion*, 10 February 1912, in Album Memento AR 1502, CAF Archives, Paris.

65. *La Montagne* (1913): 240.

66. *Revanche* for Alsace-Lorraine was not such a potent impetus for war as has been believed. It was more "a sort of sentimental reserve." In those lands most people preferred peace to the settling of the "Alsace-Lorraine question" by war. Becker, *1914*, 54.

67. Chanson, Musée du Ski, Les Rousses. Roger Tanguely, owner of this private ski museum, remembers this song sung by his aunt. A ski battalion was formed in the Jura in 1911. Yves Moralès, "La naissance du ski dans le Jura," *Travaux* (Jura) (1992): 269.

68. *La Montagne* (1914): 425.

69. Maige-Lefournier, *Ski, soleil et neige*, 10.

CHAPTER 8. THE GERMANS AND AUSTRIANS ORGANIZE

1. *Weser Zeitung* (Goslar), 10 March 1892, in E. Hepp, ed., "Militärischer Skilauf und Heeresmeisterschaften," 2. TMS in Deutscher Skiverband, Carl Luther Archiv [DSV L-A.], in Planegg, Germany, 6 box FIS/Alte JWO, envelope: Cil Skilauf im Krieg. *Tidning för Idrott*, 7 December 1893, 455, which relied on *Der Tourist* for its information. Gerd Falkner, "Goslarer Jäger," *FdSnow* 21 (July 2002): 40.

2. *Deutscher Eissport*, 14 December 1893, 52. Schneider told Carl Luther that he had suggested the use of skis, but I don't think this was a direct proposal. He had written in a positive way about the use of skis by the Norwegian military in *Der Tourist*. Letter, Max Schneider to Cil [Carl J. Luther], Berlin, 22 November 1908, and see also his letter to Cil, Rostock, 13 July 1930. HMSS in DSV L-A. *Allgemeine Sport-Zeitung*, 14 January 1894, 16.

3. Letter, Paul v. Hindenburg to Ski Club Todtnau, 5 March 1893, HMS in Ski Club Todtnau Archives. See also the photograph of the document from v. Hindenburg approving payment for twenty-four pairs of skis from Todtnau, 8 March 1893, in *Der Winter* 2 (October 1935): 18.

4. *Das Buch für Alle* 16 (1893): 393. *Illustrated London News*, 9 February 1895, 172. *L'Illustration*, 17 December 1892, 509.

5. In 1893 both young princes were given skis for Christmas. Later, in 1910 Erbprinz Johann Leopold von Sachsen Coburg und Gotha appeared on a postcard, and was mercilessly caricatured on the cover of *Simplicissimus* (10 January 1910). Max Schneider, *Praktische Winke für Wintersportler* (Berlin: Wintersportsverlag, n.d. [1895?]): 22, notes that he sold skis to six princes (*Prinz*) and one princess (*Prinzessin*), one duke (*Herzog*),

two duchesses (*Herzogin*), eight prince and princesses (*Fürst* and *Fürstin*), and eleven countesses (*Gräfinnen*).

6. Max Ehrhardt, *Die Entwicklung des Wintersports im Thüringer Walde* (Gotha: Perthos, 1908), 32–33, 37, 41. *Chronik 1906–7 Skiklub Winterberg* (Winterberg: West Deutschland Skiverband, Skiklub Winterberg [1967]), 60. "Kampf und Sieg um den Schwedenbecher," in Josef Petri, *Chronik . . . der Goslarer Jäger*, in *Mitteilungsblatt des Vereines ehem. Goslarer Jäger* 22 (15 May 1925): n.p.

7. *Allgemeine Sport-Zeitung*, 25 December 1910, 1700. *Der Winter* 7 (December 1912): 232. Hermann Czant, *Militär-Gebirgsdienst im Winter* (Wien: C. W. Sterns, 1907).

8. Czant, *Militär-Gebirgsdienst im Winter*, 10–11.

9. Igor M. Boutine, *Lyzhnyi Sport* [*The Sport of Skiing*] (Moskow: Akademia, 2000), 12. Thanks to Harold Leich for translation.

10. *Münchener Zeitung*, 8 January 1914, in E. Hepp, ed., "Militärischer Skilauf und Heeresmeisterschaften," 2. TMS in DSV L-A, 6 box FIS/Alte JWO. env. Cil im Krieg.

11. Oberleutnant Viktor Sieger, "Tagebuch: 22. Januar–7. März 1893." TMS, Wintersportmuseum Mürzzuschlag. *Allgemeine Sport-Zeitung*, 29 January 1893, 106; 5 February 1893, 127–128. F. Wedel Jarlsberg, *Reisen gjennem livet* (Oslo: Gyldendal, 1932), 78–86.

12. MS in Zdarsky Archiv, Lilienfeld. The printed version is titled *Anleitung (und Belehrung) über die Verwendung der Schneeschuhe*, 1897. For Schadek, see *Allgemeine Sport-Zeitung*, 5 February 1893, 27.

13. Karl Roll, "Ein Norweger über Wien," *Allgemeine Sport-Zeitung*, 22 March 1896, 12.

14. Raimond Udy, *Kurze praktische Anleitung über den Gebrauch, die Conservierung und Erzeugung des Schneeschuhes für Militärzwecke* (Laibach: Udy, 1894).

15. *Allgemeine Sport-Zeitung*, 23 February 1896, 164.

16. Hassa Horn, "Nogle indtryk fra en skitur i de østerrigske Alper," *Aarbog* (1905): 47.

17. *Allgemeine Sport-Zeitung*, 5 February 1893, 128; 3 March 1895, 192; 19 February 1911, 184.

18. Ibid., 20 January 1895, 68. Johan Bååarth, "Några drag ur skidlöpnings historia," *På Skidor* (1900–01): 109.

19. *Allgemeine Sport-Zeitung*, 2 March 1902, 211. Heinz Polednik, *Das Glück im Schnee: 100 Jahre Skilauf in Österreich* (Wien: Amalthea, 1991), 43–44. *Deutsche Turn-Zeitung* (1910): 175. *Der Schnee*, 16 December 1911, 4.

20. *Allgemeine Sport-Zeitung*, 8 April 1917, 195–196.

21. 3 Corps Commando to War Department, Girk, 21 September 1907. HMS in Zdarsky Archiv.

22. Jens Kruse, "Die Bedeutung von Mathias Zdarsky für die Entwicklung des modernen alpinen Skisports," Diplomarbeit, Deutsche Sporthochschule Köln, 1991, 6. In

the Marmolata avalanche in December 1916, 300 men died. Gudrun Kirnbauer, "Georg Bilgeri, (1873–1934): Persönlichkeit, Berufsoffizier, Skipionier," Ph.D. diss., Institut für Sportwissenschaften, Universität Wien (1997), 139.

23. Mathias Zdarsky, *Lilienfelder Skilauftechnik* (Hamburg: Richter, 1896).

24. Alpenski advertisement for 1902–03 season, in DSV L-A box: Large, Unnamed. Zdarsky, "Unsere Lehrwarte," *Der Schnee* 10 (1906): 2, 5. Arnold Lunn, *A History of Ski-ing* (London: Oxford University Press, 1927), 43n, 44.

25. Letter, Frl. Gusti Mannsbarth to Erwin Mehl, 26 December 1935. TMS in Zdarsky Archiv, File: Mehl. Mehl repeated the story in Erwin Mehl, *Zdarsky: Festschrift zum 80. Geburtstag des Begründers der alpinen Skifahrweise 25. Februar 1936* (Wien: Deutscher Verlag für Jugend und Volk, 1936), 55. For a critique, see Letter, Otto Lutter to R. Guttmann, Graz, May 1951. TMS in Wintersportmuseum Mürzzuschlag.

26. W. Fleischmann und E. Steinbrüchel, *Lilienfelder oder Norweger Skilauftechnik* (Diessen, 1910; Stuttgart, 1912).

27. Polednik, *Glück im Schnee*, 46.

28. Kruse, "Zdarsky," 6.

29. *Österreichische Touristen-Zeitung*, 1 March 1904, 91. Lunn, *History of Ski-ing*, 49.

30. The best account in English is E. C. Richardson, "The End of the Lilienfeld Strife," *Alpiner Wintersport*, 27 January 1905, 153–154. This had appeared two weeks before as "Ende des Lilienfelder Zwists," *Ski* [Swiss] 6 (January 1905): 11–12.

31. Horn cited in Polednik, *Glück im Schnee*, 36.

32. *Allgemeine Sport-Zeitung*, 5 February 1899, 138; 12 February 1899, 165; 26 April 1903, 470. *Wiener Mittagszeitung*, 14 January 1910, cited in Lutz Maurer, "Duell in den Bergen," in *Das grosse Buch vom Ski*, ed. Bruno Moravetz (Hamburg: Hoffmann und Campe, 1981), 40.

33. Ibid., 38–39.

34. *Wiener Mittagszeitung*, 14 January 1910, cited in ibid., 40.

35. Vivian Caulfeild, *How To Ski and How Not To* (New York: Scribners, 1912), 15–17. *Der Winter* 7 (October 1912): 30.

36. *Ski Notes & Queries* 55 (December 1934): 61, and his obituary in *British Ski Year Book* (1935): 201–203. [*BSYB.*] For his syphilis, see Kriegsministerium 1916, 1. Abt. 97–23 in Kirnbauer, "Georg Bilgeri," 68.

37. For other cycling connections, see *Österreichische Touristen-Zeitung*, 1 November 1892, 256, when the Steirische Radfahrer-Gauverband urged its members to join skiers so "muscles will grow strong, healthy and your mind and heart fresh." See also Hans Heidinger, "Der Beitrag Mürzzuschlags zur Entwicklung des Skilaufs," *Sport: Sinn und Wahn* (Mürzzuschlag: Steirische Landesausstellung, 1991), 155.

38. *Münchener Zeitung* reprinted in *Der Winter* 7 (October 1912): 29. The British estimation comes from *Country Life*, 23 November 1912, 19.

39. Ehrhardt, *Die Entwicklung des Wintersports im Thüringer Wald,* 46. For a list of venues in Lower Saxony, see *Skisport in Niedersachsen Jahrbuch* (1988/89–1989/90): 9.

40. Heinz Polednik, *Stolze Erinnerungen: Die Geschichte des Wintersportes in den Sudetenländern* (München: Buch- und Kunstdruckerei, n.d [1971?]), 45–46, 49. Polednik, *Glück im Schnee,* 19–21.

41. Ekkehart Ulmrich, "Fritz Breuer und die Gründung des Ski Club Todtnáu," *DSV Ski Schule* 2/91 (March 1991): 19–29. Before he died, Ulmrich was working on a biography of Paulcke, but I suspect his work will not be published now. Paulcke wrote extensively but never about the founding of the Todtnau club; however there is correspondence from him in the Todtnau Archives. Assmann, "Die ersten Schneeschuhe im Harz," *Der Harz,* 10 February 1909, 53–56. Eerke U. Hamer, *Arthur Ulrichs oder die Entdeckung sportlicher Winterfrische im Harz* (Hoya: Niedersächsisches Institut für Sportgeschichte, 1998). For Hauptmann O. A. Vorwerg, see *Die Wanderer im Riesengebirge* (1891), organ of the Riesengebirgsverein. In 1892 he published "Der Schneeschuh—oder Skisport?" *Mitteilungen des Deutschen und Österreichischen Alpenvereins,* 15 November 1892, 245, and the following year *Das Schneeschuhlaufen.* See also *Österreichische Touristen-Zeitung,* 15 November 1892, 270, in the *Allgemeine Sport-Zeitung,* 5 February 1893, 128, and especially 7 December 1902, 1488. Letters, O. Vorwerg to Cil, Herischdorf bei Warmbrunn, 7 February and 10 November 1908. HMS in DSV L-A 7, box: Large Unnamed. For Finsterlin, see "Zur Geschichte des Skilaufs in Bayern," *Der Winter* 8 (1908/09): 81.

42. The Todtnau Archives, held privately, contain letters, papers and articles among which are many concerning the founding of the club. A number have the dates crossed out, questions, etc. My own guess is that 20 November 1892 is the correct date for the Todtnau founding. It is based on a photo of the Fremdenbuch of the Feldberger Hof in the archives. An exhaustive analysis of the difficulties in discovering the date was made by Ulmrich, "Fritz Breuer," *DSV Ski Schule* 2/91 (March 1991): 19–29 but no certain date resulted.

43. *Rundschau vom Feldberg,* 29 November 1892.

44. Letter, Fritz Breuer to Ski Club colleagues, Düsseldorf, 7 November 1922. TMS in Todtnau Ski Club Archives.

45. Polednik, *Glück im Schnee,* 19–21.

46. *Deutsche Turn-Zeitung,* 10 February 1896, 54; also ibid. (1903): 886–887, and (1910): 208. *Allgemeine Sport-Zeitung,* 4 December 1904, 1508. Karlheinz Blechschmidt, "Die Entwicklung des Skilaufens an den Grund- und Mittelschulen seit 1925," TMS. Leipzig: Deutsche Hochschule für Körperkultur, 1958, 4–5. *Der Harz* 3 (1896): 22. *Allgemeines Korrespondenzblatt,* 22 March 1907. *Chronik 1906-7 Skiklub Winterberg,* 25, 34.

47. *Der Harz* 19 (February 1912): 2.

48. *BSYB* (1912): 98.

49. *Österreichische Turn-Zeitung*, 1 February 1892, 34. Berenc and Löbl, *Catalog* (Wien: Berenc & Löbl, n.d. [c.1900, perhaps earlier]), 20.

50. Stummer, in *Hugo's Jagdzeitung*, reprinted in Berenc and Löbl, *Catalog*, 5.

51. *Der Tourist* reprinted in *Deutsche Turn-Zeitung*, 28 January 1892, 75.

52. *Chronik 1906-7 Skiklub Winterberg*, 61.

53. For an overview, see Arnd Krüger, "There Goes This Manliness," *Journal of Sport History* 18 (Spring 1991): 137–158. See also Giselher Spitzer, *Der deutsche Naturismus. Idee und Entwicklung einer volkerzieherischen Bewegung im Schnittfeld von Lebensreform, Sport und Politik* (Ahrensburg: Czwalina, 1983), 60–76, 81–83, 131.

54. Mühlemann, "Vom Jugend-Skilauf in Österreich," *Pestalozzi Jahrbuch* (1917): 5. Erwin Jaeger, "Die Bedeutung des Wintersports für die Gesundheit unseres Volk," *Über Jugend- und Volksspiele: Jahrbuch* 20 (1911): 84–86.

55. Cil [Carl J. Luther], "Anfänge des Skilaufes in Mitteleuropa," *Ski-Chronik* 2 (1909/1910): 6. See also the cover of *Simplicissimus* (10 January 1910): "The Crown Prince Learns to Ski."

56. John E. Knodel, *The Decline of Fertility in Germany 1871–1939* (Princeton: Princeton University Press, 1974), 32.

57. Von Hindenburg, Kriegsministerium, Berlin, 5 March 1893. HMS in Ski Club Todtnau Archive. Copied document from Hindenburg, Berlin, 5 February 1893, in DSV L-A, 8 box: Large, Texte. See also how the Prussian War Ministry continued to develop ski troops. *Deutscher Eissport*, 14 December 1893, 8.

58. Unsigned [Cil], "Militärischer Skilauf und Herren-Skimeisterschaften," *Soldat der Berge, Truppenschrift*, 1 February 1961, 4.

59. Cil, "Die ersten Schisoldaten von Garmisch," *N. S. Sport* (National Socialist Sport), 1 February 1942, 4.

60. Wilhelm Paulcke, "Freiwillige Ski-Corps," *Der Winter* 6 (December 1911): 86–88.

61. Hermann Czant, *Militärgebirgsdienst im Winter* (Wien-Leipzig: Sterns, 1907). See also Paulcke, *Der Skilauf* (Freiburg i. B.: Wagner, 1908), 135–154.

62. For what follows on Max Schneider, *Der Tourist*, 15 September 1891, is the first article. For the reprinting of articles, one example for each: *Allgemeine Sport-Zeitung*, 20 March 1892, 188; *Deutsche Turn-Zeitung* (1893): 796; *Österreichische Touristen-Zeitung*, 15 November 1892, 270–271; *Der Schwarzwald*, 31 October 1892, 21.

63. Typical examples: Letter Noodt to Kleinoscheg, Trondheim, 11 December 1890. Wintersportmuseum, Mürzzuschlag. *Allgemeine Sport-Zeitung*, 23 February 1892, 183. *Der Harz* 3 (1895): 74. *Allgemeine Sport-Zeitung*, reprinted in *Deutsche Turn-Zeitung* (1894): 114. In 1892, in Bavaria, foresters from Rabenstein, Mauth, Dreisselgebiet, Buchenau, and Schlichtenberg were all supplied with skis by the landowners. Reiner Gattermann, *Skilauf im Bayerischen Wald: Anfänge und Entwicklung* (Grafenau: Morsak,

1986), 16–19. Karl Beringer, "Eduard Hauenstein: Ein Pionier des Skilaufs," *Winter Schönheit* (1949–50): 20. In Braunlage, Oberförster Ulrichs was well known for his ski activities. Eerke U. Hamer, *Arthur Ulrichs oder die Entdeckung sportlicher Winterfrische im Harz* (Hoya: NISH, 1998).

64. *Allgemeine Sport-Zeitung*, 1 January 1898, 14.

65. Letter, Schneider to Cil, Berlin, 22 November 1908. HMS in DSV L-A, 8 box: Large, Texte.

66. Cil, "On the Track of the First Tracks," *Sport* (1965): 44. My interpretation of Schneider's role was questioned by Ekkehart Ulmrich, who wondered whether Schneider was a man ahead of his time or merely a commercial charlatan. Ekkehart Ulmrich, "Max Schneider: Genialer Vordenker und Wegbereiter des Skisports—oder kommerzieller Scharlatan?" *FdSnow* 1 (1995): 33–45.

67. W. Ploch, "Ein Harzer Skipionier erzählt," *Der Winter* 27 (January–February 1934): 85–86.

68. Compare the interest that the Viennese Cycling Club, "Die Wanderer," took in skiing as early as 1888. Cil, "Anfänge des Skilaufes in Mitteleuropa,' *Ski-Chronik* 2 (1909/1910): 7.

69. Josef Müller, "Vor zwanzig Jahren," *Zwanzig Jahre Österreichischer Ski-Verein* (Wien. ÖSV, 1912), 6–13. Polednik, *Glück im Schnee*, 50.

70. Pierre Minelle, "Rössler-Orovsky," *Neige et Glace* 11 (August 1933): 273. *Majrovstvá sveta v Ly ovaní 1970 v severstych Disciplínach*, n.p. *Deutscher Wintersport*, 23 November 1906, 40–42. *Spiel und Sport* (1896): 30, 36, 176, 234; (1897): 233. *Sport im Bild* (1896): 220, (1897): 58, 143, 157, 165, 169 for photos.

71. Karel Danek, *Why Us, Here and Thus?* (Nove Město: Sporten, 1994), 2. Minelle, "Le ski dans le Tatra," *La Montagne* 230 (January–February 1931): 29.

72. Handwritten notes by Jakob Vaage taken from *Wassersport* (1893): 603 and *Sport im Bild* (1896): 220 in Vaage Papers, Holmenkollen Ski Museum.

73. Speech to the Ski Association of the Royal Kingdom of Bohemia in November 1906, in *Deutscher Wintersport*, 23 November 1906, 40–41.

74. *Allgemeine Sport-Zeitung*, 28 January 1900, 88. Thaddäus v. Kossowicz, "Skiwanderungen in den Karpathen," *Der Schnee*, 1 May 1909, 2.

75. *Der Schnee*, 8 May 1909, 3.

76. Polednik, *Stolze Erinnerungen*, 22–23. For Vorwerg, see *Allgemeine Sport-Zeitung*, 7 December 1902, 1488, and Vorwerg's bitter replies in letters to Cil, Herischdorf, 7 February, and 10 November 1918. HMSS in DSV L-A 7 box: Large Unnamed, where he objects to the Hohenelbe people and to Partsch, Paulcke, Gruber, and Madlener.

77. *Mineralogische Geschichte des sächsischen Erzgebirges*, 1775. D. J. Mierkel, *Erdbeschreibung von Kursachsen und den jetzt dazugehörenden Ländern*, 3rd ed. 1804. Engelhardt, *Vaterlandskunde*, 1824, new ed. 1824, all cited in Artur Ulbricht, "Die Entwick-

lung des Skisports in Annaberg-Buchholz," Diplomarbeit, Deutsche Sporthochschule Leipzig, 1964, 7–17.

78. For early sport skiing, see the following: "Anfänge des Skilaufs im Erzgebirge," *Skilauf in Sachsen.* Letter, Stüwe to [Cil?], Chemnitz, 30 September 1922. HMS. DSV L-A, 7 box: Large Unnamed. Stüwe speech, 19 March 1926. TMS. Ibid. *Deutsche Alpenzeitung,* 1 January 1903, 193. Kurt Spiegel, "Im Erzgebirge," *Der Winter* 23 (December 1929): 94. Ulbricht, "Entwicklung des Skisports in Annaberg-Buchholz," Leipzig DSHS, 15–16.

79. Christian Mogore, *La grande histoire du ski* (Chambéry: Agnaf, 1989), 26. *Der Winter* 25 (1931/32): 487. In 1910, British ambassador, Sir Francis Lindley, skied on the slopes of Mt. Vitosh just outside Sofia. Sir Francis Lindley, *A Diplomat Off Duty* (London: Ernest Benn, 1928), 91.

80. For Estonian skiing, see Arnold Vaiksaar and Enn Mainla, "Winter Sports in Estonian Sports Culture," in *Winter Games, Warm Traditions,* ed. Matti Goksøyr et al. (Oslo: Norwegian Society of Sport History, 1994), 65. Reet Ann Nurmberg, "Sport and Physical Education in Estonia," Ph.D. diss., University of California at Berkeley (1972), 64. TMS.

81. *Rigauer Tagblatt* 285 and 290 (1892), and *Rizhskiy Vestnik* 6 (1893). I am indebted to Professor Dr. Juris Baldunčiks of the Literaturas, Folkloras un Maklas Institute, Riga, for these references and for the translation of one from Russian. For early skiing in Latvia, see A. Bielenstein, *Die Holzbauten und Holzgeräte der Letten* (Petrograd: 1918), 2:601–602.

82. Letter, Vladimir I. Lenin to Iness Armand, December 1916, in G. S. Demeter, *Lenin o fizičeskom vospitaniji Lenin o tělesně výchově* (Praha: 1961), cited in Karel Danek, *Skiing and Poetry.* Nové Mêsto na Moravê, Czechia (Sporten: 2001), 26.

83. Heinz Hapke, "Vom Skilauf in Russland," *Der Winter* 13 (1919/20): 152–153. Ibid., 19–20 (1907/08): 188, and 22 (1928–29): 345. *Allgemeine Sport-Zeitung,* 8 December 1894, 1334. *Deutscher Wintersport,* 16 February 1906, 213. *Der Schnee,* 2 December 1911, 5. V.A. Serebriakov, "Teoria i Praktika Fizicheskoi Kultury," 3–4 (1946): 116, cited in Iwona Grys, "Foreign Influences on Russian Sport in the 19th Century," *Studies in Physical Culture and Tourism* 6 (1999): 70.

84. Max Eith, *Hinter Pflug und Schraubstock,* cited in Geka, "Skiläufer gegen Radfahrer," *Schlesische Tageszeitung Breslau,* 5 December 1936. Chernel, *A lábrzánkózás Kézikönyve,* 1898, in Jenö Serenyi, "Der Schisport in Ungarn," *Der Winter* 3 (1908/09): 182. Chernel was an ornithologist who had visited Norway in 1891. Jozéf Vetö, ed., *Sports in Hungary,* trans. István Butykay (Budapest: Corvina, 1965), 127.

85. *Budapester Politisches Volksblatt,* 27 December 1911, cited in Fritz Gött, *Der Kronstädter Skiverein in den Jahren 1905–1930* (Kronstadt: Kronstädter Skiverein, 1930), 61. See also *Der Schnee,* 20 March 1909, 20.

86. "Schneelauf in den ungarischen Schulen," *Deutsche Turn-Zeitung* (1913): 91. Jenö Serényi, "Ungarn," in *Jahrbuch des Wintersports,* ed. Emil Peege and Josef Noggler (Wien: Hof-Buchdruckerei [1914?]), 67–68.

87. Stanisław Barabasz, "Zzimowyc wycieczek w gory," *Przeglad Zakopiański* 15 (1903), and *"Na czerwonym Wirchu,"* ibid. 6 (1905). Barabasz, *Wispomnienia Narciarza* (Zakopane, 1914). Thaddäus Wilusz, "Lemberger Skibrief," *Der Schnee,* 30 January 1909, 1. Kossowica, "Das erste Lawinenopfer in der Hohen Tatra," ibid., 10 April 1909, 2. *Der Winter* 6 (April 1918): 68–69.

88. *Allgemeine Sport-Zeitung,* 19 February 1911, 184.

89. Erkki Vasara, "Maintaining a Military Capability: the Finnish Home Guard, European Fashion and Sport for War," in *Nordic World: Sport in Society,* ed. Henrik Meinander and J. A. Mangan (London: Frank Cass, 1998), 163–164.

90. *Illustrated London News,* reprinted in Walter Lorch, *Snow Travel and Transport* (Macclesfield: Coach House, Gawsworth, 1977), 125. *Universal-Kalender* (1895) seen in the Alpen- und Skimuseum, Kempten, Germany. See also *Der Winter* 9 (January 1915): 3. Letter, H. R. H. The Infanta Beatriz de Orleans-Borbon to Arnold Lunn, Cadiz, 5 Janaury 1960. TMS in box 2, folder 25, in Lunn Papers. This was later published in Lunn, ed., *The Englishman on Ski* (London: Museum Press, 1963), 51.

91. Henrik Angell, *Gjennem Montenegro paa ski* (Christiania: Aschehoug, 1893).

92. H. Archer Thomson, "Club Tour in Montenegro," *BSYB* (1909): 15–22. Thomson, "Ski-ing in the Balkans," ibid., II, 8 (1912): 111–115.

CHAPTER 9. THE LADIES SKI

1. Jean-François Regnard, *Voyage en Laponie,* cited by Yves Ballu, *L'épopée du ski* (Paris: Arthaud, 1981), 53. J. L. Gleditsch, *Historische Reisen* (Leipzig, 1699), 96. HMS copied from this work, in Deutscher Skiverband, Carl Luther Archiv [DSV L-A.], in Planegg, Germany, 7, box: Large Unnamed. Jakob Vaage, "Dameskiløpning begynner," *Norske Skiløpere: Møre, Romsdal, Trøndelag* (Oslo: Erling Ranheim, 1958), 93.

2. The term is Thackeray's. William Makepeace Thackeray, "Sketches and travels in London," in *Works* (London: Smith, Elder, 1969), 15:274.

3. *Verdens Gang,* 3 March 1893.

4. Fridtjof Nansen, *Paa Ski over Grønland* (Kristiania: Aschehoug, 1890), 115, and again in his diary, excerpts of which are published in *Sporting Days in Wild Norway* (London: Butterworth, 1925), 116–117. Compare the deserted valley in the Gudvangen region, ibid., 20.

5. Examples may be found in *Kongsberg Morgenblatt,* 23 February 1881, *Verdens Gang,* 21 February 1881, *Morgenbladet,* 3 March 1888 and 11 December 1891.

6. Helen Roberts, "The Exquisite Slave: the Role of Clothes in the Making of the Victorian Woman," *Signs: Journal of Women in Culture and Society* 2, no. 3 (1977): 568.

7. Arnold Lunn, *Ski-ing* (London: Eveleigh Nash, 1913), 188–189.

8. Tor Bomann-Larsen, *Den evige sne* (Oslo: Cappelens, 1993), 133.

9. Jakob Vaage, *Skienes verden* (Oslo: Hjemmenes, 1979), 261. Olav Bø, *Skiing Throughout History*, trans. W. Edson Richmond (Oslo: Norske Samlaget, 1993), 108. Vaage notes that there was an earlier ski club in 1887 but nothing is known about it. Vaage, *Skienes verden*, 181.

10. Reproduced in ibid., 180.

11. Ethel Tweedie, *A Winter Jaunt in Norway* (London: Bliss, Sands, 1894), 113.

12. H. Horn, "Nogle indtryk fra en skitur i de østerrigske Alper," *Aarbog* (1905): 47.

13. *Allgemeine Sport-Zeitung*, 19 February 1911, 184.

14. Max Schneider, *Praktische Winke für Wintersportler* (Berlin: Wintersportsverlag, n.d. [1895?]), 22.

15. *Public Schools Alpine Sports Club Year Book 1914* (Cheltenham: Burrow, 1914), 130–208.

16. *La Montagne*, 20 December 1908, 242. Letter, Beatriz de Orleans-Borbon, H.R.H. Infanta, to Arnold Lunn, Cadiz, 6 January 1960. TMS in box 2, folder 25a in the Sir Arnold Lunn Papers, Lauinger Library, Georgetown University, Georgetown, Md. Francis E. Brantingham, *St. Moritz, Engadine*. Brochure, n.d. but probably 1912. Item: 1969/241 in Schweizerisches Sportmuseum, Basel.

17. List in William Barton (compiler) *Engadine Year Book 1913* (Samaden and St. Moritz: Engadine Press, 1913), 189–195.

18. *The Times*, 29 March 1910, 12. W. Rickmer Rickmers had said much the same thing in 1903. " Alpine Skee and Mountaineering," *The Alpine Journal* 31 (August 1903): 454.

19. R. Gélinet, "Quelques notes sur le IIIè Concours International de Ski," *La Montagne* 5 (February 1909): 107.

20. This list is taken from Hélène Salomon, "Le corset: entre la beauté et la santé (1880–1920)," in *Histoire du sport féminin*, ed. Pierre Arnaud and Thierry Terret (Paris: L'Harmattan, 1996), 2:13.

21. *Der Winter* 6 (December 1911): 146.

22. Giselher Spitzer, *Der deutsche Naturismus* (Ahrensburg: Czwalina, 1983), 13.

23. Valerie Steele, *Fashion and Eroticism: Ideals of Feminine Beauty from the Victorian Era to the Jazz Age* (New York: Oxford University Press, 1985), 67–69.

24. Ibid., 161, 229.

25. Laurentius Urdahl, *Haandbog i Skiløbning*, 75. The translation was by Freiherr von Washington, found in a ms., 38 in DSV L-A.

26. Karl Pfeiffer, *Der Ski-Sport: Systematische Anleitung zur Erlernung des Skilaufens und dessen Anwendung im Mittel- und Hochgebirge* (Leipzig: Gloekner [1911]), 13.

27. Ibid.

28. Letter, Beatriz de Orleans-Borbon to Arnold Lunn. TMS in box 2, folder 25a, in the Sir Arnold Lunn Papers, Georgetown University.

29. Beatrix Nickolls, "In Jämtland's Mountains," *På Skidor* (1901–1902): 16.

30. *Die Alpen*, cited in Dorothea Marx, "Die Rolle der Frau im Skilauf von 1890 bis 1960." TMS. Diplomarbeit, Deutsche Sporthochschule Köln (1976), 30.

31. J. Schneider, "Die Frau im Skisport," *Der Winter* 32 (March 1939): 440.

32. "Über die schamlose Tracht der Sportweiber zu Winterberg," *Kölnisches Volksblatt*, 31 January 1914, which includes pastoral letters from Fulda dated 20 August 1913 and a police order from Münster of 5 January 1913. See also Carl J. Luther, "On the Tracks of the First Tracks," *Sport* (1965): 44. The French announcement can be found in the Musée du Ski, Besse-en-Chandesse, France.

33. H.A. Thomson and E. C. Richardson, "The Club Tour in the Tyrol," *British Ski Year Book* (1908): 27. [*BSYB.*]

34. Mathias Zdarsky, *Lilienfelder Skilauftechnik* (Hamburg: Richter, 1896; 1909 printing), 98. Anita Seck, "Die Kleidung der Schiläuferin," *Der Winter* 4 (December 1909): 70.

35. H. Pokorny, "Meine Skizeit 1905–1915," cited in Theodor Hüttenegger TMS, 5 in Wintersportmuseum Mürzzuschlag. Henry Hoek, "Frau im Schnee," in *Vom deutschen Skilauf und 50 Jahre Deutscher Skiverband*, ed. Gunter Krusche (München: DSV, 1955), 28.

36. Viscount Knebworth, "Ski-ing," in The Hon. Neville Lytton, ed., *Winter Sports*, vol. 8, Lonsdale Library of Sports, Games and Pastimes (London: Seeley, Service, 1930), 94–95.

37. Josef Wallner, TMS, 13 in Wintersportmuseum Mürzzuschlag archives.

38. *The Times*, 25 December 1909, 13; 2 December 1913, 13.

39. The elites of Europe liked to imply serious purpose to their fun and games by describing them as work. The OED gives the examples of "work's" first sporting uses in describing cricket in 1851, rowing in 1856, and track and field in 1882. Arnold Lunn in 1913 wrote that the "number of English [ski]runners who have done first-class work in the Alps might be counted on the fingers of both hands." Lunn, *Ski-ing*, 6–7.

40. Bomann-Larsen, *Den evige sne*, 133. Inge Löwdin, "Kvinnlig skidlöpning—en ny internationell tävlingssport," *På Skidor* (1952): 153. S. C. Buntenbock *1907 Festschrift zum 75 jährigen Jubiläum* (Clausthal-Zellerfeld: Piepersche Druckerei [1981]): 17. Ekkehart Ulmrich, "Zur Geschichte des Skiclubs Schwarzwald von 1895 bis 1913," *FdSnow* 3, no. 1 (1993): 6, 8. Provisional Protokoll, Freiburg Section of S.C. Freiburg, 29 November 1895. HMS in Todtnau archives, privately held. Vaage Notebook, n.p. *Norsk Idrætsblad* (1902): 115. *Der Winter* 7 (January 1913): 317; ibid. 8 (November 1913): 111. Heimat- und Ski-Tourenbuch. HMS, n.p. in Heimat- und Skimuseum, St. Anton am Arlberg, Austria. *Red Wing Republican*, 6 January, 6 February 1903.

41. For women skiing in the Black Forest, see Vera Martinelli, "Frauen in den Anfängen des Skisports. Das Beispiel Schwarzwald." Masters thesis, University of Freiburg i. Breisgau (2004), especially 57–58. TMS. My thanks to Ms. Martinelli for sending me her manuscript.

42. *Alpina* (1903) in *50 Jahre Deutscher Skiverband* (München-Passing: DSV, n.d.), 29, cited in Elisabeth Rössel, "Die geschichtliche Entwicklung des Frauenschilaufs in Deutschland bis zum Jahr 1936," 18. TMS. Deutsche Hochschule für Körperkultur, Leipzig, 1957.

43. R. Gélinet cited by Yves Moralès, "Les exercices corporels et les sports dans le Jura (1870–1914)," Université de Franche-Compté (1989–1990) thesis, TMS, 143.

44. *Allgemeine Sport-Zeitung*, 24 January 1904, 11.

45. *BSYB* (1910): 32. *The Times*, 22 January 1908, 13; 11 February 1913, 15. *Allgemeine Sport-Zeitung*, 19 February 1911, 184. I. B. "Internationalt Skirend for damer i Chamonix," *Aarbok* (1912): 129. Watkin Strang-Watkin, "Montana 1912–1913," *Public Schools Alpine Sports Club Year Book* (1914): 72.

46. Karin Berg, *Hopp, Jenter, Hopp!* (Oslo: Shipsted, 1999). Many commentators wrote against women jumping. For one, see *Pour bien faire du sport* (Paris: Pierre Lafitte, 1912), 293. For America, see E. John B. Allen, *From Skisport to Skiing: One Hundred Years of an American Sport, 1840–1940* (Amherst: University of Massachusetts Press, 1993), 62.

CHAPTER 10. THE GREAT WAR

1. W. R. Rickmers, "Alpine Skee and Mountaineering," *Alpine Journal* 31 (August 1903): 445.

2. United States: E. John B. Allen, *From Skisport to Skiing: One Hundred Years of an American Sport, 1840–1940* (Amherst: University of Massachusetts Press, 1993), 39–40. Great Britain: Explorer Frederick Jackson, the same who was the first to greet Nansen after he left the *Fram*, suggested British troops on skis in 1904. *British Ski Year Book* (1905): 40. [*BSYB.*] "Ski-running in the Highlands," ibid., I, 4 (1909): 14. Capt. Howard V. Knox, "Use of Ski, and Training British Soldiers for Duties on Snow-clad Frontiers," *Royal United Services Institute Journal* 54 (1910): 62; The British liked to heed Lt. Czant's words that "you can get a ski soldier in 2 weeks in classes of 20," ibid., 156, 161; Harry W. Chubb, "Military Ski-running," *BSYB* (1905): 36–38. Germany: *International Review* 116 (March 1910); Carl J. Luther, *Schneeschuhläufer im Krieg: über die Vergangenheit und Gegenwart des Militärschneeschuhlaufes aller Länder und von der Tätigkeit der deutschen und österreichischen Schneeschuhtruppen im Winterfeldzug 1914/15* (München: Lindauer, 1915), 46–47; *Militärische Presse* [Vienna], 2 April 1910, 2. Switzerland: Felix Schmal, "Wintersport," in G. Biedenknapp, et al., *Das grosse illustrierte*

Sportbuch (Leipzig: 1908), cited in Krüger, "History of the Olympic Winter Games," TMS, 10; O. Reimann, "Persönliche Eindrücke von Militärrennen in Andermatt, 13/14 Januar 1912," *Ski* [Swiss] (1912): 111–114. Turkey: *Allgemeine Sport-Zeitung*, 2 October 1915, 60. Lerch: Theodor von Lerch, "Takata liegt hier." Reprinted in Franz Klaus, ed., *Zdarsky-Blätter* (March 1986): 7. "Gedenken an Generalmajor Theodor von Lerch," in Klaus, ed., *75 Jahre Schifreundschaft Japan-Österreich 1911–1986*. TMS based on Lerch's diary in Zdarsky-Archiv, Lilienfeld, Austria. Lerch, "Erste Winterhochturen in Japan," *Zeitschrift des Deutschen und Österreichischen Alpenvereins* 63 (1932): 74.

3. Knox, "The Use of the Ski, or Skee, in Foreign Armies," *Royal United Services Institute Journal* 53 (1909): 225.

4. Jan Lindroth, *Idrottens väg til folkrörelse* (Uppsala: Historiska Institutionen vid Uppsala Universitet, 1974), 285–287.

5. At Laveissière, Pontarlier, and Beuil. *La Montagne*, 1 January 1913, 41. For a general overview of children and skiing in these years see, E. John B. Allen, "Skiing and the Child: Sport and Much More," in *Annual of CESH*, ed. Jim Riordan (Berlin: Tischler, 2000), 83–90.

6. Regio Decreto by General Ottolenghi, November 1902. Luciano Viazzi, "Pista! L'eroica storia del battaglione sciatori Monte Cervino, 1898–1978," 60. *Deutsche Alpenzeitung* 2 (2nd February issue 1903): 278.

7. Spartaco Targa, *La guerra di montagna e la difesa della Alpi* (Torino: Benevello: 1926), 43, n. 24. Oreste Zavattari, *Gli ski nella Guerra d'Invierno sulle nostri Alpi* (Roma: Bogera, 1900), 58.

8. *Allgemeines Korrespondenzblatt*, 10 November 1905, 10–11.

9. K. S. "Der Ski in fremden Armeen, 1. Italien," *Ski* [Swiss] 9 (1913): 75–76. *Militärische Presse* (Vienna), 30 March 1910, 2. Each mountain Artillery Regiment was to have three ski patrols of three men each.

10. *Le Monde Illustré* reprinted as "The Soldiers of the Alps," *Scientific American*, Supplement No. 1371 (12 April 1912): 21972.

11. *Le Petit Parisien*, 19 March 1905, front cover. See also the cover of *La Vie au Grand Air*, 11 January 1908, where an Alpini and a Chasseur Alpin are shaking hands.

12. Viazzi, "Pista!" 22–24.

13. *Allgemeine Sport-Zeitung*, 25 December 1910, 1700.

14. *Der Winter* 7 (October 1912): 30.

15. *Allgemeine Sport-Zeitung*, 28 October 1916, 850.

16. I follow the account of Artillery Lieutenant H. Koenig, "Anfänge des Militärski-fahrens in der Schweiz," *Allgemeine Schweizerische Militärzeitung* 1–2 (1944): 1–46. See also Knox, "Use of Ski in Foreign Armies," *Royal United Services Institute Journal* 53 (1909): 373.

17. Koenig, "Anfänge des Militärskifahrens in der Schweiz," 6–39.

18. Captain Hans Farmer, "Le développement du ski dans l'armée suisse," *Revue du Ski,* 1 January 1931, 28.

19. *Münchener Zeitung,* 8 January 1914, cited in E. Hepp, ed., "Militärischer Skilauf und Heeresmeisterschaften," 2. TMS in Deutscher Skiverband, Carl Luther Archiv [DSV L-A.], in Planegg, Germany, 6. Box: FIS/Alte JWO. Env. Cil Skilauf im Krieg.

20. Jean-Jacques Becker, *1914: Comment les Français sont entrés dans la guerre* (Paris: Presses de la fondation nationale des sciences politiques, 1977).

21. Col. Lardant, *Nos skieurs militaires pendant la guerre,* cited in Louis Helly, *Cent ans de ski français* (La Tronche-Montfleury: Cahiers de l'Alpe, 1968), 53. See also *Memento des gloires du 159è R.I.A.,* 11.

22. *La Montagne* 10, no. 8-12 (August-December 1914): 460–461.

23. "Le ski et la guerre," ibid., 1-3 (January–March 1915): 38.

24. In *Caducée,* a Parisian medical journal, Major Dr. Reichborn-Kjennerud published an article on the medical service and the use of skis on campaign. *Allgemeines Korrespondenzblatt,* 17 February 1905, 108. *La Montagne* 12, 1–3 (January–March 1916): 43. *Der Winter* 10 (October 1916): 10. Øisten Tidemand-Johannessen, "Den norske ski-ambulance i Frankrike," *Aarbok* (1916): 78–94.

25. *Daily Telegraph,* 11 January 1915, cited in *Der Winter* 9 (January 1915): 16. Cil [Carl J. Luther], *Schneeschuhläufer im Krieg: Über die Vergangenheit und Gegenwart des Militärschneeschulaufes aller Länder und von der Tätigkeit der deutschen und österreichischen Schneeschuhtruppen im Winterfeldzug 1914/15* (München: Lindauer, 1915), 31. Frank Harper, *Military Ski Manual: A Handbook for Ski and Mountain Troops* (Harrisburg: Military Service Publishing Co., 1943), 353–355.

26. *London Daily News* cited in *New York Times,* 10 February 1915, 3.

27. *The Graphic,* 3 April 1915, 432–433.

28. Capt. Ferdinand Belmont, *Lettres d'un officier de Chasseurs Alpins (2 Août 1914–28 Décembre 1915)* (Paris: Plon, 1917), 125, 127. *Der Winter* 8 (January 1933): 126.

29. *Scientific American,* Supplement, 37.

30. Eugen Kalkschmidt, "Vor 20 Jahren im Felde," *Der Winter* 28 (February 1935): 140–143. "Anruf! An alle Schneeschuhläufer des Schwarzwaldes," *Echo vom Wald,* 9 December 1914. This Triberg paper was copied. TMS in DSV L-A, 6 box: FIS/Alte JWO. Envelope: Cil Skilauf im Krieg.

31. Luther, *Schneeschuhläufer im Krieg,* 149.

32. Luther, "Skiläufer im Weltkrieg 1914/18," *N.S. Sport* 156 (December 1939): 4.

33. The best film I have seen is "Spirit of the Mountains," dir. Tom Feliu, TCC, Denver, 1992 . "Legends of American Skiing," dir. Richard Moulton, Keystone Films, Huntington, Vt., has an interesting section on the Dolomites. For still photographs see, as examples, *Le Miroir,* 16 January 1916, *Popular Mechanics* (February 1916): 208, *Scientific*

American, Supplement, 37, *Der Winter* 8 (January 1933): 127. In Ski Box 4, Folder Militär, The Swiss Sports Museum, Basel. *Das Plakat* 2 (March 1919): between 156–157.

34. Cited in Harper, *Military Manual,* 358.

35. Arnold Lunn, *A History of Ski-ing* (London: Oxford University Press, 1927), 94. Gerald Seligman, "Bilgeri Obituary," *BSYB* (1935): 201–202. The only copy of *Instruzioni al soldato per combattieri i pericolo del fredo* I know of is in Zdarsky-Archiv, 1437/26, Lilienfeld, Austria.

36. Paolo Monelli, *Toes Up,* trans. Orlo Williams (London: Duckworth, 1930), 115. Gerard Fairlie, *Flight Without Wings* (London: Hodder and Stoughton, 1957), 119–120.

37. *Der Winter* 10 (March 1917): 99.

38. Luciano Viazzi, *La guerra bianca in Adamello* (Trento: Saturnia, 1965). For the Russians into Poland, see *New York Times* (7 February 1915) and (18 February 1917). See also picture of the Red Army on skis in Swiss Sports Museum, Basel, in Ski Box 4, Folder: Militär. *Der Winter* IX, 4 (15 January 1915): 17. For Turkey: Arif Hikmet Koyunoglu, "Memoiren: Beginn des Skisportes in der Türkei," TMS in File: Fach-Beiträge Skigeschichte Wertvoll, Section T, Wintersportmuseum, Mürzzuschlag, Austria. Dr. Veitschmann, "Die österreichische Skimission bei der Kaiserlich-ottomanischen Armée," *Der Schnee* XI, 8 (31 December 1915): 55–56. *Der Winter* IX, 9 (19 April 1915). General Dosse, "Traité sur la guerre de montagne," n.d. [1920s?], TMS, 25, Regimental Archives of the 159th RIA, Briançon. For the US: *New York Times* (18 February 1917). Letter, Oliver Kaldahl to author, Glenwood, MN, 5 June 1989 in author's possession. Library of Congress, National Archives photo no. 165–470c-14 shows troops at Fort Grant, IL on skis. American troops have been on skis since 1886–87, see Allen, *From Skisport to Skiing,* 39–40.

39. *Morgenbladet,* 14 and 19 February 1893, and his book, *Gjennem Montenegro paa Ski* (Christiania, 1895).

40. *Montreal Gazette,* 24 February 1919, cited in *1918–19 Annual report of the Montreal Ski Club,* 30–31. Henrik Angell, "Norske ski paa Mourmansk-fronta 1918–19," *Aarbok* (1920): 100–103. *Norske biografisk leksikon* copied by Jakob Vaage. HMS. Lestien, "Débuts de ski en France," *Cahiers d'Inf. Des Troupes de Montagne* 23 (May–June 1953): 34, n.6. *Memento des gloires du 159é R.I.A.,* 10. My thanks to Roy Andersen who sent me a copy of his "Henrik Angell: en offiser på tvers." Foredrag i Oslo Militaere Samfund 5.2.2001, TMS which is a biographic article taken from his book *Henrik Angell: en nordmann på tvers* (Oslo: Aschehoug, 2000).

41. "Rapport," signed by Mayor, Vice-President of the Chambre d'Industrie, Chamonix, 22 February 1919. TMS copy in 8M 59, file 1911–1919, Mairie, Chamonix.

42. *La Montagne* 16 (January–February 1920): 33.

43. "Rapport." TMS in Mairie, Chamonix.

44. *La Montagne* 10 (August–December 1914): 460. Meeting of the Chambre d'Industrie Climatique, Chamonix, 23 September 1915. TMS in 8M 58: Chambre d'Industrie Climatique de Chamonix 1912–1933, in Mairie, Chamonix.

45. Carl Luther, "Der Ski im Schweizerischen Heere," *Ski* [Swiss] (1915): 26–27. Arnold Lunn, various letters, 19 September 1916–17 July 1917 in box 1, folders 3, 4, 5, 9 and 11; Diary 14 January 1917–3 May 1918 in box 9, folders 49, 50, 55. Lunn, "To be kept. Not for autobiog.," in box 7, folder 49, TMS, 6–7, all in Sir Arnold Lunn Papers, Special Collections, Georgetown University, Washington, DC, USA.

46. *La Montagne* 14 (April–May 1918): 96–97.

47. A. Bailiff, President of the TCF in *La Revue du Touring Club de France* (1916), on exhibit in Musée du Sport, Paris in 1999.

48. *La Montagne* (November–December 1919): 275–276.

CHAPTER II. UNEASY PEACE-LES ANNÉES FOLLES

1. Arnd Krüger, "The Role of Sport in German International Politics, 1918–1945," in *Sport and International Politics*, ed. Pierre Arnaud and James Riordan (London and New York: E. & F. N. Spoon, 1998), 82. Per Olof Hollmäng, "International Sports Organizations 1919–25; Sweden and the German Question," *International Journal of the History of Sport* 9, no. 2 (1992): 455–466. Jens A. Jensen, "Skisport i Tyskeland vinteren 1922," *Aarbok* (1922): 121–148.

2. José Germain in *Le Miroir des Sports*, 3 March 1921, cited in Pierre Arnaud, "French Sport and the Emergence of Authoritarian Regimes, 1919–1939," in Arnaud and Riordan, eds., *Sport and International Politics*, 120.

3. Jacques Mortane, "La Suisse, Reine de l'hiver. Quant à France . . ." *La Vie au Grand Air*, 15 October 1920, 51.

4. A. Fouillée, *Psychologie du peuple français*, 8th ed. (Paris: 1927), cited in Joseph J. Spengler, *France Faces Depopulation* (Durham: Duke University Press, 1938), 135. *Time*, 17 September 1934, 2. *New York Times*, 3 February 1920, 1.

5. Karen Offen, "Depopulation, Nationalism, and Feminism in fin-de-siècle France," *American Historical Review* 89 (June 1984): 669–670. Robert O. Paxton, *Vichy France: Old Guard and New Order* (New York: Knopf, 1972), 165–166. In Italy, also worried about the loss of youth, Mussolini presented a portrait of himself to any mother who bore six live children.

6. Letter, André Honorat, president of the National Committee against tuberculosis, to the prefect of the department of Isère, Paris, 14 October 1928, TMS. Série 113 M/9 Hygiène et Santé Publique 1925–1938, Archives d'Isère, Grenoble.

7. There is a mass of material in the departmental archives of Isère at Grenoble and Haute Savoie, Annecy. See particularly Série 113 M/8, 113 M/9 and 113 M/10 in Archives

d'Isère, and box 8M 66-69, file Mégève: 1930–31; file Mégève: Arrêtés municipaux d'hygiène in Archives d'Haute-Savoie, Annecy.

8. There is a vast literature on this subject. For an overview see Dr. F. Sandoz, "La cure solaire," *Neige et Glace*, 1 October 1935, 15–16. Middle-class publications like *L'Illustration* and *Miroir des Sports* also took it up. For France particularly, see E. John B. Allen, "French Skiing: The Way to National Health," in *Sport et santé dans l'histoire*, ed. Thierry Terret (Sankt Augustin: ISHPES, 1999), 319–326.

9. "Pacques à Val d'Isère," CAF section Vosgienne, *Revue* 14 (Winter 1937–38): 16.

10. Gaston Mortier, *Le tourisme et l'économie nationale* (Grenoble, Paris: Artaud, n.d. [1941]), 48–50.

11. *Journal Officiel de la République Française, Annexe 1927*, 744, cited in Pierre Arnaud and Thierry Terret, "Le ski, roi des sports d'hiver," in *Histoire des sports: Espaces et temps du sport*, ed. Thierry Terret (Paris: L'Harmattan, 1996), 175.

12. G. S. "Les sports d'hiver dans les Alpes de Savoie et Dauphiné," *L'Illustration*, 23 February 1929, 192. Charles Fruhinsholz, "Mégève l'ensoleillée," *Revue du Ski*, 1 April 1930, 105–106. Lucien Cavoutier, "La face cache des sports d'hiver: Les Savoyards devant l'afflux touristiques," *Mosaïques d'histoire en Savoie* (1983): 110.

13. President Lory of Isère section of CAF in 1936, in *La Montagne* 281 (July 1936): 312.

14. *La Montagne* 3-4 (March–May 1920): 68; 18 (March–April 1921): 93; 18 (January–February 1922): 27.

15. Arnaud and Terret, "Le ski, roi des sports d'hiver," in Terret, *Histoire des Sports*, 172.

16. *La Montagne* (1919): 274–276.

17. Leon Auscher, "L'Exposition du ski," *Neige et Glace*, 13 November 1924, 39–40, 42.

18. *La Montagne* 6 (November 1929): 392. *Neige et Glace*, 15 November 1929, 42. Artificial pistes were constructed at the Lyon fairs between 1934 and 1937, and could be found in the 1930s at Lillywhites of London, and in Geneva, Vienna, and Berlin. *Ski Notes & Queries* 5 (October 1931): 216 [*SN&Q.*]; *Neige et Glace*, 1 February 1931, 159; *Der Winter* 29 (January 1936): 385; M. Achard, *Histoire du ski et des sports d'hiver dans le massif du Pilat (Loire-Forez) de 1892 à nos jours* (Le Bessat-St. Etienne: Achard, 1989), 115.

19. *La Montagne* 281 (July 1936): 309, 312; 288 (April 1937): 160. Gabriel Hanot, "Les sports d'hiver en France," *L'Illustration*, 25 January 1930, n.p. E.-G. Drigny, "Le salon de ski," *Miroir des Sports*, 26 November 1929, 414. Mortier, *Tourisme et l'économie nationale*, 49. H. V. "Tourisme hivernal dans le Vercors," *Revue du TCF* 44 (December 1934): 407. Yvonne Lacroix, *Ski de Week-Ends* (Paris: Éditions de France, 1937), was an apt title.

20. *Revue du Ski* 7 (December 1936): LXI.

21. "Le grand scandale blanc," *Candide*, 6 January 1938, in L File SI-OT, Publicité Éditions 1905–1947, Archives de la Mairie, Chamonix.

22. Richard Holt, *Sport and Society in Modern France* (Hamden, Conn.: Archon, 1980), 9.

23. *Winter in Switzerland* (Zürich, Lausanne: Swiss Tourist Office, n.d. [1920?]), 7. In the Ski Club of Great Britain's *Year Book* that year there were fourteen advertisements for Switzerland and one for Norway. *British Ski Year Book* (1920): n.p. [*BSYB*.]

24. *The Times*, 1 March 1937, 17. Lunn had wondered the same thing in 1913. Arnold Lunn, *Ski-ing* (London: Eveleigh Nash, 1913), 143–144.

25. Jean Miège, "Vie touristique en Savoie," *Revue Géographique Alpine* 21 (1933): 750, n.1.

26. *Winter in Switzerland*, 9–10. *Neige et Glace*, 31 December 1933, 194.

27. *New York Times*, 21 February 1926, sect. 8, 12. E. John B. Allen, "The British and the Modernization of Skiing," *History Today* 53 (April 2003): 46–53.

28. E. John B. Allen, "St. Moritz," *Berkshire Encyclopedia of Sport* (Great Barrington, Mass.: Berkshire Publishing, forthcoming).

29. E. John B. Allen, "The Military Foundation of Civilian Skiing in Europe," in *3rd FIS Ski History Conference*, ed. Wintersportmuseum (Mützzuschlag: Wintersportmuseum, 2004), 113–120.

30. Dog: *L'Illustration*, 23 June 1928, 670; Pony: *Lake Placid Club Notes* 180 (November 1926): 1569; Yak: *BSYB* (1926): 454; Reindeer: postcard in author's collection; Motorcycle: *Der Winter* 10 (February 1933): 159; Car: ibid. Airplane: *Illustrated London News*, 14 January 1933, 48.

31. Edouard Dujardin, "Le ski, kilomètre lancé," *L'Illustration*, 2 January 1932, 6. The interest in speed skiing dropped off until the 1960s and only picked up recently as one of the extreme sports. The present record for men is 250.790 kph (155.834 mph) and for women 242.260 kph (150.530 mph).

32. A. L. [Arnold Lunn], "The Flying Kilometre," *BSYB* (1930): 699.

33. Letter, Lunn to Goodrich, *American Ski Annual* (1936): 23.

34. Best followed in *SN&Q* (1923–1926). See also *BSYB* (1920): 99; (1921): 271; and *SN&Q* 39 (October 1929): 151–152.

35. *Public Schools Alpine Sports Club Year Book* (1923): xiii. The TB restriction is in every annual from 1923 to 1929. For the prohibition of games of chance, see (1928): 13, and (1929): 12.

36. Piero Ghighlione, "Lo sci," *Rivista Mensile*, 5 October 1937, XII.

37. *BSYB* (1935): xiii; *Revue du Ski*, 5 October 1937, XIII.

38. Lunn, "The Bernese Oberland," ms. box 4, folder 22. Copy p. 6 of chapter Mürren. TMS in Lunn Papers. See also *BSYB* (19330): 708–735.

39. *L'Illustration,* 26 January 1929, 88; 22 February 1930, 249; 7 February 1931, 162; 23 January 1937, 99. *Illustrated London News,* 9 and 16 February 1935; *BSYB* (1936): xlv; (1939): 134; *Miroir des Sports,* 27 December 1931, 463; *Revue du Ski* 10 (January 1939): xxxvi; *New York Herald Tribune,* 23 January 1937, iii. Reginald Arkell, illustrations by Lewis Baumer, *Winter Sportings* (London: Herbert Jenkins, 1929), 34–35.

40. *Punch,* 19 November 1930, iii.

41. J. Marshall, *Schilaufen als Sport und Verkehrsmittel* (Leipzig: Ehlert, 1911), 20–21.

42. Valerie Steele, *Fashion and Eroticism: Ideals of Feminine Beauty from the Victorian Era to the Jazz Age* (New York: Oxford University Press, 1985), 229. Laura Troubridge, *Memories and Reflections* (London: Heinemann, 1925), 118.

43. Jean Claire-Guyot, "Les sports d'hiver à Chamonix," *L'Illustration,* 30 January 1926, 104–105.

44. J. B. Ermitage, *Ski Fever* (New York: Greenberg [1935?]), 3.

45. Arkell and Baumer, *Winter Sportings,* 15–16.

46. F. Hallbert, "L'équipement du skieur," *Revue du Ski* 2 (December 1930): 276.

47. Artist unknown. Poster executed for the Wengen Vekehrsverein, 1928.

48. Carl J. Luther, "On the Tracks of the First Tracks," *Sport* (1965): 65.

49. Dame Katherine Furse, *The Great Game* (London: F. R. Forsyth, n.d. [1924?]). Marie Marvingt, "Les femmes et le ski," in Louis Magnus and Renaud de la Fregeolière, *Les sports d'hiver* (Paris: Lafitte, 1911), 176–181.

50. Emma Borman, *Brieflicher Lehrgang des Skilaufens* (Wien: Ges. für vervielfältigende Kunst, 1922).

51. For early instructing by women, see *Allgemeine Sport-Zeitung,* 6 December 1914, 1032. For instructing troops, see J. Schneider, "Die Frau im Skisport," *Der Winter* 32 (March 1939): 440. Minutes of the Conseil Municipale, Chamonix, 22 February 1919. TMS signed by mayor, Archives de la Mairie Chamonix, 8M 59, file: 1911–1919. *La Montagne* 15 (March–April 1919): 88–89. Miège, "La vie touristique en Savoie," *Revue Géographique Alpine* 21 (1933): 810.

52. Benno Rybizka in E. John B. Allen, *Teaching and Technique: A History of American Ski Instruction* (Latham: E. P. S. I. A. Educational Foundation, 1987), Appendix.

53. *Der Winter* 26 (January 1933): 426–427; and 27 (January–February 1934): 552–553.

54. *Revue du Ski* 7 (October 1936): 229; and 8 (February 1937): xxxviii.

55. *BSYB* (1921): 214.

56. Ibid. (1928): 480. In the early days, the Inferno, run from the Schilthorn to the Lauterbrunnen valley, was really social fun and games. See A. H. D'Egville, "Three Races," ibid., 507–513.

57. Schweizerischer Damen-Club, *Frohe Stunden im Schnee* (Bern: Hallwag, n.d.), 5.

58. *BSYB* (1931): 345.

59. Ibid. (1932): 507. Heinz Polednik, *Weltwunder Skisport* (Wels: Welsermühl, 1969), 120–121.

60. *La Montagne* 236 (January 1932): 40.

61. 1958/655 in ski box 3, folder ski 1: Modekleidung. Schweizerisches Sportmuseum, Basel, Switzerland.

62. *Revue du Ski* 10 (January 1933): xxxvi. Averell Harriman in the film "Legends of American Skiing," dir. Richard Moulton, Keystone Films, Huntington, Vt., 1980.

CHAPTER 12. WINTER OLYMPIC GAMES OF CHAMONIX, ST. MORITZ, LAKE PLACID

1. G. de Lafreté, "Jeux du Nord," *La Vie au Grand Air,* 10 February 1901, 85. L.F.K. von Thiele, "The Northern Olympic Games," *Wide World Magazine* 9 (1902): 465–473. Leif Yttergren claims for the Northern Games a different ideology: Swedish opposition to the Olympics, and that the Nordic Games were held both before the Winter Olympics and after, and says rivalry between the *Nordiska Spelen* and the Winter Olympics was minimal. This chapter will dispute some of these claims. Yttergren, "The Nordic Games. Visions of Olympic Winter Games or a National Festival?," paper read to ISHPES, Lillehammer, February 1994, and in *I och ur spår!* (Lund: KFS, 2006), 35–57.

2. Pierre de Coubertin in *Revue Olympique* (April 1901): 17–24, and (February 1903): 13–14, in *Pierre de Coubertin: Textes Choisis,* 4 vols., ed. Norbert Müller (Zürich; New York: Weidmann, 1986), 2:311–319.

3. Yttergren, "Nordic Games." *Neige et Glace,* 30 November 1928, 354. Balck was a career army officer: major in 1894, colonel in 1904, and, in 1914, major general. Presently there is no biography of Balck, but that will be remedied by Jan Lindroth. For the moment, see the entry in *Nordisk Familjeboks Sportlexikon. Uppslagsverk för Sport, Gymnastik och Friluftsliv* (Stockholm: Nordisk Familjeboks Förlags Aktiebolag, 1938), 1:592–595. My thanks to Jan Lindroth for help on Swedish matters.

4. Hans Heidinger, "Der Beitrag Mürzzuschlags zur Entwicklung des Skilaufs," *Sport: Sinn und Wahn* (Mürzzuschlag: Steirische Landesausstellung, 1991), 244.

5. Jan Lindroth, "The Nordic Games, Swedish-Norwegian Relations and Politics 1905–1913. A study of Sports and Politics in Conflict." ISHPES paper, Lillehammer 1994.

6. *The Times,* 5 January, 10 February 1909.

7. Ulf Hamilton, "The Concours d'art in OS 1912," in *Memory and Beauty,* ed. Agnieszka Majkowska et al. (Warsaw: Foundation of the Olympic Education Centre and the Museum of Sports and Tourism in Warsaw, 2002), 99–106.

8. *The Times,* 10, 11, 14 February 1913.

9. Letter, J. S. Edström to Baron Pierre de Clary, Vesterås, Sweden, 14 February 1922. TMS in Coubertin Correspondance: Sigfred Edström 1908–1923. MA 5423/1 Olympic Museum, Lausanne, Switzerland. For a Swedish view of the 1922 games, see S. M. N. "Nordiska spelen 1922," *På Skidor* (1923): 55–90.

10. *Year-Book of the Ski Club of Great Britain* (1910): 91–93 [*BSYB*]; *Ski Sport* (1909–1910): 10, 12, 14, 47; "Historique de la Fédération Internationale de Ski," *Neige et Glace*, 1 December 1930, 62–63. See also Dietmar Hubrich, "Die historische Entwicklung des Internationalen Skiverbandes 'FIS'," TMS Leipzig: Deutsche Hochschule für Körperkultur, 1975, 9–26.

11. Coubertin in *Revue Olympique* (February 1908): reprinted in *Textes Choisis* II, 240.

12. *Czech Olympic Media Team Guide: XVII Olympic Winter Games Lillehammer '94* (Praha: Czech Olympic Committee, 1994), cited in Ron Edgeworth, "Nordic Games," *Citius, Altius, Fortius* 2, no. 2 (1994): 34.

13. IOC, Luxemburg, June 11–13, 1910, in Wolf Lyberg, "The IOC Sessions 1894–1955," 53. TMS in Olympic Archives, Vidy, Switzerland.

14. IOC, Paris, 15–23 June 1914, Lyberg, "IOC Sessions," 83.

15. Carl Diem, "Aufgaben für 1916," *Fussball und Leichtathletik* 14 (1913): 4654, cited in Krüger, "The History of the Olympic Winter Games." ISHPES paper, Lillehammer, 1994, TMS, 10. This has been published, but without footnotes in Matti Goksøyr, et al., *Winter Games, Warm Traditions* (Oslo: Norwegian Society of Sport History, 1994), 101–122. For the 1916 Winter Games, see *Der Winter* 8 (February 1914): 382, and ibid., 453–454. *The Times*, 20 December 1913. Norges Skiforbund, *Aarsberetning* (1914): 41–43. *Deutsche Turn-Zeitung* (1914): 528, in Karl Lennartz, *Die VI. Olympischen Spiele 1916* (Köln: Carl-Diem-Institut, 1978), 116. Dr. Müller (Progressive Party), Deutscher Reichstag, Stenographischer Bericht, 214. Sitzung 14 February 1914 (Berlin: 1914): 7339, in Krüger, "History of the Winter Olympic Games," 10.

16. Norges Skiforbund, *Aarsberetning* (1914): 41–43.

17. CIO, Antwerp 17–30 August 1920. TMS in Olympic Museum, Lausanne.

18. Norges Skiforbund, *Aarsberetning* (1921): 17–18.

19. Procès Verbal, CIO, Lausanne, 4 June 1921, 8. TMS in Olympic Museum, Lausanne.

20. Ibid., 10. Pierre Arnaud et Thierry Terret, *Le rêve blanc: olympisme et sports d'hiver en France* (Bordeaux: Presses Universitaires de Bordeaux, 1993), 58, 73.

21. Jens Ljunggren, "The Nordic Games," in Goksøyr et al., *Winter Games, Warm Traditions*, 37–41.

22. Letters, Edström to Coubertin, Vesterås, 14 February 1922. TMS copy in Coubertin Correspondance: Sigfred Edström 1908–1923, MA 5423/1 in Olympic Museum, Lausanne.

23. Letter, Edström to Clary, Västerås, 26 April 1922. TMS in Folder: Chamonix 1924, File: Chamonix General/1924. "Exposé sur la préparation, l'organisation et déroulement des Premiers Jeux Olympiques d'Hiver à Chamonix du 24 janvier au 5 février 1924." TMS in ibid. Procès Verbal, CIO, Rome 7–12 April, Lyberg, "IOC Sessions," 113.

24. *La Montagne* 19 (June 1923): 202; *Ski Notes & Queries* 22 (December 1923): 2 [*SN&Q.*]; *New York Times*, 15 December 1923), 4; *Miroir des Sports*, 14 December 1922, 370; *Neige et Glace*, 11 October 1923, cover. Briançon, "Syndicat d'Initiatif, Sports d'hiver 1924," in Bibliothèque de Briançon. Various documents on the visitors tax in 8M 58 File: Renouvellement de la taxe de séjour 1916–1934, in Archives départementales de l'Haute Savoie, Annecy, France. *L'Illustration*, 2 February 1924, cover; *Le Petit Journal* (February 1924): cover.

25. Cited by Kristen Mo, "Norwegian participation in the Winter Olympics of the 1920's: the debate in the Norwegian ski association." ISHPES paper, Athens, 1989, TMS, 4.

26. H. de Watteville, "The Olympic Winter Games at Chamonix," *BSYB* (1924): 230.

27. P. Mark, "'Den evige mumien.' Amatöfragans behandling i svensk idrott, 1890–1973," *Svenska idrottshistoriska föreningens årsskrift* 9 (1989): 73–107, cited in Krüger, "History of the Winter Olympics," 13.

28. *SN&Q* 29 (April 1926): 96–97.

29. *BSYB* (1905): 44–46.

30. E. C. Richardson, "Report on Third International Ski Congress, Munich, 24–25 January 1912," ibid., (1912): 194.

31. W. H. Weedon, "The Fifth International Ski Congress," ibid. (1914): 397–401.

32. The most accessible "history" of the FIS is in *Neige et Glace*, 1 December 1930, 62–64. For facts, such as lists of officers, see Hubrich, "Die historische Entwicklung des Internationalen Skiverbandes 'FIS'." Diplomarbeit, Leipzig, 1975.

33. Letter, Svenska Skiförbundet, Stockholm, to President of International Olympic Committee, 6 June 1924. TMS in File: St. Moritz 1928 Photocopies, Invitations 1926–1928. Commission Executive de Comité Internationale Olympique, Paris, 7 March 1926. TMS. Procès Verbal, IOC, Prague (1925) and IOC, Lisbon (1926). HMS in Olympic Museum, Lausanne.

34. Mo, "Norwegian participation," 5–6.

35. C. G. D. Hamilton, "The Swedish and Norwegian Year Books," *BSYB* (1929): 301.

36. Ibid. (1922): 392.

37. Tom Mitchell, "Finse at Easter, With Some Remarks About Norwegian Ski-Runners," ibid. (1929): 118.

38. N. R. Östgaard, "The Norwegians and Slalom and Downhill Races," ibid. (1930): 539.

39. Ibid. (1929): 109–111. *Sport* [Swiss], 24 May 1929, translated and published in *BSYB* (1929): 113–115.

40. For the FIS Oslo meeting of 1930, see the report by Fred Harris, TMS in Dewey Archives, Lake Placid Historical Society, Lake Placid, N.Y., and also E. John B. Allen, "The 1932 Lake Placid Winter Games: Dewey's Olympics," in *Olympic Perspectives: Third International Symposium for Olympic Research*, ed. Robert K. Barney et al. (London, Ontario: Centre for Olympic Studies, University of Western Ontario, 1996), 164–165. For the flag raising, see Arnold Lunn, "The Bernese Oberland," TMS in box 4, folder 22, 13–14, in Lunn Papers, Georgetown University, Washington, D.C.

41. Östgaard in *Aftenposten*, 27 February 1931, translated as "Nouvelles catégories de compétition de ski," *Neige et Glace*, 16 October 1931, 295–296.

42. Col. Holmquist of Sweden, for example, believed that although there were skiing organizations in the U.S. and Canada, "neither had the necessary competence to organize ski events." He had support from the French representative. Commission Executive de CIO, St. Moritz, 13 February 1928. TMS, Olympic Archives, Vidy, Switzerland.

43. Fred Harris, "Report of the Eleventh F.I.S Congress, Oslo, Norway, Monday February 24th and Wednesday February 26th, 1930." TMS copy, Dewey Archives, Lake Placid Historical Society, Lake Placid, New York. On the games at Lake Placid generally, see Allen, "The 1932 Lake Placid Winter Games: Dewey's Olympics," 161–171.

44. *Resolution of the California Tenth Olympiad Association*, Los Angeles, 5 January 1929. File: Lake Placid General 1932, Folder J. O. d'Hiver 1932, Lake Placid General 1928–32, Olympic Archives, Vidy. Letters and Telegrams between Dewey and William May Garland, January, February 1929, and Dewey to Donald Fair Morgan and John B. Stetson, January and August 1929. TMS, Dewey Archives, Lake Placid. Procès Verbal, CIO Lausanne, 10 April 1929, Olympic Archives, Vidy. *Oakland Tribune* enclosed in letter, Lattimer to Dewey, 23 July 1931. TMS, Dewey Archives, Lake Placid.

45. Letters to and from Dewey to Brundage, Gustavus T. Kirby, F.D. Roosevelt, Jeremiah Moses, Count de Baillet-Latour, Captain G. van Roosem, Bjorn Blix. TMSS in Dewey Archives, Lake Placid.

46. Letter, Arnulf Poulson to Dewey, Oslo, 22 January 1930; Dewey to Howard Acton, Lake Placid, 23 September 1931. TMSS, Dewey Archives, Lake Placid.

47. Telegrams and Letters, Dewey to Louis Boomer and Bjorn Blix in 1931. TMSS, Dewey Archives, Lake Placid.

48. Letters, between Dewey and Charles Lindbergh, 1932. TMSS. Dewey Archives, Lake Placid.

49. Letter, Dewey to Baillet-Latour, Lake Placid, 22 December 1931. TMS. Dewey Archives, Lake Placid.

50. Postcard, Coubertin to Dewey, Lausanne, 26 December 1931. TMS. Dewey Archives, Lake Placid.

51. George M. Lattimer, Compiler, *Official Report III Olympic Winter Games Lake Placid 1932* (Lake Placid: III Winter Olympic Games Committee, 1932), 9.

52. *Winter Sports* (February 1933): 4–6, 22. *Ski Bulletin*, 10 February 1933, 6–7. See also Harris's reply to the censure in *Winter Sports* (March 1933): 4–5.

53. Ibid. (February 1933): 4–6, 22.

54. Erling Strom, *Pioneers on Skis* (Central Valley, N.Y.: Smith Clove Press, 1977), 59.

55. The Sno-Birds Ski Club, founded in 1920 to "promote good fellowship and to originate and conduct annually a series of amusing and interesting competitions." *Lake Placid Club Notes* (November 1920): 886.

56. Ibid. (March 1905): n.p.; (March 1913): 417; (December 1917): 639; (March 1929): 2017.

CHAPTER 13. EUROPEANS ABROAD IN THE EAST

1. The states of China and Japan are bordered by exact boundaries today, but into the nineteenth and even early twentieth centuries, border regions were defined more by tribal areas than exact frontiers with customs' posts. Thus, for one example, the Ghiliaks lived both on the northern part of Sakhalin as well as in the coastal area both north and south of the Amur river. Our modern sense of order would like to characterize them as Russian tribes, yet some lived in China. The Ainu lived on south Sakhalin as well as on Hokkaido, the northernmost island of Japan. There is not, then, a neat "fit."

Early travel reports on winter in Korea describe people on snowshoes; "they wear small boards like battledores," is how one 1662 description has it. Hendrik Hamel, quoted in William E. Griffiths, *Corea, Without and Within* (Philadelphia: Presbyterian Board of Publications, 1885), 114. Witsen's well-known *Noord en Oost Tartary* (Amsterdam, 1705), 148, also related the use of snowshoes in Korea. See also Leopold von Schrenck, *Reisen und Forschungen im Amur-Lande in den Jahren 1854–1856* (St. Petersburg: Commissionaire der kaiserlichen Akademie der Wissenschaften, 1881), 472–478.

2. Jakob Vaage, *Norske ski erobrer verden* (Oslo: Gyldendal, 1952); Vaage, *Skienes verden* (Oslo: Hjemmenes, 1979); Vaage, "Milepeler af merkedager gjennom 4000 ar," *Norske Skiloper: Østlandet Nord* (Oslo: Erling Ranheim, 1955), 9–42.

3. I have had my own run-ins with Vaage, and so has Karin Berg, curator of the Holmenkollen Ski Museum. Vaage died in 1994.

4. Vaage, *Norske ski erobrer verden*, 209–210.

5. Shang Caizhen et al., eds., *The History of Skiing in China* (Wuhan: Chinese Ski

Association and the Cultural and Historical Working Association of the State Sports Association, 1993), Chapter 1. I am indebted to Dr. Xiaoxiong Li for translation. A table of contents in English appears on pp. 234–237. See also Liu Qilu and Liu Yueye, "Sports on Ice and Snow in Ancient China." ISHPES paper, Lillehammer, 25–30 January 1994. Li Di, "Some Records about the Arctic in Early Chinese Books," *Earth Sciences History* 10, no. 2 (1991): 219–222. Wilhelm Schott, "Über die ächten Kirgisen," *Abhandlung der königlichen Akademie der Wissenschaften zu Berlin 1864*, 429–474.

6. Vaage, *Norske ski erobrer verden*, 211.

7. "Skifahrt in Peking," *Der Winter* 20 (1926–27): 203–204.

8. A Japanese hut was virtually taken over in 1936 by the Ski and Winter Sports Club of China, whose members were Germans, Czechs, and a few Britons. D. Gordon Evans, "Ski-ing in Sogadaira," *Ski Notes & Queries* 60 (October 1936): 333. [*SN&Q.*]

9. Anton Obholzer, *Geschichte des Skilaufs* (Wien, Leipzig: Deutscher Verlag für Jugend und Volk, 1935), 14. This is another undocumented ski history written by a man who went on to write two other, well-documented books.

10. Schrenck, *Reisen*, 472–478. See also de la Brunière, "Excursion en Mandchourie en 1845," *Nouvelles annales des voyages*, 5th series, vol. 16 (1848), 110, quoted in E. G. Ravenstein, *The Russians on the Amur* (London: Trubner and Co., 1861), 92, 94.

11. According to John Batchelor, *The Ainu of Japan* (New York: Revell Co., 1854), 186.

12. Y. Yamamoto, *Karafuto Ainu Jukyo to Mingu* (Tokyo: Sagami Shobe, 1970), 236, 239, 255. See also N. Okada, "Suto," *Karafuto Jiho* 35 (1940): 92–97. I am indebted to Professor Emiko Ohnuki-Tierney for these references. See also Mamiya-Rainshu, *Hoku-Ezo zusetsu* (Edo: 1855), 6a, b, and 13, in Anton Obholzer, *Geschichte des Skis und des Skistockes* (Schorndorf: Karl Hofmann, 1974), 17.

13. *Eine Reise nach dem Norden Japans* (1804), in A. E. von Nordenskjöld, *Die Umseglung Asiens und Europas auf der Vega* (Leipzig: 1882), 101. Compare George Montadon, *La civilisation Aïnou* (Paris: Payot, 1937), 129–131. Montadon was among the Ainu in 1919. The depiction of the Ainu drawn by reindeer has found its way onto T-shirts.

14. G. B. Sansom, *The Western World and Japan* (New York: Knopf, 1973), 382–3.

15. 1897 in Carl J. Luther, Untitled TMS in Deutscher Skiverband, Carl Luther Archiv [DSV L-A.], in Planegg, Germany, 8, box: Large Unnamed: Europe, Japan, China, Korea. 1901 in Vaage, *Norske ski erobrer verden*, 211. No date by Wilhelm Paulcke, *Der Skilauf* (Freiburg i. Breisgau: Wagner'sche Universitäts-Buchhandlung, 1908), 141. January 1902 in Jirō Nitta, *Death March on Mount Hakkōda. A Documentary Novel* (Berkeley: Stone Bridge Press, 1992), 189. "Skidsport i Japan," *Ny Tidning för Idrott* 12 (March 1903): 101–102.

16. *Norsk Idrætsblad* and *Ny Tidning for Idrott* published in The Export Council of Norway, "Norwegians Introduced Skis to Japan," TMS.

17. *Morning Post* (Tokyo) in *Allgemeines Korrespondenzblatt*, 17 February 1905, 109; and 24 February 1905, 119.

18. "Use of the Ski, or Skee, in Foreign Armies," trans. by permission of the Minister of War from the *Revue Militaire des armées etrangères*, in *Royal United Services Institute Journal* 53 (1909): 375.

19. *A History of Ski in Hokkaido, and a Guide to Main Ski Ground* (1972): n.p.

20. Fritz Paravicini, "Ski in Japan," *Ski* (Mitteleuropäischer Ski Verband) 16 (March 1906): 256; *History of Ski in Hokkaido*, n. p.

21. See von Kratzer's call for skiers in *Deutsche Japan-Post* cited in *Der Schnee*, 17 February 1912, 5–7. See also ibid., 13 January 1912; 31 January 1914, 122; 4 April 1914, 207. E. von Kratzer, "Meine erste Skitour in Japan," ibid., 25 March 1911, 1–3; Leopold von Winkler, "Die Entwicklung des Skilaufs in Japan," ibid., 10 November 1925, 30–32.

22. Theodor von Lerch, "Takata liegt hier," reprinted in Franz Klaus, ed., *Zdarsky-Blätter* (March 1986): 7. "Gedenken an Generalmajor Theodor von Lerch," in Klaus ed., *75 Jahre Schifreundschaft Japan-Österreich 1911–1986*. TMS based on von Lerch's diary in Zdarsky-Archiv, Lilienfeld, Austria. J. Müller, "Die Entwicklung des militärischen Skilaufs," *Schwarztaler Zeitung*, 15 November 1913, 3. Winkler, "Die Entwicklung," *Der Winter* 21 (November 1925): 11–13. Von Lerch, "Erste Winterhochturen in Japan," *Zeitschriften des Deutschen und Österreichischen Alpenvereins* 63 (1932): 74.

23. Von Lerch, "Gedenken," *Zdarsky-Blätter* (March 1986): 5.

24. Koichi Ikeda and Masaharu Ohashi, "A Historical Study of Skiing with in [sic] the Realm of School Physical Education in Taisho Era: in the Case of Niigata Prefecture," *Japanese Journal of Physical Education* 23 (September 1978): 99–108. English summary, p. 99.

25. C. A. de Linde, "A Ski-ing Holiday in Japan," *British Ski Year Book* (1930): 390. [*BSYB.*]

26. Kenju Takahashi, "Berge und Bergsteigen in Japan," *Deutsche Alpen-Zeitung* 9 (September 1929): 257.

27. *Ski-Sport* (1924–25): 57. Winkler, "Die Entwicklung," *Der Schnee*, 10 November 1925, 30–332.

28. Hiroshi Arai, "The Opening of Ski Slopes During the Period in which Skiing was Spreading Over Japan," in *International Ski History Congress 2002: Collected Papers*, ed. E. John B. Allen (New Hartford, Conn.: I.S.H.A., 2002), 258–267.

29. *BSYB* (1927): 151.

30. Cil [Carl J. Luther], "Untitled" TMS. DSV L-A 8. Box: Large Unnamed: Europe, Japan, China, Korea.

31. *Der Winter* 32 (December 1938): 309.

32. Foreningen til Ski-idretten fremme, *Arbok* (1928): 43, 47–48.

33. Lt. Olaf Helset letters to *Aftenposten* in February, April and May, 1929 published in Helset, "Norwegian Skiers in Japan, 1929," TMS. The three Norwegians arrived on 6 January 1929. For the trip and initial impressions only, see Olaf Helset, "Norske Skiløpere i Japan: ankomsten til arbeitsfeltet," *Arbok* (1920): 109–114.

34. *Ski-idrett* 1 (December 1928): 27.

35. De Linde, "Ski-ing Holiday in Japan," *BSYB* (1930): 383; de Linde, "Further Notes on Ski-ing in Japan," *SN&Q* (October 1931): 208. De Linde, "A Memory of Japan," in *The Englishman on Ski,* ed. Arnold Lunn (London: Museum Press, 1963), 88. *Neue Zürcher Zeitung* quoted in *Ski* [Swiss] (1936): 71. *Ski* [Swiss] (1931), quoted in *Der Winter* 26 (October 1932): 277.

36. Hannes Schneider, *Auf Schi in Japan* (Innsbruck: Tyrolia, 1935).

37. Takazumi Fukuoka, "Schilauf in Japan an der Jahrhundertwende," *FdSnow* 22 (January 2003): 26.

38. Japan Tourist Bureau, *Skiing in Hokkaido* (Tokyo: Japan Tourist Bureau, 1935).

39. "75 Jahre Skifreundschaft Japan-Österreich 1911–1986." TMS, n.p. Zdarsky-Archiv, Lilienfeld.

40. *Der Völkische Beobachter,* 19 February 1936.

41. Ilse Ruef-Rohde und Dr. Ernst, "Deutscher Skikurs in Japan, Take Asos Skihütte und Skilauf in Korea," *Der Winter* 29 (March 1936): 161. The Japanese, according to an Englishman, knew little about downhill or slalom in 1937, but enjoyed "a gruelling langlauf." *SN&Q* 62 (May 1937): 437.

42. *Der Winter* 32 (December 1938): 309.

43. Vaage, *Norske ski erobrer verden,* 214, 218. The information came from Bjerknes' nephew.

44. A. Warburton, "Early New Zealand Ski-ing," in *The Australian and New Zealand Ski Year Book,* ed. Stewart Jamieson (Sydney, 1936): 121.

45. G. E. Mannering, "The Early Use of Ski in the New Zealand Alps," ibid. (1938): 52–53.

46. Diary excerpts, *BSYB* (1910): 23–24.

47. Letter, B. Head, Christchurch, NZ, to *Winter Sports Review* (1911–1912): 204. *The Press* (Christchurch), 22 May 1912.

48. A. Anderson, "Early Ski-ing at Mount Cook: Reminiscences of Peter Graham," *The Australian and New Zealand Ski Year Book* (1940): 13–17.

49. For Tryggve Gran's Antarctic experiences, see *The Norwegian with Scott. Tryggve Gran's Antarctic Diary 1910–1913,* trans. Ellen Johanne McGhie (née Gran) (London: HMSO, 1984). See also Tor Bomann-Larsen, *Den evige sne* (Oslo: Cappelens, 1993), 181–189.

50. *The Press* (Christchurch), 22 May 1912.

51. Letter, George W. Cuthpium (?), department of Tourist and Health Resorts,

Christchurch, to General Manager, Wellington, NZ, 24 July 1914. TMS in Mount Cook archives; box: Skiing, Mount Cook, New Zealand.

52. Letter, Department of Tourist and Health Resorts to Chief Guide, Wellington, 21 August 1918. TMS in Mount Cook Archives; box: Skiing, Mount Cook, NZ.

53. *Skiing the Volcano: Historical Images of Skiing on Mt. Ruapehu* (Wellington, NZ: Ruapehu Alpine Lifts and Tourism Resource Consultants, 1986), 7–8.

54. R. C. Morie, "New Zealand Ski-ing," *SN&Q* 53 (May 1934): 297–303.

55. J. C. Graham, *Ruapehu. Tribute to a Mountain* (Wellington: Reed, 1963), 32–33. L. V. Bryant, "The Ski Championship at Mount Cook, August 1932," *The Australian and New Zealand Ski Year Book* (1933): 244–246.

56. "A Letter from New Zealand to B. S. R.," *Ladies Ski Club Bulletin* 6 (October 1931): 270. Compare his remark with those made in central Europe when the first Norwegians appeared; they, too, had no idea of how to instruct. See Chapter 4.

57. *SN&Q* 53 (May 1934): 270.

58. *Skiing the Volcano*, 21. It is curious that in G. C. Lockwood, "New Zealand Skiing to Date," *The Australian and New Zealand Ski Year Book* (1940): 2–5, there is great emphasis put on the 1930s, the "hey-day of our racing. . . . All were obsessed with the necessity of learning turns and speed running," yet no mention of Skardarasy.

59. *The Story of Arthur's Pass* (Christchurch: Arthur's Pass National Park, 1986), 104. See also Robert Logan, *"Waimakariri," Canterbury's River of Cold Rushing Water* (Gisborn: Robert Logan, 1987), 177.

60. Vaage, *Norske ski erobrer verden*, 215–216. In Vaage's *Skienes verden*, 256, he was on skis in 1854. The information came from Bjerknes' nephew.

61. The Kiandra gold rush started in 1859. Probably 1860 was the first season miners wintered over. Edward Axford, "Last Words on our First Skiers," *Australian Ski Year Book* (1952): 11.

62. For the Swede Bumpstone (anglicization of names was common), see W. Hughes, "Old Kiandra," ibid. (1931): 53. See also Stewart Jamieson, "Ski-ing in Australia," *The Australian Quarterly* (14 March 1932): 106. Other writers refer to a Swede, see *Tidning för Idrott* (1895) in Artur Zettersten, HMS, 460, in Svenska Skidmuseet, Umeå, Sweden. Arnold Lunn, *The Story of Ski-ing* (London: Eyre and Spottiswoode, 1952), 141.

63. *Monaro Mercury* in *Sydney Morning Herald*, 6 August 1861. *Yass Courier*, 10 August 1861. See also *Braidwood Observer* in *Sydney Morning Herald*, 12 August 1861.

64. Hughes, "Old Kiandra," *Australian Ski Year Book* (1931): 53–55.

65. Percy Hunter, "History of the Australian Ski-ing Clubs," ibid., (1928): 5.

66. Many of Kerry's photographs have been published, some made into postcards. The description comes mostly from C. D. Paterson, "Kosciusko," *BSYB* (1911): 52.

67. For the Kiandra ski lasting into the 1930s, see Hunter, "History of the Australian

Ski-ing Clubs," *Australian Ski Year Book* (1928): 5. Amundsen, thought by some to be a relative of the explorer, Letter W. P. Bourke to *Norsk Idrætsblad*, 20 November 1895, 383. For importing Norwegian skis, see B. Head, "Five Weeks in New South Wales," *BSYB* (1911): 54. The Huitfeldt binding was much criticized by locals.

68. E. John B. Allen, *From Skisport to Skiing: One Hundred Years of an American Sport, 1840–1940* (Amherst: University of Massachusetts Press, 1993), 21–28.

69. For two descriptions see Letter, Bourke, *Norsk Idrættsblad*, 20 November 1895, 383. W. R. Rickmers, "Skilauf in Australien," *Deutsche Wintersport*, 29 October 1902, part of which Rickmers translated from "Kiandra in Winter," *Wide World Magazine*.

70. Probably the *Sydney Mail* (3 August 1901) excerpted in E. C. Richardson, "Ski-riding in Australia," *BYSB* I, 2 (1906): 23–24. This account found its way into the European sporting press. See *Deutsche Alpenzeitung* 2 (January 1903): 193, *Le Sport Universel illustré*, 23 March 1902, 45. Vaage, *Norske ski erobrer verden*, 216–218 makes much of Winther.

71. C. D. Satersch, "Mt. Kosciusko," *Alpine Ski Club Annual* 4 (1911): 18. "Skilauf in Australien," *Der Winter* 6 (February 1912): 235. Percy Hunter talked to the Premier of New South Wales, the Honourable Joseph Carruthers, about a hotel. Janis Lloyd, *Skiing into History 1924–1980* (Toorak: Ski Club of Victoria, 1986), 42–43.

72. "The Ski Club of Australia," *SN&Q* 47 (May 1932): 350–352. Jamieson, "Ski-ing in Australia," *Australian Quarterly* (14 March 1932): 106.

73. "Stewart Jamieson," *SN&Q* 58 (December 1935): 213–214.

74. Alois Mock, "Skilauf in Australien," *Der Winter* 23 (1929–1930): 64. See also Klaus Hueneke, "Skiing around the Gum Trees," *Hemisphere* 19 (August 1975): 27, which claims that the Austrian Georg Aalberg was the first. He was instrumental in promoting touring.

75. Letter, Percy W. Pearson to Editor, Sydney, 6 September 1927, *SN&Q* 34 (December 1927): 349.

76. *Australian and New Zealand Ski Year Book* (1938): 17. For the Austrians, see Lloyd, *Skiing into History*, 556–557; Ainslie Douglas, "Skiing in Australia," *Hemisphere* (July 1957): 21 maintains that Ernst Skardarasy "did more to put the sport on its feet in Australia than anyone else." For Pfeifer, see Friedl Pfeifer with Morten Lund, "The Making of the Aspen Dream," TMS, 124, 128, 130–131. This is the manuscript of *Nice Goin': My Life on Skis* (Missoula: Pictorial Histories Publishing Company, 1993), 53, 57–60. My thanks to Morten Lund for the TMS.

77. For the two advertisements see Charles M. Dudley, *60 Centuries of Skiing* (Brattleboro, Vt.: Stephen Daye Press, 1935), 180, and Jamieson, "Ski-ing in Australia," *Australian Quarterly* (14 March 1932): 110.

78. J. Jacot Guillarmod, "Un record dans l'Himalaya," *Jahrbuch des Schweizer Alpenclub* 38 (1902): 226.

79. William H. Workman, "Some Obstacles to Himalayan Mountaineering and the History of a Record Attempt," *Alpine Journal* 169 (August 1905): 492.

80. *Alpiner Wintersport*, 2 December 1904, 27. Letter, C. Kirkpatrick to Editor, Khyber Pass, 1 August 1908, *BSYB* (1908): 49–50.

81. Ibid. (1907): 5; (1908): 50. See also Kenneth Mason, "Two Himalayan Passes and a Note on the Snow Conditions in the Pamirs," ibid. (1913): 314.

82. Lt. Col. A. G. Dyce, "Ski-ing in India," ibid. (1944): 217. See also ibid. (1905): 39.

83. What follows comes from Dyce and Captain C. I. Curteis, "Ski-ing in Kashmir," *Journal of the Royal Artillery* 57 (1930–31): 382–384.

84. By Dr. H. de Terra, member of the German central Asian expedition. *Der Winter* 21 (1927–28): 450.

85. *Winter Sports in India* (1932–33), brochure published by the Indian State Railways.

86. See also Enid Fernandez, "Forty Years Back," *Eagle Ski Club Year Book* (1969): 55.

87. Georg Buschan, *Illustrierte Völkerkunde* (Stuttgart: Strecker und Schröder, 1923), 2:415. Captain A. C. Galloway, "Ski-ing in Afghanistan," *BSYB* (1936): 247–249.

88. *Münchener Illustrierte Presse*, 19 November 1936, 636–637. See also *Der Winter* 29 (February 1936): 501. For those looking for more obscure ski developments, they might follow the monks from the Grand St. Bernard who searched out a new hospice on skis in Tibet in 1929. They came to a suitable pass at about 4,000 meters in their new paradise between the sources of the rivers Mekong and Salween in northeast Tibet. Ibid., 23 (December 1929): 278.

89. G. B. S. Hindley, "A New Ski Club," *SN&Q* 45 (October 1931): 192.

CHAPTER 14. EUROPEANS ABROAD IN THE AMERICAS

1. Frank Leslie's *Illustrated Weekly*, 2 February 1893, 70.

2. *Billed-Magazin*, 1 May 1869, 172. Norwegians settled mostly in the nineteenth century in Iowa, Michigan, Minnesota, and Wisconsin, then called the Northwest. The present term is Midwest, and I use that to avoid any misunderstanding. There were, of course, communities of immigrants elsewhere, such as Swedes in New Sweden, Maine, Norwegians in Berlin, New Hampshire, and some Finns in Newport, Vermont, to pick three examples outside the Midwest.

3. Detailed analysis is in E. John B. Allen, *From Skisport to Skiing: One Hundred Years of an American Sport, 1840–1940* (Amherst: University of Massachusetts Press, 1993).

4. G. Hendel, "Snow-Shoeing in the Californian Sierras," *The Mining and Scientific Press*, 3 January 1874, 1, 9. See also William H. Brewer, *Up and Down in California in 1860–1864*, ed. Francis P. Farquhar (New Haven: Yale University Press, 1930), 435, and John R. Gillis, "Tunnels of the Pacific Railroad," *Transactions of the American Society of Civil Engineers* (1874): 114. For the use of the term "snowshoe" into the 1930s, see

W. Mosauer, "Skiing on the East Side of the Sierra," *Sierra Club Bulletin* 21 (February 1936): 55.

5. The literature on Thompson is extensive and hagiographic. Most accounts rest on D. de Quille, "Snowshoe Thompson," *Territorial Enterprise,* 13 February 1876. The most balanced treatment is K. Bjork, " 'Snowshoe' Thompson: Fact and Legend," *Norwegian-American Studies and Records* 19 (1956): 62–88.

6. E. John B. Allen, "Skiing Mailmen of Mountain America: U.S. Winter Postal Service in the Nineteenth Century," *Journal of the West* 29 (April 1990): 76–86.

7. Nevada *Union,* 29 January 1866, cited in P. Fatout, *Meadow Lake Gold Town* (Bloomington: Indiana University Press, 1969), 56–57. Silver Mountain *Alpine Chronicle,* 1 April 1876.

8. *Sacramento Daily Union,* 14 December 1867.

9. Prize money was almost always listed in the published results of a race. For one example, see *Daily Union,* 28 March 1868. For miners' wages, see W. A. Thayer, *Marvels of the New West* (Norwich: Henry Bill, 1892), 455, and J. Marx, *The Magic of Gold* (Garden City: Doubleday and Doubleday, 1978), 391–392.

10. E. John B. Allen, "Sierra 'Ladies' on Skis in Gold Rush California," *Journal of Sport History* 17 (Winter 1990): 347–353.

11. Sacramento *Daily Union,* 14 December 1867.

12. Marquette (Michigan) *Mining Journal,* 21 January 1905. R. Hubbell, "Ski Running," *Frank Leslie's Popular Monthly* 35 (January 1893): 64. The Red Wing (Minnesota) *Daily Republican,* 13 February 1905, said the same thing in a different spirit: "Winter in California—don't mention it. No sleighing, no skiing, no skating, no Minnesota ozone—nothing that makes life worth living."

13. *The Skisport* (1906–07): 2. These sorts of words can be found in the daily papers from time to time. For one example, see *The North,* 22 January 1890.

14. For the formation of the National Ski Association, see E. John B. Allen, "The Modernization of the Skisport: Ishpeming's Contribution to American Skiing," *The Michigan Historical Review* 16 (Spring 1990): 1–20. The one non-midwestern club was "The First Kingdom of the Ski" of Utica, N.Y., comprising a group of middle-class social skiers. One wonders what the National Ski Association leadership thought of a club whose motto was "Soc et Tuum." MS of the constitution of The First Kingdom of the Ski. My thanks to Mrs. Emily Williams of Turin, N.Y. See also D. H. Beetle, "The First Kingdom of the Ski," *Ski Time* [1951?]: 29–31.

15. *The Skisport* (under varying titles and with an occasional lapse in publication (1906–1925).

16. Ibid. (1907–08): 19–20.

17. K. H. R., "Skisport in America," *Der Winter* (1909), reprinted in *The Skisport* (1909–10): 10, and (1910–11): 69.

18. Ibid. (1909–10): 10, and (1910–11): 78.

19. These were the first movies taken of skiing. G. Newett, "History of Ishpeming Ski Club," in *History of the National Ski Association and the Skisport in America, 1840–1930,* ed. H. A. Grinden (Duluth: National Ski Association [1931?]), 16. *The Skisport* (1913–14): 39. See also "Bobsled Used in Taking Motion Pictures," *Popular Mechanics* (February 1916): front cover and 171. *Harper's Weekly,* 9 January 1883, 365; 4 March 1899, front cover; and *Frank Leslie's Illustrated Weekly,* 2 February 1893, front cover.

20. The best source for early Lake Placid Club activity is the *Lake Placid Club Notes.* For discrimination and anti-Semitism, see ibid., 1 (March 1905): n.p.; 63 (March 1913): 417; 204 (March 1929): 2017. *Petition to the Regents of the State of New York Respectfully Asking for the Removal from office of Melvil Dewey, the Present State Librarian, whose Tenure of Office is dependent upon your Action, December 20, 1904,* 3, and Dewey's reply, pp.6–20, in New York State Archives, Albany, N.Y. The Californian threat is found in *Nevada State Journal,* 11 April 1929.

21. *The Dartmouth,* 7 December 1909. For the development of Harris as a skier, see E. John B. Allen, "The Making of a Skier: Fred H. Harris 1904–1922," *Vermont History* 53 (Winter 1985): 5–16.

22. F. H. Harris, "Skiing Over the New Hampshire Hills," *National Geographic* 37 (February 1920): 133–166. In a typed list of Harris's articles is the following note after the above title: "Secretary of Dartmouth College stated that this article increased Freshmen applications in one year from 800 to over 2600." Harris papers, in possession of Harris heirs, Brattleboro, Vt. See also D. Bradley, "Dartmouth in the Old Days," *Ski* (January 1959): 19. Bradley told me he had received confirmation of his figures in 1958, from 824 to 2,625.

23. T. Hook, "Ski Clubs Boom Throughout America," *The Ski Annual* (1960–61): 13.

24. U.S.E.A.S.A., *The Ski Annual* (1934): 122–153, *American Ski Annual* (1935): 179–188.

25. O. E. Schniebs, "Sanity in Ski Competition," ibid. (1938–39): 149.

26. E. D. Woolsey, *Off the Beaten Track* (Wilson: Wilson Bench Press, 1984), 58. *Boston Herald,* 7 February 1939.

27. F. Donaldson, "With the First American Ski Team in Europe," *Appalachia* (November 1935): 404.

28. *Ski Bulletin,* 25 February 1938, 8.

29. E. John B. Allen, *Teaching and Technique: A History of American Ski Instruction* (Latham: E.P.S.I.A. Educational Foundation, 1987), see especially 9–27.

30. Lowell Thomas, "Let's Ski for Fun," *American Ski Annual* (1937–38): 158–159.

31. Boston and Maine Railroad pamphlets in the New England Ski Museum, Franconia, N.H. The annual snow train statistics from Boston give a good idea of the increasing clientele—1931: 8,371; 1932: 10,314; 1933: 7,703; 1934: 14,974; 1935: 17,943; 1936:

24,240. For a discussion of snow train activity, see E. John B. Allen " 'Millions of Flakes of Fun in Massachusetts': Boston and the Development of Skiing 1870–1940," in *Sports in Massachusetts: Selected Essays,* ed. R. Story (Westfield: Institute of Massachusetts Studies, 1991), 82–84.

32. S. Hannah interviewed by C. Morrissey, Franconia, N.H., 14 January 1981, for the documentary film *Legends of American Skiing,* dir. Richard W. Moulton, Keystone Productions, 1982.

33. In the New England Ski Museum. This has been published in black and white in E. John B. Allen, *New England Skiing 1870–1940* (Dover: Arcadia, 1997), 88.

34. Jeffrey R. Leich, "Winter Work: The CCC and New England Skiing," *Journal of the New England Ski Museum* 61 (Autumn 2004) and 62 (Spring 2005). See also *Appalachia* (December 1933): 600–601. P. Merrill interviewed by R. W. Moulton, Montpelier, Vt., 24 August 1981 for the film *Legends of American Skiing.* G. Mazuzan, "Skiing is not Merely a Sport: the Development of Mt. Mansfield as a Recreation Area," *Vermont History* 40 (Winter 1972): 47–63. Allen, "Millions of Flakes of Fun," 90–94.

35. *Ski Bulletin,* 13 March 1936, 10. M. Dole, *Adventures in Skiing* (New York: Franklin Watts, 1965), 50–59. For an overview of the NSPS, see G. Besser, *The National Ski Patrol: Samaritans of the Snow* (Woodstock: Countryman Press, 1983).

36. First at Woodstock, Vt. *Rutland Daily Herald,* 27 January 1934. The tow was more or less copied from the rope tow at Shawbridge, Quebec, Canada.

37. The advertising slogan will be found in the *Ski Bulletin,* 9 December 1938, 11. For an overview, see E. John B. Allen, "The Development of New Hampshire Skiing: 1870's–1940," *Historical New Hampshire* 35 (Spring 1981): 32.

38. Theodore A. Johnsen, *The Winter Sport of Skeeing* (Portland, Maine: 1905). Letter M. A. Strand to F. C. Barton, New Richmond, Wisc., 10 March 1914. Letter 14.023, Apperson papers, Adirondack Research Center, Schenectady, N.Y.

39. *Boston Herald,* 13 March 1936.

40. The best contemporary overview is E. R. Warren, "Snow-Shoeing in the Rocky Mountains," *Outing* (January 1887): 350–353.

41. *Middle Park Times,* 16 February 1912.

42. For the King's medal, see *Aarbog* (1903): list immediately following page 115. Leif Hovelsen, *The Flying Norseman* (Ishpeming: National Ski Hall of Fame, 1983), 27–34.

43. See the reports in the *Steamboat Pilot,* 16 and 23 February 1916.

44. Erling Strom, *Pioneers on Skis* (Central Valley, N.Y.: Smith Clove Press, 1977), 26–34.

45. G. C. Torguson, "Skiing," *Outers' Recreation* 62 (February 1920): 109.

46. Averell Harriman interviewed by Moulton, August 1981, Washington, D.C., for *Legends of American Skiing.* The Hannigan quote appears in Doris Taylor, *Sun Valley* (Sun Valley: Ex Libris, 1980), 28.

47. V. S. Morrow, "Skiing America First," *The Ski Annual* (1934): 16–17.

48. *Boston Evening Transcript,* 14 December 1934; *Boston Globe,* 8 January 1937.

49. Allen, *From Skisport to Skiing,* 145–170, for an economic analysis of U.S. skiing.

50. The resort was going to use Mt. Hayden. T. Ryan interviewed by Moulton, Sharon, Conn., 25 August 1981, for *Legends of American Skiing.* Film clips of Fiske's burial bring the film to a close. See also R. Hough and D. Richards, *The Battle of Britain* (New York: Norton, 1989), 188–189, 194, 336.

51. *Aftenposten,* 21 March 1872. Skis #506, Documentation #787 in Svenska Skidmuseet, Umeå. My thanks to Kenneth Åstrom for translation of documentation concerning the 1878 skis. See also E. John B. Allen, "Early Canadian Skis: Notes from Europe," *Canadian Journal of History of Sport* 17 (May 1986): 88–89. On Norwegian immigrant Birch, see *Le Courrier de Ste. Hyacinthe,* 4 February 1879, *Canadian Illustrated News,* 8 February 1879 (with woodcut), *La Minerve,* 22 April 1879. Lord Frederick Hamilton, *Vanished Pomp of Yesterday* (London: Hodder and Stoughton, 1937), 265. At Dorset, North Baffin Island, what is most probably a model ski, dated to 1000 AD has been found. Local Eskimos know nothing of ski culture. The find remains a mystery. Mary Rousselière, "Dorset Finds," *Arctic* 32 (March 1979): 26–28.

52. H. P. Douglas, "Early Days in Montreal," *Canadian Ski Annual* (1923–1924): 62. Douglas, *My Ski-ing Years* (Montreal: Whitcomb and Gilmour, 1951), 15–16. Percy E. Nobbs, "Reminiscences," *Canadian Ski Annual* (1927–1928): 42. *Iron Ore,* 13 February 1903.

53. Visiting British skier Gerald Seligman remarked on the rivalry of the snowshoe and ski in 1905. Gerald Seligman, "United States and Canada," *British Ski Year Book* (1905): 35. [*BSYB.*] Douglas, "Early Days in Montreal," *Canadian Ski Annual* (1923–1924): 64.

54. Reprinted articles from various papers, most not named, but all dated: 1887, 18 February 1888, 15 February 1896, 7 March, 3 December 1897, 3 February, 4 November 1898, *Kootenay Star* 1891, 9 December 1892, in Sam Wormington, *The Ski Race* (Sandpoint: Selkirk, 1980), 5–11.

55. *Manitoba Morning Free Press,* 6 January 1897.

56. Ibid., 4 March 1897, and 29 November 1911.

57. Unnamed paper (28 January 1899) in Warmington, *Ski Race,* 13.

58. Unnamed paper (18 February 1900) in ibid., 17.

59. Unnamed paper (18 February 1915) in ibid., 65.

60. Unnamed papers (18 February 1905, and 17 February 1907) in ibid., 36, 40.

61. *Manitoba Morning Free Press,* 18 February 1907.

62. Unnamed paper (12 February 1908) in Wormington, *Ski Race,* 44–45.

63. *Daily Pioneer Press,* 3 January 1886, printing a report from Montreal.

64. Unnamed paper (12 February 1908; 11 February 1916; and 13 February 1919) in Wormington, *Ski Race* 46, 67, 148–149.

65. *Phoenix Pioneer,* 30 January 1915, in ibid., 86.

66. *Montreal Gazette,* 7 and 11 February 1907; 2 March 1908.

67. *BSYB* (1910): 10. John Marsh, "Changing Skiing Scenes in Canada," *Canadian Geographical Journal* 90, no. 2 (1975): 4. C. Lund, "Development of Skiing in Banff," *Alberta History* 25, no. 4 (1977): 26–30. Wormington, *Ski Race,* 274.

68. V.V.Kutschera, "Alpine Ski-ing in the Canadian Rockies," *BSYB* (1936): 257.

69. Avis E. Newhall, "Spring Skiing in Assiniboine Park," *Appalachia* 21 (June 1928): 215–219.

70. John A. Holden Jr., "The Laurentians as a Ski Country," *Appalachia* 21(June 1928): 153. For an account of the Appies' 1930 trip from Grey Rocks, Ste. Jovite, to Shawbridge, see ibid. 24 (June 1930): 84–85.

71. Brian Powell, comp., *Jackrabbit: His First Hundred Years* (Don Mills: Collier Macmillan Canada, 1975). Emil Cochand interviewed by Allen for the film *Legends of American Skiing.*

72. "Our First Ski Funicular," *Canadian Ski Annual* (1933): 50. The date has recently been questioned, see Neil and Catharine McKenty, *Skiing Legends and the Laurentian Lodge Club* (Montreal: Price Patterson, 2000), 52–55. For Shawbridge in the 1920s, see *BSYB* (1926): 507.

73. *Ski Bulletin,* 16 December 1932–14 February 1936.

74. John and Frankie O'Rear, *The Mont Tremblant Story* (New York: A.S. Barnes, 1954).

75. *Verdens Gang,* 2 December 1889. K. J. Johansen, "Norske skilöbere i Sydamerica," 9, 10, 49, 73, 98. HMS Vaage Papers, Holmenkollen Skimuseet. The phrase is Tom Mitchell's, "Ski-ing in Chile and the Argentine," *BSYB* (1939): 45.

76. Ibid. (1939): 45. Eugene Du Bois, "Chilean Skiing," *Ski Bulletin,* 12 February 1937, 6–7.

77. Josef Koch, "Der Schi erobert die Anden," 274. Printed article (1938?) found in Deutscher Skiverband, Carl Luther Archiv [DSV L-A.], in Planegg, Germany. Eilert Sundt letter to Editor, Valparaiso, Chile, October 1919, *Aarbok* (1920): 126–136.

78. Gordon B. Dukes, "Doing the Devil's Own Corner on Skis," *Outing* 81 (October 1922): 23.

79. Koch, "Schi erobert die Anden," 275. DSV L-A.

80. Mitchell, "Ski-ing in Chile and the Argentine," *BSYB* (1939): 23–24.

81. L. Cousiño, "Le sport du ski au Chili," *Ski* [Swiss] (1936): 78. A. Edwards, "Ski-ing in Chile," *BSYB* (1936): 259. *Der Winter* 29 (September 1936): 613, for an account of a twenty-seven-person excursion that became snowbound.

82. Edwards, "Ski-ing in Chile," *BSYB* (1936): 259.

83. Ibid., 263.

84. Ibid.

85. There were other places to ski, of course. Chillàn, ten hours by train south of Santiago, then a narrow gauge railway for three hours to Recinto, followed by 12 miles further on to the hut.

86. Ibid., 260. One Swiss was Wendelin Hilty, who ran one of the first South American ski schools, trained the Chilean army, and emigrated to the United States, where he owned Wendy's Ski School in Plymouth, N.H., for some years.

87. *Revue du Ski* 7 (November 1936): XL. Mitchell, "Ski-ing in Chile and the Argentine," *BSYB* (1939): 43.

88. *Boston Herald*, 3 March 1939.

CHAPTER 15. SKIING UNDER SIEGE

1. (Schacht) *New York Times*, 10 February 1939, 26. (Speer) Albert Speer, *Inside the Third Reich: Memoirs*, trans. Richard and Clara Winston (New York: Avon, 1970), 428–9. (Hitler) Ibid., 83. Hitler wished all male youths to have an hour's physical exercise during the morning and again in the afternoon "covering every sport," but particularly boxing. Adolf Hitler, *Mein Kampf*, trans. Ralph Manheim (Boston: Houghton Mifflin, 1943; edition 1971), 409–410.

2. Gigliola Gori, *Italian Fascism and the Female Body: Sport, Submissive Women and Strong Mothers* (London: Routledge, 2004), 22–25.

3. Bernard Janin, "Tourisme dans les Grandes Alpes italiennes: Breuil-Cervinia et Valtournanche," *Revue Géographie Alpine* 52 (1964): 219. Ski Club di Torino, *Itinerari Skiistici* (Torino: Ski Club di Torino, 1920). Piero Ghiglione, "Le ski en Italie," *Neige et Glace*, 1 January 1926, 116; *Lo storia dello Ski Club Torino e le Origini dello sci in Italia* (Torino: Ski Club Torino, 1971), 80.

4. A. P. Caliari, "Il tricolore italiano nel cielo di Garmisch," *Neve e Ghiaccio* 1, no. 6 (1936): 1, cited in Gigliola Gori, "Mussolini's Boys at Hitler's Olympics," in The *Nazi Olympics: Sport, Politics and Appeasement in the 1930s*, ed. Arnd Krüger and William Murray (Urbana: University of Illinois Press, 2003), 117.

5. Albert Dunant, "Ski autour de Rom," *Die Alpen* 14 (1938): 604

6. Mario Impiglia, "The 'Fascist Holiday': The *Afterwork Association* and the Beginning of Mass Tourism in Italy 1926–1940," in *Europäische Perspektiven zur Geschichte von Sport, Kultur und Tourismus*, ed. Arnd Krüger et al., CESH vol. II (Berlin: Tischler, 2000), 97.

7. Le Semanier, "En blanc et noir," *L'Illustration*, 24 February 1934, 236.

8. B. Preve, "Ave Caesar . . . ," *L'educazione fisio-psichica* 9 (1928): 144–148, cited in Angela Teja, "Italian Sport and International Relations under Fascism," in *Sport in*

International Politics, ed. Pierre Arnaud and James Riordan (London and New York: E. & F. N. Spoon, 1998), 152.

9. *Gerarchia* (November 1930): 952, 954. Translation by Gigliola Gori. See also Dennis Mack Smith, *Mussolini: A Biography* (New York: Vintage, 1983), 161.

10. Felice Fabrizio, *Storia dello sport in Italia* (Rimini-Firenze: Guaraldi, 1977), 112, cited in Allen Guttmann, *Women's Sports: A History* (New York: Columbia University Press, 1991), 181.

11. Federico Terschak, "Cortina d'invierno," *Rivista Mensile* 12 (December 1934): clv–clix.

12. Janin, "Tourisme dans les Alpes italiennes," *Revue de Géographie Alpine* 52, no. 2 (1964): 221–222.

13. Guido Tonella, *Skiing at Sestrières,* trans. Katherine Natzio (Sestrières: Movemento del Sestrières, 1934), 13.

14. Sestrières was in immediate competition for English visitors with the nearby French resorts. The English, reported *Le Petit Briançonnais,* "cross the entire country of France to go further to look for what we are unable to give them," cited in Roger Merle, *Histoire du ski dans le Briançonnais* (Gap: Ophrys/Alpes et Midi, 1989), 75.

15. "L'attrezzatura turistica di un grande centro invernali: Sestriéres [sic]," *Rivista Mensile* 12 (January 1934): V.

16. See the photos of a woman from Pragelato in Tonella, *Skiing at Sestrières,* 46.

17. Ibid., 13.

18. A sign in the center of Garmisch reading "Jews: Your Entry is Forbidden" had disturbed the American Committee for Fair Play. It was removed later. Richard D. Mandell, *The Nazi Olympics* (New York: Macmillan, 1971), 59, 93–94. See also William L. Shirer, *Berlin Diary: The Journal of a Foreign Correspondent 1934–1941* (New York: Knopf, 1941), 44–45. The term *anti-Semitism* came into use in 1879 when Wilhelm Marr founded an Anti-Semitic League. Bruce Pauley, *From Prejudice to Persecution: A History of Austrian Anti-Semitism* (Charlotte: University of Carolina Press, 1992), 5.

19. Wolfram Manzenreiter, review of Rainer Armstaedter, *Der Alpinismus, Kultur-Organisation-Politik* (Wien: Universitätsverlag, 1996), in *Journal of Sport History* 28 (Spring 2001): 109–110.

20. Toni Schruf, "Schneeschuhsport," *Obersteirerblatt* in *Dillingers Reisezeitung,* 1 December 1892. TMS copy in Wintersportmuseum Mürzzuschlag.

21. Pauley, *From Prejudice to Persecution,* 79–80.

22. Heinz Polednik, *Das Glück im Schnee: 100 Jahre Skilauf in Österreich* (Wien: Amalthea, 1991), 56. "Der Skilauf in Österreich," *Jahrbuch des Österreichischen Ski-Verbandes,* 155–157.

23. Pauley, *From Prejudice to Persecution,* 119.

24. "Der Skilauf in Österreich," *Jahrbuch des Österreichischen Ski-Verbandes,* 155.

25. Pauley, *From Prejudice to Persecution*, 119.

26. Alexander Bronische et al., *Hahnenkamm. The Chronicle of a Myth: 100 Years of the Kitzbühel Ski Club* (Munich: Kitzbühel Ski Club, 2003), 34. See also Andrea Wachter, "Antisemitismus im Österreichischen Vereinswesen für Leibesübungen 1918–38 am Beispiel der Geschichte ausgewählter Vereine," Ph.D. diss., University of Vienna (1983), TMS, 137. For the Arlberg, see Gerhard Strohmeier, "Snow: Cultural Constructions," paper read to the American Society for Environmental History, Tacoma, Wash., March 2000, TMS, 8.

27. Arnold Lunn, *Unkilled For So Long* (London: Allen and Unwin, 1968), 57.

28. *Der Winter* 1 (1932): 247. By way of comparison, the Swiss Ski Association had 19,000.

29. Ibid. On a local level, the numbers for Garmisch increased over three seasons from 1925–28 from 7,135 to 14,140 to 15,597, and in Partenkirchen from 9,110 to 10,162 to 13,306. Figures from Günter Scharf und Manfred Thiess, "Die Entwicklung des Skilaufs in Deutschland bis 1933," *Theorie und Praxis der Körperkultur* 3 (1968): 202.

30. *Deutsche Turn-Zeitung* (1919): 69.

31. *Der Winter* 20 (March 1927): 472. See also the front cover of Theo Reinwarth, *Der Skisport* (Berlin: Ullstein, 1925).

32. Scharf und Thiess, "Die Entwicklung des Skilaufs in Deutschland," *Theorie und Praxis der Körperkultur* 3 (1968): 202. Erik Bogdanovics, "Der Arbeitersport und die 2. Arbeiter-Olympiade 1931," *Sport: Sinn und Wahn* (Mürzzuschlag: Steirische Landesausstellung, 1991), 137–138.

33. R. Planque, in Sports d'Hiver section, *Miroir des Sports*, 15 April 1919, 38. Gabriel Hanot, "L'inauguration de la 1ère saison des sports d'hiver à Font Romeu, dans les Pyrénées," ibid., 6 January 1921, 12. The phrase "crusade for the ski" was used in the Réunion des Hoteliers, 2 April 1927, when CAF's 16th international meet ended with a Chamonix-Briançon trip. TMS Réunion des Hoteliers, 2 April 1927, Archives Mairie, Chamonix.

34. E.-G. Drigny, "L'ouverture de la saison," *Miroir des Sports*, 22 December 1921, 386.

35. Drigny, "Pour les fanatiques des sports d'hiver les centres se multiplient, dans le Jura, les Alpes, et les Pyrénées," ibid., 18 December 1928, 418.

36. Drigny, "Des demonstrations de ski pour instituteurs et institutrices des régions de montagne," ibid., 12 February 1929, 106.

37. Arnold Lunn, "A Fortnight in Scandinavia," *British Ski Year Book* (1930): 537. [*BSYB.*]

38. *Neige et Glace*, 31 January 1924, 149.

39. Advertisement for "Le Bois Bakélisé" in CAF *Revue* de la section Vosgienne, 1

(Hiver 1932–33): 5. See also A. Dauvillier, "Essais de skis bakélisés," *La Montagne* 230 (January–February 1931): 37–43.

40. *Revue du Ski* 7 (October 1936): XI. See also R. G. "Comment sont fabriqués vos skis," ibid., 3 (October 1932): 182–6.

41. Auguste Mottet, "Erfahrungen mit metallisierten Ski," *Ski* [Swiss] 13 (1918): 61; (duraluminum) Letter, T. C. Paynter to Editor, *Ski Notes & Queries* [*SN&Q*] 46 (December 1931); (heavy hinges) *BSYB* (1938): 306–8; (Laminated) ibid. (1935): 110; (Gabrac) ibid. (1937): 111–112; (Swedes) *Der Winter* 26 (February 1933): 471; (steel) *SN&Q.* G. S. [Seligman], "Steel-soled Ski," ibid., 45 (October 1931): 207; (rudder skis) *BSYB* (1937): 112; (roller skis) *Der Winter* 26 (February 1933): 135, and (November 1934): 300–301; (adjustable tip) *BYSB* (1926): 543.

42. CAF was criticized for sponsoring parties to Norway, Switzerland, Czechoslovakia, and the Arlberg. *Neige et Glace,* 15 October 1934, 56. *La Montagne* 265 (January 1935): 37. Antoine Borrel, "Pour une politique française des sports d'hiver," *Revue du Ski* 5 (November 1934): 264, 267.

43. Maurice Bernard, "Sports d'hiver en France," *La Montagne* 264 (December 1934): 370–371, and 272 (October) 1935: 321–324.

44. F. H., "Concours de chasse-neige," *L'Illustration,* 22 February 1930, 261, and "Le IIe concours international de chasse-neige," ibid., 7 March 1931, 280.

45. "L'automobile dans les neiges," ibid., 31 March 1928, 323. Tracked vehicles had been up the Kitzbühelerhorn in November 1930 and such vehicles were used on a number of routes in the Salzburg region. In 1932 they took visitors from St. Anton and St. Christoph to the hospice on the Arlberg Pass. *Der Winter* V (December 1932): 76–77.

46. R. Peyronnet de Torres, "Le chamoniard Martial Payot est Champion de France de ski," *Miroir des Sports,* 31 January 1928, 70.

47. G. Bargillat, "Méthode française de ski," *La Montagne* 245 (January 1933): 28–30.

48. A. Fanck et H. Schneider, *Les merveilles du ski* (Paris: Fasquelles, 1930). *Revue du Ski,* 5 December 1937, xxx.

49. Mario Baracci, *50 Jahre Schweizer Skischule Celerina 1932–1982* (Kärnten: Theiss [1982?]), 9, 13–22. To follow how the Swiss accomplished this, see W. Grob, "La nouvelle école Suisse de ski," *Revue du Ski* 4 (November 1933): 241–243. Theodor Wyder, "Skiführer + Skisoldaten = Skischulen," *Skilehrer + Bergführer,* 1 December 1989, 43. *Der Winter* 29 (November 1935): 299.

50. Bargillat, "Méthode française de ski," *La Montagne* 245 (January 1933): 28–30.

51. Gabriel Hanot, "Le ski, mondain et sportif, dans les Alpes et dans les Pyrénées," *L'Illustration* (18 February 1933): 201.

52. For bindings: *BSYB* (1937): 117–118. Edges have a long history culminating in the patented Lettner edge of 1928. In 1934, the *BSYB* (1934): 559ff. advertised thirteen different edges made in Norway, Switzerland, Austria, and Germany. There was even a whalebone edge in 1938. Ibid. (1938): 316.

53. Emile Allais, Paul Gignoux, and Georges Blanchon, *Ski Français* (Grenoble: Arthaud, 1937). Roland Palmedo review in *Ski Bulletin*, 13 January 1939, 5–6.

54. Lunn's innovations in slalom were translated and published in the *Bulletin Pyrénéen* (January–March 1928). See also *La Montagne* 209 (February 1928): 73.

55. *Revue du Ski* 8 (January 1937): XLVI. See also *BSYB* (1935): 215 for FIS revision of rules. See also photo in *IV. Olympische Winterspiele 1936, Amtlicher Bericht,* 255.

56. *SN&Q* 6 (October 1933): 173.

57. For what follows, see Lunn, "The FIS Meeting at Innsbruck," *BSYB* (1933): 233–253, and "The World Championship at Innsbruck, 1936," ibid., (1936): 337–360. René Levainville, "F.I.S. 1936," *Neige et Glace,* 1 March 1936): 344–347. For an analysis of FIS 1933, see Anneliese Gidl, "Die FIS-Wettkämpfe 1933 in Innsbruck—eine moderne Grossveranstaltung?" in *Internationale Skihistoriographie und Deutscher Skilauf,* ed. Gerd Falkner (Planegg: DSV, 2005), 93–104.

58. *BSYB* (1928): 572. *Der Winter* 26 (January 1933): 445–446. The amateur-professional debate can be followed in *BSYB* (1931): 324–325; (1932): 600–601. A. Virot, "Une conversation à Chamonix avec le norvégien, Petersen," *Miroir des Sports,* 7 February 1928): 95.

59. N. Östgaard in *Norges Skiforbund* (1929), translated and printed in *BSYB* (1930): 570.

60. "Davos et son monte pente," *Neige et Glace* 13 (June 1935): 460. *Motor im Schnee* (November 1993): 38, (November? 1995): 48. *Revue du Ski* 8 (November 1936): n.p.

61. *Neige et Glace,* 16 March 1937, 286.

62. Charles F. Dwyer, "Aerial Tramways in the United States—an Historical Overview," communication from Kirby Gilbert, 26 February 1999.

63. Photo in *Revue du Ski* 2 (March 1931): 94.

64. *Der Winter* 27 (May 1934): 633. See also ibid., cover; and 15 (November 1933).

65. Ibid., 28 (October 1934), and 28 (November 1934).

66. *Harzer Rundschau* 12 (1933): II.

67. Hans Eichhorn-Sens, "Die Entwicklung des Skilaufs in Lauscha von der Entstehung bis zum Ausbruch des zweiten Weltkrieges." Diplomarbeit Leipzig DHfK, 1965. TMS, 126.

68. *Der Winter* 29 (December 1935): 340. *Skiführer.* Frankfurt Fachamt Skilauf Gau XII–XIII: [1938], 8

69. *Ski-Sport,* 22 March 1938, 4. Günter Krusche, "Sudetendeutsches Skiland kommt heim ins Reich!" *Der Winter* 32 (November 1938): 33–36.

70. Speer, *Inside the Third Reich*, 83.

71. Procès-Verbal, CIO, Athens, 19 May 1935. TMS in Olympic Archives, Vidy.

72. Ibid.

73. Sir Eric Phipps to Foreign Office, Berlin, Dispatch 204, 13 February 1936, cited in Martin Polley, "Olympic Diplomacy," *Journal of the History of Sport* 9, no. 2 (1992): 173.

74. Speeches and interviews reported in the *New York Times*, 25 October 1935, and 9 March, 5 October 1936. Roger F. Langley, *A Survey of Skiing in the United States*. M.Ed. thesis, State Teachers College of Fitchburg, Mass. (1946), 147. TMS.

75. Letters to and from Arnold Lunn to Archbishop of York in April and May 1935. TMSS in box 2, folder 31, Lunn Papers, Georgetown University, Washington, DC.

76. *Neige et Glace*, 1 March 1936, 327. Poetic license taken in the translation; the last two lines translate as: Skiers, have faith in the divine order.

77. Letter, Dr. Karl Rösen to Arnold Lunn, cited in "Skiing Events in the Olympic Games," 15–16. TMS copy. box 7, folder 47, Lunn Papers.

78. Cited in Gigliola Gori, "Fascist Italy in the 1936 Games," in Goksøyr, *Winter Games, Warm Traditions*, 305–309. Angela Teja, "Central Military School," in ibid., 214. See also Ulzega, Maria Piera, and Angela Teja, *L'addestamento Ginnico-Militare nell'esercisto italiano (1861–1945)* (Roma: Ufficio Storico SME, 1993), 136.

79. Jacques Dieterlen, "Garmisch-Partenkirschen," *Revue du Ski*, 3 March 1936, 64.

80. Reported in *Newsweek*, 22 February 1936, 33.

81. Claude Ferrière, member of the French Academy. William Murray, "France: Liberty, Equality, and the Pursuit of Fraternity," in Krüger and Murray, eds., *The Nazi Olympics*, 94.

82. Guttmann, *Women's Sports*, 183–185.

83. *Der Winter* 28 (December 1934): 377; 7 (January 1939): 353. *Ski-Sport*, 16 February 1937, 5.

84. *Neuzeitlicher Skilauf: Amtlicher Lehrplan* (Berlin: Limpert, 1937). *Der Winter* 29 (January 1936): 416–7; 32 (January 1939): 354.

85. "Congrès National de la Fédération Française de Ski: Marseilles 24–28 septembre 1936," *Revue du Ski* 7 (October 1936): 227.

CHAPTER 16. THE SCHNEIDER PHENOMENON

1. Hannes Schneider, "Wie ich Skifahrer und Skilehrer wurde," Feierabend Wochenbeilage zum *Vorarlberger Tagblatt* 12 (1930): 44–46, and Schneider, "The Development of the Ski School in Austria," in *Skiing: The International Sport*, ed. Roland Palmedo (New York: Derrydale Press, 1937), 89–112.

2. Mathias Zdarsky, *Lilienfelder Skilauftechnik* (Hamburg: Richter, 1896). Zdarsky's heritage is guarded in the Zdarsky-Archiv, Lilienfeld, an archive and a museum.

3. *British Ski Year Book* (1910): 34. [*BSYB.*] *Allgemeine Sport-Zeitung*, 2 February 1913, 114.

4. Cited in Arnold Lunn, *A History of Ski-ing* (London: Oxford University Press, 1927), 384. According to Lunn, Bernays considered Schneider "more Papal than the Pope." Ibid.

5. Raimond Udy, *Kurze praktische Anleitung über den Gebrauch, die Konservierung und Erzeugung des Schneeschuhs für Militärzwecke* (Laibach: Udy, 1896). Hermann Czant, *Militärgebirgsdienst im Winter* (Wien-Leipzig: Sterns, 1907). Georg Bilgeri, three articles in *Ski-Chronik* 1 (1908–1909): 76–92; 2 (1909–1910): 156–170; 3 (1910–1911): 105–121.

6. Arnold Fanck, *Er führte Regie mit Gletschern, Stürmen und Lawinen: Ein Filmpionier erzählt* (München: Nymphenburger, 1973), 113–119. For the success of the film, see the reviews in *Die Lichtbühne* (19 February 1921) and *Dresdener Volkszeitung* (11 March 1921), quoted in ibid., 124.

7. Fanck, *Er führte Regie mit Gletschern*, 90–93. *Allgemeine Sport-Zeitung*, 22 March 1914, 163. *Der Schnee*, 17 February 1912, 6. *Popular Mechanics* (February 1916): cover and 171. For what follows on films, see Fanck, cited in Klaus Spathelf, ed., *100 Jahre Freiburger Ski-Geschichte* (Freiburg im Breisgau: Kehere, 1995), 105. "'Film' vom Skifilm," in Günter Krusche, ed., *50 Jahre Deutscher Skiverband* (München: DSV, 1955), 119–128. Erwin Lauterwasser et al., eds., *Faszination Skilauf* (Heidelberg: Braus, 1995), 52. Glen B. Infield, *Leni Riefenstahl: the Fallen Film Goddess* (New York: Crowell, 1976), 21–29. Sepp Allgeier, *Die Jagd nach dem Bild: 18 Jahre als Kameramann in Arktis und Hochgebirge* (Stuttgart: Engelhorn, 1931), is actually more on his Arctic photography, but there is interesting material on his experiences with alpine shoots. Leni Riefenstahl's *Kampf in Schnee und Eis* (Leipzig: Hesse & Becker, 1933) and her autobiography of sixty years later, *A Memoir* (New York: St. Martin's Press, 1993), also hold interest. The most interesting of all, though, is Fanck's autobiography.

8. Arno Klien, "Sepp Allgeier and the First High Mountain Ski Movie," in *3rd FIS Ski History Conference*, ed., Wintersportmuseum (Mürzzuschlag: Wintersportmuseum, 2004), 11.

9. Friedl Pfeifer and Morten Lund, *The Making of the Aspen Dream*, TMS, 49. Riefenstahl, *Memoir*, 59–60, 133–134. *Der Winter* 28 (November 1934): 285.

10. Fanck, *Er führte Regie mit Gletschern*, 115.

11. *Der Filmkurier* and *Die Weltbühne*, cited in ibid., 130, 237.

12. Siegfried Kracauer, *From Caligari to Hitler* (Princeton: Princeton University Press, 1947), 112.

13. Susan Sontag, "Fascinating Fascism," *New York Review of Books* (6 February 1975): 23.

14. Schneider, "The Development of the Ski School," 101.

15. "Die Heiligsprechung Hannes Schneiders," *Ski* [Swiss] 20 (1925): 110–112. See

also the critique by the Norwegian Thor Tangvald: "Your 'school' . . . is a mixture of bluff and ignorance." *BSYB* (1929): 120. Dr. Hoschek who ran the ski school at Hinterglem, near Saalbach found the Arlberg method "rather slow and laborious." *The Times,* 15 February 1935, 17.

16. Christian Rubi, "Ski Instruction in Switzerland," in Palmedo, *Skiing: The International Sport,* 115–142. There was also a St. Moritz school of instruction. Hans Georg, "St. Moritz Ski Technique," *American Ski Annual* (1940–41): 81–84. B. "Arosa Notes," n.d. [1927?], Deutscher Skiverband, Carl Luther Archiv [DSV L-A.], in Planegg, Germany, 6 Env: Wintersportsaison-Verlängerungen. TMS.

17. The word *Schuss* first appeared in the French literature during the 1932–3 season. *Ski-Sports d'Hiver* 11 (December 1932): 233, cited in Monique Jacquemin and Christiane Tetet, *Datations et Documents Lexicographiques 36. Matériaux pour l'histoire du vocabulaire français: les sports de montagne. Le Ski (fin XIXe s. –. 1960)* (Paris: Centre National de la Recherche Scientifique, 1990), 212.

18. *Der Winter* 28 (November 1934): 317. Paris boasted also a Swiss ski school. For Otto Schniebs, see E. John B. Allen, *From Skisport to Skiing: One Hundred Years of an American Sport, 1840–1940* (Amherst: University of Massachusetts Press, 1993), 102–103, 166; and Ulmrich, "Otto Schniebs, ein Pionier des amerikanischen Skilehrwesens aus Deutschland—wer war er?" *DSV Ski Schule* 1 (October 1991): 5–10. For those who went to Australia and New Zealand, see E. John B. Allen, "The Modernization of Skiing in the British Colonies, c. 1900–1940," in *History of Skiing Conference. Holmenkollen Oslo, 16–18.9.1998,* ed. Karin Berg, et al. (Oslo: Skiforeningen, 1998), 6, 8.

19. *The Times,* 15 February 1935. H. de Watteville, "On Ski-ing Schools and Styles," *BSYB* (1931): 219.

20. A. H. d'Egville, "Three Races," ibid. (1928): 516–524. R. J. E. Bracken, "The Arlberg-Kandahar, 1930," ibid. (1930): 677–686.

21. Hannes Schneider, *Auf Schi in Japan* (Innsbruck: Tyrolia, 1935). He had help in writing the book from Rudolf Gomperz. Hans Thöni, "Fremdenverkehrspionier am Arlberg. Das Schicksal des Rudolf Gomperz," in *"Wir lebten wie sie . . .": Jüdische Lebensgeschichten aus Tirol und Vorarlberg,* ed. Thomas Albrich (Innsbruck: Haymon, 1999), 129.

22. *BSYB* (1934): 661; (1935): 194–195; (1936): 366, 369–370.

23. Lunn's report is based on Othmar Gurtner's article in *Sport. BSYB* (1934): 660–661.

24. Alexander Bronische et al., *Hahnenkamm. The Chronicle of a Myth: 100 Years of the Kitzbühel Ski Club* (Munich: Kitzbühel Ski Club, 2003), 40.

25. Franz von Papen interrogation at Nuremberg, 8 October 1945. (www.nizkor.org). *Der Winter* 29 (September 1936): 614. Gert Ammann, *Alfons Walde 1891–1958* (Innsbruck, Wien: Tyrolia, 2001), 146–147.

26. *BSYB* (1936): 365–366. Thöni, *Hannes Schneider zum 100. Geburtstag des Ski-pioniers und Begründers der Arlberg-Technik* (Innsbruck: Tyrolia, 1990), 45, 49, 51, 124. Thöni, "Fremdenverkehrspionier am Arlberg," in Albrich, *"Wir lebten wie sie,"* 124–137. Gerald Aichner, *Die weisse Spur. Tyroler Skitouren-Geschichten: 100 Jahre Tourenskilauf* (Thaur: Druck- und Verlagshaus Thaur, 1996), 163–166. Franz X. Gabl, *Franzl II. From Four Years on the Russian Front to Standing on the Olympic Podium in 1948* (Missoula: Pictorial Histories, 2000), 77–78, 216. F. Sandoz, "Le Bluff des méthodes nationales," *Neige et Glace* 17 (July 1939): 379.

27. Friedl Pfeifer and Morten Lund, "The Making of the Aspen Dream," TMS, 49, 124. According to Pfeifer, Riefenstahl spoke to him after the Anschluss and was happy to see Schneider imprisoned in Landeck. Ibid., 129. The French expression comes from *Revue du Ski* 9 (July 1938): vii.

28. *BSYB* (1937): 157–158.

29. "Die zwei 'Herren' von St. Anton," *Der Rote Adler*, 2 February 1934, 11. Copy, Nachlass Schneider.

30. [Schneider], "Vorfälle nach meiner Verhaftung." TMS copy, Nachlass Schneider.

31. Thöni, *Hannes Schneider*, 106. [Schneider], "Mein Verhalten zu Herrn Bürger-meister Moser." Unsigned TMS copy. *Anlage* 2 in letter, Schneider to *Reichsführer SS Heinrich Himmler*, Gasthof Melber, Garmisch-Partenkirchen, 14 November 1938. Nach-lass Schneider.

32. "Die Herrscher von St. Anton," *Das Schwarze Korps*, 27 October 1938, 19. Photo-copy Nachlass Schneider. Letter, Schneider to Himmler, 14 November 1938, Nachlass Schneider.

33. Pfeifer and Lund, "The Making of the Aspen Dream," 106. Thöni, "Fremden-verkehrspionier am Arlberg," in Albrich, *"Wir lebten wie sie,"* 132.

34. Allen, *From Skisport to Skiing*, 119–120.

35. Thöni, *Hannes Schneider*, 111. *Der Rote Adler*, 2 February 1934, 11.

36. *BSYB* (1938): 412. Arnold Lunn, *Unkilled For So Long* (London: Allen and Unwin, 1968), 57.

37. Arnd Krüger, "German Way of Worker Sport," in Arnd Krüger and James Rior-dan, *The Story of Worker Sport* (Champaign: Human Kinetics, 1996), 19.

38. *BSYB* (1938): 42.

39. *Der Winter* 12 (March 1938); 485–486.

40. Besprechung Dr. Rösen. Marktarchiv Garmisch-Partenkirchen 1814 EAPL: 02–025, Bürgermeister Scheck 1938–1944. TMS copy. My thanks to Christof Thöny for sending me a copy.

41. Denver newspaper in Pachman Scrapbook, Denver Historical Society, Denver, Colorado. *New York Times*, 17 and 25 March 1938.

42. For what follows, see *Der Hitler-Prozess vor dem Volksgericht in München*

(München: Knorr und Hirth, 1924; reprinted Glashütten im Taunus: Detlev Auermann, 1973). Ernst Deuerlein, *Der Hitler Putsch. Bayerische Dokumente zum 8./9. November 1923* (Stuttgart: Deutsche Verlags-Anstalt, 1962). Hanns Hubert Hoffmann, *Der Hitler-putsch. Krisenjahre deutscher Geschichte 1920–1924* (München: Nymphenburger Verlags-handlung, 1961). Alice Kiaer, "Hannes Schneider," *Ski* [U.S.] (October 1955): 46. Otto Lang, "A Bird of Passage," TMS II, 15–19.

43. Kiaer, "Hannes Schneider," *Ski* [U.S.] (October 1955): 46.

44. Lang, "Bird of Passage," TMS II, 15–19. Herbert Schneider, Hannes's son, and others said the same thing. Conversations with Otto Lang, Seattle, Wash., Herbert Schneider, North Conway, N.H., and Nicolas Howe, Jackson, N.H., April and May 1999.

45. Lunn, *Unkilled For So Long*, 60–61. Yet Rösen was of sufficient stature to send an affidavit on behalf of Walther Funk for his trial after the war. Rösen affidavit in International Military Tribunal, *Trial of the Major War Criminals before the International Military Tribunal, Nuremberg, 14 November–1 October 1946* (Nuremberg, 1947–1949), 15:188–189.

46. "Besprechung Dr. Rösen," Marktarchiv Garmisch-Partenkirchen 1814 EAPL: 02–025 Bürgermeister Scheck 1938–1944. TMS copy, and E. John B. Allen, "Hannes Schneider and the Germans," in *Internationale Skihistoriographie und Deutscher Skilauf,* ed. Gerd Falkner (Planegg: Deutscher Skiverband, 2005), 9–12..

47. Lady Londonderry had written to Göring on 15 March 1938. See also Göring's reply in Public Record Office of Northern Ireland, Belfast, D/30999/3/35/34A, letter Hermann Göring to Lady Londonderry, in Ian Kershaw, *Making Friends with Hitler* (London: Penguin, 2005), 422, fn. 60. Anne de Courcy, *Circe. The Life of Edith, Marchioness of Londonderry* (London: Sinclair-Stevenson, 1992), 271–272, 286.

48. For this and what follows, see Besprechung Dr. Rösen. Marktarchiv Garmisch-Partenkirchen 1814 EAPL: 02–025, Bürgermeister Scheck 1938–1944, and Allen, "Hannes Schneider and the Germans," 9–12.

49. "Mein Verhalten zu Herrn Bürgermeister Moser," 2. TMS, Nachlass Schneider.

50. Letter Hannes Schneider to SS Reichsführer Himmler, Gasthof Melber, Garmisch Partenkirchen, 14 November 1938. TMS copy. Nachlass Schneider. The supporting documents were as follows: "Mein Verhalten zu Herrn Bürgermeister Moser" (TMS copy); "Vorfälle nach meiner Verhaftung" (TMS copy); "Anlage gegen Hannes Schneider" (TMS copy); "Betreff Hannes Schneider: Allgemeines, Stellungnahme zu Vorwürfen, insbesonders zu einem Artikel im Roten Adler" (TMS copy); list of Schneider's household belongings; two letters: from the Bergbahn A. G. St. Anton am Arlberg to Hannes Schneider, Innsbruck, 9 July 1938; and Schneider's reply, Garmisch-Partenkirchen, 13 July 1938 (TMS copies); "Die zwei Herren von St. Anton," *Roter Adler,* 2 February 1934, 11 (copy); "Skischule Arlberg unter neuer Leitung," *Innsbrucker Nach-*

richten, 21 September 1938 (typed copy); "Der Fall Hannes Schneider," *Das Schwarze Korps,* 27 October 1938 (copy); and "Die Herrscher von St. Anton," ibid. (copy).

51. *BYSB* (1939): 285.

52. Lang, "Bird of Passage," TMS II, 22–23.

53. *New York Times,* 10 February 1939, 26.

54. No contract has been found. The New England Ski Museum holds what was probably a tentative contract which Gibson sent round to a very few friends for comment. There are no figures given. TMS copy, Shedd Papers, New England Ski Museum.

55. *New York Times,* 19 February 1939.

56. Besprechung Dr. Rösen. Marktarchiv Garmisch-Partenkirchen 1814 EAPL:02–025, Bürgermeister Scheck 1938–1944.

CHAPTER 17. THE RUSSO-FINNISH WAR

1. London *Times,* 11 December 1939.

2. John Langdon-Davis, *Invasion in the Snow: A Study of Mechanized War* (Boston: Houghton-Mifflin, 1941), 18–29.

3. Nikita Khrushchev, *Khrushchev Remembers,* trans. Strobe Talbot (Boston: Little Brown, 1970), 153.

4. Carl Mydens, *More Than Meets the Eye* (New York: Harper, 1959), 23–24. See also his article and photos in *Life,* 29 January 1940, 57–63.

5. The Social Democratic Party and the Finnish Trade Union Congress invited the (British) National Council of Labour to send a fact finding team. The trip was not a huge success as two of the three sent did not know how to ski. Walter Citrine, *My Finnish Diary* (London: Penguin, 1940), 12, 82, 128.

6. Alfred Fabre-Luce, *Journal de la France, Mars 1939–Juillet 1940* (Trévoux: Imprimerie de Trévoux [Ain], 1940), 246.

7. Arthur Koestler, *Scum of the Earth* (New York: Macmillan, 1968), 162.

8. Fabre-Luce, *Journal de la France,* 247.

9. The *Times,* 9 March 1940.

10. Ibid., 4 March 1940.

11. Max Jakobson, *The Diplomacy of the Winter War* (Cambridge: Harvard University Press, 1961), 273, fn.32.

12. William B. Trotter, *A Frozen Hell* (Chapel Hill: Algonquin Books of Chapel Hill, 1991), 199. See also the fanciful remarks by a French correspondent claiming that he saw Americans from Broadway and Florida ski training for nine to ten hours a day. Edmond Demaître, "Quelques révélations," *L'Illustration,* 6 April 1940, 341.

13. *American Ski Annual* (1940–41): 50. *Ski Bulletin,* 19 January 1940, 7.

14. *Life,* 22 January 1941. American troops had first donned skis in the nineteenth century, and there had been units with skis before World War I, and in the 1920s and

1930s. E. John B. Allen, " 'Calling All Skiers': The Formation of the 10th Mountain Division, U.S. Army," in *Actas del Congreso Internacional ISHPES 1991, Proceedings of the 1991 International ISHPES Congress,* ed. Roland Renson et al. (Madrid: Instituto Nacional de Educación Física de Madrid, 1993), 273–274.

15. Eloise Engle and Lauri Paananen, *The Winter War* (New York: Scribners, 1973), 18.

16. *Neige et Glace* 18 (January 1940): 23.

17. Langdon-Davis, *Invasion in the Snow,* 2.

18. F. Sandoz, "Les Finlandais et le sport," *Neige et Glace* 18 (January 1940): 23.

19. Fabre-Luce, *Journal de la France,* 249.

20. The *Times,* 8 December 1939.

21. Richard Elwes, *First Poems* (London: Hodder and Stoughton, 1941), 16.

EPILOGUE

1. Odd Nansen, *Langs veien* (Oslo: Gyldendal, 1970), 40, cited in Roland Huntford, *Nansen: The Hero as Explorer* (New York: Barnes and Noble, 1998), 537.

2. *Der Winter* 26 (January 1933): 444–445.

3. Otto Lang, *Downhill Skiing* (New York: Holt, 1936), 76.

BIBLIOGRAPHIC NOTE ON SELECTED ARCHIVES

Most countries have one or two libraries specializing in skiing, some of which also hold archival sources of documents, papers, diaries, and scrapbooks. Institutions like the Deutsche Sporthochschule in Cologne and the Ski Club of Great Britain in Wimbledon, however, are more book- and journal-oriented than they are stocked with primary sources. (There are two outstanding ski bibliographies: Heiner Brinkmann's *Skisport Bibliographie*, 5 vols. [Köln: Deutsche Sporthochschule, 1989–2000], and Henry M. Yaple's *Ski Bibliography*, 2 vols. [Woodbury, Conn.: International Skiing History Association, 2004].) The Carl Luther archive and Arnold Lunn's papers used to be held by the two institutions named above but are now housed, in the case of the Luther archive, in the German Ski Association's headquarters in Planegg, outside Munich, and in the case of the Lunn Papers, in the Lauinger Memorial Library of Georgetown University, Washington, D.C.

The three Scandinavian countries have one major ski museum each and any number of smaller ones, often associated with regional interest. The Norwegian Holmenkollen Skimuseet (under the jump) is a national shrine and concentrates on display, special exhibitions, and guardianship. The library is surprisingly unorganized, but the papers of the longtime curator Jakob Vaage are a major source for information on skiing all over the world. Umeå, 600 kilometers north of Stockholm, is home to the Svenska Skidmuseet, which has a good library and marvelous collections; the Artur Zettersten archives there contain many letters concerning ski-related matters. The earliest extant Canadian ski can be seen in Umeå along with documentation of killing wolves in Alaska by an immigrant Sami. Lahti, Finland is home to the Hiihtomuseum, whose small display area confines the exhibits. The library is about 70 percent Finnish language and 30 percent other languages, mostly English and German books and periodicals. Many documents concerning modern competitions, many of which have been held in Lahti's jumping and cross-country arenas, comprise a major source.

In Germany, there are many small museums and collections; some, like the Ski Club Todtnau's archives, remain private. These archives contain letters from Paul von Hindenburg, Fritz Breuer, Wilhelm Paulcke, and others vital to any understanding of skiing in the Black Forest and, indeed, of early skiing in Germany and the Alps.

The Carl Luther archive in the German Ski Association's offices and museum in Planegg is extensive, ranging widely both geographically and chronologically and covering most facets of skiing—as one might expect from Luther, who, as longtime editor of *Der Winter* and author of many books, had a continuing interest in ski history for fifty years. The archive contains the best collection of early manufacturers' catalogs, which he obtained from Max Schneider, and Luther's correspondence with many of the pioneers is of great importance. In 2006, the library was modernized, and reorganization is in progress. The notation system of Luther's archive used in this book may change. There is much material in handwritten documents (HMS) and in typescript (TMS).

In Austria, the Lilienfeld Heimat-Museum also houses Mathias Zdarsky's archive containing documents on his activities and those of his protégé, Theodor von Lerch, who had so much to do with the propagation of skiing in Japan before the First World War. There remains a strong tie between Lilienfeld and Japan today.

About an hour south of Lilienfeld, the Wintersportmuseum in a new building in downtown Mürzzuschlag is the most important repository. Its good library also has a wide selection of pioneers' correspondence and documents from men like Toni Schruf, Max Kleinoscheg, Oskar Schadek, and Josef Wallner. These were mostly collected by the founder of the museum, Theodor Hüttenegger, and his archive is of interest as well, containing letters concerning the early history of skiing in Austria.

In neighboring Switzerland, the Swiss Sport Museum in Basel contains much ski material with an extensive collection of prints. There is a filial—exhibit only—in Mürren, and a new museum opened in Glarus recently. Of course, the International Olympic Committee's museum in Lausanne has much documentation and many papers concerning all the Olympics from 1924 on. The Dewey papers, vital for any understanding of the 1932 Olympics, remain with the Lake Placid Historical Society in Lake Placid, New York.

France is well served by a large section of the Musée Dauphinois in Grenoble that has been given over to skiing. Along with interesting artifacts, a good library, and a superlative collection of prints, it holds a few letters and documents. Others may be found in any number of institutions: departmental archives of Haute Savoie and Isère in Annecy and Grenoble, in municipal libraries of Grenoble and Briançon, in the Salle d'Honneur of the 159th Régiment de la Neige, whose barracks are in Briançon, and in the town offices of Chamonix. In Paris, the Club Alpin Français' headquarters holds interesting club material, but this should be supplemented by regional CAF archives such as those at Nancy and Gérardmer.

Two other museums, neither with large libraries, but both with occasional archival material of considerable interest on Jura skiing, are in Roger Tangueley's private museum at Les Rousses and, on the subject of the Abbé Blot, in Pierre Chauvet's museum in the Auvergne at Besse-en-Chandesse. Both have outstanding collections of early regional artifacts.

The Canadian Ski Museum in Ottawa is strong in eastern Canadian material. For western artifacts and documentation one must go to the Whyte Museum in Banff and to Revelstoke.

In the United States, the Western Skisport Museum in Boreal Ridge, California, has an outstanding collection of gold rush skis and much archival material but is closed for the foreseeable future. The Midwest is well served by the National Ski Hall of Fame in Ishpeming, Michigan, especially with respect to documentation on early immigrant skiing and the formation of the National Ski Association. In the East, the New England Ski Museum at Cannon Mountain, New Hampshire, has a good library and a growing archive of papers relating to New England skiing.

For artwork, indispensable is the Mammoth Mountain Educational Foundation's Beekley collection in the village and ski resort of Mammoth, California. Its library is of equal importance, although there are few papers, letters, or other documentation.

The impressive Japan Ski Museum at Nozawa, besides having excellent collections of artifacts, has a good library, with books in English and German that many a Western European or English-speaking country would envy. The Goro Sakabe collection of letters, and of photos of General Nagaoka, von Lerch, and Schneider, is particularly valuable.

For those who feel this list is too selective, turn to the website of the International Skiing History Association, www.skiinghistory.org, which contains a list of the ski museums of the world along with opening hours, costs, phone numbers, and other details. Like all such lists, it is seldom up to date and details should be checked before visiting.

INDEX

Skade (goddess of skiers), 13–16, 18–19, 42

Skardarasy, Ernst (Austrian instructor to Australia), 208, 212

Skardarasy, Franz (Austrian instructor to New Zealand), 212

Skazel, Alois (Austrian instructor), 261

ski advertising: bulletins, club journals, newspapers, periodicals, 80, 82–84, 204–205, 213, 346n. 56; postcards, 79, 82; posters, 79, 81, 85; promotional cards, 79, 82; stamps, 11, 252

ski catalogs, 48, 131–134; French, 74, 76, 82; German, 48, 75, 82

ski clubs and associations: American, 67, 217, 220–224, 227, 355n. 14; Australian, 67, 209–210; Austrian, 65–66, 71–72, 77, 82, 98, 124, 127, 245–246; Bohemian, 135; British, 77, 92–93, 105; Canadian, 233–235; Chilean, 237–239; Czech, 135; Danish, 49; Estonian, 136; French, 74, 249; German, 71, 75, 129–130, 133-136, 185, 245–246, 254; Hungarian, 137; Indian, 213; Italian, 241–242; Japanese, 202–205; New Zealander, 207–208; Norwegian, 24–25, 65, 182, 194; Polish, 138; Russian, 49, 137; South African, 67; Swedish, 154, 185; Swiss, 99; women's, 140–141, 148–149. *See also Club Alpin Français*

ski competitions pre-1914: in Australia, 209–210; in Austria, 47–48, 124; in Bohemia, 135; in Canada, 233–234; in France, 76, 79; in Germany, 44; in Norway, 44, 50; in Switzerland, 100–101, 152; in USA, 361, 364–365

ski films: Arnold Fanck, 253, 262–264; Japan, 203, 205, 222; New Zealand, 207; USA, 229

ski instruction: in Australia, 212; in Austria, 26, 47, 66, 125–129, 135–136, 156, 261–265; in Canada, 235; in France, 158, 249–250; in Germany, 83, 257; in India, 213; in Italy, 244; in Japan, 201, 204–205; Otto Lutter on, 66; in Morocco, 177; in New Zealand, 207–208; in Norway, 66–67; in Switzerland, 66, 79, 83, 156–157, 249; in USA, 226; women, 177–178

ski jumping, 45, 67, 190, 208, 220–222, 230–231, 233–234, 250; indoor, 167; women, 152

ski lifts: in Australia, 212; in Canada, 235–236; in Czechoslovakia, 254; in France, 169, 253; horse drawn, 88; in Italy, 243–244; mountain railways, 85, 88; in New Zealand, 208; in Switzerland, 253; in USA, 89, 229, 231–232, 254; water powered, 88–89, 316n. 88

ski manufacture: in Australia, 209–210; in Austria, 66, 75, 311n. 22; in Canada, 247; in Finland, 71, 279; in France, 74, 76, 117, 247; in Germany, 74–75, 117, 311n. 32; in India, 213; in Japan, 202–206; in New Zealand, 206; in Norway, 70–72, 117; in Russia, 117; in Sweden, 72; in Switzerland, 20, 67, 74–76; in USA, 73–74, 225, 229–230, 233, 311n. 23

ski material: aluminum, 247–248; ash, 22, 66, 70, 75, 206; aspen, 233; bamboo, 205; birch, 22, 60, 70; copper, 247; duraluminum, 247; fir, 22; hickory, 22–23, 76, 247; metal sheaths, 60, 247; oak; 22, 60; pine, 22, 70, 233; steel, 248; teak, 248

ski mountaineering, 97–99, 106, 203–204; background of, 94–96; in Caucasus, 98; in Japan, 204; Mont Blanc, 97; Norwegians on, 97; in Switzerland, 98–99. *See also* Kurz, Marcel

ski museums, 373–375; in Finland, 17; in France, 307n. 10, 312n. 27; in Holland, 301n. 47; in Japan, 23, in Norway, 52, 71; in Russia, 10; in Sweden, 71; in USA, 250

ski shops: in Austria, 76, 134; in France, 76; in Japan, 205; in Latvia, 136; in Switzerland, 76; in USA, 229–230

ski terminology and language, 19–20, 26, 29, 174, 217; in Austria, 17; in China, 17; in Finland, 17; in Germany, 17–18, 300n. 42; in New Zealand, 207; in Norway, 17–18; for races, 103–104; in USA, 18, 217, 224

Ski-Idræt (Norwegian), *Ski-Idrott* (Swedish), 126, 183, 190, 193–194, 218–220; decline of, 45, 220, 222; and health, 41–42, 50, 218; history of